STUDIES IN ORIENTAL CULTURE

Number 5

A History of Islamic Philosophy

Majid Fakhry

A HISTORY OF ISLAMIC PHILOSOPHY

1970

COLUMBIA UNIVERSITY PRESS

New York & London

Majid Fakhry is Chairman
of the Department of Philosophy
at the American University of Beirut

The Publications Committee of the American University of Beirut
has generously provided funds to assist in the publication
of this volume.

ISBN: 0 231 03231 5
Library of Congress Catalog Card Number: 71-110144
Printed in the United States of America

STUDIES IN ORIENTAL CULTURE

Edited at Columbia University

PREFACE

THE INTEREST of Western scholars in the development of Islamic philosophical thought has been comparatively small. There appear to be two reasons for this neglect: the nature of the subject matter and the character of Western scholarship itself. The main body of Islamic thought, in so far as it has any relevance outside the scope of Islam, belongs to a remote past. In fact, as this book will show, Islamic philosophy is and continues to be, even in the twentieth century, fundamentally medieval in spirit and outlook. Consequently, from the time of Thomas Aquinas and Roger Bacon until now, interest in this thought has been cultivated in the West only in so far as it could be shown to have a direct or indirect bearing on the development of European philosophy or Christian theology. More recently, attempts have been made by Western scholars to break away from this pattern and to approach Islamic philosophy as an intellectual concern in its own right, but the fruits of these efforts remain meager compared to the work of scholars in such cognate fields as the political, economic, and social development of the Muslim peoples.

Second, we note the radically modern direction that philosophy has taken in the West, from the seventeenth century on. Fresh attempts are continually being made to formulate a coherent world view for modern man, in which the role of ancient (Greek) and medieval (both Arabic and Latin) thought is progressively ignored or minimized. In this way Islamic philosophy suffers the same fate as European medieval philosophy. Furthermore, the role that Arabic philosophy played in preserving and transmitting Greek thought between A.D. 800 and 1200 has become much less significant for Western scholarship since the recovery of the original Greek texts.

It can hardly be denied that the system of ideas by which the Muslim peoples have interpreted and continue to interpret the world is not without relevance to the student of culture. Nor is the more abstract formulation of this system, in theology or metaphysics, devoid of intrinsic value. For it should be recalled that Greek philosophy, in which modern Western thought has its origins, has played a crucial role in the formulation of Islamic philosophy, whereas it has made almost no impact on other cultures, such as the Indian or Chinese. This consideration alone should be sufficient to reveal the close affinities between Islamic and Western thought.

The first important modern study in the general field of Arabic philosophy is Amable Jourdain's *Recherches critiques sur l'âge et l'origine des traductions d'Aristote et sur les documents grecs ou arabes employés par les docteurs scholastiques*, which appeared in 1819. This book helped to underscore the influence of Arabic philosophy on Western, particularly Latin, scholastic thought. It was followed in 1852 by Ernest Rénan's classic study, *Averroês et l'averroïsme*, which has since been reprinted several times. In 1859 appeared Solomon Munk's *Mélanges de philosophie juive et arabe*, a general survey of Jewish-Arabic philosophy which is still of definite value. Early in the twentieth century appeared T. J. de Boer's *Geschichte der Philosophie im Islam* (1901), which was translated into English in 1903 and continues to be the best comprehensive account of Islamic philosophy in German and English. A more popular but still useful survey, *Arabic Thought and Its Place in History* by de Lacy O'Leary, appeared in 1922. The many surveys by Carra de Vaux, G. Quadri, and L. Gauthier are listed in the Bibliography.

We must mention, however, three historical narratives which appeared in very recent years. M. Cruz Hernandez, *Filosofía hispano-musulmana* (1957), though primarily concerned with Spanish-Muslim philosophy, contains extensive and valuable accounts of the major "Eastern" philosophers and schools. W. Montgomery Watt's *Islamic Philosophy and Theology* (1962), which is part of a series entitled "Islamic Surveys," is weighted in favor of theology and therefore does not add much to our knowledge of Islamic philosophy. Henry Corbin's

Histoire de la philosophie islamique (1964), though very valuable, does not recognize the organic character of Islamic thought and tends to overemphasize the Shi'ite and particularly Isma'īlī element in the history of this thought. M. M. Sharif's *History of Muslim Philosophy* is a symposium by a score of writers and lacks for this reason the unity of conception and plan that should characterize a genuine historical survey.

In the field of Greco-Arab scholarship, Islamic philosophy owes much to the studies of Richard Walzer, now available in the one-volume *Greek into Arabic* (1962), and to the critical editions of texts prepared by M. Bouyges, S. J. (d. 1951) and 'Abdu'l-Raḥmān Badawī. Bouyges made available to scholars, in the *Bibliotheca Arabica Scholasticorum*, a series of fundamental works in unsurpassed critical editions. A. R. Badawī has edited, over a period of two decades, a vast amount of philosophical texts which have considerably widened the scope of Arabic philosophical studies. As for the Ishrāqī tradition, Henry Corbin is a pioneer whose studies will probably acquire greater significance as the post-Averroist and Shi'ite element in Muslim philosophy is more fully appreciated. Finally, the studies of L. Gardet, Mlle. A. M. Goichon, L. Gauthier, I. Madkour, S. van den Bergh, G. C. Anawati, S. Pines, M. Alonso, and L. Massignon are among the most important contemporary contributions to the study of Muslim thought; these books are listed in the Bibliography.

An argument against the attempt to write a general history of Islamic philosophy might be based on the fact that a great deal of the material involved must await critical editions and analysis before an attempt can be made to assess it. I believe that this objection is valid in principle. However, a fair amount of material is now available, either in good editions or manuscripts, and the collation of the two should make interpretation relatively accurate. Moreover, the writing of a general history that would give scholars a comprehensive view of the whole field is a prerequisite of progress in that field, since it is not possible otherwise to determine the areas in which further research must be pursued or the gaps which must be filled.

We might finally note that the writing of a history of philosophy, as distinct from a philosophical chronicle, must involve a considerable element of interpretation and evaluation, in addition to the bare narrative of events, the listing of authors, or the exposition of concepts; without such interpretation the dynamic movement of the mind, in its endeavor to comprehend the world in a coherent manner, can scarcely be understood. In taking this approach a writer might find it valuable to reexamine areas which others have studied before him. In this hazardous undertaking I have naturally tried to learn as much as possible from other scholars. However, in the exposition of philosophical concepts or problems I have relied primarily on the writings of the philosophers themselves. Sometimes the interpretation of philosophical or theological doctrines has compelled me to turn to the studies of contemporary authorities. I did not feel, however, once those doctrines had been sufficiently clarified, that it was necessary to multiply these authorities endlessly. The purpose of the Bibliography at the end of the book is to acquaint the interested reader with the work of other scholars in the field and to indicate the extent of the material used in the writing of this book.

I wish to acknowledge my debt to the many persons and institutions that have made the publication of this work possible. In particular, I thank the librarians at Istanbul, Oxford, the Escurial, Paris, London, the Vatican, and the Library of Congress who have generously given their assistance. To the Research Committee and the Arabic Studies Program of the American University of Beirut I am particularly indebted for financing the research and travel that I did in connection with writing large parts of this book. To the Publications Committee of this University I am indebted for a generous subsidy to meet the editorial costs of preparing the manuscript for press. I also wish to thank the former Dean of the School of Arts and Sciences of the American University of Beirut, Professor Farid S. Hanania, for his encouragement in the early stages of writing the book, and Professors Arthur Sewell and David Curnow for their help in editing the manuscript, at least up to Chapter Seven. And to the many unnamed scholars and colleagues, from whose advice and criticism I have profited more than I can say, I extend a warm expression of thanks. Finally to Georgetown University I am grateful for assistance in the final preparation of the manuscript and the opportunity, while engaged in teaching, to complete the last chapters of this book, and to the staff of Columbia University Press for their courtesy and efficiency in producing this volume.

Majid Fakhry

CONTENTS

A History of Islamic Philosophy

NOTE ON TRANSLATION OF ARABIC PASSAGES. Unless otherwise indicated, the translation of Arabic excerpts is the work of the author. The system of translation of Arabic terms and proper names adopted in this book is, with slight modifications, that of the *Encyclopaedia of Islam.*

INTRODUCTION

ISLAMIC philosophy is the product of a complex intellectual process in which Syrians, Arabs, Persians, Turks, Berbers, and others took an active part. The Arab element is so preponderant, however, that it might be conveniently termed Arabic philosophy. The medium in which writers, hailing from such distant countries as Khurāsān and Andalusia, chose to express their thoughts from the eighth to the seventeenth centuries was Arabic. The racial element that provided the cohesive force in this cosmopolitan endeavor and determined its form and direction, at least in the early stages, was Arabic; without the Arabs' enlightened interest in ancient learning, hardly any intellectual progress could have been made or maintained. Moreover, it was the Arabs who, while they assimilated the customs, manners, and learning of their subject peoples, contributed the one universal element in the whole complex of Muslim culture, i.e., the Islamic religion.

As we proceed we shall note the role of each racial group in the development of Islamic philosophy. We observe here that the intellectual history of the Arabs, to whom the development of philosophy and science in the Near East owed so much, virtually begins with the rise of Islam. The chief cultural monuments of the Arabs, before the rise of Islam, were poetry and literary traditions that were transmitted orally and embody a record of the social, political, religious, and moral aspects of Arab life. However, this record was primitive, regional, and fragmentary. Islam not only provided the Arabs with a coherent and bold world-view, which sought to transcend the narrow confines of their tribal existence, but thrust them almost forcibly upon the cultural stage of the ancient world and set before them its dazzling scientific and cultural treasures.

The pivot round which the whole of Muslim life turns is, of course, the Koran. Revealed to Muḥammad by God between 610 and 632 from an eternal codex (the Preserved Tablet), according to Muslim doctrine, the Koran embodies the full range of principles and precepts by which the believer should order his life. The Koran is supplemented, however, by a mass of utterances attributed to Muḥammad and constituting, together with circumstantial reports of the actions and decisions of the Prophet, the general body of Muḥammadan Traditions, properly designated in Muslim usage as the Prophetic "Way" (*al-Sunnah*).

Overwhelmed by the awesome sacredness of the divine Word (*kalām*) and the Prophetic Way, the first generation of Muslim scholars dedicated themselves wholly to the fixing of the sacred canon, commenting upon it and drawing the legal or moral corollaries implicit in it. Thus arose the sciences of reading (*'ilm al-qirā'āt*), exegesis (*tafsīr*), and jurisprudence (*fiqh*), the only basic sciences the nascent community needed in order to assimilate or live by the divinely revealed ordinances of the Koran. From these sciences, however, there soon stemmed the whole body of subsidiary disciplines, collectively referred to as the linguistic or traditional sciences, as distinct from the rational or philosophical sciences.[1] Grammar, rhetoric, and the allied studies were developed during the first two centuries of the Muslim era, chiefly as a means of adequately interpreting or justifying the linguistic usages of the Koran and the Traditions. Even the study of literature, and particularly pre-Islamic poetry, appears to have been stimulated by the desire to find a venerable basis in ancient usage for the many unfamiliar terms or idioms in the Koran and the Traditions.

The canonical text of the Koran was finally fixed during the reign of the third caliph, Uthmān (644–656), and in honor of him the authorized version of the Koran ever since has been called "Muṣḥaf Uthmān".[2] A few minor refinements of a purely grammatical and orthographic nature were made in the tenth century. The Traditions,

[1] See for this general classification of the sciences Ibn Khaldūn, *al-Muqaddimah*, pp. 435 f, and al-Fārābī, *Iḥṣā' al-'Ulūm*, pp. 58 f.

[2] Arthur Jeffery, *Materials for the History of the Text of the Qur'ān*, pp. 1–10.

on the other hand, circulated orally for almost two centuries, and in consequence a vast amount of apocryphal material was added to what must have been the original core. By the middle of the ninth century, however, elaborate criteria for sifting this material were developed and compilations of "sound" or canonical Traditions were made, the best known and most authoritative of which is that of al-Bukhārī (d. 870).[3]

As one might expect, the greatest scholars of the early period were primarily linguists or exegetes who addressed themselves to the study and analysis of the texts of the Koran and the Traditions, on the one hand, or the interpretation of the juridical aspects of Scripture and their application to concrete cases, on the other. The first function was discharged by the commentators and Traditionists, and the second by the jurisconsults (*fuqahā'*), upon whom also devolved, in the absence of an organized teaching authority in Islam, the task of doctrinal definition as well.

The criteria for settling juridical or even doctrinal problems by the early jurisconsults were often purely linguistic or textual. However, there soon arose a class of scholars who were willing to permit the use of analogy (*qiyās*) or independent judgment (*ra'y*) in doubtful matters, especially when a specific textual basis for a decision could not be found in Scripture. Of the four major legal schools into which Muslim jurisprudence eventually crystallized, the school of Abū Ḥanīfah (d. 767) and that of al-Shāfi'ī (d. 820) were much more liberal than the two rival schools of Mālik b. Anas (d. 795) and Aḥmad b. Ḥanbal (d. 855).

The implications of this bipolarity for the subsequent development of scholastic theology (*Kalām*) are not far to seek. The conservative "people of Tradition," as the Malikites and the Ḥanbalites are generally called, tended to repudiate the use of any deductive method. Their position is best epitomized by the comment of Mālik on the koranic reference to God's "sitting upon the throne" (Koran 7, 54 and 20, 5). "The sitting," he is reported to have said, "is known, its modality is unknown. Belief in it is an obligation and raising questions regarding it is a heresy [*bid'ah*]."[4]

[3] See Guillaume, *The Traditions of Islam*, pp. 9 ff.

[4] Al-Shahrastānī, *al-Milal wa'l-Niḥal*, p. 17 (hereafter cited as *al-Milal*).

This somewhat narrow approach to the questions raised by the study of koranic texts could not long withstand the pressures of the times. There was first the inevitable confrontation of Islam with paganism and Christianity, both at Damascus and at Baghdad, and the numerous tensions it generated. Second, there were the moral and legal questions raised by the gloomy picture of God's overwhelming supremacy in the world as depicted in the Koran, and its bearing on the responsibility of human agents. And there was finally the necessity of safeguarding what one may call the unity of the Islamic view of life, which could not be achieved without a systematic attempt to bring the conflicting data of revelation (in the Koran and the Traditions) into some internal harmony.

The attempt to grapple with these complex problems is at the basis of the rise and development of Islamic scholastic theology. A good deal of the work of the earliest theologians consisted in the rebuttal of the arguments leveled at Islam by pagans, Christians, and Jews. Significantly, the early Muʿtazilite doctors are often commended for their defense of Islam against the attacks of the Materialists (*al-Dahriyah*) and the Manichaeans.[5] Indeed, heresiographers explicitly state that scholastic theology arose as a means of buttressing Islamic beliefs by logical arguments and defending them against attack.[6]

Within the confines of Islam itself, discussion began to center by the seventh century around the questions of divine justice and human responsibility. Authorities report that a cluster of early theologians engaged in the discussion of the problem of free will and predestination (*qadar*), an issue generally recognized as the first major one broached by the early theologians. The Muʿtazilah, who continued this line of speculation, asserted the freedom of the individual on the one hand and the justice of God on the other. And although they naturally supported their positions by quotations from the Koran, their general tendency was to advance arguments of a strictly ethical or rational character in support of these positions.

Moreover, the anthropomorphic passages in which the Koran abounded made it imperative to resort to some process of allegorical

[5] See al-Khayyāt, *Kitāb al-Intiṣār*, p. 21.

[6] Al-Shahrastānī, *al-Milal*, pp. 17 f., and al-Farābī, *Iḥṣā' al-ʿUlūm*, pp. 107 f.

interpretation in order to safeguard the immateriality and transcendence of God. Here again the Mu'tazilah were undoubted pioneers. The koranic references to God's "sitting upon the throne," as well as the possibility of seeing Him on the Last Day (Koran 75, 22, etc.), are interpreted as allegories for the divine attributes of majesty or royalty on the one hand, or the possibility of contemplating Him mystically on the other.[7]

The proper prosecution of discussions of this kind naturally called for a high degree of sophistication, which, prior to the introduction of Greek philosophy and logic, was rather difficult, if not impossible. Scholastic theology therefore gave the Muslims, as it had given the Christians of Egypt and Syria centuries earlier, the incentive to pursue the study of Greek philosophy.

Not much progress was made in that direction during the Umayyad period (661–750). The Umayyad caliphs, especially during the first few decades of their rule, were concerned primarily with the consolidation of their political power and the solution of the numerous economic and administrative problems which governing a vast empire raised.

However, souls thirsting after knowledge were not altogether wanting even during this period. We might mention, as a striking instance, the Umayyad prince Khālid b. Yazīd (d. 704), who appears to have sought consolation in alchemy and astrology for his disappointed claims to the caliphate. According to our most ancient sources, Khālid provided for the first translations of scientific works (medical, astrological, and alchemical) into Arabic. Nevertheless, the development of philosophy and theology in Islam is bound up with the advent of the 'Abbāsid dynasty in the middle of the eighth century. Interest in science and philosophy grew during this period to such an extent that scientific and philosophical output was no longer a matter of individual effort or initiative. Before long, the state took an active part in its promotion and the intellectual repercussions of this activity acquired much greater scope. Theological divisions, growing out of philosophical controversy or inquiry racked the whole of the Muslim community. Caliphs upheld one theological view against another and demanded adherence to it, on political grounds, with the inevitable

[7] See Wensinck, *The Muslim Creed*, pp. 63 f.

result that theology soon became the handmaid of politics. As a consequence, freedom of thought and conscience was seriously jeopardized.

A fundamental cause of this development is, of course, the close correlation in Islam between principle and law, the realm of the temporal and the realm of the spiritual. But such a development required the challenge of foreign ideas and a release from the shackles of dogma. This is precisely the role played by the introduction of Greek ideas and the Greek spirit of intellectual curiosity, which generated a bipolar reaction of the utmost importance for the understanding of Islam. The most radical division caused by the introduction of Greek thought was between the progressive element, which sought earnestly to subject the data of revelation to the scrutiny of philosophical thought, and the conservative element, which disassociated itself altogether from philosophy on the ground that it was either impious or suspiciously foreign. This division continued to reappear throughout Islamic history as a kind of geological fault, sundering the whole of Islam. As a result, throughout Muslim history reform movements have not been marked by a great degree of release from authority or dogma or a quest for the reinterpretation or reexamination of fundamental presuppositions in the realms of social organization, theological discussion, or legal thought. Instead, like the reform of al-Ash'arī (d. 935) in the tenth century, that of Ibn Taymiya (d. 1327) in the fourteenth century, or that of Muḥammad 'Abdu (d. 1905) in the nineteenth century, they were marked by a deliberate attempt to vindicate the old, Traditionist concepts and assumptions of the earliest protagonists of Muslim dogma, the so-called good forebears (*al-salaf al-ṣāliḥ*) of the Muslim community.

One lasting consequence of the introduction of Greek philosophy and the Greek spirit of inquiry, however, was that the "Traditionism" of early theologians and jurists, such as Mālik b. Anas, was no longer tenable in its pure or original form. The great Ash'arite "reformers," committed as they were to the defense of orthodoxy against heretics and free thinkers, could no longer do so without recourse to the weapons which their rationalist opponents had borrowed from the Greeks. It was as though the ghost of Greek dialectic could no longer be exorcised without recourse to the formula of exorcism which it had itself enunciated in the first place.

Moreover, the varying degrees of allegiance to Greek philosophy and logic not only gave rise to the diverse theological schools of thought, but generated the more distinctly Hellenic current of ideas, which we shall designate as the Islamic philosophical school.

The rise and development of this school is the primary concern of the present history. Scholastic theology will be discussed only in so far as it absorbed, reacted to, or by-passed Islamic philosophy. To theology might be added another movement whose relation to philosophy has also fluctuated between the two poles of total endorsement or total disavowal—mysticism or *Sūfism*. Mysticism is ultimately rooted in the original matrix of religious experience, which grows in turn out of man's overwhelming awareness of God and his sense of nothingness without Him, and of the urgent need to subordinate reason and emotion to this experience. The mystical experience, it is often claimed, is distinct from the rational or the philosophical, and, less often, it is said to be contrary to it. But, whether it is distinct or not, it can hardly be irrelevant to man's rational or philosophical aspirations, since it allegedly leads to the very object which reason seeks, namely, the total and supreme apprehension of reality. In fact, the history of Muslim mysticism is more closely bound up with that of philosophy than other forms of mysticism have been. The mysticism of some of the great *Sūfis*, such as Ibn 'Arabī (d. 1240), culminated in a grandiose cosmological and metaphysical world-scheme, which is of decisive philosophical significance. Conversely, the philosophical preoccupations of some philosophers, such as Ibn Bājjah (d. 1138) and Ibn Ṭufayl (d. 1185), led logically and inevitably to the conception of mystical experience (designated "illumination") as the crowning of the process of reasoning.

The beginnings of the Islamic philosophical school coincide with the first translations of the works of the Greek masters into Arabic from Syriac or Greek. We might accept as credible the traditional account that scientific and medical texts were the earliest works to be translated into Arabic. The Arabs, as well as the Persians, who contributed so abundantly to the scientific and philosophical enlightenment in Islam, are a practical-minded people. Their interest in the more abstract aspects of Greek thought must have been a subsequent development.

Even the Christian Syrians, who paved the way for the introduction of the Greek heritage into the Near East shortly before the Arab conquest in the seventh century, were interested primarily in Aristotelian logic and Greek philosophy as a prelude to the study of theological texts. These were not only written originally in Greek, but also were rich in logical and philosophical terms that previously had been unknown to the Semites.

In addition to scientific and medical works, collections of moral aphorisms ascribed to Socrates, Solon, Hermes, Pythagoras, Luqmān, and similar real or fictitious personages appear to have been among the earliest texts to be translated into Arabic. The Arab accounts of Greek philosophy abound in such apocryphal literature, whose exact origin is sometimes difficult to ascertain. It might be assumed that it was the affinity of these writings to belles lettres (*adab*) and their literary excellence which insured their early vogue among the elite. Translators had naturally to depend upon the generosity of their aristocratic or wealthy patrons, who, even when they affected interest in other than the purely practical disciplines of astrology or medicine at all, were content with this species of ethical and religious literature, which was cherished and disseminated partly as a matter of social refinement and partly as a matter of moral edification.

Interest in the more abstract forms of ancient, especially Greek, learning was bound to follow in due course, however. First, the translators themselves, having mastered skills required for translating into Arabic more practical works, proceeded next to tackle works of a greater speculative interest, and eventually to induce their patrons to provide for their translation. Secondly, the theological controversies had reached such a point of sophistication by the end of the eighth century that the old weapons were no longer sufficient for the defense of orthodoxy, which had now been given the authority of the state. Abstract philosophy was further popularized through the personal idiosyncrasies of such men as the Umayyad prince Khālid b. Yazīd, the ʿAbbāsid caliph al-Maʾmūn (d. 833), and the Persian vizier Jaʿfar the Barmakid (d. 805), who had acquired more than a conventional zeal for ancient learning in its Persian, Indian, and Babylonian forms in general, and its Greek and Hellenistic forms in particular.

The greater translators, most of whom were Syriac-speaking Christians, of the unorthodox Nestorian and Monophysite communions, were not mere translators or servile imitators of Greek or other foreign authors. Some of them, such as Ḥunain (d. 873) and Yaḥiā b. ʿAdī (d. 974), are credited with a series of important scientific and philosophical works. Ḥunain's interests seem to have been chiefly medical and scientific, whereas Yaḥiā seems to have been more interested in theological and philosophical questions. To a famous pupil of his, Ibn al-Khammār (d. 940), is ascribed a treatise on the *Agreement of the Opinions of the Philosophers and the Christians*, which belongs to the same literary lineage as the parallel treatises of the Muslim philosophers (such as Ibn Rushd, d. 1198) who dealt systematically with the questions of reason and revelation in their works.

The works of those early translators were on the whole compilations which lacked originality. They contained ideas that had been gleaned at random from the works they had translated. The first genuine philosopher to write in Arabic was al-Kindī (d. ca. 866), a contemporary of the great Ḥunain. Like the rest of the Arab philosophers and expositors, he differed from the Christian translators in two important particulars: his religion and his total ignorance of Syriac or Greek, the two chief languages of the times, besides Arabic. It is surprising that even the greatest admirers of Greek philosophy, such as Averroes, lacked even a perfunctory knowledge of Greek. The chief reason appears to have been the contempt of the Arabs for all foreign tongues, which seems to have spread like an infection, even to non-Arabs of the most bigoted type. Some philosophers, it is true, chose to write in their native tongues, in addition to writing in Arabic, as is illustrated by Ibn Sīnā's and al-Ghazālī's Persian writings. This was probably a gesture of nationalist loyalty, not the manifestation of a genuine desire for a polyglot erudition or distinction.

As a result of their total ignorance of Greek, those philosophers tended to be less slavish in their interpretation of Greek texts, if a trifle less exact, than the early Greek commentators, such as Themistius and Alexander. Being Muslims by faith, they were naturally anxious to justify their interest in the pagan philosophers of antiquity. Indeed, almost from the beginning it was standard for the orthodox to reproach all those who "looked into the books of the [Greek] philosophers"[8]—even presumably when they did not understand them. Such theological preoccupation was a distinctive feature of the development of Islamic philosophy. Al-Kindī, the first genuine philosopher, was more than a philosopher with a theological bent; he was to some extent a theologian with an interest in philosophy. We might say that al-Kindī still stands on the borderline of philosophy and theology, which the later philosophers tried more boldly, perhaps, to cross. How far they succeeded in so doing and how far it was possible for them to span the distance separating Islamic belief from Greek speculative thought will be seen in later chapters. But it might be mentioned at this stage that al-Kindī's theological interests did act as a safeguard against the total submersion of religious belief in the current of abstract philosophical thought, and the total subordination of the supernatural light of faith to the light of reason—a devastating temptation which Islamic philosophy could not ultimately resist. For the subsequent "illuminationist" trend in the history of Islamic philosophy amounted precisely to this: the vindication of the right of reason to scale the heights of knowledge unaided and to lift the veil of mystery which shrouded the innermost recesses of reality. The ultimate goal of reason, according to Ibn Bājjah, Ibn Rushd, Ibn Ṭufayl, and others, is "contact" or "conjunction" (*ittiṣāl*) with the universal mind or active intellect, not the enlightenment which the *visio Dei* promises, by admitting the soul graciously into the company of the elect, who are blessed with understanding. In this respect, it is clear that the Islamic philosophers remain true to the Greek ideal, in its exaltation of man and its faith in his boundless intellectual prowess and his ability to dispense altogether with any supernatural light.

This is the sense in which Islamic philosophy can be said to have followed a distinctive line of development which gave it that unity of form which is a characteristic of the great intellectual movements in history. We should, however, guard against the illusion that the course of its development was perfectly straight. Some of the most fascinating Muslim thinkers, such as al-Naẓẓām (d. 845?), al-Rāzī (d. 925?), and al-Maʿarrī (d. 1057), fall outside the mainstream of thought in Islam.

[8] *Al-Milal*, p. 18. See al-Ashʿarī, *Maqalāt al-Islāmiyin*, p. 485.

Their dissident voices lend a discordant note to an otherwise monotonous symphony. The difficulty of expounding their thought with any degree of completeness is bound up with its very nonconformist character. Islam did generate such dissentient and solitary souls, but it could not tolerate or accept them in the end. The historian of Islamic thought cannot overlook them, however, without distorting the total picture.

CHAPTER ONE

The Legacy of Greece, Alexandria, and the Orient

I

THE NEAR EASTERN SCENE IN THE SEVENTH CENTURY

THE Arab conquest of the Near East was virtually complete by 641, the year in which Alexandria fell to the Arab general 'Amr b. al-'Āṣ. Greek culture had flourished in Egypt, Syria, and Iraq since the time of Alexander the Great, but the capture of Alexandria brought them under Arab rule and put an end to the centuries-old dominion of Persia and Byzantium in that area.

Numerous factors contributed to the swiftness with which this conquest was carried out. The accession of the Roman Emperor Heraclius in 610 heralded a period of bitter fighting between the Persians and the Byzantines, who had been involved in a prolonged struggle for military hegemony in the Near East. This struggle had weakened the two belligerent powers to such an extent that the Arab armies were able to score a series of decisive victories against those two far superior and larger armies, despite the fact that the Arabs were not experienced in large-scale warfare.

Moreover, the religious differences and squabbles in which the Nestorians, the Monophysites, and the Melchites (Orthodox) were engaged contributed greatly to the general malaise and the disaffection of the subject peoples of Egypt, Syria, and Iraq. It is not surprising, in these circumstances, that the Arabs were welcomed as liberators by the vast majority of those peoples who hoped that the Arab conquest would lift the oppressive yoke of Constantinople, committed as it was to the defense of orthodoxy, especially since the reign of Justinian (527–565).

Alexandria was the most important center for the study of Greek philosophy and theology in the seventh century, but by no means the only one. In Syria and Iraq Greek was studied as early as the fourth century at Antioch, Ḥarrān, Edessa, and Qinnesrīn in northern Syria, and at Nisibis and Ras'aina in upper Iraq. Some of these centers were still flourishing when the Arab armies marched into Syria and Iraq. The study of Greek had been cultivated chiefly as a means of giving the Syriac-speaking scholars of those venerable institutions access to Greek theological texts emanating chiefly from Alexandria. At the same time numerous theological treatises were translated into Syriac, notably Eusebius' *Ecclesiastical History*, the *Recognitiones*, attributed to St. Clement of Alexandria, the *Theophany* of Eusebius, the *Discourses* of Titus of Bostra against the Manichaeans, and the works of Theodore of Mopseustia and Diodorus of Tarsus.[1]

With the translation of theological texts went very often the translation of works in logic. This was dictated by the need to probe more deeply into the meaning of theological concepts and the dialectical processes involved in the christological debates of the time. It is significant, however, that the translators did not proceed beyond the *Isagoge* of Porphyry, the *Categories*, the *Hermeneutica*, and the *Analytica Priora*.[2] As borne out by a tradition associated with al-Fārābī's name in the Arabic sources, logical studies were not pursued beyond the *Analytica Priora* because of the dangers inherent in the study of demonstrative and sophistical arguments.[3]

[1] Duval, *Histoire d'Edesse*, p. 162, and Wright, *History of Syriac Literature*, pp. 61 f.

[2] See Georr, *Les catégories d'Aristote dans leurs versions syro-arabes*, p. 14; Baumstark, *Geschichte der Syrischen Literatur*, p. 101; and Wright, *History of Syriac Literature*, pp. 64 f.

[3] See Ibn Abī Uṣaybi'ah, '*Uyūn al-Anbā'*, II, 134 f.; cf. infra, p. 127.

The Arab conquest did not, on the whole, interfere with the academic pursuits of scholars at Edessa, Nisibis, and the other centers of learning in the Near East. An indication of this is the fact that Edessa (Arabic: *al-Ruhā*) continued to flourish well into the late decades of the seventh century. The vast theological and philosophical output of one of its chief doctors, Jacob of Edessa (d. 708), is a monument to the freedom of thought which he and his colleagues enjoyed.[4]

Theological studies were also still pursued undisturbed in the seventh century at the Monophysite monastery of Qinnesrīn in northern Syria. Founded by John bar Aphtonia (d. 538) in the sixth century, it produced numerous scholars, the most distinguished of whom was Severus Sebokht (d. 667). He composed commentaries on the *Hermeneutica* and the *Rhetorica* of Aristotle and wrote a treatise on the *Syllogisms of Analytica Priora*.[5] Severus' most famous disciple was Jacob of Edessa, whose learning ranged widely over theology, philosophy, geography, grammar, and other subjects. Of Jacob's philosophical works we have a *Treatise on Technical Terms*, the *Enchiridion*, and a Syriac version of the *Categories*.[6]

The monastery of Qinnesrīn produced two other distinguished scholars: Athanasius of Balad (d. 696) and his disciple, George, Bishop of the Arabs (d. 724), who both produced translations and commentaries on the *Categories*, the *Hermeneutica*, and the first book of the *Analytica Priora* of Aristotle, as well as the *Isagoge* of Porphyry.[7] Rénan rates the work of George so high that, in his estimation, "among the Syriac commentators, none can match him, in regard to the importance of his output or the accuracy of his method of exposition."[8]

There were two other important institutions of Greek learning in the seventh century, at Ḥarrān and Jundishapūr. Ḥarrān, in northern Syria, had been the home of a sect of star-worshipers, who were

[4] For Jacob's literary activity see Duval, *Histoire d'Edesse*, pp. 244–51.

[5] Georr, *Les catégories*, pp. 25 f.; Duval, *La littérature syriaque*, p. 257; Wright, *History of Syriac Literature*, p. 138.

[6] Georr, *Les catégories*, p. 27, and Baumstark, *Geschichte*, pp. 248–56. Wright has contested Jacob's authorship of the latter work (*History of Syriac Literature*, p. 91, notes).

[7] Wright, *History of Syriac Literature*, pp. 155 ff., and Duval, *La littérature syriaque*, pp. 258 ff.

[8] Rénan, *De philosophia peripatetica apud Syros*, p. 33.

erroneously identified during the 'Abbāsid period with the Sabaeans (*al-Ṣābi'ah*) mentioned in the Koran. Their religion, as well as the Hellenistic, Gnostic, and Hermetic influences under which they came, singularly qualified the Ḥarrānians to serve as a link in the transmission of Greek science to the Arabs and to provide the 'Abbāsid court from the beginning of the ninth century with its greatly prized class of court astrologers. We shall have occasion to consider the contribution that some of the chief scholars of Ḥarrān, such as the famous Thābit b. Qurra (d. 901), his son Sinān, and his two grandsons, Thābit and Ibrāhīm, made to mathematical and astronomical studies, and in this way played their part in the diffusion of Greek science among the Arabs.

The School of Jundishapūr, founded by Chosroes I (Anūshirwān) around the year 555, stands out as a major institution of Hellenic learning in Western Asia, whose influence was destined to extend to the world of Islam in 'Abbāsid times. Its Nestorian teachers, allowed by the enlightened Chosroes to pursue their scientific studies, continued the tradition of Syriac-Greek scholarship. Greek teachers were welcomed by the Persian court when the School of Athens was closed by order of Justinian and its pagan teachers were forced to flee from persecution in 529. In time the School of Jundishapūr, with its medical faculty, its academy, and observatory, achieved great fame and was still flourishing when Baghdad was founded in 762 by the 'Abbāsid caliph al-Manṣūr. Since Jundishapūr was near Baghdad, the Persians were in close political contact with the 'Abbāsid caliphate. Consequently, it was from this school that important scientific and other intellectual developments spread throughout the Muslim empire. From the beginning, Jundishapūr provided the caliphs at Baghdad with court physicians, such as the members of the famous Nestorian family of Bakhtishū', who served the caliphs loyally for over two centuries and were instrumental in setting up the first hospital and observatory at Baghdad, modeled on those of Jundishapūr, during the reigns of Hārūn al-Rashīd (786–809) and his successor al-Ma'mūn (813–833).[9] Even interest in Greek philosophy and theoretical science owes a great

[9] Ibn al-'Ibrī, *Mukhtaṣar Tārīkh al-Umam*, pp. 130 f., and Hitti, *History of the Arabs*, pp. 309, 365, 373 f.

deal to the School of Jundishapūr, for it was a Persian, Yaḥia al-Barmakī (d. 805), the vizier and mentor of Hārūn, whose zeal for Hellenic studies was instrumental in promoting the translation of Greek works into Arabic. And it was a disciple of Jibrīl b. Bakhtishū', Yuḥanna b. Māsawaih (d. 857), teacher of the great Ḥunain, who became the first outstanding Arabic translator of Greek works and the first head of the School of Baghdad (*Bait al-Ḥikmah*), founded in 830 by al-Ma'mūn.

II

THE TRANSLATIONS OF PHILOSOPHICAL TEXTS

For a century or so following the conquest of the Near East, Arab rulers were occupied with the new problems of administering their far-flung empire and consolidating their military and political gains. The Umayyad caliphs (661–749) particularly were involved in the process of adjustment to this situation. Among the most pressing issues was simply the practical problem of keeping the accounts and records of state, for the Arabs had had no experience of this in their desert homeland. At first, the Umayyads were content to leave matters as they were, ignoring not only the books but the bookkeepers as well, many of whom like Sarjūn b. Manṣūr, the finance minister of Mu'āwiya and the grandfather of St. John of Damascus, had been in the service of the Byzantines. The urge to initiate change soon took hold, however, during the reign of the Umayyad caliph 'Abd al-Malik (685–705) and continued with his immediate successors. One such change was the use of Arabic as the new language in which the public records and accounts were to be kept, instead of Persian and Greek.[10]

[10] Ibn al-Nadīm, *al-Fihrist*, pp. 352 f.

The substitution of Arabic for Persian and Greek as the official language of the state by the end of the seventh century marks the first attempt of the Arab rulers to assert their literary supremacy, just as they had asserted their military and political supremacy over the subject peoples. Whether, as our sources indicate, this change of language was due to the jealousy the Muslims felt for the monopoly which non-Muslims (mostly Christians and Jews) held as officials of the caliph or not, practical considerations also made the switch to Arabic imperative.

Practical considerations also called for the translation of the earliest scientific and medical texts into Arabic, although they were limited at first to the purely pragmatic or semi-pragmatic disciplines of medicine, alchemy, and astrology. According to the most ancient and reliable authority, Ibn al-Nadīm (d. 995), the credit for initiating the process of translating alchemical, astrological, and medical works must be attributed to Khālid b. Yazīd (d. 704),[11] the Umayyad prince who turned to the study of alchemy for consolation when his claims to the caliphate were thwarted. Various poems and treatises ascribed to him have come down to us, but it is impossible to determine their authenticity or the debt of their alleged author to his Greek or other foreign sources.[12]

A more reliable tradition attributes to the Jewish physician Māsarjawaih (Marsarjuis) the Arabic translation of the medical compendium (Syriac: *kunnāsh*) of the Alexandrian Monophysite physician Aaron, during the reign of the Umayyad caliph Marwān (683–685).[13] This work had acquired a considerable reputation among the Syriacs, and was without doubt one of the earliest medical translations into Arabic.

Of major importance to the history of translation was the contribution made in the next five decades by ʿAbdullah b. al-Muqaffaʿ, a Persian convert from Zoroastrianism, who died a violent death in 757. To him we owe the translation into Arabic from Pahlevi of the fables of the Indian sage Bidpai, known as *Kalilah wa Dimnah*, a literary classic which continues even now to be regarded as a model of Arabic prose.

[11] Ibn al-Nadīm, *al-Fihrist*, p. 511, and Ṣāʿid, *Ṭabaqāt al-Umam*, pp. 48, 60.

[12] For critical discussion, see Ruska, *Arabischen Alchemisten*, pp. 8 f.

[13] Ibn Juljul, *Ṭabaqāt al-Aṭibbā'*, p. 61; Ibn al-ʿIbrī, *Mukhtaṣar*, p. 112; *al-Fihrist*, p. 427; al-Qifṭī, *Tārīkh al-Ḥukamā'*, p. 334 f.

In addition, he translated the Persian *Khudai-Nāmeh*, or *History of Persian Kings*, as well as the *Ayin-Nāmeh*, the *Book of Mazda*, a *Biography of Anūshirwān*, and numerous original literary and ethical treatises.[14]

Much more important for our purposes, however, is the tradition which ascribes to this 'Abdullah (or to his son Muḥammad) the translation of Aristotle's *Categories*, *Hermeneutica*, and *Analytica Posteriora*, as well as Porphyry's *Isagoge*, for the 'Abbāsid caliph al-Manṣūr (754–775).[15]

Whether or not Ibn al-Muqaffa' is to be credited with the translation of the latter logical treatises, it is certain that the process of translating scientific and philosphical works did not begin in earnest until the 'Abbāsid period, and in particular until the reign of al-Manṣūr, who is said to have been "proficient in jurisprudence and fond of philosophy and astronomy."[16] This caliph, who is portrayed as an austere figure, employed the most eminent physicians, scholars, and astrologers in his service. The most illustrious of the physicians were the first representatives of the famous medical family of Bakhtishū', Georgius b. Jibrā'īl, head of the medical school of Jundishapūr in Persia, and his disciple 'Isā b. Shahlāthā. Of the astrologers, the best known was a Persian from an equally renowned family of scholars and astrologers, al-Naubakhtī.[17] As for the scholars whom al-Manṣūr commissioned to translate medical and other works for him, the most famous was al-Biṭrīq (Greek: *Patrikios*), who is credited with numerous medical and astrological translations.[18]

The reign of the same caliph is said by some authorities to be the period also when several treatises of Aristotle, the *Almageste* of Ptolemy, the *Elements* of Euclid and several other Greek works were translated.[19] However, the truth of such reports cannot always be ascertained. The general impression one gathers from classical sources is that al-Manṣūr

[14] *Al-Fihrist*, p. 178. Other translators from Persian included al-Naubakhtī, al-Ḥasan b. Sahl, the astrologer, Ishāq b. Yazīd, Zadāwaih, Bahrām (*ibid.*, pp. 355–56).

[15] Al-Qifṭī, *Tārīkh*, p. 220, and Ṣa'id, *Ṭabaqāt al-Umam*, p. 49. See manuscript at University of St. Joseph, Beirut, No. 338. Cf. Kraus in *Rivista degli Studi Orientali*, 1933, No. 4, pp. 1–14.

[16] Ibn al-'Ibrī, *Mukhtaṣar*, pp. 135 f.

[17] *Ibid.*, pp. 124–25.

[18] *Al-Fihrist*, p. 354, and Dunlop, "The Translations of al-Biṭrīq and Yaḥia (Yūḥanna) b. al-Biṭrīq," in *Journal of Royal Asiatic Society*, 1959, pp. 140 f.

[19] Al-Mas'ūdī, *Murūj al-Dhahab*, VIII, 291–92.

took a keen interest in scientific and philosophical works and lent his support and patronage to the activity of translators, but that owing to the scarcity of either competent scholars or Greek scientific and philosophical material, the process did not make much headway before the beginning of the ninth century. It was then that al-Manṣūr's great-grandson, al-Ma'mūn, made a systematic and determined effort to acquire and translate the chief monuments of Greek science and philosophy.

None of al-Manṣūr's two immediate successors concerned themselves much with the literary and scientific activity he had initiated at Baghdad. Hārūn al-Rashīd, however, appears to have shown considerable interest in the progress of learning. His court physician, Yūḥanna (Yaḥia) b. Māsawaih, stands out as the greatest scientific and literary character of the period. Ibn al-'Ibrī states that Hārūn, in addition to employing him in his service as his private physician, "entrusted him with the task of translating ancient medical works,"[20] and this is borne out by the role al-Ma'mūn later assigned to him as the first head of the academy he founded at Baghdad in 830.[21] Whether Ibn Māsawaih produced any translations himself is difficult to ascertain, but he composed a number of works, mostly medical, which are only of incidental interest to us here.[22]

It was during Hārūn's reign (or possibly during al-Manṣūr's) that a famous Indian treatise on astronomy, the *Siddhanta* (Arabic: *Sindhind*) was translated by Muḥammad b. Ibrāhīm al-Fazārī (d. 806). He and his father, Ibrāhīm (d. 777), who reportedly built the first astrolabe in Islam, are considered to be the first two Islamic astronomers.[23]

There were other astronomers who made significant contributions during Hārūn's time. 'Umar b. Farūkhān is said to have composed a commentary on the *Quadripartitus* of Ptolemy, translated by al-Biṭrīq in the reign of al-Manṣūr.[24] Māshallah (d. 820), a Jewish astronomer of

[20] *Mukhtaṣar*, p. 131. Cf. Ibn Abī Usaybi'ah, *'Uyūn*, I, 175; Ibn Juljul, *Ṭabaqāt*, p. 65; al-Qifṭī, *Tārīkh*, p. 380.

[21] See *infra*.

[22] Hitti, *History of the Arabs*, p. 364, and *al-Fihrist*, pp. 425–26; Ibn Juljul, *Ṭabaqāt*, pp. 65–66.

[23] Ṣā'id, *Ṭabaqāt*, pp. 49–50; al-Qifṭī, *Tārīkh*, p. 270; al-Mas'ūdī, *Murūj*, VIII, 290–91; *al-Fihrist*, p. 395.

[24] *Al-Fihrist*, p. 395.

Persian origin during the reigns of al-Manṣūr, Hārūn, and al-Ma'mūn, has received Ibn al-Nadīm's tribute as the "unique astronomer" of his day and is reported by him to be the author of works on astronomy, astrology, meteorology, and even a heresiography.[25] Another Persian astronomer was Abū Sahl al-Faḍl al-Naubakhtī of the famous Shī'ite family of Naubakht, whose founder was converted from Zoroastrianism and was attached to the service of al-Manṣūr as his court astrologer. Abū Sahl, who succeeded his father in this office, is said to have been the librarian and astrologer of Hārūn and to have translated astronomical works from Persian into Arabic.[26]

The preponderance of astronomical and astrological works is linked to a significant feature of the reign of Hārūn, and indeed most of the early 'Abbāsid caliphs. The political upheavals which had followed the downfall of the Umayyad dynasty and the succession of the 'Abbāsids had convinced the latter that the secrets of human destiny and the rise and fall of empires were securely committed to the stars, and that it belonged to the wise alone to unravel them. Hence their keen interest in the acquisition, as well as the translation, of ancient works on astrology. Even the most enlightened caliphs of the period, like al-Ma'mūn, did not escape this dependence on the stars. Not only did he attach an astrologer-royal to his service, but he made no important military or political move without first consulting him.

Most of the translations mentioned so far, it will be noticed, were in the practical disciplines of medicine and astrology. Although a certain departure from this practice can be seen in some works, such as that of Māshallah's heresiography or treatise on the *States and Creeds* (*Kitāb al-Dual wa'l-Niḥal*), which became a favorite theme of later authors, the first translations of philosophical texts appear to be the work of Yaḥia (Yūḥanna) b. al-Biṭrīq, who lived during the reigns of Hārūn and al-Ma'mūn. Most sources report that, although he was interested in medicine and produced translations in that field, he excelled primarily in philosophy.[27]

The most important philosophical work Yaḥia is credited with translating is undoubtedly Plato's *Timaeus*. This work, according to

[25] *Al-Fihrist*, p. 396, and al-Qifṭī, *Tārīkh*, p. 337. [26] *Al-Fihrist*, pp. 396–97.
[27] Ibn al-'Ibrī, *Mukhtaṣar*, p. 138; Ibn Juljul, *Ṭabaqāt*, p. 67.

al-Fihrist, consisted of three books (*maqālāt*).[28] Although it cannot be ascertained from the scant data in *al-Fihrist* and similar sources whether the whole *Timaeus* or Galen's compendium of that work is meant,[29] it is more likely that Galen's shorter version of that remarkable and baffling dialogue is here in question.

Equally important is Ibn al-Biṭrīq's translation of the paraphrase of Aristotle's *De Anima*, probably in Themistius's version, which together with that of Alexander of Aphrodisias played a decisive role in the development of the Arab conception of Aristotle's psychology, and especially his doctrine of the intellect.

The other philosophical works this scholar is said to have translated are all Aristotelian: the zoological corpus (in nineteen books),[30] *Analytica Priora*,[31] and the apocryphal *Secret of Secrets*, which had a considerable vogue among medieval Latin authors and which Ibn al-Biṭrīq supposedly discovered during his search for the *Politics* of Aristotle at the behest of the caliph.[32]

The example Ibn al-Biṭrīq set in the translation of philosophical texts was subsequently emulated by more competent scholars than himself. Many of his own translations were revised and fresh translations made as the demand for greater textual accuracy increased. The beginnings of the ninth century witnessed a genuine scramble for philosophical and scientific material, in which well-to-do patrons vied with the caliphs themselves. At no time had the process of translation grown out of individual initiative or devotion to pure scholarship. Like most of the literary disciplines which the Arabs cultivated, such as belles lettres, verse writing, and narrative, the philosophical and scientific output was dependent on the generosity or interest of wealthy patrons. In fact, the more rarefied the discipline the more urgent was the need for lavish patronage. We have already mentioned the case of the Umayyad Khālid b. Yazīd, who subsidized the translation of astrological and alchemical works as early as the seventh century. But it was more than half a century later that the movement caught on

28 *Al-Fihrist*, p. 358; see also Mas'ūdī, *Al-Tanbīh wa'l-Ishrāf*, p. 163; al-Qifṭī, *Tārīkh*, pp. 131, 18.

29 Cf. Steinschneider, *Die Arabischen Uebersetzungen aus dem Griechischen*, pp. 58 f.

30 *Al-Fihrist*, p. 366.

31 Cf. Dunlop, "Translations," p. 145.

32 *Ibid.*, p. 147, and Ibn Juljul, *Ṭabaqāt*, pp. 67–68.

during the reign of the second ʿAbbāsid caliph, al-Manṣūr. A decisive factor in the process was the enthusiasm which the Barmakid family, especially Yaḥia, showed for Greek learning, which had been cherished and pursued in Persia from the time of Emperor Anūshirwān onward, and had made considerable strides at Jundishapūr and Merw.[33]

Other patrons of science and philosophy included the members of the opulent and influential family of Banū Mūsā, who provided generously for the acquisition and translation of scientific and philosophical works. Ibn al-Nadīm singles out three representatives of this distinguished family, who could boast not only vast wealth, but true intellectual brilliance. They vied with the caliphs in sending out emissaries to purchase Greek texts from Byzantium and engaging the most expert translators throughout the empire. In consonance with the trend of the times, their mathematical and astronomical interests dominated these pursuits, but a *Treatise on the Atom* and another *Treatise on the Eternity of the World*, ascribed to a distinguished member of the family, Muḥammad, testifies to the broad range of their intellectual interests.[34]

None of the patrons of Greek learning mentioned hitherto could match in zeal, liberality, or intellectual distinction the great ʿAbbāsid caliph al-Ma'mūn, whose reign marks a turning point in the development of philosophical and theological thought in Islam. To the luster of the caliphal office, al-Ma'mūn added the very rare distinction of profound intellectual dedication. He not only presided over assemblies of scholars at which theological and philosophical disputations of the most radical type were conducted according to the strictest rules of intellectual candor,[35] but he himself composed a number of treatises, which dealt mainly with theological questions in a Muʿtazilite spirit, such as a *Treatise on Islam and the Confession of Unity* (*Tauḥīd*) and another treatise on the *Luminaries of Prophecy*,[36] as well as a series of aphorisms and adages, which are preserved in ancient sources and testify to his brilliance.[37]

[33] *Supra*, p. 15.

[34] *Al-Fihrist*, pp. 392–93, 353; al-Qifṭī, *Tārīkh*, pp. 315–16, 441 f.

[35] Masʿūdī, *Murūj*, VII, 38–43.

[36] *Al-Fihrist*, p. 174.

[37] See, e.g., *Murūj*, VII, 7–10, 39 f.

Al-Ma'mūn was the greatest patron of philosophy and science in the whole checkered history of Islam. The accounts of his *salons*, at which theological and philosophical questions were broached with unusual boldness, shed much light on the intellectual preoccupations as well as the general climate of opinion prevalent at the time.[38] If such accounts are to be trusted, al-Ma'mūn's liberal mindedness was such that he entertained the most adverse commentaries on his reign with great openness and equanimity. The story is told of a *Ṣūfī* who, having been brought before the caliph, put to him the searching question: "This position [of preeminence] you assume over the Muslims, was it universally consented to by them all, or was it simply the outcome of subjection or of superior power to which they have had forcibly to submit?"[39] In reply to this bold question, the caliph is reported to have engaged in a subtle defense of political authority as the indispensable antidote to anarchy, and then to have offered to resign his office if this now-disgruntled interlocutor could find another candidate to the caliphal office who would be acceptable to the whole Muslim community.

Despite al-Ma'mūn's obvious liberality and undoubted munificence, his reign can hardly be commended for its tolerance. In fact, it was perhaps his very interest in theological discussions that led by degrees to not only the promotion of a popular interest in theology, but also to the support of the cause of a theological party (the Mu'tazilite) that had sought to apply the categories of Greek thought to Muslim dogmas and the use of the decisive resources of the state in the defense and consolidation of this position. In pursuance of such a policy, he marshaled the executive and judicial powers of the state in a determined effort to enforce the Mu'tazilite theologico-political credo upon the reluctant Muslim theologians and masses in 827 and in 833.[40]

Al-Ma'mūn's rationalist interests and his definite theological bias undoubtedly enhanced his interest in Greek science and philosophy. Ibn al-Nadīm, however, cites the following episode, in the traditional

[38] *Murūj*, *VII*, pp. 38 f., and Suyūṭī, *Tārīkh al-Khulafā'*, p. 310.

[39] *Ibid.*, pp. 40 ff.

[40] Hitti, *History of the Arabs*, p. 429, and Patton, *Aḥmad b. Ḥanbal and the Miḥna*, pp. 50 f. and *infra*, p. 78 f.

manner of Arab historians, as a decisive factor in prompting al-Ma'mūn to bend his energies toward the acquisition and translation of Greek philosophical works. In a dream, Aristotle appeared to al-Ma'mūn in the guise of a hoary old man of "overwhelming dignity," with whom he engaged in a dialogue about the nature of the good. Aristotle is said to have defined it, in the first instance, as "what is rationally good," in the second instance, as "what is religiously good," and in the third and final instance, as "what is conventionally of popularly good." This encounter ends significantly with the advice of the Greek sage to the Muslim prince "to cling to the confession of unity [or monotheist creed]."[41]

Although a start had been made by al-Ma'mūn's two predecessors, al-Manṣūr and Harūn, the young caliph set up in 830 the famous *Bait al-Ḥikhmah* or the House of Wisdom, an official institute and library for translation and research. In order to stock the library with important scientific and philosophical works, al-Ma'mūn sent emissaries to Byzantium to seek out and purchase for him books of "ancient learning," which were then ordered to be translated by a panel of scholars. These translators included a number of illustrious names such as Yaḥia b. Māsawaih, who had been in the service of both al-Manṣūr and Hārūn and who was now appointed head of the new institute; al-Ḥajjāj b. Maṭar; Yaḥia b. al-Biṭrīq; and a certain Salmā, whom *al-Fihrist* describes as "the keeper of the House of Wisdom."[42]

But by far the foremost figure in the history of the translation of Greek philosophy and science is that of Ḥunain b. Isḥāq (809–873), disciple and colleague of Ibn Māsawaih, who based the art of Arabic translation on a scientific footing. Sources indicate that, although he presided over *Bait al-Ḥikmah* for a short period and was presumably in the service of the caliph, most of his scientific output was subsidized by Banū Mūsā, the outstanding family mentioned among the leading patrons of philosophy and science. Whatever his relation to the caliph, Ḥunain should be counted as one of the most important figures in that caliph's reign.

[41] *Al-Fihrist*, p. 353; Ibn Abī Uṣayb'ah, *'Uyūn*, I, 186–87.

[42] *Al-Fihrist*, p. 353. See also al-Qifṭī, *Tārīkh*, pp. 97–98, and *'Uyūn*, I, 187, for the same tradition.

Ḥunain's activity marks a decisive stage in the history of translation. A new preoccupation with greater accuracy made it necessary either to retranslate current philosophical and scientific texts or to improve upon already existing translations by a closer scrutiny of the original texts. Ḥunain reportedly took a leading part in these efforts, although he was aided by a team of equally competent translators, the most important of whom were his son Isḥāq (d. 911), his nephew Ḥubaish, and his disciple 'Īsā b. Yaḥia.

The measure of Ḥunain's accuracy can be gauged by the fact that he made numerous translations of many of the works he cites in an epistle he wrote in 856.[43] For instance, he states that as a young man of twenty he made a Syriac translation of Galen's treatise "On the Order of Studying his Own Works" (π. τῆς τάξεως τῶν ἰδίων βιβλίων) from a mediocre Greek version.[44] However, twenty years later he says: "Having acquired a number of Greek versions of this work, I carefully collated them together, until I had in my possession one sound version, which I further collated with the Syriac version and corrected it. I then retranslated it for the second time." "And this," he adds significantly, "has been my wont in everything I have translated shortly after into Arabic for Abū Ja'far Muḥammad b. Mūsā [his already-mentioned patron],"[45] for whom he also made an Arabic translation of this work.[46]

Of the strictly philosophical works of Galen, Ḥunain cites his *Treatise on Demonstration*, *Hypothetical Syllogisms*, *Ethics*, his paraphrases of Plato's *Sophist*, *Parmenides*, *Cryatylus*, *Euthydemus*, *Timaeus*, *Statesman*, *Republic*, and *Laws*,[47] and tells us that either he or his disciple 'Īsā b. Yaḥia rendered them for his patron Muḥammad b. Mūsā.[48] Another tradition attributes to him the translation, or in some accounts

[43] See Ayasofia Ms No. 3631. This epistle was edited and translated by Bergsträsser as "Über die Syrischen und Arabischen Galen-Übersetzungen," in *Abhandlungen für die Kunde des Morgenlandes*, XVII, 2. See also XIX, 2.

[44] Ayasofia Ms. Bergsträsser's edition has Galen's *Treatise on the Classes of Learners* (π. αἱρέδεων τοῖς εισαγομένοις) p. 22.

[45] Ayasofia Ms. [46] Cf. Bergsträsser, "Über die Syrischen," p. 5.

[47] *Ibid.*, and Ibn Abī Uṣaybi'ah, '*Uyūn*, I, 101.

[48] Bergsträsser, "Über die Syrischen," p. 5 f. The Ms tradition here appears to be defective. Cf. Walzer and Kraus, *Galeni compendium Timaei Platonis*, pp. 18 ff.

the revision of the paraphrase, of the *Timaeus*, also attributed to Yaḥia b. al-Biṭrīq, as well as a translation of the *Laws*.[49]

Of the Peripatetic works of Galen, Ḥunain claims to have translated his *Treatise on the Immovable Mover* into Arabic and Syriac and his *Introduction to Logic* into Syriac only. The *Numbers of the Syllogisms* he translated into Syriac, whereas his son Isḥāq subsequently translated it into Arabic.

In addition, numerous Aristotelian works were translated, although hardly any directly into Arabic,[50] by Ḥunain's associates, working no doubt under his supervision. Thus his son Isḥāq, his nephew Ḥubaish, and his disciple 'Īsā b. Yaḥia were responsible for translating almost the whole Aristotelian corpus, as well as a series of Platonic and Peripatetic works. To Isḥāq is attributed the translation into Arabic of the *Categories*, the *Hermeneutica, De Génération et Corruptione*, the *Ethica* in Porphyry's Commentary,[51] parts of the *Metaphysica*, Plato's *Sophist*, parts of *Timaeus*, and finally the spurious *De Plantis*.[52] Many of these translations are available even now.

Ḥubaish, like his uncle, appears to have excelled in medical translations, and it is possible, as a number of authorities attest, that many translations executed by Ḥubaish were erroneously ascribed to Ḥunain, either because of his seniority or because of the curious circumstance that a careless scribe could not easily distinguish his name from that of Ḥunain, owing to their morphological similarity in Arabic script. *Al-Fihrist* puts the matter thus: "It was one of Ḥunain's tokens of good fortune that what Ḥubaish b. al-Ḥasan and 'Īsā b. Yaḥia and others translated into Arabic has been fathered on him."[53] And although only a few nonmedical translations are attributed to him, it is quite possible that he has simply been overshadowed by the celebrated uncle.[54]

Ḥunain's chief interests were medical, and we owe to him the translation of almost the whole medical corpus of Galen and Hippocrates, a good deal of which has survived in Arabic to the present day.

[49] *Al-Fihrist*, pp. 357 f., 419; al-Qifṭī, *Tārīkh*, p. 131.

[50] *Al-Fihrist*, pp. 395 f.

[51] *Al-Fihrist*, p. 361, and al-Qifṭī, *Tārīkh*, p. 35.

[52] *Al-Fihrist*, pp. 361, 366, 358.

[53] *Al-Fihrist*, p. 417.

[54] The philosophical works credited to him are *The Ethics of Galen* (De Moribus) and *The Introduction to Logic by Galen* (*al-Fihrist*, p. 419).

But this versatile scholar also made a valuable contribution to the translation of philosophical texts. The small number of philosophical works whose translation is attributed to him should not detract from the importance of his work. Many of the translators of Greek works, such as his son Isḥāq, Ibn al-Biṭrīq, and others, are said to have submitted their translations to him for correction or revision. Moreover, he composed a number of original scientific and philosophical works, which compel us to look upon this remarkable scholar as more than a simple dragoman of Greek learning. The titles of some of these works are enough to command our admiration: *A Greek Grammar*, *A Treatise on the Tides*, *A Treatise on the Salinity of Sea Water*, *A Treatise on Colors*, *A Treatise on the Rainbow*, *The Truth of Religous Creeds*, *The Analects of the Philosophers*,[55] *A Universal History*, and even a *Work on Alchemy*, plus numerous medical treatises and philosophical paraphrases, such as a paraphrase of Aristotle's *De Caelo* and his apocryphal *Physiognomy*.[56]

The other great translators included Ibn Nā'imah al-Ḥimṣī (d. 835), Abū Bishr Mattā (d. 940), Yaḥia b. 'Adī (d. 974), Qusṭā b. Lūqā (d. 900), Abū 'Uthmān al-Dimashqī (d. 900), Abū 'Alī b. Zur'a (d. 1008), and al-Ḥasan b. Suwār (d. ca. 1017), also called Ibn al-Khammār, Yaḥia b. 'Adī's best-known disciple; and finally a scholar who falls in a class of his own, the pseudo-Sabaean astrologer-philosopher Thābit b. Qurra of Ḥarrān.

The scholar who was without doubt the equal of Ḥunain in the scope of his learning and his versatility was Qusṭā b. Lūqā, who was born in Ba'albeck, Lebanon, and was possibly of Greek extraction. In his account of Qusṭā's literary and scientific output, Ibn al-Nadīm finds it necessary to apologize for mentioning Ḥunain before him, despite the fact that he was, in this authority's estimation, his undoubted peer. In addition to medicine, he appears to have excelled in philosophy, geometry, and astronomy, and to have distinguished himself by his revisions of many existing translations from Greek, a language which he is said to have mastered.[57] The list of his philosophical writings includes *The Sayings of the Philosophers*, *The Difference between Soul and*

[55] German translation by K. Merkle, Leipzig, 1921.

[56] *Al-Fihrist*, p. 423, and Ibn Abī Uṣaybi'ah, *'Uyūn*, II, 200.

[57] *'Uyūn*, I, 244, and *al-Fihrist*, p. 424.

Spirit,[58] *A Treatise on the Atom, An Introduction to Logic, A Political Treatise, An Exposition of the Doctrines of the Greeks, An Historical Treatise Entitled al-Firdaus*.[59]

The chief philosophical translations attributed to Qusṭā are the first four books of Aristotle's *Physica* (together possibly with Books V and VI), *On Generation and Corruption* (Book I),[60] and pseudo-Plutarch's *Opinions of the Physicists*, or *Placita Philosophorum*.[61]

The two tenth-century translators Abū Bishr Mattā and his disciple Yaḥia b. 'Adī deserve special mention because of their contribution to the translation and exposition of Aristotle, and in particular Aristotelian logic. In addition to a long list of translations which included Alexander's commentaries on *Metaphysica* L, *De Caelo*, and *De Generatione et Corruptione*, Mattā is credited with commentaries on Aristotle's four logical works: *Categories*, *Hermeneutica*, *Analytica Priora*, and *Analytica Posteriora*,[62] as well as a *Commentary on Porphyry's Isagoge*, an *Introduction to Analytica*, and a *Treatise on Conditional Syllogisms*. These commentaries, which apparently achieved great fame, served as the basis of logical studies during this period and earned their author the title of the chief logician of his day.[63]

His disciple, the Jacobite Yaḥia b. 'Adī, also earned a fine reputation in logic and was known on that account as the Logician (*al-Manṭiqī*). In addition to Aristotle's *Poetica*, *Sophistica*, *Topica*, and possibly *Metaphysica*,[64] he is credited with a translation of Plato's *Laws*, a commentary on *Topica* and parts of *Physica VIII* and *Metaphysica*, and the whole of *De Generatione*, as well as a series of original philosophical treatises, some of which have come down to us.[65] As might be expected, many of those texts dealt with logic, such as the *Treatise on the*

[58] Shaykho, *Maqālāt Falsafiya*, no. 11.

[59] *Al-Fihrist*, p. 425; Ibn Abī Uṣaybi'ah, *'Uyūn*, I, 245; al-Qifṭī, *Tārīkh*, p. 263.

[60] Al-Qifṭī, *Tārīkh*, pp. 38–39, 40. [61] *Al-Fihrist*, p. 368.

[62] The Arabic version of *Analytica Priora* is probably the work of Theodorus Abū Qurra (d. 820), disciple of St. John of Damascus and Bishop of Ḥarrān (al-Qifṭī, *Tārīkh*, p. 36, *al-Fihrist*, p. 362, and Walzer and Kraus, *Galeni*, p. 99).

[63] Cf. al-Qifṭī, *Tārīkh*, pp. 278, 323, and *al-Fihrist*, p. 382.

[64] Averroes, *Grand commentaire de la Métaphysique* (*Tafsīr*), Tome V, I (Notice), p. CXXII.

[65] Al-Qifṭī, *Tārīkh*, p. 362; *al-Fihrist*, p. 248 *passim*, and Périer, *Yaḥīa b. 'Adī*, pp. 71 f., and British Museum Ms, Orient, 8069. *Infra*, p. 216 f.

Nature of Logic and numerous works on the (Aristotelian) categories and on the division of the six genera of Aristotle. Others, however, dealt with purely physical and metaphysical questions, such as the *Refutation of Atomism*, the *Impossibility of the Existence of the Infinite, Either in Number or in Magnitude*, and treatises on the *Whole and the Parts* and the *Nature of the Possible*. Further works dealt with theological questions, which appear to have been discussed in Yaḥia's school or were broached in theological discussions with Muslims. These included: *A Refutation of the Arguments of Those Who Maintain That Acts Are Created by God and Acquired by Man*, obviously directed at the Ash'arite view of human action, a treatise on the *Unity of God*, as well as a refutation of the (Ash'arite) view that bodies consist of atoms and accidents.[66]

All of the translators discussed so far have been Christians of the Nestorian or Jacobite sect. The most outstanding exception to this general rule is without doubt the great pagan astrologer-philosopher Thābit b. Qurra, who hailed from Ḥarrān in north Syria, settled in Baghdad, where he was attached to the service of the famous patrician family of Banū Mūsā. He subsequently became astrologer-royal and companion of the caliph al-Mu'taḍid (892–902). He was the sire of a long line of distinguished scholars, who like their great forebear, devoted themselves to the study of astrology and mathematics. His extraordinary mathematical-philosophical output, which was by no means limited to translations from Greek and Syriac, includes a commentary on the *Physics* of Aristotle, treatises on the *Nature of the Stars and Their Influences*, *Principles of Ethics* and *Music*, paraphrases of *Analytica Priora* and *Hermeneutica*, as well as numerous mathematical-astrological works with which we are not concerned here.[67] His translations included a medical compendium and an Arabic version of *Almageste* of Ptolemy and the *Elements* of Euclid, which were definite improvements on the earlier versions.

Abū 'Uthmān al-Dimashqī was another leading figure in the ninth-century tradition of Aristotelian scholarship. He was responsible for translations of *Topica*, *Ethica Nicomachaea*, *Physica* IV, *De Generatione et*

[66] Al-Qifṭī, *Tārīkh*, p. 362.

[67] *Ibid.*, pp. 116–20, for a list of Thābit's works.

Corruptione, Euclid's *Elements*, Porphyry's *Isagoge*,[68] and Alexander's three treatises on *Colors*, *Immaterial Substances*, and *Growth*,[69] as well as a number of medical works.

Two rather late noteworthy translators were 'Īsā b. Zur'ah and Ibn al-Khammār. They belonged to the school of the Jacobite Yaḥia b. 'Adī, who cultivated particular interest, as we have seen, in Aristotelian logic. The former is credited with the translation from Syriac of Aristotle's *De Generatione Animalium*, *Metaphysica* L, *Sophistica*, and of Nicolaus' *Five Books on the Philosophy of Aristotle*.[70] Many other philosophical works are attributed to him,[71] but none of them is of primary importance.

Ibn al-Khammār's output is even more impressive. His translations, mostly from Syriac into Arabic, include Aristotle's *Meteorologica*, the four books on logic (i.e., *Isagoge*, *Categories*, *Hermeneutica*, and *Analytica Priora*) in the version of the commentator Albinus, *The Problems of Theophrastus*, and a treatise on *Ethics*. He also is said to have composed a long and a short commentary on *Isagoge*, and treatises on *Matter*, *Friendship*, and the *Philosophical Life*, as well as a series of medical writings. But perhaps his most interesting work is the previously mentioned treatise on the *Agreement between the Opinions of the Philosophers and the Christians*, which emphasizes the theological interests of this scholar and his school and their preoccupation with the problem of the harmony between philosophy and dogma, which greatly concerned the Muslim philosophers as well. Of equal theological interest are his other works: an *Exposition of the Opinions of the Ancient (Philosophers) on God Almighty and on the Holy Laws and Their Transmitters*, and the *Creation of Man and his Anatomical Make-up*.[72]

We need not concern ourselves here with any but two other noteworthy names: Ibn Nā'imah al-Ḥimṣī, translator of the apocryphal *Theology of Aristotle*, destined to play such a far-reaching role in the

[68] Ahwānī's edition, Cairo, 1952.

[69] Al-Qifṭī, *Tārīkh*, pp. 36 f., 64, and 257; and Ibn Abī Uṣaybi'ah, '*Uyūn*, I, 234. See also Badawī, *Manṭiq Arisṭu*, II, 467–672, and Escorial Ms No. 798 (fol. 69–71, 100–102).

[70] *Al-Fihrist*, pp. 383 f. and al-Qifṭī, *Tārīkh*, p. 246.

[71] *Al-Fihrist*, p. 384; al-Qifṭī, *Tārīkh*, p. 246; Ibn Abī Uṣaybi'ah, '*Uyūn*, I, 235 f.

[72] Ibn Abī Uṣaybi'ah, '*Uyūn*, I, 323; al-Qifṭī, *Tārīkh*, p. 164; *al-Fihrist*, p. 384.

history of Islamic Neo-Platonism, and a certain Asṭāt (Eustathius), about whom very little information can be gleaned from the ancient sources but who is responsible, according to the most reliable tradition, for the integral translation of the *Metaphysica* of Aristotle. *Al-Fihrist*, which appears to be the basis of all subsequent accounts, states in connection with Aristotle's major speculative treatise:

The *Book of Letters*, known as *Theologica* [*Metaphysica*]. This book is arranged according to the order of the letters of the Greek alphabet; the first book being 'a' Minor, which was translated by Isḥāq, and of which we have up to Mu, which was translated by Abū Zakariya, Yaḥia b. 'Adī. The letter Nu might be found in Greek, in Alexander's Commentary. And these letters were translated by Asṭāt for al-Kindī,[73] and in this connection a tale is told [?]. Abū Bishr Mattā translated Book L, in Alexander's Commentary, into Arabic; this being the eleventh of the letters.[74] On the other hand, Ḥunain b. Isḥāq translated this book into Syriac. Themistius also commented on Book L, and Abū Bishr Mattā translated it in Themistius's Commentary. Shamlī also translated it, and Isḥāq b. Ḥunain translated a number of other books as well. Syrianus commented on Book B, which has been done into Arabic and I have seen it in Yaḥia b. 'Adī's hand, in his book collection.[75]

From this statement it appears that the Arabs were in possession of twelve[76] out of the fourteen books of the *Metaphysics* by the middle of the ninth century, and that, in addition, a number of Greek commentaries upon it were also available to them in Arabic. Not only Eustathius, but Yaḥia b. 'Adī also appears to have made integral translations of the twelve books,[77] which can now be studied in the edition of Averroes' *Commentary on the Metaphysics* which the late Jesuit Father Maurice Bouyges prepared and which was published between 1938 and 1952.

[73] Al-Kindī, the first creative Arab philosophical writer, died around 866, which would place the previously mentioned Asṭāt in roughly the same period.

[74] But the book in question is definitely the twelfth of the *Metaphysics*, allowing for the traditional designation of the first two books as A and 'a' Minor.

[75] *Al-Fihrist*, p. 366. Cf. al-Qifṭī, *Tārīkh*, pp. 41–42.

[76] Book K appears to have been unknown to the Arabs, as can be inferred from the previous statement of Ibn al-Nadīm that L was the "eleventh of the letters" (i.e., books) and from Ibn Rushd's extant Commentary.

[77] See *supra*, p. 28.

III

NEO-PLATONIC ELEMENTS: THE APOCRYPHAL THEOLOGIA ARISTOTELIS AND THE LIBER DE CAUSIS

THE Greek work whose impact was most decisive on Arab philosophical thought was not, as might be expected, Aristotle's greatest venture into the realm of speculative thought, i.e., the *Metaphysica*, which had, as we have seen, found its way into Arabic as early as the middle of the ninth century. It was rather the *Theologia Aristotelis*, an alleged Aristotelian compilation whose Greek author is unknown. It was translated into Arabic for al-Kindī, the first purely philosophical Arab writer, around the same time as the *Metaphysica* by a Syrian Christian, ʻAbd al-Masīḥ b. Nāʻimah of Emessa.[78] The historical value of this work is considerable; it has been described as the epitome of Greek philosophy as it strove in Hellenistic times to blend into a whole all the elements generated during the period of greater creativity.[79] The Arabs, who as we have mentioned were preoccupied with the task of harmonizing not only Greek philosophy and Islamic dogma, but also the divergent elements in Greek philosophy itself, must have looked upon the apocryphal *Theologia* as a real boon. Although the Arabic version of Ibn Nāʻimah purports to be a translation of Porphyry's commentary upon the alleged text of Aristotle, none of our sources ascribes such a commentary to this Syrian Neo-Platonist. Curiously enough, however, a *Theologia* is credited to Diodochus Proclus (d. 485),[80] the other great exponent of Neo-Platonism and the last great pagan representative of Greek thought. This work is almost certainly the same as the one known as Proclus' *Elements of Theology*,

[78] Cf. Badawī (ed.), *Plotinus apud Arabes*, pp. 1–164, and Kraus, "Plotin chez les Arabes," *Bull. de l'Institut d'Egypte*, 23 (1941), p. 267. Cf. English version, *Plotini Opera*, II, ed. Henry and Schweyzer (hereafter cited as "Henry").

[79] Cf. Duhem, *Le système du monde*, IV, 325.

[80] *Al-Fihrist*, p. 367.

or Στοιχείωσις Θεολογική, which went into the pseudo-Aristotelian corpus in Arabic. The Scholastic authors of the thirteenth century, such as St. Thomas and St. Albert the Great, studied or commented on this work under the rubric of *Liber de Causis* (Arabic: *Fi'l Khair al-Maḥḍ*).[81]

Both the *Theologia* and the *De Causis* are enormously remote from the genuine teaching of Aristotle. The former work has been shown to be a paraphrase of Books IV, V, and VI of the *Enneads* of Plotinus, which explains in part Porphyry's association with it in the Arabic tradition. Why the *Enneads*' genuine author is not mentioned in connection with this compilation, however, is due primarily to the startling fact that this great Greek thinker was almost unknown to the Arabs by name. The name of Plotinus, in its Arabic form of *Fluṭīnus*, occurs once or twice in our sources quite casually, among Aristotle's commentators.[82] He is, however, sometimes referred to as *al-Shaykh al-Yūnānī* or "Greek Sage."

In both the *Theologia* and *De Causis*, the doctrine of emanation, which served as the cornerstone of almost the whole of Arab philosophical thought, is fully expounded and discussed. Here Plotinus' doctrine of the One and the manner in which it generates the whole order of being beneath it is set forth at length. The nobility of its Plotinian theme and the boldness of its conceptions reportedly moved al-Kindī to write a commentary on this work.[83] Unfortunately this commentary has not reached us, but it must have set the tone for subsequent metaphysical discussions and made the already elaborate account of the origination of creatures from the One, as outlined by the author of the *Theologia*, more elaborate still.

The author of the *Theologia* states in the opening chapter that his aim is

To discuss the divine nature and exhibit it, by showing that it is the First Cause and that time and the *aeon* [*al-dahr*] are both beneath it, and that it is the cause of causes and their author, after a fashion; and that the luminous

[81] Cf. Anawati, "Prolégomènes à une nouvelle édition du *De Causis* Arabe," *Mélanges Louis Massignon*, pp. 75 ff.; also Duhem, *Le système du monde*, IV, 332.

[82] *Al-Fihrist*, p. 371, and al-Qifṭī, *Tārīkh*, p. 258.

[83] *Al-Fihrist*, p. 366; al-Qifṭī, *Tārīkh*, p. 43.

virtue (or power) shines forth from it upon Reason; and through the intermediary of Reason upon the universal and heavenly Soul; and from Reason, through the intermediary of the Soul upon Nature; and from the Soul through the intermediary of Nature upon the objects of generation and corruption; and that this action [of the One] issues forth from it without movement; and that the movement of all things is from it and through it; and that things gravitate toward it through a species of desire or appetite.[84]

In this movement of desire, the author finds the clue not only to the nature of the Soul, which acts as the link between the sensible and the intelligible worlds, but also the emanation of all things from the One (or First). Thus the Soul, which is none other than Reason in the guise of desire,[85] performs one of two functions: it orders or governs either the world of forms or that of particulars, depending upon whether it is moved by desire for the universal or for the particular.[86] When it desires the particular, owing to its yearning to reveal its active nature, it moves downward, dominated and directed by Reason, and dwells in animals, plants, or humans, in the form of an indivisible, incorporeal substance which, upon the disintegration of the body, will rejoin the realm of separate substances (or forms), after passing through a series of progressive purifications.[87] In support of this view, the author invokes the authority of Heraclitus, Empedocles, Pythagoras, and Plato, who are all said to have held that the Soul descends into the body from the intelligible world and will rejoin it upon its release from the bondage of the body. This body Plato has described as a dungeon to which the Soul is temporarily consigned, whereas Empedocles has described it as the rust which attacks it.[88]

The author of the *Theologia* also gives Plato the credit for introducing the distinction between sensible and intelligible entities and for ascribing to the latter the character of permanence and immutability and to the former that of perpetual flux. Despite this distinction, however, Plato held that the cause of corporeal and incorporeal entities is the same, i.e., the First True Entity (*Ens Realissimum*), the Pure Good, or God.[89]

[84] See *Theologia Aristotelis* in Badawī, *Plotinus apud Arabes*, p. 6, and English version in Henry, *Plotini Opera*, II. The Greek *Loca Parallela* are given in this edition.

[85] Badawī, *Plotinus apud Arabes*, p. 10 (Henry, p. 219).

[86] *Ibid.*, pp. 18 f. (Henry, pp. 219 f.).

[87] *Ibid.*, p. 20 (Henry, p. 221).

[88] *Ibid.*, pp. 23 f. (Henry, pp. 225 f.).

[89] *Ibid.*, p. 26 (Henry, p. 231).

A too literal interpretation of Plato might lead one to believe that the Pure Good was supposed to have created Reason, Soul, and Nature in time. However, Plato introduced the concept of time in his account of the beginning of creation, in emulation of the ancient philosophers, simply to underscore the distinction between the superior, primary causes and the inferior, secondary causes. For one cannot talk of cause without reference to the concept of time, since a cause is assumed to be prior to its effect. Such priority, however, need not necessarily refer to temporal priority. Of the two classes of agents, those which are subject to time and those which are not, only the former can be said to act in time, and accordingly can be described as *prior* to their effects. Indeed, the agent or cause reveals the very nature of the effect, and whether it is subject to time or not will depend not on its own nature as effect, but rather on that of its causes.[90]

In Chapters Two and Three, the author examines the manner in which the Soul becomes cognizant of things in the world of sense and raises three questions: (1) whether, upon rejoining the intelligible world, it retains such cognition; (2) whether the Soul is divisible or not, and (3) whether it is material or immaterial. To the first question, he replies that, in the intelligible realm, the Soul possesses knowledge of all things in a permanent, unchanging, and perfect manner, akin to the nature of that realm, and is accordingly in no need of recollecting those mutable cognitions which it acquired during its excursion into the world of sense. To the second question, he replies that divisibility is predicated of the Soul *per accidens*, not absolutely, since in essence it is one, eternal, and indivisible. However, through its union with the body it is divided into the animal, the appetitive, the irascible, and the cognitive, depending on the part of the body in which it dwells.[91]

In his account of the nature of the Soul, the author criticizes the view that the Soul is a harmony of the parts of the body.[92] He refers disparagingly to those who support this view as the materialists or physiologists. The Soul, he argues, cannot reasonably be identified

[90] Badawī, *Plotinus apud Arabes*, pp. 27 f. (Henry, p. 231).

[91] *Ibid.*, pp. 38 f. (Henry, pp. 63 f.).

[92] The reference is to the view of Empedocles and Pythagoras and their followers. Cf. Aristotle *De Anima* I, 408*a*.

with the harmony which belongs to the body, since it is the principle or cause of such harmony itself. Moreover, harmony is an accident which supervenes upon the body through the agency of the Soul, whereas the Soul itself is a substance which is distinct from the body and independent of it and stands to it in the capacity of guardian or ruler.[93]

Even the view that the Soul is an actuality (or *entelecheia*) of the body, which is advanced by the "more notable among the philosophers,"[94] must be carefully examined. The term "*entelecheia*" might mean the actuality or form of a natural object or an artifact to which the *entelecheia* belongs purely passively and with which it is indissolubly bound up. However, the relation of the Soul to the body is that of an active *entelecheia*, i.e., the principle or cause of the actuality proper to body.[95]

In Chapters Four and Six, the author dwells eloquently on the beauty and excellence of the intelligible world, which rises above the sensible and imparts to it all the perfections with which it is endowed. The intelligible world, according to him, is the locus of forms, which are the prototypes of objects found in the world of nature, and the immaterial paragons of beauty and perfection. This world is, moreover, the abode of spiritual beings—the pure intellects or separate intelligences, which are different from inferior intellects in that the objects of their knowledge are everlasting and unchanging.

As to the mode of being of these spiritual beings, about whom Aristotle had spoken only briefly, the writer explains that each one of them "dwells in the universality of the sphere of the heaven to which it belongs," while remaining locally distinct from the others, not in the manner in which corporeal entities are said to be distinct from each other, but in an entirely different manner. These "luminous" beings are not mutually exclusive, but rather complementary and interdependent in such a way that each one "perceives itself in the other."[96] in addition to perceiving everything else, whether intelligible or sensible, in a purely intellectual and instantaneous fashion.[97]

[93] Badawī, *Plotinus apud Arabes*, p. 53 (Henry, pp. 207, 199 f.).

[94] I.e., Aristotle and his school; see *De Anima* II, 412*b*5.

[95] Badawī, *Plotinus apud Arabes*, p. 55 (Henry, pp. 209 f.).

[96] *Ibid.*, p. 63 (Henry, p. 385). [97] *Ibid.*, pp. 63 f. (Henry, pp. 383 f.).

Perhaps the knottiest problem in the metaphysical doctrine of emanation that we shall find at the very center of Arab philosophical thought is the problem of plurality, or the emanation of the many from the One.[98] To furnish a clue to the solution of this problem, which Plato and the Eleatics had bequeathed to ancient philosophy, the author urges the searcher "to fix his gaze upon the True One alone, and leave behind all other things—and return to himself and pause there. For he will see, through the eye of the mind, the True One, motionless, rising aloft, above and beyond everything else, both intelligible and sensible, and will perceive all things, as images emanating[?] from him and tending toward him,"[99] actuated by their yearning (*shauq*) for him, as their origin or principle.

In order to grasp the emanation of the "nobler essences or Forms" from the One, however, it is necessary to abstract from all modes of temporal generation. For unlike their particular representations, these forms were generated by the One outside time (*bi ghair zamān*) and "without the interposition between them and their Creator-Author of any agency."[100] How indeed could they be supposed to have been generated in time, seeing that time and temporal entities are caused by those forms themselves? "The cause of time is not subject to time, and comes to be in a higher or nobler mode, similar to that of the shade in relation to the object causing it."[101]

Being the cause or principle of all things, the One is nevertheless thoroughly other than they. And whereas all things abide in it, it is not immanent in any of them. For all things have proceeded from it, subsist in it, and will ultimately return to it. It is precisely because the One is none of the things that emanate from it, that it is possible for all things to issue forth from it. The first emanation from it is Reason, which is also the first essence and the first perfect entity, from which the essences of all things, both in the higher and the lower worlds, emanate.

Paradoxically enough, the One which causes all being and perfection is nevertheless above being and perfection, since it lacks nothing.

[98] Badawī, *Plotinus apud Arabes*, p. 113.
[99] *Ibid.*, p. 114 (Henry, pp. 273 f.).
[100] *Ibid.*
[101] *Ibid.*

Indeed, it is on account of its superlative perfection that the first perfect being (i.e., Reason) has issued forth from it.[102]

The Perfect (*al-Tāmm*), which is also the first being or essence, trains its gaze upon its author, is filled with light and beauty, and thereby becomes Reason. As a result, its actions have come to resemble those of the True One, from which it derived, and by which it was endowed with "great and numerous powers," whereupon it produced the Soul, in a motionless manner, analogous to the manner in which the One produced Reason in the first place. The Soul, however, being "the effect of an effect," is unable to act without motion, the product of its action being an image, i.e., an entity "which is continually revolving and is neither permanent or lasting," as indeed are all the products of motion. This image is the world of Nature or sense.[103]

Being intermediate between the world of Reason and the world of sense, the Soul is able to direct its gaze upward toward its author and acquire thereby "power and light," or downward, and produce thereby the world of Nature. The abject destiny of the Soul, according to the author of the *Theologia*, is bound up with its preoccupation with the "ignoble" objects of sense, in preference to the "noble" objects of reason.[104]

In its degeneration, the Soul passes through the three successive stages: the vegetable, animal, and human modes of being. The lower the mode, the lower the condition to which the Soul sinks. When conjoined to man, the Soul regains its kinship to Reason, since it recovers, in addition to the faculty of motion, the faculties of sense and thought. And even in its association with the vegetable or animal species, it never completely loses its intelligible character. For upon being released from its temporary dwelling in the world of Nature, it rejoins the intelligible world, which is its genuine locus or abode. Not being confined to place, the Soul is able to subsist everywhere and to pervade the whole world, without partaking of the divisibility of the whole.[105]

[102] Badawī, *Plotinus apud Arabes*, pp. 138 f. (Henry, pp. 291 f.). The writer, who sometimes describes the One as the acme of perfection, is not consistent in his claim that it is above perfection. In general, he refers to the One as superior to the First Perfect Being, i.e., Reason.

[103] *Ibid.*, p. 136 (Henry, p. 293).

[104] *Ibid.*, pp. 136 f. (Henry, pp. 293 f.).

[105] *Ibid.*, pp. 137 f. (Henry, p. 295).

If it is asked now what is the locus of the intelligible essences or forms, the author's answer is that it is the First Reason, which is expressly described as the locus of forms. "All things," says the author, "are found in the First Reason, since the First Agent [the One] has made this first product [Reason] to contain many Forms, and each of these Forms to contain all the particular objects corresponding to that Form."[106] These forms, however, are conceived of not merely as the universal prototypes of things, but as their creative principles as well. Called the "active logoi" by the author, they correspond to the "*λογοὶ σπερματικοὶ*" or *rationes seminales* of the Stoics and the early church fathers.[107]

The manifestation of Reason in Creation is all pervasive. At the lowest levels of animate life, we find unconscious reason (*ghair nāṭiq*), which manifests itself not only in the vital functions which the lower beasts possess, but also in "its endeavor to make up for the imperfection [of the animal], by providing it with certain organs [such as teeth, claws, horns, etc.] which contribute to rendering it perfect. Since it is due to every living thing to be perfect or complete, in so far as it is alive and is rational."[108]

Higher up in the scale of being we encounter conscious reason, which is a kind of light emanating from the First Reason. It permeates the rational animal or "natural man," who is an image or copy of the "intelligible man" but is so engrossed in the world of sense that he is unable to rise above the plane of opinion or discursive thought. If, however, like "the Divine Plato," he can transcend the world of sense, he will be able to gaze upon the intelligible world in the fullness of its beauty and splendor, and apprehend the truth of things without mental discourse or exertion.[109] Having attained this level, he would have justified his kinship to the "intelligible man," who is his prototype, and his citizenship in the intelligible world, which is his true abode.

The *Liber de Causis* consists of thirty-one or thirty-two propositions which, like the *Theologia*, expound succinctly the chief tenets of

106 Badawī, *Plotinus apud Arabes*, p. 139 (Henry, pp. 441 f.).
107 *Ibid.*, pp. 113, 141, 143, 144, *et passim* (Henry, pp. 273, 447, 449).
108 *Ibid.*, p. 151 (Henry, p. 459).
109 *Ibid.*, pp. 142 f., 157 f. (Henry, pp. 449, 389).

emanationism. How early this work was translated into Arabic is difficult to determine. Ibn al-Nadīm, who wrote his bibliographical dictionary (*al-Fihrist*) in 987, ascribes to Proclus in addition to the *Elementatio Theologica* a treatise on the *First Good*, which appears to be the same as the *Liber de Causis*.[110] An earlier work, the *Ṣuwān al-Ḥikmah* of al-Sijistānī (tenth century), cites excerpts that are purported to be taken from Proclus' book entitled *Niskus* [?] *Minor* or the *Pure Good*.[111] This would strengthen the supposition that the book was probably in circulation in the tenth century as borne out also by a treatise ascribed to the great naturalist and physician al-Rāzī (d. ca. 925) and entitled the *Arguments against Proclus*.[112] His arguments for the eternity of the world, as well as John Philoponus' counterarguments, had acquired considerable vogue among the Muslim theologians and philosophers of that century.[113]

The *Liber de Causis* ranks with the *Theologia Aristotelis* as a major Greek source of the emanationist world-view to which the Muslim philosophers adhered almost without exception. The book embodies the substance of Neo-Platonic thought[114] as it was partially modified by the great Neo-Platonist of the fifth century, Proclus, a pupil of Syrianus and a familiar name in the Arabian rosters of Aristotelian "commentators."

The introductory propositions deal with the Proclean tetrad of One, Essence, Reason, and Soul, which already involves a development of the Plotinian triad in which Essence has no distinct place. The *Liber de Causis* interposes Essence between Reason and the One, stating expressly (Prop. 4) "that the first created being is Essence—since it is above sense, above Soul and above Reason,"[115] and it is on that

[110] *Al-Fihrist*, p. 367; Ibn Abī Uṣaybi'ah, *'Uyūn*, I, 69. See also Anawati, "Prolegomènes," pp. 77–78.

[111] Cf. Al-Bayhaqī, *Muntakhab Ṣuwān al-Ḥikmah*, Bodleian Ms, *Marsh* 539 and *Koprülü Ms*, 902.

[112] *Al-Fihrist*, p. 432; al-Qifṭī, *Tārīkh*, p. 275; Ibn Abī Uṣaybi'ah, *'Uyūn*, I, 319.

[113] Al-Bīrūnī (d. 1048) quotes two passages from this book in his *Indica*; see pp. 17, 32.

[114] For a summary of the thirty-two propositions into which the book is divided see Hauréau, *De la phil. scholastique*, I, 384–90. See also St. Thomas Aquinas, *In Liber de Causis*, in *Opuscula Omnia*, X, etc.

[115] See Badawī, *Neoplatonici apud Arabes*, p. 6. "Essence" (*anniyah*) is rendered in the Latin version as "*esse*" or "to be." Cf. Duhem, *Le système du monde*, Vol. IV, p. 334.

account the most comprehensive created being, as well as the highest and the most unified, by virtue of its proximity to the One from which it directly springs. But it is not for that reason entirely free from plurality, since it is composed of the two contrary elements of finitude and infinity. In so far as it is contiguous to the first cause, "it is perfect, complete and all-powerful Reason," containing within itself all the intellectual virtues and forms, in the highest degree of universality; but in so far as it is not, it is an inferior reason, containing in itself the intellectual forms, in a lesser degree of universality. Multiplicity arises within it by virtue of the above-mentioned duality, and this is what gives rise to a multiplicity of intellectual forms. For the same form, when diversified in the lower world, gives rise to an infinite number of particular objects corresponding to it. However, this multiplicity does not impair the intrinsic unity of Essence, since its effects are not as distinct from it as the particular objects of sense are from the forms to which they correspond. Essence, then, is "one without corruption, diverse without distinctness; being a unity in plurality and a plurality in unity."[116]

The third entity in the scale is the Plotinian Reason, which shares in the nature of Essence, in so far as they are both caused and are intellectual entities. However, they both differ from the One in that the One is above time and the *aeon*, whereas Essence and Reason are above time, but subsist in the *aeon*, which is the duration of the eternal entities subsisting in the intelligible world. The Soul, which is the fourth emanation from the One, is beneath the *aeon*, but above time, being the cause of time and of motion, which is a concomitant of time (Prop. 2).

Reason differs from the Soul in other respects also. It is an "indivisible substance," which is not subject to the categories of magnitude, body, or motion (Prop. 6). Its mode of cognition is twofold: it knows what is beneath it, in so far as it is its cause, and it knows what is above it, in so far as it is its effect. However, its cognition of the particulars that are generated by it is not particular but universal, for even the particular subsists in Reason in an intellectual, or universal, way

[116] Badawī, *Neoplatonici apud Arabes*, p. 7.

(Prop. 7). In this manner, Reason apprehends all things, through the power conferred upon it by the One, and in so apprehending them preserves and orders them. However, its apprehension of the inferior objects of generation is mediated by the Soul's apprehension of Nature and Nature's apprehension of the objects of generation beneath it. Accordingly, Reason might be described as the "ruler of all the things beneath it and their preserver through the divine power which belongs to it and through which it is the cause of all things" (Prop. 8).

What Reason knows or cognizes are the forms of things, which, according to the author of *Liber de Causis*, as indeed according to Plato himself, must differ in the degree of their universality; the higher the rank of the reason in question in the hierarchy of being, the greater the universality of the forms contained in it (Prop. 9). These forms, being the subject matter of the cognition of Reason, are not to be conceived of, however, as distinct from the essence of Reason itself, since according to the famous Aristotelian dictum which the author here invokes, "every reason-in-act is both object and subject [thinker and thought]" and, in thinking itself, thinks all the things inferior to it in a universal manner (Prop. 12). Not only in the point of knowledge, but also in the point of being, Reason stands to the whole order of being inferior to it, as indirect source or fountainhead. Like the One, which it emulates, Reason communicates its essence to the things beneath it in the same manner in which the One communicates its goodness to all things (Prop. 22).

Whereas both the One and Reason are above time and movement, the Soul, which is generated by the One through the agency of Reason, is essentially the principle of motion and time. "It moves the first sphere, as well as all the natural spheres, being at the same time the cause of the movement of the spheres and the activity of Nature" (Prop. 3). Standing on the periphery of the intelligible world, it bridges the gulf between the world of "immovable, intelligible entities" and the world of movable, sensible entities. Since they subsist in the Soul, *qua* universal prototypes or forms of things, the Soul might be said to be the "formal cause" of these sensible entities. And being the principle of motion imparted to them, it might be said to be their "efficient cause." In fact, the writer states, "by Soul, I mean the power which causes sensible things to be" (Prop. 13). This active or creative power of the Soul, however, should not be compared to material or physical powers, since it belongs to the Soul to contain "sensible, physical, movable entities" in a unitary and immaterial fashion, whereas "intellectual, unitary, and immovable entities" are contained in it accidentally in a movable and multiple manner (Prop. 13).

The One, which stands at the apex of the hierarchy of being which proceeds eternally from it, is sometimes called by the author the First Entity, sometimes the First Cause, the One True Being, the Pure Good, or the Pure Light. One wonders, in view of this great diversity of names, whether the author, in the manner of most mystical writers, is not concerned to underscore the fact that the One is featureless and nameless. As the principle of all things, the entity above which there is no other entity, the One must forever elude the grasp of the mind. For, of the two classes of things, the sensible and the intelligible, the former are objects of sense and imagination, the latter objects of discursive thought. Being above both classes, the First Cause cannot be grasped either by sense or reason. Only its existence can be inferred from the consideration or perusal of the first[117] caused being, i.e., Reason (Prop. 5).

As further proof of the One's transcendence, the author of *Liber de Causis* observes that the First Principle is above infinity and perfection, both of which he identifies with Reason (Prop. 15). For the perfect, being self-sufficient, is incapable of producing anything else (Prop. 21), and the infinite is the principle of the endless series of things below it only.

The clue to the emanation of things from the One is found, as with Plato and Plotinus, in its character as the Chief Good, which communicates its goodness or essence necessarily to all things, in a uniform manner. Diversity arises from the different dispositions of things and their diverse natures, which cause them to receive the uniform outpouring of the goodness of the First Principle in different ways and in

[117] The text says "second," but this might refer to its position next to Essence, which is sometimes identified with, sometimes distinguished from, the *First* caused entity, i.e., Reason.

varying degrees. That is how diversity arises in a world otherwise dominated by a supreme principle of unity.[118]

Not only the generation of things, but their preservation in being is due to the One, who safeguards the order and permanence of the universe through the same act which posits them in being. The One preserves and orders the universe in a faultless and superior manner, being free from composition itself (Prop. 19).

The other attributes of the One upon which the author dwells should be briefly listed here. It is wholly self-sufficient (Prop. 20), nameless (Prop. 21), all-knowing and all-preserving (Prop. 22), all-present and all-permeating (Prop. 23), absolutely incomposite (Prop. 24), incorruptible (Prop. 25, 26), simple and indivisible (Prop. 27), and the ultimate principle of all unity and being in the world (Prop. 31).

Those two Neo-Platonic compilations contain virtually all the germinal elements that went into Islamic Neo-Platonism: the utter transcendence of the First Principle or God; the procession or emanation of things from Him; the role of Reason as the instrument of God in his creation, and the locus of the forms of things, as well as the source of the illumination of the human mind; the position of the Soul at the periphery of the intelligible world and the link or "horizon" between the intelligible and the sensible worlds; and finally the contempt in which matter was held, as the basest creation or emanation from the One and the lowest rung in the cosmic scale.

Other documents of lesser importance also expound or develop the same Neo-Platonic themes of emanation and the absolute transcendence of the First Principle. These works reflect the eclectic spirit of the late Hellenistic period, as illustrated by Porphyry (d. ca. 304), Jamblichus (d. ca. 330), Damascius (d. 553), Syrianus (d. ca. 450), and Simplicius (d. 533). Such, for instance, is the character of a treatise on metaphysics (*Fi'l-'Ilm al-Ilāhī*) attributed to al-Fārābī, one attributed to 'Abd al-Laṭīf al-Baghdādī, as well as a whole series of fragments ascribed to al-Shaykh al-Yūnānī (Plotinus).[119]

[118] Badawī, *Neoplatonici apud Arabes*, Props. 19, 21, and 23.

[119] Badawī, *Plotinus apud Arabes*, pp. 165–240; and Rosenthal, "As-Šaykh al-Yunānī, and the Arabic Plotinus Source," in *Orientalia*, Vol. 21 (1952), pp. 461–529; Vol. 22 (1953), pp. 370–400; Vol. 24 (1955), pp. 42–66; and Henry, II, *passim*.

IV

PERSIAN AND INDIAN INFLUENCES

ALTHOUGH their cultural debt to the Greeks was very great, the Arabs did not escape the influence of the Persians and Indians, particularly in the positive sciences, medicine, and political institutions. Contact with these two cultures began as early as the eighth century.

We have already noted that one of the earliest works to be translated into Arabic was an Indian astronomical treatise, the *Siddhanta* of Brahmagupta, which in the Arabic version of al-Fazārī played an important role in the development of Islamic astronomy.[120] In addition, numerous Indian medical works were translated during the reigns of al-Manṣūr and Hārūn, at the instance of the great Persian vizier Yaḥia al-Barmakī, who is reported in the Arabic sources to have made a decisive contribution to the cause of scientific and cultural progress among the Arabs.[121]

The interest of the Muslims in Indian and Persian philosophical literature, however, does not appear to have been as extensive as their interest in Indian astronomy and medicine. But the measure of their acquaintance with this literature might be gauged from the fact that an anonymous treatise on the *Religious Beliefs of the Indians* was in circulation among the Arabs by the end of the eighth century. Ibn al-Nadīm, who reports this, states in his bibliographical dictionary that he saw a copy of this work in the handwriting of al-Kindī,[122] the great Arab philosopher whose interest in philosophical and theological literature has been repeatedly mentioned. Other works of a moral or religious nature are quoted or listed by the same authority in his account of Indian religious beliefs and in his catalogue of Indian,

[120] *Supra*, p. 19. [121] *Al-Fihrist*, pp. 435, 498.

[122] *Ibid.*, p. 498. Al-Kindī died around 866; however Ibn al-Nadīm states that he saw another anonymous copy of this book dated 863 which was purported to have been written by an Indian scholar for Yaḥia al-Barmakī.

Persian, and Greek works on moral philosophy known to the Arabs.[123]

If we turn now to the more philosophical elements in Indian thought which might have influenced the Arabs, we are at once struck by their relative scarcity, or their triviality when compared with the rich stream of ideas that came from Greece. The chief Muslim writer on India, al-Bīrūnī (d. 1048), writing in 1030, devoted a number of chapters in his treatise *On the Truth about the Beliefs of India*[124] to philosophical and religious matters. Al-Bīrūnī's account, however, came too late to make any decisive impact upon Arab philosophy in its formative stages. But the great Muslim astronomer pays an almost unknown but interesting character, al-Irānshahrī (second half of the ninth century), a singular compliment by naming him as the only writer to have aimed at objectivity in his account of the religious beliefs of the Indians.[125] Unfortunately, however, the works attributed to al-Irānshahrī by the only other authority to have referred to him, the Persian Ismā'īlī author Nāṣir-i-Khusrū (d. 1061), have not come down to us.[126] But his association with one of the greatest figures in the history of Islamic philosophy and science, al-Rāzī, emphasizes his importance in the history of religio-philosophical nonconformism in Islam and lends his name a particular luster among the solitary, searching spirits of the ninth century. If it is true, as Nāṣir-i-Khusrū states, that al-Rāzī took over from al-Irānshahrī some of his views on matter, space, and time, we might seek in the philosophical doctrines of the latter the possible influence of India on the philosophers of Islam. The problem is complicated, however, by the circumstance that al-Rāzī has had to pay the classic price for his intellectual boldness: the consignment of most of his literary output to oblivion. However, enough has survived of al-Rāzī's philosophical writings to enable us to reconstruct his view of the world and of man with a certain measure of completeness. The most distinctive aspect of that view of man and the world is his belief in five eternal principles encompassing every aspect of the world, his conception of the atomic composition of bodies, and perhaps, for a Muslim, his boldest view, belief in the transmigration of the Soul. Although the

[123] *Al-Fihrist*, pp. 501, 452 f. [124] Edited by Sachau. [125] *Ibid.*, p. 4.

[126] *Zād al-Musāfirīn*, pp. 98, 343. See also Pines, *Beiträge zur Islamischen Atomenlehre*, pp. 34 f.

influence of Plato and Pythagoras is undoubted, some aspects of his theory of the Soul and its reincarnations, of time and the composition of matter, cannot be fully explained in terms of Greek philosophy, and therefore a possible Indian influence naturally suggests itself.[127]

Apart from al-Rāzī, atomism was in great vogue among the Muslim theologians. These theologians had evolved, chiefly as a reaction against Aristotelianism, a distinctive theory of the world resting upon the cardinal dualism of substance and accident, which was identified before long with orthodoxy. With hardly a single exception, the Muslim theologians accepted the atomic view of matter, space, and time, and built upon it an elaborate theological edifice over which God presided as absolute sovereign.[128] We shall have occasion to consider this atomic theory later, but it is noteworthy that some of its important divergences from Greek antecedents, such as the atomic nature of time, space, and accidents, the perishability of atoms and accidents, appear to reflect an Indian influence. The two Buddhist sects of Vaibhashika and Sautrantika, the two Brahmin sects of Nyaya and Vaishashika, as well as the Jaina sect, had evolved by the fifth century an atomic theory, apparently independent of the Greek, in which the atomic character of matter, time, and space was set forth and the perishable nature of the world resulting from their composition was emphasized.[129] Accidents were recognized, in the manner of the Muslim theologians, as a distinct class of entities and were defined simply as what supervenes upon the atom. Like the accidents of the Ash'arites, they were incapable of duration in their own right.[130]

Many other similarities between Islamic and Indian atomism and their implications may be noted. Perhaps the most significant feature which the two theories have in common is the vindication of the ephemeral character of being and its fundamental metaphysical

[127] Both al-Rāzī's atomism and his concept of the five eternal principles exhibit a striking similarity to the teaching of the Nyaya-Vaishishka sect as well. See Radhakrishnan, *History of Philosophy, Eastern and Western*, I, 227–28, and *infra.*

[128] See Fakhry, *Islamic Occasionalism*, pp. 37 f., 71 f.

[129] See Hastings, *Encyclopaedia of Religion and Ethics*, Atomic Theory (Indian), II, 200; and Pines, *Beiträge*, pp. 102 ff.; Radhakrishnan, *History of Philosophy, Eastern and Western*, I, 143 f., 224–29. Cf. Fakhry, *Islamic Occasionalism*, pp. 26 f., 34 f.

[130] See, e.g., al-Baghdādī, *Uṣūl al-Dīn*, p. 56; al-Bāqillānī, *al-Tamhīd*, pp. 18 f., and *infra.*

contingency, which is at the very root of both Islamic and Indian thought.

There are other instances of the Arabs' acquaintance with Indian thought. Muslim writers ascribe to an Indian sect, generally designated as *Barāhima* (i.e., Brahmins), the view that prophethood or the commissioning of prophets by God is altogether unnecessary, and therefore theological treatises generally devote considerable space to the vindication of prophethood against these Brahmins and against the rationalists who argue that thanks to unaided reason we can dispense with revelation altogether.

Another mysterious Indian sect, the Sumaniya, which appears to have had some following among the Muslims, is mentioned in Arab sources. Very little is known about this sect, but it is significant that the Arab theologians who were not sufficiently familiar with the Greek skeptics, cite the Sumaniya as the exponents of an agnostic or skeptical epistemology in which any supersensible knowledge is impossible.[131]

The Persian influence on Islamic philosophical thought was equally restricted and consisted chiefly of a certain amount of moral or aphoristic traditions. We owe to one of the earliest translators into Arabic, the Persian Ibn al-Muqaffa', a masterly translation from Pahlevi of a book of fables, *Kalīla wa Dimna*, originally written in Sanskrit and attributed to Bidpai, the Indian sage. This translation has always occupied a prominent position in the history of Arabic prose, as well as in moral exhortation. A mass of aphoristic literature, of which a major part is attributed to such sages as Anūshirwān, Buzurjumhr (Vuzurgmihr), or Kisrā (Khosroes), has somehow and at some time trickled from Persian sources. It is possible that Persian authors, writing in the tenth century, found it necessary to concoct compilations of moral or religious aphorisms in order to substantiate the Persian nationalist contention that the ancient Persians were the peers of the Greeks or the Arabs in wisdom. An important collection of this kind, still extant, is attributed to the Persian philosopher Miskawayh (d. 1030); the title of it, translated from Pahlevi, is *Jawidān Khirad*. It consists of the exhortations, among others, of the prehistoric Iranian king Ushahang (Hoshang) to his son. The moral aphorisms of such

[131] Al-Bīrūnī, *Indica*, pp. 10 f.; *al-Fihrist*, p. 498; Pines, *Beiträge*, pp. 107, 110.

notable Persian, Arab, and Greek sages as Anūshirwān, Luqmān, Hermes, Diogenes, and many others, are added by Miskawayh.[132]

Other moral treatises were written by authors of Persian origin, not least of which is a *Treatise on Morals* by Ibn al-Muqaffa', bearing on such matters as the manner in which one should treat one's associates, or one's superiors, the nature of virtue, etc. It is written in that florid, rhetorical style in which the Persian Ibn al-Muqaffa' sought obviously to rival Arab stylists.[133]

In the speculative domain, the Persian influence centered almost exclusively on the religious and philosophical implications of Manichaean dualism,[134] which appears to have had a great vogue among Arab authors. Some of the fiercest polemics against heretics, known by the Persian name of Zindigs, are aimed at Manichaeanism.[135] These polemics are in themselves symptomatic of the diffusion of Manichaeanism in Islam, echoes of which ring not only in philosophical and theological works or disputations but even in purely literary works as well. It would be pointless to attempt a historical survey of a current of ideas which we meet at almost all the junctions of intellectual life in Islam. The professional philosophers themselves did not escape its influence and most discussions of the problem of unity as predicated of God are written with the Manichaean heresy as a background.

Although the comparative insignificance of the Persian metaphysical element in Muslim thought is apparent, it should be remembered that the Persian contribution to the mainstream of philosophical thought in Islam came from the new generation of Persian thinkers and philosophers. Having imbibed Greek ideas and the few vestiges of ancient Persian culture they could find, they left an indelible mark upon the history of thought in Islam. Indeed their preeminence was such that after 750 almost all the chief luminaries of Islam were of Persian origin:

[132] See *Jawidān Khirad*, Badawī's edition. See also Henning, "Eine Arabische Version Mittel-Persischen Weisheitschriften," in *Zeitschrift der Deutschen Morgenlandischen Gesellschaft*, Vol. 106, I (1956), pp. 73–77, and *Islamic Culture*, Vol. 35, 4 (1961), pp. 238–43.

[133] Istanbul Ms., Nurosmaniye, 2392.

[134] See discussion of Mani and his views in *al-Fihrist*, pp. 470–87.

[135] A long list of Zindigs, including such notorious characters as Ibn al-Muqaffa', Bashshār the poet, the members of the Barmakī family, and even an Umayyad caliph, Marwān (744–750), is given in *al-Fihrist*, pp. 486 f.

the greatest grammarian, Sībawayh (d. ca. 793), the greatest philosopher, Ibn Sīnā (d. 1037), the greatest physician, al-Rāzī, and the greatest theologian, al-Ghazālī (d. 1111). What they owed to the Arabs, with whom they entered into such active competition and rivalry after the accession of the ʿAbbāsids in 750, was their cultural language as well as their religion. But it is a measure of the cultural climate of the times that racial allegiance counted for little as compared with the more overriding religious loyalty in which Persians and Arabs shared, and to which most of them subordinated their intellectual interests and pursuits.

CHAPTER TWO

Early Political and Religious Tensions

I

THE RELIGIO-POLITICAL FACTIONS

THE full impact of Greek philosophy on Islamic thought came in the wake of the introduction and diffusion of Greek philosophical texts in the ninth century. Prior to that period, the Muslims were largely preoccupied with the pressing political and military problems that confronted them; apart from poetry, which often served a political purpose, their cultural interests were somewhat limited. However, the close interrelation between Islamic politics and religion, the order of law and that of belief, was certain to breed, almost from the start, labyrinthine religio-political controversies as soon as the first political rifts had broken the crust of religious unity in the early period.

Despite the remote bearing of Islamic religious belief on the development of philosophy, we should at least cast a brief glance at the first attempts to define some of these basic concepts. Formulations of religious concepts often were made in the process of bolstering up conflicting political positions and then took on decisive significance in the subsequent development of Islamic theology.

The first serious political rift grew out of a struggle for the leadership of the Muslim community by the two able contestants for the caliphate, 'Alī, son-in-law of Muḥammad and fourth caliph, and Mu'āwiyah, governor of Damascus and founder of the Umayyad dynasty. According to the traditional account, just as 'Alī was about to snatch the fruit of victory in a battle at ṣiffīn in 657, Mu'āwiyah tricked him into calling off the fighting and consenting to arbitration, which eventually resulted in 'Alī's downfall.[1] As a consequence, a section of his army mutinied, allegedly because his consent to arbitration cast suspicion upon his legitimate claims to the caliphate. Whether there were other factors at work need not concern us here. The important point is that these mutineers, called thereafter the Khārijites or Secessionists, raised for the first time in the history of Islam the question of the ground and limits of political authority; they even went as far as repudiating the necessity of the caliphal office altogether and advocating tyrannicide.[2] Their encouragement of anarchy and political assassination, however, was bound up with a precise view of the nature and scope of orthodoxy (or piety), which set them apart from revolutionary groups elsewhere. According to the Khārijites, a Muslim who committed a grave sin (*kabīrah*), political or other, would cease to be a Muslim, and if he were the caliph he could be deposed or killed legitimately as an infidel.[3] From this it followed that orthodoxy was not only the natural basis of political authority but of membership in the Muslim community as well.

This extremist position did not go unchallenged by other Muslim sects, such as the Shī'ah, who pledged 'Alī their unquestioning support, and the Murji'ah, who challenged the Khārijites' hidebound conception of faith (*imān*). Whereas the Khārijites had tended to equate belief with outward conformity to the Holy Law, the Murji'ah identified it with "the knowledge of, submission to, and love of God" and urged

[1] Al-Mas'ūdī, *Murūj*, IV, 391 f.; al-Ṭa. arī, *History*, I, 3340–60 f.; Hitti, *History of the Arabs*, pp. 181 f.

[2] Al-Shahrastānī, *al-Milal*, pp. 92 ff.

[3] *Ibid.*, p. 91. See also al-Baghdādī, *al-Farq bain al-Firaq*, p. 62 (hereafter cited as *al-Farq*).

that acts of piety (or good works) were no indication of genuine faith.[4] The faithful will be consigned to paradise according to their sincerity and love, rather than their knowledge or obedience to God. Should one in whose heart "submission to and love of God" are firmly rooted nevertheless commit a sin, it will not impair his faith or cause him to forfeit his rightful place in paradise.[5] The ultimate verdict should, at any rate, be left to God, and political authority should not be questioned on theological grounds since it belongs to God alone to determine the genuineness of the faith of rulers, as indeed of all Muslims.[6]

On the crucial question of eligibility to the caliphate, the Murji'ah agreed with the Khārijites in one important particular: any pious Muslim who was deemed worthy by the community was eligible to that office, regardless of whether he descended from Quraysh, the Prophet's tribe, or even was of Arab stock, as the conservatives had stipulated.[7]

Other extremely liberal views of the Murji'ah included the claim, ascribed to some of their leading theologians, that verbally professing the most heterodox beliefs (such as tritheism) does not necessarily entail infidelity, and that committing the gravest sin does not lessen the faith or jeopardize the salvation of the Muslim who died professing belief in God's unity, which was the sole prerequisite of salvation, according to them.[8]

The third major religio-political sect to emerge during the upheavals that shattered the unity of Islam shortly after Muḥammad's death, was the Shī'ah. It was by far the most important faction to break away from the main body of Islam. Like the other two sects considered above, the Shī'ah sprang out of the political struggles of the times and the attempt to find an adequate answer to the problem of political authority which the Khārijites had so dramatically raised. If the Khārijites are said to have revolted against the fourth caliph out of jealousy for the unquestioned constitutional prerogatives of the duly elected caliph, and the Murji'ah to have voiced a mild protest against

[4] Al-Shahrastānī, *al-Milal*, p. 104; al-Baghdādī, *al-Farq*, pp. 191 ff.

[5] *Ibid.*, p. 104.

[6] Cf. Goldziher, *Le dogme et la loi de l'Islam*, p. 68.

[7] Al-Shahrastānī, *al-Milal*, p. 106, and cf. p. 86; al-Baghdādī, *al-Farq*, p. 190.

[8] *Ibid.*, pp. 104, 107; al-Baghdādī, *al-Farq*, p. 195; Goldziher, *Le dogme*, pp. 180 f.

fanaticism, but left all answers to God, the Shī'ah simply pledged their absolute and unqualified support to 'Alī as the sole legitimate claimant to the caliphate.[9] In trying to give substance to their claims for 'Alī's legitimacy, the Shī'ah often resorted to *de jure* rather than *de facto* arguments and rested most of their claims on an a priori or idealized conception of the caliph (whom they call *Imām*, i.e., head or master) and his functions. The *Imām*, they contended, was not only the sole rightful successor of Muḥammad, whose succession can only run in his progeny (the so-called House of the Prophet), but also was the only authoritative interpreter of the Holy Law.

Unlike the Khārijites, who did not flinch from the prospect of political anarchy, the Shī'ites stood for a monarchy of the strictest theocratic and absolutist type. They maintained that the caliph or *Imām* is not chosen by popular election, as had been the constitutional fiction underlying the election of the first three caliphs, but rather by divine designation. The Prophet, in nominating him, simply acts as the mouthpiece of God.[10] Since the chief characteristic of the *Imām* is his inability to err or to sin (*'uṣmah*), it follows that the charge of violating the Holy Law or the precepts of God can never be leveled at him or used as a pretext for deposing him, as the Khārijites had done; to do this would be to jeopardize both the political unity of the community and the purity of the Holy Law.[11] Moreover, in view of the importance of his function as the vicegerent of God on earth and the infallible teacher or supreme pontiff of the Muslim community, his office can neither be dispensed with nor the line of succession guaranteeing it be broken. In the absence of the "visible" *Imām*, it can only be assumed that he is in temporary "concealment" (*ghaibah*) and the Muslim community must manage its affairs on some kind of interim basis as best it can until his eventual return at the end of time (*raj'ah*).[12]

Although the original supporters of 'Alī sought to find a textual basis in the Koran or the Traditions for their legitimist constitutional claims, it is clear that they drew their theological arguments mainly

[9] Goldziher, *Le dogme*, p. 165 f.; al-Shahrastānī, *al-Milal*, pp. 108 f.

[10] Al-Shahrastānī, *al-Milal*, pp. 108 f.

[11] Al-Naubakhtī, *Firaq al-Shī'ah*, pp. 16, 91.

[12] *Ibid.*, p. 91; al-Shahrastānī, *al-Milal*, pp. 122, 131; Goldziher, *Le dogme*, p. 165; Hitti, *al-Bābu'l-Ḥādī 'Ashar: A Treatise on the Principles of Shī'ite Theology*, passim.

from the realm of a priori speculation. They were so engrossed with the concept of the faultless *Imām* that they proceeded without hesitation to invest him with divine or semi-divine qualities. One of the earliest Shī'ites, 'Abdulla b. Saba', a convert from Judaism, is said to have taught that 'Alī was undying and that he would return at the end of time to "inherit the earth."[13] Other advocates of Shī'ism, while accepting in principle the concept of the undying *Imām*, reserved this privilege for their own *Imāms*. Thus the Ismā'īlis consider Ismā'īl, second son of Ja'far, who died in 760, the last *Imām* and claim that he is in temporary concealment, whereas the Twelvers look upon the twelfth *Imām*, Muḥammad Abu'l-Qāsim (d. 878), as the *Mahdī* or Guided One, who will return at the end of time to "fill the earth with justice, as it had been filled with injustice."[14]

On the other major issue that the Khārijites had raised and thereby bequeathed to subsequent theologians—the nature of belief or faith (*īmān*)—the Shī'ite position presents certain revolutionary features that are of considerable interest to the historian of Islamic ideas. Whereas, for instance, the Khārijites had declared the "Book of God" to be the ultimate court of appeal for the settlement of religio-political differences, the Shī'ites proclaimed the *Imām* as the ultimate theological and judicial authority in Islam and recognized him as the fount of religious instruction (*ta'līm*); hence the name *Ta'līmīs* is sometimes applied to the extreme Shī'ah, particularly the Ismā'īlis.

Moreover, since throughout Muslim history the Shī'ites had been forced into the position of a disgruntled minority whose political ambitions were repeatedly thwarted, it was natural that they should rebel intellectually against the facts of religio-political reality and seek in the realm of abstract constructions a spiritual haven to which they could turn in adversity. This tendency would probably account not only for the revolutionary spirit that fired many Shī'ite leaders throughout Muslim history and the occultism characterizing Shī'ite thought and attitude, but also their association with the leading school of rationalist theologians in Islam, i.e., the Mu'tazilah,[15] their recognition

[13] Al-Ash'arī, *Maqālāt*, p. 15; al-Naubakhtī, *Firaq al-Shī'ah*, pp. 18–20.

[14] Al-Naubakhtī, *ibid*, and Hitti, *al-Bābu'l-Ḥādī 'Ashar*, pp. 440 f.

[15] Goldziher, *Le dogme*, pp. 188 f.

of the validity of the independent judgment (*ijtihād*) of qualified jurists in matters of jurisprudence, even to the present day and their readiness to assimilate Greek philosophy without any hesitation. Paradoxically enough, however, some of the grossest forms of anthropomorphism were entertained by Shī'ite doctors,[16] probably as a means of bridging the gap between God and man, which their doctrine of the *Imām* required. And the Shī'ites' most excessive emphasis on the ritual aspects of belief, such as levitical cleanliness, was made possibly as a device for marking them off from the main body of orthodox Islam. Although allowance is made for the permissibility of circumspection (*taqiyah*) in outward observances, the fundamental difference between the Shī'ite and Sunnite sects of Islam, we think, should be sought in the Shī'ites' self-conscious and deliberate assertion of their inalienable identity. The negativism which stems from this assertion often reaches disproportionate dimensions, as expressed in the generally received Shī'ite maxim "Whatever runs counter to [the practice of] the community is the token of rectitude."

II

THE RISE OF ISLAMIC SCHOLASTICISM (KALĀM)

MUCH more important for our purposes than the religio-political factions discussed above are the more strictly theological divisions which began to split the ranks of Islam from the earliest times but apparently gained momentum with the introduction of Greek philosophy in the eighth and ninth centuries. The early jurists (*fuqahā'*) and Traditionists (*Muḥaddithūn*), despite their avowed literalism, did not fail altogether to perceive the obvious logical incongruencies of the sacred

[16] Al-Ash'arī, *Maqālāt*, pp. 15 f.; al-Shahrastānī, al-*Milal*, pp. 14, 143 ff.

texts and the problem of interpretation and harmonization which they inevitably raised. It appears, however, that only when more was at stake than the niceties of textual exegesis or linguistic analysis did theological schools begin to take shape and the protagonists of conflicting theological views begin to engage in debates of dogma. Political factors, Judaeo-Christian influences, as well as Greek philosophical ideas seem to have been the chief forces contributing to the acceleration of this process.

Most ancient authorities agree that the first abstract issue on which the earliest theological controversies hinged was the question of free will and predestination (*qadar*). Some of the first theologians to discuss this subject were Ma'bad al-Juhanī (d. 699), Ghailān al-Dimashqī (d. before 743), Wāṣil b. Aṭā' (d. 748), Yūnus al-Aswārī, and 'Amr b. 'Ubaid (d. 762).[17] Other theologians, like the famous Ḥasan al-Baṣrī (d. 728), who is at the center of many later theological developments, tended to confirm the traditional repudiation of free will in the interest of a quasi-absolute predestinarian eschatology. Some ancient authorities, however, attribute to him belief in free will.[18]

The theological claims of the proponents of free will (*Qadarīs*) would probably not have caused so much concern if it had not been for the political implications thought to be involved. Both Ma'bad and Ghailān were executed by order of the Umayyad caliphs 'Abdul-Malik (685–705) and Hishām (724–743) respectively, apparently on account of the challenge to the authority of the caliph and the threat to the stability of the political order which their concept of free will posed. A belief in free will meant, of course, that the caliph could no longer be relieved from the responsibility for his unjust deeds on the ground that they were the result of the inexorable decree of God.[19] And although two of the Umayyad caliphs, Mu'āwiyah II and Yazīd III, are said to have inclined toward the libertarian (or Qadarī) view,[20]

[17] Al-Shahrastānī, *al-Milal*, p. 17, and Watt, *Free Will and Predestination in Early Islam*, pp. 40 f.

[18] *Ibid.*, p. 32; Ibn Qutaybah, *Kitāb al-Ma'ārif*, p. 285; Watt, *Free Will*, pp. 54 f.

[19] Ibn Qutaybah, *Kitāb al-Ma'ārif*, p. 301; al-Ṭabarī, *History*, II, 1733; Watt, *Free Will*, pp. 40 f.; Browne, *Literary History of Persia*, I, 282 f.; al-Shahrastānī, *al-Milal*, p. 105.

[20] Browne, *Literary History*, p. 283; and Hitti, *al-Bābu'l-Ḥādī'Ashar*, p. 245.

the Qadarī movement was never in great vogue during the Umayyad period.

The strictures of the orthodox against the advocates of free will took on increased strength with the allegation that Greek or Christian thought was behind this notion. According to al-Shahrastānī, the early theological discussions on "fundamentals of belief" (*uṣūl*) during the latter part of the seventh century were vitiated by dialectical elements derived from the "books of the (Greek) philosophers,"[21] and a similar charge of Greek influence is continually leveled by orthodox writers at those they claim to be heretics.

Moreover, a Christian influence appears to have been at work during the early period at Damascus, where contact between Muslim and Christian theologians may be presumed to have been frequent, as evidenced by an extant tract purporting to summarize a discussion on free will and related subjects between a Christian and a Saracen. This work is attributed to Theodore Abū Curra (d. 826), Bishop of Ḥarrān, and disciple of St. John of Damascus (d. ca. 748), the last great theologian of the Eastern Church.[22] Also, reports of a conversation between Maʿbad, who initiated this whole current of discussion on free will, and a Christian from Iraq called Sausan are given by later authors.[23]

These early ventures into the realm of speculative theology naturally required the sharper tools of dialectic, which the Muslims were to borrow from the Greeks before the eighth century was over. So little is known about the early discussions on free will that it is not possible to reconstruct the theological picture of the period with any completeness, especially since our information about the Qadarī movement is mostly derived from later, hostile authors. Nevertheless, an advanced degree of refinement cannot be assumed before the movement became incorporated into the first major school of theology, i.e., the Muʿtazilah, whose leading doctors flourished during the ninth century and whose

[21] Al-Shahrastānī, *al-Milal*, p. 17.

[22] Migne, *P.G.* XCIV, Col. 1589 f.; Anawati and Gardet, *Introduction à la théologie musulmane*, pp. 201 f., 36 f.

[23] Ibn Ḥajar alʿ-Asqalānī, *Tahdhīb al-Tahdhīb*, X, 225 f.; Wensinck, *Muslim Creed*, p. 53; Browne, *Literary History*, pp. 280 ff.

cause was so zealously championed by the great 'Abbāsid caliph al-Ma'mūn.

According to the traditional account, the founder of the Mu'tazilite school was Wāṣil b. 'Aṭā' (d. 748), originally a pupil of al-Ḥasan al-Baṣrī, who was a central figure in the history of Islamic jurisprudence, asceticism, and theological dogma. His differences with his master are said to have centered around the vexed question the Khārijites had so dramatically raised: whether a Muslim who committed a grave sin (*kabīrah*) could still be rightly regarded as a Muslim. The Khārijites had answered this question in uncompromising negative terms, the Murji'ites in a liberal, if noncommittal, manner, and Wāṣil now, in a new, but subtle, fashion. The grave sinner, he urged, must be placed in an intermediary position between infidelity (*kufr*) and faith (*īmān*). Indeed such a sinner, Wāṣil appears to have contended, is what he is semantically acknowledged to be, a grave sinner (*fāsiq*), no more and no less.[24]

The primary interest of this solution is that it recognizes an essential distinction between three different concepts—infidel, sinner, and believer—which in the heat of theological polemics tended to be thoroughly confused. And although not very original or startling, Wāṣil's view underscores the difficulty that the theological bigot faces in keeping his balance on this kind of intellectual tight-rope. The moderation which Wāṣil and his followers showed in this regard is best illustrated by the attitude that they and even those among them who openly professed Shī'ism took concerning the crucial political issue of the unjust or sinful caliphs, as well as that of the legitimate successor of Muḥammad. Wāṣil is reported to have suspended judgment on the ground of insufficient evidence.[25]

Very little is known of Wāṣil's views on the other central questions that in time formed the basis of Mu'tazilite doctrine. It is important to note, however, an early and significant association between the Mu'tazilah and a contemporary of Wāṣil, Jahm b. Ṣafwān (d. 745), founder of the rival Jahmite school, which upheld the unqualified doctrine of divine omnipotence and the consequent absolute determination

[24] Al-Khayyāṭ, *Kitāb al-Intiṣār*, pp. 118 f.; al-Shahrastānī, *al-Milal*, pp. 17 ff.
[25] *Ibid.*, pp. 73 ff.

of all human actions by God. Other theologians must be assumed to have subscribed to this view, which with minor refinements was later identified with the orthodox belief and whose exponents are generally referred to as Jabrites (Determinists), without being identified by name. A controversy between Jahm and an emissary of Wāṣil is reported by a later authority,[26] and echoes of the polemics between the two schools ring through the old doxographical treatises. The striking point, however, is that on some basic propositions, such as the creation of the Koran, Jahm and the Muʿtazilah were in complete agreement—a circumstance that apparently led some of the adversaries of the Muʿtazilah and others to consider him one of them.[27] Jahm also appears to have held the view that God's attributes are identical with His essence, another cornerstone of Muʿtazilite doctrine and the key to their claim to be the only true confessors of divine unity (*Muwaḥḥidūn*), a name also applied to Jahm and his followers.[28]

Jahm maintained, however, in addition to his denial of free will, a belief in the ultimate destruction of heaven and hell, together with all their occupants,[29] a view which was entirely at variance with the Muʿtazilite concept of eternal punishment and reward and the consequent eternity of heaven and hell, which will be discussed in due course. In advancing this extraordinary view, Jahm appears to have been inspired by the desire to place a purely literal construction upon those verses in the Koran that speak of God as the "First and Last" (Koran 57, 3), or of the perishability of everything at the end of time, "save His face" (55, 27). However, it is significant that despite their differences, Jahm and Wāṣil, the founders of the two earliest schools of systematic theology, dealt roughly with the same cluster of theological problems, which split the Muslim community asunder as early as the beginning of the eighth century.

Although it is not possible to trace fully the development of the Muʿtazilite movement from Wāṣil's time onward because most writings of its early doctors have been lost, enough has survived to

26 Ibn al-Murtaḍa, *Al-Munia*, p. 19; and Pines, *Beiträge*, Appendix.

27 Al-Khayyāṭ, *Kitāb al-Intiṣār*, p. 92.

28 *Ibid.*, p. 92; al-Ashʿarī, *al-Ibānah*, p. 45; Pines, *Beitrgäe*, Appendix; Watt, *Free Will*, p. 103.

29 *Ibid.*, p. 18; al-Ashʿarī, *Maqālāt*, p. 542.

enable us to reconstruct the teaching of the Muʿtazilite school during its greatest period, the first half of the ninth century.

Almost all authorities agree that the speculation of the Muʿtazilah centered around the two crucial concepts of divine justice and unity, of which they claimed to be the exclusive, genuine exponents. Although other propositions were debated by them, it is noteworthy that many could be logically reduced to the two fundamental ideas of justice and unity. Thus, according to a leading Muʿtazilite authority of the end of the ninth century, five basic tenets make up the strict Muʿtazilite creed: justice and unity, the inevitability of God's threats and promises, the intermediary position, the injunction of right, and the prohibition of wrong.[30] Of these five, the latter three will be shown to follow logically from the Muʿtazilite doctrine of the all-pervasive justice of God. It was doubtless their interest in vindicating this justice that led the Muʿtazilite doctors to resolve rationally the problems raised by the Koran's doctrine of God's unlimited sovereignty, and to engage in those ethico-theological polemics concerning their assertion of free will.

Although the Koran emphatically affirms the justice of God and denies equally emphatically His injustice or wickedness, a number of Koranic verses bearing on such concepts as the guidance or misguidance of God (Koran 7, 178; 32, 13; 3, 154; 18, 16; 24, 21, etc.), the "sealing of the heart" (2, 5–6; 6, 125; 16, 95; 61, 5, etc.), the appointed term (*ajal*) (6, 2; 7, 32, etc.), provision for human needs (*rizq*), the book of fate (69, 17, 27), and especially the overwhelming picture of hell it depicts, exhibit a dazzling spectacle of the unlimited and arbitrary power of God, which can hardly leave scope for any power other than God in the world.

Moreover, the concept of the inexorable decree of God, as set forth both in the Koran and the Traditions of Muḥammad (in which an even gloomier picture of divine predestination is painted) strip divine justice or human responsibility of any positive meaning altogether.[31] The early traditionist view, which culminated in the thoroughgoing determinism of Jahm b. Ṣafwān and his followers, simply confirmed

[30] Al-Khayyāṭ, *Kitāb al-Intiṣār*, p. 93.

[31] Wensinck, *Muslim Creed*, pp. 56 f.

the view implicit in the Traditions that man can have no part in determining his action, in any real sense. Indeed, argued Jahm, a man's life is so thoroughly predestined that we only impute his actions to him figuratively, in very much the same way as we impute "the bearing of fruit to the tree, flowing to the stream, motion to the stone, rising or setting to the sun—blooming and vegetating to the earth." God creates the actions of both animate and inanimate beings, and man, like other creatures, has neither power, will, nor choice.[32]

It was apparently against the determinism of the Jahmites, with whom they came into active contact, that the Mu'tazilah reacted so vehemently, and this reaction led them to try to vindicate God's justice. The early Muslim theologians had naturally been unanimous in denying that God could be unjust,[33] but the problem of the reconciliation of the justice of God and the glaring reality of evil in the world does not appear to have disturbed them particularly. And it was precisely this problem that became, from Wāṣil's time on, the crucial issue with which the Mu'tazilah and their adversaries grappled.

What set the Mu'tazilah apart, from the outset, was their revolutionary vindication of what might be called the rationality of God's ways, which they sought to subtantiate intellectually without necessarily repudiating the authority of Scripture. Especially significant in this regard was their contention that good and evil are not conventional or arbitrary concepts whose validity is rooted in the dictates of God, as the Traditionists and later the Ash'arites held, but are rational categories which can be established through unaided reason.[34] From this as a major premise the Mu'tazilah proceeded to argue that God cannot enjoin what is contrary to reason or act in total disregard for the welfare of His creatures, in so far as this would compromise His justice

[32] Al-Shahrastānī, *al-Milal*, pp. 59 f.; al-Baghdādī, *Uṣūl al-Dīn*, p. 134; Watt, *Free Will*, pp. 96 ff.

[33] Paradoxically enough, a section of the Mu'tazilah reportedly dissented from this view; see al-Khayyāṭ, *Kitāb al-Intiṣār*, p. 22. Al-Ṣāliḥī, a contemporary of al-Khayyāṭ, placed sometimes among the Murji'a, sometimes the Mu'tazilah, appears to be the chief exponent of this view; see al-Ash'arī, *Maqālāt*, pp. 309 f., and Ibn al-Murtaḍa, *al-Munia*, p. 40.

[34] Al-Baghdādī, *Uṣūl al-Dīn*, pp. 26 f.; al-Shahrastānī, *al-Milal*, p. 31; al-Ash'arī, *Maqālāt*, p. 356.

and His wisdom.[35] Unlike the Traditionists, those ethical rationalists could not reconcile themselves to the concept of an omnipotent Deity who could act in total violation of all the precepts of justice and righteousness, torture the innocent, and demand the impossible, simply because He was God.[36]

A related thesis was the belief in man's capacity to act freely in the world. To substantiate this thesis, some Mu'tazilite doctors led by Abu'l-Hudhail (d. 841?) advanced the concept of generation (*tawallud*), or the causal relation between the action of the doer and the deed. According to al-Ash'arī, Abu'l-Hudhail and his followers held that the acts "generated" by man can be divided into those acts of which he knows the modality (*kaifiya*) and those he does not.[37] An example of the former is the flight of the arrow or the sound caused by the impact of two solid objects. An example of the latter is pleasure, hunger, knowledge, smell, etc. Man, he argued, can rightly be said to be the author of those acts of which he knows the modality, whereas acts which he cannot observe or scrutinize must be attributed to God. In this regard he seems to have departed from the teaching of Bishr b. al-Mu'tamir (d. 825), head of the rival school of Baghdad, who inaugurated this decisive doctrine of "generation" (or *tawallud*)[38] and held that "whatever is 'generated' from our deeds is of our doing,"[39] irrespective of whether we can scrutinize it. Abu'l-Hudhail's motive in making this subtle distinction is not clear, but it is very likely that he sought thereby to ward off one of the charges which the anti-Mu'tazilite polemicists directed against their notion of man "as the creator of his deeds." According to the anti-Mu'tazilites, whom al-Shahrastānī calls the "Orthodox," the notion of creation implies knowledge of the effects of creation, "in every respect," on the part of the Creator, and is consequently not predicable of man, who has only a "general" knowledge

[35] *Al-Milal*, pp. 31 f.; *Uṣūl*, pp. 150 f.

[36] Fakhry, *Islamic Occasionalism*, pp. 68 ff.; al-Baghdādī, *Uṣūl al-Dīn*, pp. 150 f., 240 f.

[37] al-Ash'arī, *Maqālāt*, p. 402 f., and Fakhry, "Some Paradoxical Implications of the Mu'tazilite View of Free Will," *Muslim World*, XLIII (1953), 98–108. I have drawn on this article in writing the above section.

[38] As al-Shahrastānī relates in *al-Milal*, p. 44. He aptly remarks that Bishr took his doctrine over from the "physical philosophers." See also al-Khayyāṭ, *Kitāb al-Intiṣār*, pp. 6, 171.

[39] Al-Ash'arī, *Maqālāt*, pp. 401, 403; al-Baghdādī, *al-Farq*, p. 143.

of the effects of his actions.[40] Despite this minor disagreement, Bishr and Abu'l-Hudhail agreed on two points that are central to any solid belief in moral freedom: (1) First, that in the inward domain of willing and choosing man exercises a definite freedom of initiative.[41] (2) Second, that man can accomplish certain deeds in the outward sphere of nature by causing (or generating), through his will, such acts. In this way, the concept of a causal connection between the will as cause and the event as effect is tacitly presupposed and a certain measure of consistency achieved.

It would be a grave illusion to imagine that the Mu'tazilah generally concurred in these two elementary propositions, much as it would appear that they constitute the irreducible minimum of any effective belief in moral freedom. It is true that the Mu'tazilah generally concur in acknowledging the reality of free will, that is, of man's initiative in the inward world of volition, as we have seen. But when it comes to the second proposition, their teaching reveals a wide measure of divergence, which in certain cases endangers their whole ethical structure and militates against the claim that they were genuine believers in free will.

To overcome the difficulties involved in the antithesis of human capacity and divine power, some ingenious thinkers such as al-Naẓẓām (d. 835 or 845) resorted to various philosophical expedients. Both in his concept of an inherent nature (*ṭab'*) and that of God's initial creation of the latent properties of things (*kumūn*), subsequently manifested

40 Al-Shahrastānī, *Nihāyat al-Iqdām*, pp. 68 f. See also al-Ghazālī, *Iqtiṣād*, p. 42. What gave point to this highly speculative matter seems to have been a purely legal consideration, namely, whether a man is responsible for deeds caused (or generated) posthumously by his action. The classical instance is that of an archer who kills a man but dies, himself, before his victim does; see al-Ash'arī, *Maqālāt*, p. 403, and al-Baghdādī, *Uṣūl al-Dīn*, p. 137.

41 Al-Ash'arī, *Maqālāt*, p. 403. Abu'l-Hudhail distinguishes between "what man causes or effects in himself [*yaf'alu fī nafsihi*]" and "what he causes in other things." The former, he held, is the cause of the latter. He names will among the things man "causes in himself." Recognizing the role of the will as the "principium primum" of action, the majority of the Mu'tazilites (with the notable exception of al-Jubā'i) denied that "the will has a will" (p. 149) or "that it is generated" (p. 414), avoiding thus the "regressus ad infinitum." It is worth noting here that the Ash'arites disputed the reality of the self-determination of the will itself and referred this to God. Al-Ghazālī, who exemplifies their teaching, relates the notion of choosing (*ikhtiyār*) to that of good (*khayr*), and this he ascribes to the agency of God, see *Iḥyā'*, IV, 219 f.

externally (*ẓuhūr*), he appears to have sought to refer every activity in the world indirectly to God and directly to secondary natural agents.[42]

The exponents of the theory of *kumūn* appear to have proposed it with a view to relieving God from the cumbrous task of continuous intervention in the course of natural events without however compromising His indirect sovereignty in the world. But this modified version of determinism did not satisfy either the believers in divine omnipotence, like Ibn Karrām (d. 869) and his school, or the advocates of man's right to act freely in the domain of nature, like Bishr and Abu'l-Hudhail. It is no wonder that the Mu'tazilah and their opponents alike assailed al-Naẓẓām with great bitterness.[43]

With regard to the notion of nature (*ṭab'*) as the decisive principle of activity inherent in things, al-Naẓẓām seems to have followed the lead of Mu'ammar b. 'Abbād, teacher of Bishr b. al-Mu'tamir.[44] Mu'ammar, who pushed this notion of *ṭab'* to its logical limit, argued that the existence of bodies is to be ascribed to God, whereas the existence of accidents must be ascribed to the "action" of bodies themselves. This action is brought about either by natural necessity (*ṭab'an*), as in the case of inanimate things such as fire, or in a voluntary manner (*ikhtiyāran*), as in the case of animate beings such as man.[45] To prove this, he presented to his opponents the following example. A body might be susceptible of a given accident (e.g., color) or it might not be. In the first case, color would belong to it by nature and is of its "doing" (*min fi'lihi*), since what is natural to a thing cannot be said to be the action of another agent. In the second case, God might decide to color the body, and yet the body might not receive the color of which it is not susceptible.[46] Consequently, God cannot be said to cause the

[42] Al-Shahrastānī, *al-Milal*, p. 39; al-Baghdādī, *al-Farq*, p. 129; al-Khayyāṭ, *Kitāb al-Intiṣār*, p. 44.

[43] Abu'l-Hudhail, Ja'far b. Ḥarb, al-Iskāfī, and al-Jubā'ī are reported to have written polemics against him; see *al-Farq*, p. 115. Of the Ash'arites, al-Baghdādī mentions al-Ash'arī, al-Bāqillānī, and al-Qalānisī.

[44] Contemporary of al-Naẓẓām, Abu'l-Hudhail, and the Caliph Hārūn (786–809); see Ibn al-Murtaḍa, *al-Munia*, pp. 31–32.

[45] Al-Shahrastānī, *al-Milal*, p. 46, see also al-Khayyāt, *Kitāb al-Intisār*, p. 54; al-Baghdādī, *al-Farq*, p. 137, and al-Ash'arī, *Maqālāt*, p. 548.

[46] *Maqālāt*, p. 406, and *Kitāb al-Intiṣār*, p. 54.

accidents, except indirectly, that is, through the agency of the body which causes its own accidents naturally.[47]

The motive of Mu'ammar in following this notion of *ṭab'* to its logical consequence was obviously the desire to relieve God completely of any responsibility for evil in the world.[48] But his opponents not unnaturally interpreted this lack of responsibility as synonymous with impotency, which made mockery, they said, of God's title as author of life and death, etc., in the Koran.[49]

On the question of human action, Mu'ammar's teaching was very akin to that of al-Naẓẓām. "Man," according to him, is a "substance or an entity distinct from the body and is endowed with power, initiative, and knowledge, unsusceptible of movement, rest, development, or spatiality and is invisible, untouchable, and imperceptible." It is free from the conditions of space and time and exercises over the body the function of "guardianship" (*tadbīr*) only.[50] Al-Ash'arī adds a further note to this account: man, according to Mu'ammar, is an "indivisible particle" or atom directing the body, which is its instrument through will, without contact with it.[51] As to what man can accomplish in the external world, Mu'ammar, like al-Naẓẓām whose view differed only in one particular from his conception of the nature of man,[52] held that man acts in the inward world of the will (*fī nafsihi*). Thus he is capable of knowledge, will, hate, and representation, but is incapable of accomplishing anything at all in the outward world. Whatever is generated in the world of nature, therefore, and whatever inheres in bodies, such as motion and rest, color, and taste, heat or cold, etc., is the work of the body in which it inheres, through a necessity of nature.[53]

[47] This is actually the point of al-Khayyāṭ's defense of Mu'ammar against the allegations of Ibn al-Rāwandī; see *Kitāb al-Intiṣār*, p. 54.

[48] Al-Shahrastānī brands Mu'ammar the "foremost heretic" for repudiating the thesis "that *qadar*, whether good or evil, is from God" (*al-Milal*, p. 46).

[49] Al-Baghdādī, *al-Farq*, p. 137; al-Ash'arī, *Maqālāt*, p. 548; al-Shahrastānī, *al-Milal*, p. 46.

[50] *Al-Milal*, p. 47; *al-Farq*, p. 140.

[51] Al-Ash'arī, *Maqālāt*, pp. 331–320.

[52] Namely, that of its intermingling with the body. Al-Naẓẓām defines man as "a spirit which is interpenetrant with the body and is commingled with it as the whole in the whole, the body however being a mere infirmity [*āfah*] and constraint thereto" (*Maqālāt*, p. 331).

[53] Al-Ash'arī, *Maqālāt*, pp. 405, 332; al-Baghdādī, *al-Farq*, p. 140.

It is difficult to see what positive advantage Muʿammar's view of freedom could have gained from this extraordinary conception of man as an "intellectual substance."[54] Al-Naẓẓām, whose view of man resembles that of Muʿammar to a considerable degree, was able however to insure the partial unity of man through his notion of man's spirit as an entity commingled with his body in its entirety.[55] But neither version of the dualism of body and spirit was favorable to the solution of the moral dilemma which faced the Muslim theologians.

The example of Muʿammar was followed by another leading representative of the School of Baghdad, Thumāma b. Ashras (d. 828). Starting from the same viewpoint of man and the world, Thumāma was so baffled by the inscrutable character of the dilemma of moral action that he surrendered it altogether as insoluble and relapsed into a position of complete agnosticism. Like the rest of the Muʿtazilah, he was committed to the vindication of God's justice and the consequent necessity of imputing responsibility to man. Man, he argued, "acts" only in the domain of the will,[56] but outside this domain he cannot do anything. Whose responsibility then are the effects of man's willful action? Bishr, as we have seen, had assigned the consequence of his decisions in the external world to man, as had Abu'l-Hudhail, with certain qualifications. Muʿammar and al-Naẓẓām, on the other hand, had ascribed these consequences to nature, in which al-Naẓẓām at least saw the invisible tool of God. Thumāma's solution, if solution it could be called, differed radically from all these answers. To ascribe the "generated act" to man, he reasoned, would involve us in the paradox of Bishr and his followers, that a given act of a man which resulted in an evil posthumous effect (such as the injury of another man) would have to be imputed to him. And consequently, we should be imputing activity to the dead.[57] If, on the other hand, such an effect is imputed to God, then He would be responsible for the evil deeds of

[54] Al-Shahrastānī actually states that Muʿammar "took this over from the 'philosophers' who held that the Soul was a self-subsisting essence which is neither in space nor in time" (*al-Milal*, p. 47). Al-Baghdādī more aptly remarks that he had in fact ascribed to man the traits proper to the Deity (*al-Farq*, p. 140).

[55] Al-Naẓẓām's view was not altogether free from paradox, since he ascribed "power, capacity, life, and will" to the spirit alone (al-Shahrastānī, *al-Milal*, p. 38).

[56] Al-Ashʿarī, *Maqālāt*, p. 407.

[57] Al-Shahrastānī, *al-Milal*, p. 49.

man. The only alternative, he argued, is to say that generated effects have no author at all.[58] With one stroke, Thumāma relieved both God and man from moral responsibility, without advancing a single step toward a rational solution of the ethical dilemma.

Unfortunately, our information on Thumāma's teaching is so scanty that it is difficult to determine how seriously one should take him. A number of anecdotes, reported by both Ibn al-Murtaḍa and al-Baghdādī,[59] seem to give point to al-Shahrastānī's remark that Thumāma "combined levity of religion with vileness of character."[60]

Despite their assumption that man was the creator of his deeds, the Mu'tazilah posited a contingent metaphysics of atoms and accidents, generally designated as "occasionalism."[61] The cardinal tenet of this metaphysics was that everything in the world (defined as everything other than God) consisted of two distinct elements, atoms (or indivisible particles) and accidents (*a'rāḍ*). Muslim authorities report that this "atomistic metaphysics" was accepted by all Muslims with the exception of al-Naẓẓām,[62] who seems to have adhered to the Aristotelian thesis of the divisibility of substance *ad infinitum*. Although al-Naẓẓām should be regarded as the major dissident of atomistic metaphysics, he was by no means alone. Ḍirār b. 'Amr, a contemporary of Wāṣil (d. 748), rejected the whole notion of atom (or substance) and reduced the body to an "aggregate of accidents, which, once constituted, becomes the bearer (or substratum) of other accidents."[63] Hishām b. al-Ḥakam (who died at the end of the eighth century or the beginning of the ninth) and al-Aṣamm his contemporary, disputed likewise the orthodox dualism of substance and accident and reduced everything to the one notion of body.[64] Yet there seems to have been

[58] Al-Shahrastānī, *al-Milal*, p. 49; also al-Ash'arī, *Maqālāt*, p. 407, and al-Baghdādī, *al-Farq*, p. 157.

[59] Ibn al-Murtaḍa, *al-Munia*, pp. 36, 37; *al-Farq*, p. 158.

[60] Al-Shahrastānī, *al-Milal*, p. 49.

[61] See Fakhry, *Islamic Occasionalism*, pp. 33 f.

[62] Al-Baghdādī, *Uṣūl al-Dīn*, p. 36; al-Shahrastānī, *al-Milal*, p. 38; Ibn Ḥazm, *al-Fiṣal*, V, 92; al-Ash'ari, *Maqālāt*, pp. 308 f.; and al-Nīsābūrī, *Kitāb al-Masā'il*, pp. 2 ff.

[63] Al-Ash'arī, *Maqālāt*, pp. 305, 345; cf. Ibn Ḥazm, *al-Fiṣal*, V, 66.

[64] *Maqālāt*, p. 343; *Fiṣal*, V, 66; al-Shahrastānī, *al-Milal*, p. 38; al-Baghdādī, *al-Farq*, p. 114. Hishām, according to one account reported in *Maqālāt*, p. 345, conceded the existence of notions (*ma'ānī*) in addition to body.

very little disagreement on the question of accidents, outside the limited following of al-Aṣamm.[65] Al-Naẓẓām himself, while denying the existence of substance, reduced all accidents to the one accident of motion.[66] Within the Ash'arite school, however, there was total agreement on this question, so much so that al-Baghdādī equates belief in accidents with orthodoxy.[67] Thus the Ash'arites taught that a body cannot be divested of positive or negative accidents, such as color, smell, life, knowledge, or their opposites.[68] This view was accepted by the majority of the Mu'tazilite doctors but was disputed by Ṣāliḥ Qubba and al-Ṣāliḥī, who, in line with their notion of God's absolute power, held that He could create an "atom" devoid of any accidents.[69] Abū Hāshim, son of al-Jubā'ī (d. 933), and al-Ka'bī both agreed partially with this view and held that a body could be stripped of all accidents except the accidents of color and of being (*kaun*).[70]

The most important characteristic of those accidents, from our standpoint, was their perishable nature. The Mutakallims, as a whole, held that accidents do not endure for two moments. Al-Bāqillānī (d. 1013), who is credited with refining the atomism of Islam, defines the accident "as that which cannot endure . . . but perishes in the second instant of its coming-to-be"[71] and finds a basis for this definition in the Koran, following in this the lead of his master, al-Ash'arī.[72]

As one might expect, the Mu'tazilah, notably those who believed in "generation," found this teaching inimical to their doctrine of freedom. Consequently many of them disputed this thesis and assigned a certain durability to some accidents. Abu'l-Hudhail, for instance, assigned to

[65] Among the notable representatives of this school of negators of accidents we ought to mention al-Jāḥiẓ (d. 868); see *al-Milal*, p. 53.

[66] Al-Baghdādī, *Uṣūl al-Dīn*, pp. 46–47, and *al-Farq*, pp. 114, 131.

[67] *Uṣūl al-Dīn*, pp. 36 ff.; see also *al-Farq*, p. 316.

[68] Al-Baghdādī, *Uṣūl al-Dīn*, p. 56.

[69] Al-Ash'arī, *Maqālāt*, p. 570; also pp. 307, 310; *Uṣūl al-Dīn*, pp. 56–57; and al-Juwaynī, *al-Irshād*, p. 14.

[70] Al-Baghdadī, *Uṣūl al-Dīn*, p. 56. The former is the view of al-Ka'bī, the latter that of Abū Hāshim. From al-Baghdādī's statement, it appears that they both had their following.

[71] Al-Bāqillānī, *al-Tamhīd*, p. 18; Ibn Khaldūn, *al-Muqaddimah*, p. 326; and Anawati and Gardet, *Introduction à la théologie musulmane*, pp. 62 ff.

[72] Al-Ash'arī, *Maqālāt*, p. 370; the Koranic passages invoked are 8, 67 and 46, 24, which speak of the "transient things" of this world (*a'rāḍ*).

the category of perishable accidents those of will and motion, and to the category of durable accidents a number of others, such as color, life, and knowledge, as did Bishr b. al-Mu'tamir, al-Jubā'ī (d. 915), his son Abū Hāshim, al-Najjār, Ḍirār, and others. Al-Naẓẓām, who reduced all accidents to that of motion, as we have seen, held that it was impossible for motion to endure.[73]

Now the interest of the Mutakallims (especially the Ash'arites) in this contingent metaphysics of atoms and accidents (as Maimonides aptly remarks)[74] was simply the desire to vindicate the absolute power of God and to ascribe to His direct intervention not only the coming of things into being, but their persistence in being from one instant to another as well. Consequently, they argued, things would cease to exist the minute God ceases to create in them the accidents that cast them into being and which include, in the first instance, the accident of being (*kaun*) itself.[75] This in itself is sufficient to explain why the Ash'arite doctors adhered solidly to this particular view of the universe in preference to any other. The Mu'tazilah, however, could not without self-contradiction subscribe wholly to such a world-view; that is why many of them, as we have seen, endeavored to modify it in a manner which would safeguard their notion of man as "the creator of his deeds."

Other ethico-religious corollaries flowed from the Mu'tazilite vindication of divine justice. Chief among them were the denial of intercession (*shafā'ah*), the inevitability of divine judgment, and the eternity of punishment in hell. Concerning divine judgment, the Mu'tazilah argued that the justice of God entails necessarily the inexorability of his decrees and in particular "his promise" to reward the faithful with eternal bliss and his "threat" to consign the wayward

[73] *Maqālāt*, pp. 358–59; and al-Baghdādī, *Uṣūl al-Dīn*, pp. 50–51.

[74] Maimonides, *Guide des égarés*, pt. 1, ch. 73, 6th proposition.

[75] This is the official Ash'arite view according to which "everything in the world comes to be through God's fiat . . . and ceases through His commanding it to cease" [*kun* or *ifna*] (al-Baghdādī, *Uṣūl al-Dīn*, p. 50). However, the duration (*baqā'*) of a body is the result of God creating in it the accident of duration. If God were to withhold from it this accident it would cease to exist. Some Mu'tazilah (notably al-Jubā'ī and his son, Abū Hāshim), however, disputed this thesis and argued that God would have to create the accident of extinction (*fanā'*) in no substratum, if He wished to annihilate the universe (*ibid.*, pp. 45, 67 ff.).

eternally to hell.[76] Neither the intercession of prophets or saints nor the mercy of God could alter what His justice decreed, since this would jeopardize His righteousness and leave the creature in total ignorance of his ultimate destiny.

What appears to have added significance to this question was the claim of Jahm and his followers that God, who is "the First and the Last" according to Koran 57,3, will eventually cause heaven and hell to perish, so that He alone might endure everlastingly.[77] The Traditionist view, which had left greater scope to divine mercy while tending to abolish the distinction between heaven and hell, insisted on the eternity of heaven as the abode of the blessed (which included ultimately all Muslims), and that of hell as the abode of infidels.[78] Even the prerequisites of salvation tended to diminish progressively in the early theological squabbles. Eventually the profession of the unity of God became the only condition of salvation, or at any rate of the cessation of punishment in hell.[79]

The more abstract theological assumptions of the Mu'tazilah revolved round their second major thesis, the unqualified unity of God (*tauḥīd*), which was aimed primarily at the Manichaeans on the one hand and the anthropomorphists and other Attributists (*Ṣifātiyah*) on the other. The latter two heterodox groups predicated, in perfect consonance with the literal pronouncements of the Koran, a series of positive attributes (*ṣifāt*) of God, ranging from such abstract qualities as wisdom, life, and will, to such gross traits as bodily form, face, and limbs. Neither the moderate Attributists nor the extreme anthropomorphists, of course, can be assumed to have proceeded beyond the explicit statements of the Koran in this regard. Thus the references in Koran 75,22 to the possibility of seeing God, or His face (55,27), as well as His "sitting upon the throne" (7,54 and 20,5), are either taken at their face value, without much ado, or the logical inference is made that God is possessed of corporeal and other characteristics which He

[76] Al-Khayyāṭ, *Kitāb al-Intiṣār*, pp. 13 f.; *Uṣūl al-Dīn*, pp. 238 f.; al-Bāqillānī, *al-Tamhīd*, pp. 365 f.

[77] *Kitāb al-Intiṣār*, p. 18; *Uṣūl al-Dīn*, pp. 238 *et passim*.

[78] Al-Baghdādī, *Uṣūl al-Dīn*, pp. 238, 242 f.

[79] Al-Bukhārī, *Ṣāḥīḥ*, p. 19, and Muslim, *Ṣāḥīḥ*, I; 217, respectively; see also *Uṣūl Dal-īn*, pp. 242 f.

shares with man. The latter extreme view appears to have been strengthened by doctrinal considerations of a more abstract character. As the earliest exponents of this thesis were mostly Shī'ites, we might safely assume that their anthropomorphism was dictated by the urge to ascribe a divine or semi-divine status to their *Imāms*, in whom according to the extreme Shī'ites God became periodically incarnate. The introduction of this gross view is attributed to a Jewish convert, 'Abdulla b. Saba', who earned the wrath of 'Alī, it is said, by deifying him in his own lifetime[80] and thus initiating the whole notion of anthropomorphism in Islam, to which a number of Shī'ite subsects, such as the Bayānites, the Hishāmites, the Mughīrites, the Mūsawites, the Khaṭṭābites, and the Karrāmites, actually subscribed.[81]

The less extreme literalists and Traditionists were content to assert that God was endowed with a series of attributes, distinct from His essence, which were reduced in time to the seven *essential* attributes of power, knowledge, life, will, hearing, sight, and speech, stated to subsist eternally in God. To these, other *active* attributes such as creation, justice, munificence, etc., were added.[82]

The Mu'tazilah, despite the allegation of their adversaries that they were out to strip God of all positive characteristics, appear to have simply sought to safeguard the unity and simplicity of God, which the thesis of a series of positive attributes distinct from His essence and inhering eternally in Him tended to jeopardize in so far as it involved, according to them, a plurality of eternal entities other than He.[83] Even the chief antagonist of the Mu'tazilah, al-Ash'arī, brings out vividly, in his account of their view of the unity of God, their preoccupation with safeguarding His otherness and His transcendence above everything else:

The Mu'tazilites are unanimous that God is unlike anything else and that He hears and sees and is neither body, ghost, corpse, form, flesh, blood,

[80] Al-Ash'arī, *Maqālāt*, p. 15; al-Naubakhtī, *Firaq al-Shī'ah*, pp. 19–20; al-Baghdādī, *Uṣūl al-Dīn*, p. 332; al-Jurjānī, *Kitāb al-Ta'rīfāt*, p. 79.

[81] *Ibid.*, pp. 15 f.; al-Baghdādī, *Uṣūl al-Dīn*, pp. 331–32; al-Naubakhtī, *Firaq al-Shī'ah*, pp. 28, 39, 67; al-Shahrastānī, *al-Milal*, pp. 134 f.; al-Malaṭi, *Kitāb al-Tanbīh*, p. 15.

[82] *Uṣūl al-Dīn*, p. 90, and al-Bāqillānī, *al-Tamhīd*, p. 272.

[83] Al-Shahrastānī, *al-Milal*, p. 30.

substance, or accident and that He is devoid of color, taste, smell, tactual traits, heat, cold, moistness, dryness, height, width, or depth . . . , and that He is indivisible . . . and is not circumscribed by place or subject to time . . . and that none of the attributes of the creature which involve contingency can be applied to Him . . . , and that He cannot be perceived by the senses or assimilated to mankind at all . . . , and that He has always been the First, prior to all contingent things . . . and has always been knowing, powerful, and living and will always be so. Sight cannot perceive Him . . . and the imagination cannot encompass Him . . . the *only* eternal Being, beside whom there is no other eternal being, and no God or associate to share His realm with Him.[84]

In rationalizing their view of the unity of God, the Mu'tazilite doctors apparently were influenced by the Aristotelian concept of God as the pure actuality of thought, in whom essence and attribute, thought and the object of thought, are identified, as well as the Plotinian view that God, who transcends thought and being altogether, can only be known negatively.[85] Curiously enough, however, this view is attributed in the Arabic sources to a more ancient Greek authority than either Aristotle or Plotinus, namely, Empedocles, generally credited by Muslim authors with the doctrine of the unity of essence and attribute in God.[86]

In rejecting the thesis of a series of eternal attributes inherent in God, the Mu'tazilah hoped to vindicate His absolute unity. The koranic view of a personal Deity of such overwhelming concreteness, however, made it virtually impossible to give up altogether the positive attributes of God, especially that of power. Recognizing this difficulty, many Mu'tazilite scholars sought earnestly to rationalize the divine attributes in a manner which, while it safeguarded God's unity, did not at the same time jeopardize the fullness of His Godhead. Four different attempts to wrestle with this problem are distinguished by al-Ash'ari in his account of Mu'tazilite doctrine.[87]

1. Some held, he states, that in saying that God has knowledge, power, or life, etc., we simply assert that He is knowing, powerful,

[84] Al-Ash'arī, *Maqālāt*, pp. 156–57. [85] *Ibid.*, p. 483.

[86] Ṣā'id, *Ṭabaqāt al-Umam*, p. 6; al-Shahrastānī, *al-Milal*, p. 317.

[87] Al-Ash'arī, *Maqālāt*, pp. 177 f.; also pp. 483 ff.; and Wensinck, *Muslim Creed*, pp. 75 f.

living, etc. and that consequently He is *not* ignorant, impotent, or dead, etc., since this would not become Him. This is reported as the view of al-Naẓẓām[88] and the majority of the Mu'tazilah of both the Schools of Baghdad and Basra.

2. Others are said to have interpreted the statements that God has knowledge or power as referring not to the two attributes of knowledge or power as applied to God, but to the *objects* thereof.

3. Some, who included the famous Abu'l-Hudhail and his followers, conceded the fact that God *has* power, knowledge, life, etc., but only in the sense that His knowledge, power, etc. are identical with Him.[89]

4. Finally, some contested the very legitimacy of stating the question in these terms and held that it is equally wrong to say that God has power, knowledge, life, etc., or that He does not. This appears to have been the view of another leading doctor, 'Abbād b. Sulaymān, and his followers.[90]

Other theologians, prompted by the desire to overcome the difficulty of predicating positive attributes of God, resorted to other dialectical devices. Thus Ibn al-Ayādī, a contemporary of al-Ash'arī, argued that attributes are to be predicated of God only figuratively or metaphorically.[91] Another notorious but subtle dialectician, Abu'l-Ḥusain al-Ṣālihī (ninth century), maintained that there is nothing more to the statement that God is knowing, powerful, living, etc. than the recognition that He is distinct from other beings so qualified or the confirmation of the substance of the koranic verse that "He is unlike anything else" (Koran 42,11),[92] a thesis which reduced the attributes of God to empty verbal utterances. Later doctors, such as al-Jubā'i (d. 915), the famous teacher of al-Ash'ari, while asserting the attributes of God, simply reduced them to corollaries or, if our authorities are correct, *effects* of the essence of God, and to have denied that some of those attributes (such as hearing and seeing) could be predicated of God unless they are in an active relationship with their object or subject matter (i.e., the thing heard or seen).[93] This original view

[88] Al-Baghdādī, *Uṣūl al-Dīn*, p. 91, and *Maqālāt*, p. 486.
[89] *Uṣūl*, p. 91; al-Shahrastānī, *al-Milal*, p. 34; and al-Khayyāṭ, *Kitāb al-Intiṣār*, p. 59.
[90] See also al-Ash'arī, *Maqālāt*, p. 497. [91] *Ibid.*, p. 184. [92] *Ibid.*, p. 501.
[93] *Ibid.*, pp. 175 f. 492, 522; see also al-Baghdādī, *Uṣūl al-Dīn*, p. 92.

would have rendered the attributes of God purely contingent accidents of His essence, dependent as they were held to be on their contingent object, but al-Jubā'ī, like most Mu'tazilah, declared that prior to their coming-to-be things were nonetheless real entities (singular: *shay'*), which could enter into a positive relationship with God's activity or will.[94]

A leading Mu'tazilite doctor, Abū Hāshim (d. 933), son of al-Jubā'ī, refined his father's view by declaring the attributes of God to be states or conditions (singular: *ḥāl*) of His essence, which are neither existent nor nonexistent, or even knowable except through the entity to which they belong, but are nevertheless that which sets one entity apart from another.[95] However, unlike other exponents of this view, Abū Hāshim appears to have assigned a certain priority to some attributes, such as life, over others, such as knowledge, power or will, which were stated to be concomitant conditions or effects of life.[96] It is not clear what Abū Hāshim and others such as the Ash'arite al-Bāqillānī might have gained from this peculiar thesis, except possibly the recognition of the priority of essence over attribute in God, in the first instance, and the priority of certain essential attributes over others, in the second instance. It is nevertheless obvious that this subtle distinction between state and attribute was an instance of the tendency to resort more and more to linguistic devices of this kind as a means of explaining away some of the crucial theological difficulties confronting the later Mu'tazilite and post-Mu'tazilite doctors, without offering any genuine solution of them.

On the other central problems of the eternity of the attributes of God, the Mu'tazilite position exhibited the same degree of complexity and intricacy. Even when applied to God, the concept of eternity (*qidam*) was viewed with suspicion by some Mu'tazilite scholars, who were anxious to remove the barest hint of plurality in God. Thus Abu'l-Hudhail retained the concept and subsumed it under the same category as the other attributes, which he identified, as we have seen, with the essence of God. Mu'ammar made its application to God conditional upon the inception of contingent entities (*ḥudūth*), whereas

[94] Al-Shahrastānī, *Nihāyat*, pp. 150 f.; *Uṣūl al-Dīn*, pp. 70–71.
[95] *Ibid.*, pp. 132 f. [96] *Ibid.*

others challenged the validity of this approach to the problem and even denied that God could in any way be described as eternal.[97]

However, with regard to the other attributes of God, the Mu'tazilites made a distinction between essential and active attributes. In accord with their rejection of the concept of eternal attributes, many of them made a semantic concession which amounted to admitting the eternity of these attributes but not of their distinctness from God. Essential attributes such as life, power, and knowledge, they argued, are such that their opposites could not be affirmed of God, so that it would be illegitimate to speak of God, who is living, powerful, and knowing, as nonliving, impotent, or ignorant. Active attributes, on the other hand, such as love, will, munificence, speech, mercy, justice, and creation, could be affirmed or denied of God.[98] This amounted to the admission that the latter class of attributes, which are in some relation to their object, are neither essential to our conception of God nor belong eternally to Him, as the former class does, but are merely accidental or contingent.

The two attributes over which the fiercest controversy raged in theological and philosophical circles were will and speech. In view of the logical correlation between the divine will and its contingent or created object, a number of Mu'tazilites, particularly the Basrah section of the school, with Abu'l-Hudhail at its head, declared the divine will to be a contingent accident (*ḥādith*), and as such to inhere in no substratum, since it could not without logical inconsistency be said to inhere in God Himself.[99] The head of the Baghdad section, Bishr b. al-Mu'tamir, and his followers, however, distinguished between an essential and an active will in God,[100] thereby emphasizing the bipolarity of this elusive concept in its double relation to God on the one hand and to the creature on the other.

Others, such as al-Naẓẓām and al-Ka'bī, went one step further and denied altogether that this attribute could apply to God. Presumably perceiving the impossibility of any discrepancy between willing and

[97] Al-Ash'arī, *Maqālāt*, p. 180. [98] *Ibid.*, pp. 187, 508 f.

[99] Al-Baghdādī, *Uṣūl al-Dīn*, pp. 90 f., 103; al-Ash'arī, *Maqālāt*, pp. 189 f., 510. An inconsistency in Abu'l-Hudhail's view is noted in *Maqālāt*, pp. 190, 511.

[100] Al-Ash'arī, *Maqālāt*, p. 190.

doing in God, al-Naẓẓām is said to have held that God's willing of the creation or production of an object is simply the *act* of creating or producing it, His willing of the deeds of man simply the *act* of commanding them, and finally His willing of future events the *act* of recognizing or declaring them to be forthcoming.[101]

Owing to its analogy with will, the divine attribute of speech raised a whole host of similar difficulties, which the Mu'tazilah sought to overcome. Furthermore, the christological controversies, of which we encounter distinct echoes in the treatises of Kalām,[102] apparently contributed to the articulate formulation of the problem of the "Word of God," which not unnaturally the Muslim theologians identified with the Koran. And it is significant that the adversaries of the Mu'tazilah frequently castigated them for having borrowed their belief in the creation of the Koran from the Christians, who believed that the "Word of God" could become incarnate in a creature,[103] i.e., Jesus Christ, whereas the Mu'tazilah denounced these critics for believing the Koran to be, like Christ, the eternal Word of God.[104]

In keeping with their denial of the eternal attributes generally, the Mu'tazilah also denied the eternity of God's word or speech (*kalām*) and declared it to be a created accident.[105] The subtler exponents of this view, like the oft-mentioned Abu'l-Hudhail, preoccupied with the task of assigning a substratum or locus in which such an accident could inhere, found it necessary to distinguish between two aspects of God's speech: the primary created fiat (*kun*), through which, according to the Koran, God created the world by ordering it to be, and the subsequent or secondary fiats, through which the creation of particular entities is effected by God. The former could not inhere in God, who is not a "bearer of accidents," nor in the world, which had not as yet come into being. Instead it inhered in "no substratum," whereas

[101] Al-Ash'arī, *Maqālāt*, pp. 190 f.; al-Baghdādī, *Uṣūl al-Dīn*, pp. 90, 103.

[102] See, e.g., al-Bāqillānī, *al-Tamhīd*, pp. 75 f., 89, 95, 101; cf. Anawati and Gardet, *Introduction à la théologie musulmane*, pp. 38 f.

[103] *Al-Tamhīd*, p. 253, and al-Ash'arī, *al-Ibānah*, p. 21.

[104] Al-Ash'arī, *Maqālāt*, pp. 192 ff.

[105] See al-Ma'mūn's letter to the chief judge of Baghdad, in al-Ṭabarī, *Tārīkh*, Vol. 7, p. 198, and Ibn al-Nadīm, *al-Fihrist*, pp. 269–70.

the secondary particular fiats of God inhered in their corresponding created object.[106]

Other scholars, like al-Naẓẓām, distinguished between human speech, which they declared to be an accident, and divine speech, which they declared to be an audible sound caused by God.[107] However, despite their many refinements upon the grand theme of created speech, the Mu'tazilah generally concurred in the proposition that the Koran, as the speech of God, was created. But lest it should be imagined that the creation in question referred to its actual revelation to Muḥammad between the years 610 and 632, we might note that this creation bore on a purely academic or abstract point that had little to do with the concrete problems of the historical revelation or transmission of the Koran. Like the Traditionists and the orthodox generally, the Mu'tazilah retained the concept of the Preserved Tablet (*al-Lauḥ al-Maḥfūẓ*), or original codex, which was kept in heaven and upon which the Koran was inscribed[108] *prior* to its revelation to Muḥammad through Gabriel, the Faithful Spirit and mouthpiece of God. From this heavenly phase, so to speak, the Koran passed through two human phases: that of writing and that of recitation; in all those phases, however, they believed the Koran to be created.[109]

Be this as it may, of the early theological schools, not only the Mu'tazilah as a whole but the Khārijites, the majority of the Murji'ites, the Shī'ites, and the Jahmites appear to have subscribed to the thesis of the created Koran.[110] And had the issue of the creation of the Koran remained what in fact it was, a purely academic or theoretical question, it would doubtless not have released such passion or caused such furor throughout the early part of the ninth century. What added point to the controversy between the proponents of this view and its critics, who clung obstinately to the thesis of the uncreated Koran, was the dramatic manner in which the caliph al-Ma'mūn publicly championed the Mu'tazilite cause, which had always been suspect in the eyes of the

[106] Al-Baghdādī, *Uṣūl al-Dīn*, p. 106; al-Ash'arī, *Maqālāt*, p. 598; al-Shahrastānī, *al-Milal*, p. 34.

[107] *Maqālāt*, pp. 191, 588.

[108] Koran 85,21.

[109] Al-Ash'arī, *Maqālāt*, pp. 598 f.

[110] *Ibid.*, pp. 582, 589; al-Khayyāṭ, *Kitāb al-Intiṣār*, pp. 92 ff.

orthodox masses, and proclaimed the thesis of the creation of the Koran in 827 and 833 official state doctrine throughout the empire. This so-called *Miḥna* or Inquisition simply dramatized the theological divisions within Islam and led to the gradual rallying of the conservative and reactionary elements around the standard bearer of the orthodox party, the learned and pious Aḥmad b. Ḥanbal (d. 855), whose single-mindedness and courage alone were sufficient to thwart the designs of three caliphs and to blunt by degrees the edge of the inquisitorial wrath of the state, and to cause irreparable and lasting damage to the cause of the Mu'tazilah.[111]

The tendency of the Traditionists, from Mālik b. Anas (d. 795) on, had been to rule out every attempt at rationalizing dogma, as synonymous with heresy. Ibn Ḥanbal's stand on this question is illustrated by his reaction to the otherwise moderate approach to the question of the creation of the Koran of a leading theologian of the period, al-Ḥusain al-Karābīsī (d. 859), who despite his accredited sound learning, we are significantly told, inclined toward scholastic theology. Having declared on one occasion that whereas the Koran, as the speech of God, is uncreated, its words, as recited by readers, are created, he submitted his view to Ibn Ḥanbal for his verdict. Ibn Ḥanbal declared it to be a heresy (*bid'ah*). Perfectly willing to modify his stand, al-Karābīsī then declared both the Koran and its written and spoken words uncreated. Instead of being appeased by such latitude, Ibn Ḥanbal declared the latter view equally heretical, thereby underscoring the futility and perniciousness of the very inquiry into the nature of the Koran, that the ancients, he maintained, had so piously avoided.[112]

The political star of the Mu'tazilah continued to rise following the death of al-Ma'mūn in 833. The reign of his two successors, al-Mu'taṣim and al-Wāthiq, who sought to carry out his decrees with comparative nonchalance, was simply an extension of the political and religious policies he had initiated. The accession of al-Mutawakkil in 847, however, completely reversed the situation. Amends were made to Aḥmad b. Ḥanbal, who had stood up heroically to persecution at the hands of three caliphs, and the notion of the Koran's creation

111 Patton, *Aḥmad b. Ḥanbal and the Miḥna*, pp. 50 f.

112 *Ibid.*, pp. 33 f.; see also al-Ash'arī, *Maqālāt*, p. 602.

became public anathema, as the view of its being eternal had been under his three predecessors.[113]

However, it would be a mistake to assume that with its falling out of favor the Mu'tazilite school, which had caused such a stir in the intellectual world of Islam, simply came to a close. In theological circles, its influence will continue for a long time to come, not only through the teaching of its later doctors, but through the impact it left upon the subsequent history of orthodoxy itself, as well as the moderation of its extremist claims. The Ash'arite school, which as we shall have occasion to see, stemmed from the Mu'tazilite in the tenth century, despite its deference for tradition as embodied in the teaching of the early theologians, took over almost without modification the methods that the Mu'tazilah had introduced in theology, as well as the whole legacy of problems and concepts which they were the first in the history of Islam to broach.

Without attempting to give an exhaustive account of the subsequent history of this revolutionary movement, we might note here the names of its leading scholars, up to the rise of the Ash'arite school, which fell heir to it. They are traditionally subdivided into two branches: the Basrite and the Baghdadī. The following list gives the names of their leading representatives up to the middle of the tenth century. Thereafter it is the Ash'arites who dominate the theological scene.

The Basrite Branch

Wāṣil b. 'Aṭā' (d. 748)
'Amr b. 'Ubaid (d. 762)
Abu'l-Hudhail al-'Allāf (d. 841 or 849)
Ibrāhīm al-Naẓẓām (d. 835–845)
'Alī al-Aswārī (contemporary of al-Naẓẓām)
Mu'ammar b. 'Abbād (contemporary of al-Naẓẓām)
Hishām al-Fuwaṭī (flourished during al-Ma'mūn's reign, 813–833)
Al-Shaḥḥām (d. 847)
'Abbād b. Sulaymān (d. 864)
Al-Jāḥiẓ (d. 868)

[113] Patton, *Aḥmad b. Ḥanbal and the Miḥna*, pp. 139 f.

Al-Jubā'ī (d. 915)
Abū Hāshim, son of al-Jubā'ī (d. 933)

The Baghdadī Branch

Bishr b. al-Mu'tamir (d. 825)
Abū Mūsa al-Murdār (d. 841)
Ja'far b. Mubashshir (d. 849)
Thumāma b. Ashras (d. 828)
Al-Iskāfī (d. 855)
Aḥmad b. Du'ād (d. 855)
Abu'l-Ḥusain al-Khayyāṭ (d. 902)
Abū Qāsim al-Balkhī al-Ka'bī (d. 931)

CHAPTER THREE

Beginnings of Systematic Philosophical Writing in the Ninth Century

I

THE FIRST CREATIVE PHILOSOPHICAL WRITER IN ISLAM: AL-KINDĪ

THE author unanimously hailed as the first Arab philosopher, both in the strict ethnic and the less strict cultural sense, is Abū Yūsuf Ya'qūb b. Isḥāq al-Kindī, a scion of the great South Arabian tribe of Kindah. It was this tribe that also gave Arabic literature one of its greatest figures, the poet-prince Imru'l-Qais (the Child of Hardship), referred to also as the Itinerant Prince (al-Malik al-Ḍillīl) (d. ca. 540) on account of his abortive struggle for restoration to the throne of Kindah following his father's assassination.

We have already met al-Kindī as a promoter or patron of the translation movement and a champion of the introduction of Greek and Indian writings into the Muslim world.[1] Some authorities even

[1] *Supra*, pp. 31, 32, 35.

ascribe to him the translation of "numerous philosophical" works,[2] mistakenly no doubt on account of his role in revising or paraphrasing several philosophical treatises. Nevertheless, al-Kindī's contribution to the nascent philosophical and theological movement in ninth-century Islam and his endeavor to counter the natural aversion of his co-religionists to the reception or assimilation of foreign concepts and methods entitle him to a place entirely his own in the history of philosophical thought in Islam.

Little is known of al-Kindī's early life in al-Kūfa. He seems to have been born toward the end of the eighth century during his father's governorship of that Irāqī city.[3] From al-Kūfa, he apparently migrated to al-Basra, an important center of grammatical and theological studies, and finally settled down as a young man in Baghdad, the capital of the empire, and the hub of intellectual life in the ninth century.[4] Here he enjoyed the patronage of three 'Abbasid caliphs: al-Ma'mūn (813–833), al-Mu'taṣim (833–842), and al-Wāthiq (842–847), whose interest in the dissemination of philosophical studies and especially their championship of the Mu'tazilite cause have already been discussed. During the reign of al-Mutawakkil (847–861), who reacted violently against the philosophical and theological sympathies of his three predecessors, al-Kindī suffered a reversal in his personal fortune.[5] He did, however, survive al-Mutawakkil by five years. According to the most likely conjectures, he died in 866 or shortly after.[6]

We are just as poorly informed about al-Kindī's education, background, and character as we are about his birth and death. Miserliness, however, is generally attributed to him by his biographers, and accounts of his avarice are given in the *Book of Misers*, written shortly before

[2] Ibn Juljul, *Ṭabaqāt*, p. 73; al-Qifṭī, *Tārīkh*, p. 98; and Ibn Abī Uṣaybi'ah, '*Uyūn*, I, 207.

[3] Ṣā'id, *Ṭabaqāt al-Umam*, p. 51; al-Qifṭī, *Tārīkh*, p. 347; Ibn Abī Uṣaybi'ah, '*Uyūn*, I, 206.

[4] *Ṭabaqāt al-Umam*, p. 51; '*Uyūn*, I, 206 f.; Ibn al-Nadīm, *al-Fihrist*, p. 371.

[5] See the account of his flogging by order of this caliph in Ibn Abī Uṣaybi'ah, '*Uyūn*, I, 207.

[6] I.e., 252 A.H., as suggested by 'Abdul-Rāziq, in *Failasūf al-'Arab wa'l Mu'allim al-Thānī*, p. 51. For other suggestions see Massignon, *Recueil des textes inédits concernant l'histoire de la mystique*, p. 175, and Nallino, *Tarikh al-Falak 'inda'l-'Arab*, p. 117.

al-Kindī's death by the litterateur and Mu'tazilite author al-Jāḥiẓ (d. 868).[7] Certain maxims justifying and praising thrift are attributed to him by later authors such as Ibn Abī Uṣaybi'ah.

Fortunately, we have much better information about al-Kindī's voluminous philosophical and scientific output, which certainly places him in the forefront of encyclopedic writers in Islam. Most of this work unfortunately has disappeared but, to judge from the remaining treatises recently published in Egypt,[8] the 242 works attributed to him by Ibn al-Nadīm must have been essays or epistles dealing with, according to that bibliographer's classification, logic, metaphysics, arithmetic, spherics, music, astronomy, geometry, medicine, astrology, theology, psychology, politics, meteorology, topography, prognostics, and alchemy.[9]

In view of the extraordinary scope of his scientific learning and writing, some historians such as al-Sijistānī have seen him solely as a scientist or mathematician.[10] Others have more justly recognized him as one of the great exponents of Arab philosophy and theology, as well as science and mathematics.[11] It is perhaps this comprehensive character of his genius that has earned him the title of the "Philosopher of the Arabs" and the praise of the most competent authorities. Some writers, it is true, have leveled the charge of mediocrity against him, chiefly in the field of logic. They claim that he did not proceed analytically to the first principles of that science,[12] but we cannot properly assess the merits or demerits of this charge since none of his logical works is extant.

A striking agreement among both al-Kindī's detractors and his admirers appears, however, concerning his role in seeking to bridge the gap between philosophy and dogma.[13] His recently published treatises confirm that the first systematic philosophical writer in Islam was also one of the great advocates of applying the rational process to

[7] *Kitāb al-Bukhalā'*, pp. 18, 83 ff.

[8] Abū Rīda, *Rasā'il al-Kindī al-Falsafiyah* (hereafter cited as *Rasā'il*).

[9] Ibn al-Nadīm, *Kitāb al-Fihrist*, pp. 371–79, and McCarthy, *al-Taṣānīf al-Mansūbah ilā Failasūf al-'Arab* (hereafter cited as *al-Taṣānīf*).

[10] *Tārīkh Ḥukamā' al-Islām*, p. 47. [11] Ibn Juljul, *Ṭabaqāt*, pp. 73 f.

[12] Ṣā'id, *Ṭabaqāt al-Umam*, p. 52, and echoed by other authors.

[13] *Ibid.*, Ibn Juljul, *Ṭabaqāt*, pp. 73 ff.; al-Bayhaqī, *Tārīkh Ḥukamā' al-Islām*, p. 47.

revealed texts. Al-Kindī's work indeed should be placed in the mainstream of theological ideas that we associate with the Mu'tazilah, the real originators of scholastic theology in Islam. Another indication of his affinity with the Mu'tazilah is the fact that several of his treatises, such as *First Philosophy*, *Prostration of the Outermost Heavenly Body and its Submission to God*, and *Proximate Cause of Generation and Corruption*, are addressed to the caliph al-Mu'taṣim, or to his son Aḥmad, his pupil, who were both well known for their Mu'tazilite sympathies.[14]

More significant in this regard, perhaps, is the tenor of his theological writings, some of whose titles reveal a distinct Mu'tazilite leaning: *Justice of God's Actions*, *God's Unity*, *Refutation of the Manichaeans*, *Capacity* [*Istiṭā'ah*] *and the Moment of its Inception*,[15] which were among the more favorite themes explored by Mu'tazilite doctors. Even the treatises that have come down to us show quite conclusively that al-Kindī, contrary to the opinion of some ancient critics,[16] departed from the teaching of Aristotle on a number of major issues and remained thoroughly imbued with the spirit of Islamic dogma. Take for instance his contention that the truth of Muḥammedan revelation can be demonstrated syllogistically in a manner which only the ignorant would contest,[17] or that the superiority of revealed truth over human wisdom is an instance of the privileged status of the prophets, who are God's spokesmen and the bearers of a "divine science" transcending human capability.[18] Furthermore, he joined the ranks of theologians who stoutly championed many fundamental Islamic beliefs in the face of attacks by Materialists, Manichaeans, or Agnostics, and disavowals by other philosophers. For instance, he defended the doctrine of the creation of the world *ex nihilo*, the resurrection of the body, the possibility of miracles, the validity of prophetic revelation, and the origination and destruction of the world by God.

We shall note in due course that, by the beginning of the eleventh century, and chiefly as a reaction against the emanationist world-view of al-Fārābī and Ibn Sīnā, the two cognate problems of the eternity of

[14] See Abū Rīda, *Rasā'il*, I, 97–162, 214–37, and 244–61; also Walzer, "New Studies on al-Kindī," in *Greek into Arabic*, pp. 175–205.

[15] Ibn al-Nadīm, *al-Fihrist*, p. 372, and McCarthy, *al-Taṣānīf*, p. 29.

[16] Ibn Juljul, *Ṭabāqāt*, p. 73; Ibn Abī Uṣaybi'ah, *'Uyūn*, I, 207.

[17] Abū Rīda, *Rasā'il*, I, 244 ff.

[18] *Ibid.*, p. 372.

the world and its creation *ex nihilo* became the touchstone of orthodoxy at the philosophical level, whereas orthodoxy at the practical, religious level was characterized by the admission of the possibility of miracle in general, and of prophetic revelation as a specific instance of miracle. On all these fundamental issues, al-Kindī had taken a positive stand against the Neo-Platonists and the Peripatetics, and in support of the theologians.

At a time when the theologians inveighed vehemently against Indian and Hellenistic exponents of the idea that revelation was superfluous,[19] since this notion undercut the claims of the prophets to be the privileged bearers of God's message to mankind, al-Kindī invoked the authority of the Koran and interpreted allegorically its abstruse statements. He never questioned their validity and he even composed a treatise to vindicate the prophets' assertions. Like another work, *Refutation of the Arguments of Atheists*, mentioned by Ibn al-Nadīm, this was directed no doubt against those who denied the truths of prophecy.[20]

Before we turn to an analysis of al-Kindī's theological thought, let us examine his conception of the nature and scope of philosophy and the manner in which it differs from other disciplines. In *First Philosophy*, a major treatise addressed to the caliph al-Mu'taṣim, he defines philosophy as "the knowledge of the realities of things, according to human capacity," and first philosophy or metaphysics, more specifically, as the "knowledge of the First Reality which is the Cause of every reality."[21]

Metaphysical knowledge, he explains, in unmistakable Aristotelian fashion, is the knowledge of the causes of things. To the extent we know the causes of an object, our knowledge is nobler and more complete. These causes are four: the material, the formal, the efficient (or moving), and the final. Philosophy is concerned with four questions also, since as "we have shown in numerous places,"[22] writes al-Kindī, the philosopher inquires into "the *whether*, the *what*, the *which*, and the *why*"; or the existence, the genus (or species), the *differentia*, and the final cause of things. Thus whoever knows the matter knows the

[19] *Supra*, p. 48. [20] Ibn al-Nadīm, *al-Fihrist*, p. 376.
[21] Abū Rīda, *Rasā'il*, I, 97 f. [22] *Ibid.*, p. 101.

genus, whoever knows the form knows the species, as well as the *differentia* which it entails; and once the matter, form, and final cause are known, the definition and, *eo ipso*, the reality of the *definiendum* are known also.[23]

In a noteworthy tribute to the ancients, al-Kindī stresses the cumulative character of philosophy, the debt of the philosopher to his predecessors, and his duty to receive gratefully the truth from whatever source it comes, even if this source should happen to be foreign:

We owe great thanks to those who have imparted to us even a small measure of truth, let alone those who have taught us more, since they have given us a share in the fruits of their reflection and simplified the complex questions bearing on the nature of reality. If they had not provided us with those premises that pave the way to truth, we would have been unable, despite our assiduous lifelong investigations, to find those true primary principles from which the conclusions of our obscure inquiries have resulted, and which have taken generation upon generation to come to light heretofore.[24]

Al-Kindī quotes Aristotle as saying, "We ought to be grateful to the progenitors of those who have imparted to us a measure of truth, just as we are to the latter, in so far as they have been the causes of their being, and consequently of our discovery of the truth."[25]

Our aim should be to welcome truth from whatever source it has come, for "nothing should be dearer to the seeker after truth than truth itself." And, dedicated to the quest of truth, we ought to begin by setting forth the views of our predecessors as readily and as clearly as possible, supplementing them where necessary, "according to the norms of our own language and times." We should avoid prolixity in discourse, which has allowed false seekers after truth to misinterpret and repudiate the study of philosophy in the name of religion, of which they are devoid, and which they merely exploit for their personal aims and ambitions. Whoever repudiates the quest for truth as blasphemous (*kufr*), must himself blaspheme, for the knowledge of truth involves the knowledge of the divine, of the unity of God, of whatever is virtuous or useful, as well as the means for clinging to it and shunning its opposite. This, al-Kindī wrote, is precisely what all the genuine apostles of God have taught.[26]

[23] Abū Rīda, *Rasā'il*, I, p. 101. [24] *Ibid.*, p. 102. [25] *Ibid.*, p. 103.
[26] *Ibid.*, p. 104.

Moreover, no one can reasonably deny that such a quest is necessary, for, if he admits that it is necessary, then it is necessary. If he refuses, he must give his reasons for this refusal; and this is already to admit that it is necessary, since no one can reason without knowing the reason[27] or (as Aristotle put it) no one can refuse to philosophize without actually engaging in philosophizing.[28]

As to the various divisions of philosophy, al-Kindī establishes them on the basis of the different channels of human knowledge. To begin with, there is the channel of sense experience, which is bound up with our apprehension of external objects in an effortless and immediate manner through our senses. Such an apprehension, like its sensible object, is in a state of continuous flux and may increase and decrease incessantly. The act of sensation results in the formation of certain images in the representative faculty and these images are subsequently committed to the retentive faculty for safe-keeping, and acquire in this fashion a certain permanence.[29]

Next comes the channel of rational cognition, which is "more akin to the nature of things," though less akin to our nature, than sensation. The object of such cognition is the universal, which is immaterial, and of which neither a representation nor a sense image can ever be formed, since both sensation and representation are concerned with particulars, whose existence is material. The mode of our apprehending it, however, is mediate or inferential: we recognize its truth, as following logically and necessarily from the "first principles of cognition," which are intuitively known to us. Thus our recognition of the truth of the proposition that outside the world there can be neither vacuum nor plenum is by way of inference from a series of premises from which this conclusion logically follows.[30]

Of immaterial entities which, as such, can never become objects of representation, some can nevertheless be associated with matter accidentally, and this might give rise to the illusion that they are susceptible of representation. Such, for instance, is the case with shape, which exists in conjunction with matter, and is nevertheless a purely rational concept, arrived at by abstraction and independently

[27] Abū Rīda, *Rasā'il*, I, p. 105.
[28] Ross, *Select Fragments*, Fr 51 (Protrepticus).
[29] Abū Rīda, *Rasā'il*, I, 106.
[30] *Ibid.*, pp. 107, 109.

from the sensible object in which it inheres.[31] This is clear in the case of immaterial entities which are never conjoined with matter and which we apprehend purely intellectually.

The distinction between material and immaterial entities corresponds for al-Kindī to the broad twofold division of philosophy into physics and metaphysics (or as the author calls it here hyper-physics). The Aristotelian concept of nature as a principle of movement enables him to distinguish further between physics and metaphysics, as the science of the movable and the immovable respectively.[32] Here he appears to simplify the Aristotelian formula by recognizing two, as against Aristotle's three, theoretical sciences.[33] Elsewhere, the twofold distinction between material and immaterial entities is broadened to correspond to that between "divine" and "created" things, and the two major divisions of philosophy are called the science of divine and that of created objects.[34] A class of entities falling halfway between the two, and described as immaterial though susceptible of conjunction with matter, is not precluded, but the only instance thereof he gives is that of the Soul.[35] The relation of mathematical entities to the two major branches of philosophy is left undetermined. For, although psychology is fitted into an intermediary scheme, contrary to the Aristotelian classification,[36] it is difficult to see how mathematics could differ from metaphysics in scope, despite al-Kindī's contention that it should serve as a propaedeutic to the study of philosophy proper.[37] Al-Kindī in fact states explicitly that the mathematical method should be applied exclusively in the domain of immaterial entities, i.e., metaphysics.[38]

The same conclusion would follow from al-Kindī's statement that to each science pertains a particular type of proof. In metaphysics and mathematics we seek demonstration (*burhān*), whereas in the subordinate sciences, such as physics, rhetoric, and history, we look for assent, representation, consensus, or sense perception. Nothing but confusion

[31] Abū Rīda, *Rasā'il*, I, p. 108. [32] *Ibid.*, p. 111; cf. p. 165.
[33] *Met.* IV. 1026ᵉ, 10 f. [34] Abū Rīda, *Rasā'il*, II, 8, 10.
[35] *Ibid.*, II, 10, and I, 265 f.
[36] Aristotle, *De Anima*, I, 403ᵃ 27; cf. Walzer, "New Studies on al-Kindī," in *Greek into Arabic*, pp. 229 f.
[37] Abū Rīda, *Rasā'il*, I, 369 f., and *infra*, p. 110. [38] *Ibid.*, pp. 111 f.

will result from applying the wrong method to the wrong subject matter.[39] We should guard, however, against the illusion in demonstrative matters that there is a demonstration of every proposition, for this would involve an infinite regress and would lead ultimately to the impossibility of demonstration altogether. Demonstration should rest in the last analysis upon self-evident primary principles, the knowledge of which is prior to the knowledge of the propositions resting upon them.[40]

After these introductory remarks on the nature of metaphysics, or first philosophy, as distinct from the philosophical sciences, and the method proper to each, al-Kindī proceeds to examine some of the cardinal themes with which this "divine science" is concerned. Not unnaturally, he begins by considering the First principle of all things, which he sometimes calls the Eternal, sometimes the True One. This One he defines as that which cannot be conceived not to exist or to have a cause for its being other than itself.[41] In short, it is for him the Necessary and Uncaused Being, which as such has neither genus nor species, since the species is made up of a genus and a *differentia* and involves the composition of subject (i.e., the genus) and predicate (i.e., the specific form).

Moreover, the Eternal Being is unchanging and indestructible, since change in general and destruction in particular result from the supervention upon the subject of the "common contraries," such as hot and cold, moist and dry, sweet and bitter, which belong to the same genus. But since, as already stated, the Eternal is not in a genus, it is not susceptible of change or destruction. In so far as it is being (*ais*) per se, it cannot possibly cease to be, nor change into a more perfect being, on the one hand, or into a less perfect being, on the other. Being necessarily perfect, it is in a state of permanent excellence, which can never be exceeded.[42]

Such a being is naturally not a body, for a body answering to the description of the Eternal would have to possess quantity or plurality and to be actually infinite. But the actually infinite is logically absurd; if we

[39] Abū Rīda, *Rasā'il*, I, pp. 110, 112.

[40] *Ibid.*, p. 112, and cf. Aristotle, *Anal. Post.* I. ch. 3, and *Met.* IV. 1006ᵉ 1–12.

[41] *Ibid.*, 113, 169. [42] *Ibid.*, p. 114.

were to remove a finite portion of this supposedly infinite body the remainder would be either finite or infinite. If finite, we might restore to it the finite portion removed from it, and thereby make up the original magnitude, which would be clearly finite, although the whole was originally supposed to be infinite. If, however, the remainder is said to be infinite, when the portion removed from it is restored the resulting body would be either greater than the original or equal to it. If greater, then one infinite body would be said to be greater than another, and this is absurd. If equal to it, then a body has remained constant despite the addition to it of another mass, and this is equally absurd since it would imply that the part is equal to the whole.[43]

By this process of *reductio ad absurdum*, the proposition that a body can be eternally infinite is shown to be untenable, as is the proposition that any of its attributes in the category of magnitude, such as space, time, and motion, are infinite. Now the universe and motion are concomitant or concurrent, since the supposition that the universe (or its body, as al-Kindī has it) was at first motionless and was subsequently set into motion is absurd. And whether we suppose the universe to have been created *ex nihilo* or to have existed eternally, the same conclusion would follow: namely, that motion and the universe are inseparable—in the first case, because the act of bringing the universe into being, out of nothing, is a form of change or motion; in the second case, because the universe, supposed to exist eternally, must have always been at rest or in motion, since the eternal is not susceptible of change or motion (as has been shown), and the universe is known in fact to be in motion. Therefore, it must, on the supposition of its existing eternally, be eternally in motion.[44]

The same might be said about time in its relation to body. Time being the measure of motion, it is impossible that one should precede the other; consequently, it is impossible that either should precede the "body of the universe." From this it would follow that in so far as the "body of the universe" has been shown to be finite, motion and time, as its necessary concomitants, would also be finite.[45]

[43] Abū Rīda, *Rasā'il*, I, pp. 115 f.; see also pp. 191 f., 194 f., and 202 ff., where this argument is repeatedly advanced.

[44] *Ibid.*, pp. 118 f. [45] *Ibid.*, pp. 119, 120.

Other arguments might be advanced to prove that time cannot be actually infinite. Suppose time to be infinite in duration; then every period of time will be preceded by another period and so on ad infinitum, in such a way that we can never come to a first period. And if we can never come to a first period from which the reckoning of time can start, there will be no given period, such as the present day, in which the temporal series terminates since an infinite series cannot be traversed.[46] Nor will it be possible, on the supposition of the infinity of time, to traverse the temporal series, as it extends into the future, and to come thereby to an end of time. But, at any given time, say the present, we have actually traversed the series, which cannot on that account be infinite. And if we proceed to add to the present time successive, finite periods, the result will be a given finite duration, not an infinite time. Therefore, both with regard to its beginning and to its end, the temporal series can actually be circumscribed and is on that account finite or determinate.[47]

Al-Kindī's preoccupation with the concept of infinity, as it applies to time, motion, and magnitude generally, to which he returns in three other treatises,[48] might seem to be disproportionate. But his interest was not inspired by idle theoretical considerations; it arose instead out of his theological concern with such crucial problems as the demonstration of God's existence, the possibility of creation *ex nihilo*, the ultimate cessation or destruction of the world at the behest of God, etc., all of which rested, in his view, on the thesis of the impossibility of an actually infinite series. Although he borrowed this thesis from Aristotle, he exploited it for entirely different metaphysical purposes.

In proving the existence of God, al-Kindī sometimes used the teleological argument,[49] which has always enjoyed a particular preeminence in circles where religious or esthetic feeling has been intense. It is, however, the argument from the beginning or novelty of the world which he more generally used. Indeed, the finitude of time and motion

[46] Abū Rīda, *Rasā'il*, I, pp. 121 f. [47] *Ibid.*

[48] Cf. *On the Infinity of the Body of the World, the Nature of What Can Be and What Cannot Be Said To Be Infinite, the Unity of God and the Finitude of the Body of the World*, in *Rasā'il*, I, 186–92, 194–98, and 201–207.

[49] *Ibid.*, pp. 214 f., 236 f. *et passim.*

is advanced by al-Kindī as a clue to the beginning of the world in time (Arabic: *ḥudūth*), and this in turn as the clue to the existence of its author. Thus, having established that it is impossible for the world to be infinite and *eo ipso* eternal, the author proceeds to make the inescapable inference that "it must therefore be generated [*muḥdath*] of necessity. Now what is generated is generated by a generator [*muḥdith*], since generator and generated are correlative terms. The world as a whole must be generated out of nothing."[50]

Part of the plausibility of al-Kindī's argument arises from the purely linguistic circumstance that the Arabic term "*muḥdath*," as applied to the world, and which I have intentionally translated as "generated" rather than "created" so as to remove the obvious impression of circularity, bears the dual connotation of creation *ex nihilo* and *in time*. It is obvious that the first connotation would yield no more than a tautological conclusion, since if it is assumed that the world is created, the conclusion is inevitable, at least verbally, that it has a creator. But the crux of the matter is precisely whether or not it is created. The argument simply begs this question. With the second connotation, however, the argument could have a far greater cogency, and its validity would depend simply on whether the major premise has or has not been successfully established. I do not propose to enter into the substance of this question here, however, except to remark that al-Kindī, like the majority of the scholastic theologians of Islam, appears to have drawn upon a common historical source. According to the best evidence available, this source was the Alexandrian commentator and theologian John Philoponus, who was the last great champion, in the pre-Islamic era, of the Semitic concept of creation *ex nihilo*, which he opposed to the traditional Hellenic and Hellenistic thesis of an eternal universe as advanced by Aristotle and Proclus.[51] Philoponus' polemics against both Proclus and Aristotle seem to have

[50] *Rasā'il*, I, p. 207.

[51] Walzer, "New Studies on al-Kindī," in *Greek into Arabic*, pp. 218 f. A Platonic influence is also noticeable in the form of the argument as set forth by al-Kindī and which resembles the argument of the *Timaeus* in Galen's paraphrases translated during al-Kindī's lifetime. See Walzer and Kraus, *Galeni Compendium Timaei Platonis*, pp. 4–5. Timaeus is said to have argued that "whatever is generated [*kā'in* — *ḥādith*] must be produced by a cause necessarily."

been known to the Arabs,[52] and it is possible that his theological and philosophical views were actively disseminated by fellow Monophysite or Jacobite writers, who, as we have seen, were instrumental in translating Greek philosophical and theological works into Syriac and Arabic. According to a short treatise ascribed to a disciple of the great Jacobite theologian and logician Yaḥia b. ʿAdī, known as Ibn al-Khammār (d. 1017), Philoponus' argument rested on the thesis that the body of the universe, being finite, cannot be eternal; it was identical with the argument from *ḥuduth*, or *a novitate mundi*. Philoponus' argument, according to this writer, was nevertheless superior to the parallel ones of the Muslim theologians. Their proof was based on the proposition that the universe is generated (*ḥādith*), since it cannot be divested of generated accidents (singular: *ḥādith*) and is a purely dialectical premise, according to him.[53]

The chief attribute of God as the author of the world, argued al-Kindī, is unity. This, like eternity, was recognized also by the Muʿtazilite doctors as one of God's essential attributes. Things that have unity derive it from God, the principle of all unity; consequently their unity is a secondary and, as it were, derivative or figurative unity.[54]

In an argument that appears to have been taken over by all writers from al-Fārābī on, al-Kindī urges that if the author of the world were more than one, each one of its associates would share in a common characteristic with the others and would be differentiated from them by some distinguishing attribute or property. Consequently this author would be composite. But as the composite would require an "agent of composition," the author of the world would be this prior agent. Otherwise, the process would go on ad infinitum.[55]

Moreover, such a being must be uncaused, for, as the cause of all things, it can only be self-caused. This is impossible, since prior to its being it is nothing and, as such, is incapable of imparting being to

[52] Ibn al-Nadīm, *al-Fihrist*, p. 370; Steinschneider, *Die Arabischen Uebersetzungen*, pp. 141 f.

[53] Badawī, *Neoplatonici apud Arabes*, pp. 243–47.

[54] Abū Rīda, *Rasā'il*, I, 160 f. [55] *Ibid.*, pp. 160 f.

itself or to anything else—a proposition that despite its self-evidence is not established without a certain amount of logical quibbling.[56]

As the cause of everything, the First Being must be superior to everything else and have no analogy with anything created. In particular it must possess the character of unity, i.e., be free from all plurality, composition, or correlation with anything else.[57] It must also be simple, having no matter or form, and be independent of any of the four Aristotelian forms of motion.[58] Cognition, which implies a certain movement of the Soul and a certain plurality corresponding to its ability to encompass the whole class of universals, cannot be identified with the First Being, so it is impossible for it to be either Soul or Reason.[59]

Al-Kindī's account of creation *ex nihilo*, in a treatise entitled *The True and Perfect Primary Agent, as against the Imperfect, Figurative One* and others, brings out vividly his intellectual kinship with the Muslim theologians of the ninth century and sets him definitely apart from later Arab Neo-Platonists and Peripatetics, who either evaded this issue or allowed it to drown in a flood of ambiguous verbiage. Action in the primary sense, he argued, as did al-Ghazālī later in the eleventh century in his rebuttal of Neo-Platonic emanationism, is a process of bringing things forth into being out of nothing, and this is God's exclusive prerogative. Action in the secondary sense simply denotes the effects of such action on the object, and this is truly passion not action. That is how creatures are sometimes referred to as agents, in a figurative sense, for in reality they are mere recipients of the impact of God's sovereign action, who then pass it on successively.[60]

God is therefore the only Real Agent or cause in the world. Al-Kindī, however, who shared this dictum with the Muslim theologians, remained sufficiently imbued with the Greek spirit to recognize the

[56] Abū Rīda, *Rasā'il*, I, pp. 123 f.

[57] *Ibid.*, pp. 143 f. In a treatise *On the Refutation of the Christians* (preserved in Yaḥia b. 'Adī's retort; see *Revue de l'Orient Chrétien*, Vol. 22 (Tome II, XXII [1920], pp. 4 ff.), al-Kindī polemizes against the doctrine of the Trinity on the grounds that (a) the three Divine Persons, sharing in the same essence, must be composed of essence and *differentia*, and (b) unity is either numerical, specific, or generic, and in any of these senses the concept of a triune God would involve plurality. *Infra*, pp. 221f.

[58] *Ibid.*, pp. 153 f. [59] *Ibid.*, pp. 154 f. [60] *Ibid.*, pp. 182 ff.

necessity of positing what might be called the great causal chain of being, more in the spirit of Aristotelianism than that of Neo-Platonism, which later was to acquire greater vogue. The Muslim theologians in general, and the Ash'arites in particular, reacted violently against the concept of "secondary" causality and the inevitable concept of mediation implicit in it. They felt that it resulted in the interposition of a series of active entities between God and the creature, and thereby curtailed God's unqualified omnipotence and sovereignty in the world.[61] Al-Kindī, however, despite his concern to vindicate the sovereignty of God as the *ultimate* cause of creation, did not ignore the role of secondary agents in the processes of nature. In a treatise on the *Proximate, Efficient Cause of Generation and Corruption*, he inquires into the function of such an intermediate or *subordinate* agent, so that the manner of "God's universal disposition of things, through the decrees of His wisdom," as he puts it, might be clearly brought out.[62]

Generation and corruption, for al-Kindī, belong to whatever is susceptible of the four primary qualities, i.e., heat and cold, moisture and dryness. The upper sphere, defined as the region between the perigee of the moon and the extremity of the "body of the outermost sphere," i.e., the heavenly realm, is not susceptible of any of the four qualities, and therefore not subject to generation and corruption, which belong solely to the sublunary world, comprising the four elements and whatever is compounded from them. The four elements themselves, al-Kindī observed, are not generable or corruptible, only their compounds, which will endure for as long as God has decreed. Those compounds include minerals, vegetables, and animals, and are subject to generation and corruption qua individual substances, but their "forms" are as durable as the elements they are made of.[63] Not only generation and corruption, but time, space, and motion are predicable of the four elements and substances compounded from them. Each of the elements moves naturally toward its natural locus. The locus of earth and water is the center of the world, and that of air and fire is the region enclosed between the center of the universe and

[61] Fakhry, *Islamic Occasionalism*, pp. 56 ff., and *infra*, p. 240.

[62] Abū Rīda, *Rasā'il*. I, 219. [63] *Ibid.*, p. 220.

the lower extremities of the celestial sphere, which surrounds the spherical regions of these elements.

The proximate cause of generation and corruption in the sublunary world is either one or more than one of the elements of which this world is made up, on the one hand, or something extraneous to them, on the other. In the former case, the part of the element or elements which is the cause of the generation and corruption of the rest will be altogether incorruptible, which is disproved by the fact that every part of the elements making up the world is generable and corruptible. A subsidiary alternative is that each one of the elements is the cause of the generation and corruption of the rest, from which it would follow that each one is both cause and effect of the generation and corruption of the rest, in such a way that they would all interact among themselves uniformly, despite the distance separating them. But this is absurd, unless we suppose that their natures are homogeneous, and we reduce them in this manner to one simple generic element instead of the acknowledged four.[64]

An extraneous agent therefore must be supposed to be the cause of generation and corruption in the world. This agent is found, upon investigation, to be one or the other of the heavenly bodies, whose movements away from and toward the earth generate heat and cold, the two active primary qualities involved in the generation and corruption of animate or inanimate entities.[65] We need only observe the movements of the sun and the other planets to realize their influences upon earthly phenomena. The sun, in particular, being (relative to its mass) in the most active relationship to the earth, influences earthly phenomena to the highest degree and determines the distribution of prosperity and fertility. Thus some regions such as the arctic and antarctic circles and adjacent territories, on the one hand, and the equatorial regions, on the other, are found to be sparsely populated and barren on account of excessive heat or cold, whereas intermediary regions, being at an optimum distance from the sun, are more dense and fertile.[66]

Moreover, it is by virtue of the fluctuations of the distance of the sun from these regions that the variations of day and night and the

[64] Abū Rīda, *Rasā'il* I, pp. 221 f. [65] *Ibid.*, 224; II, 41 f. [66] *Ibid.*, 228.

succession of the seasons arise, causing thereby the intermittent changes that are a part of generation and corruption. From all this, remarks al-Kindī,

> it appears clearly that the subsistence of things in the world of generation and corruption, the perdurance of their proper forms, as long as the Creator of the universe (may He be praised) has decreed for them, and the preservation of their orderly disposition, are in fact due to the proportionate distance of the sun from the earth, and its particular motion in the ecliptic and its concurrence with the motion of the "outermost sphere," which causes it to move from east to west; they are due likewise to the ex-centricity of its sphere, relative to the center of the earth, namely, its periodic progression toward and its recession from the center of the earth.[67]

A similar role is ascribed to the moon, which because of its smaller distance from the earth determines the orderly succession of meteorological phenomena. Thus, were it any nearer to the earth, there would be neither clouds nor rain. The excessive brightness and the great heat that the moon imparts to the atmosphere, al-Kindī believed, would disperse the cloud formations, and when the moon is full there would be no rain.

Similarly, had its course coincided with the meridian, the propitious meteorological phenomena that result from the moon's rotation in the ecliptic would have been canceled. Its action in tempering the atmosphere and moderating its humidity would be barred.[68] This would happen especially during summer nights, when the growth of vegetation requires the dissemination of heat, and during winter nights, when heat is not required.

In the same way, the other planets of the Ptolemaic cosmology, according to al-Kindī, influence earthly phenomena through their rotations in the ecliptic or in their particular orbits and cause the changes in epochs, and ultimately in the very make-up of people, their character and mores; this results in the rise of new political regimes as decreed by the all-mighty and all-wise Creator of the universe.[69]

As to the nature of the heavenly bodies, al-Kindī explains in a commentary upon a koranic verse which speaks of the "stars and the

[67] Abū Rīda, *Rasā'il*, I, p. 231; cf. Aristotle, *De Caelo* I. 289[a].
[68] *Ibid.*, 231 f. [69] *Ibid.*, pp. 236 f.

trees" prostrating themselves before God,[70] that those "superior entities" must be affirmed to possess both life and intelligence. For, as the proximate causes of the generation and corruption of animate entities in the world, those heavenly bodies impart to such entities, created *ex nihilo* by God, "the form of animate body" proper to them.[71]

Next, from the major premise that the "efficient cause, in so far as it is a cause, is nobler than the effect, in so far as it is an effect," al-Kindī argues that the Outermost Sphere, which imparts life to animate entities in the sublunary world, either directly or indirectly, must on that account be itself animate. Being superior to the objects of generation and corruption it must also be free from generation and corruption and, *eo ipso*, must possess life essentially and everlastingly, whereas life belongs to the lower *generabilia* accidentally and transitorily.[72]

The preeminence of the heavenly bodies, as compared to the terrestrial entities, is therefore twofold: they possess life and they possess it everlastingly. This blissful state belongs to them by virtue of the fact that they have no opposites and are not composed of any of the four elements;[73] and, being alive, they must be capable of sense and motion, in the manner of all living entities. We might distinguish, however, between those faculties of sense that exist for the sake of growth, and those that exist for the sake of something nobler or higher. Now, taste, smell, and touch contribute directly to the acquisition of food, and indirectly to the growth of the animal. The heavenly bodies do not grow and therefore could dispense with these three faculties, but not with the two higher faculties of hearing and sight, which exist for the sake of acquiring knowledge and virtue and which the heavenly bodies must consequently possess.[74]

In keeping with the foregoing premise that the causes of generation and corruption must be superior to their effect, al-Kindī next asserts that the heavenly bodies must also possess intelligence. For, since the two faculties of hearing and sight were said to be necessary to the acquisition of knowledge and virtue, to maintain that the heavenly

[70] *Koran*, 55,6. [71] Abū Rīda, *Rasā'il*, I, 248. [72] *Ibid.*, pp. 251 f.

[73] *Ibid.*, p. 253, and II, 40 f.; cf. Aristotle, *De Caelo* I. 270[b].

[74] *Ibid.*, 254. This was the view of the early Aristotle and of Proclus; see Walzer, "New Studies on al-Kindī," in *Greek into Arabic*, p. 231, quoting Ross, *Fragmenta*, pp. 94 f.

bodies did not possess intelligence would amount to saying that the possession of the two faculties in question is in vain. But this is contrary to the ways of nature, which does nothing in vain.

Second, since the rational creature is superior to the irrational, were the heavenly bodies devoid of Reason, they would be inferior to us.

Third, being the proximate causes of our being, in accordance with God's decree, the heavenly bodies must be the causes of our being rational, since this is our specific "form." If they were lacking in reason themselves, it would be impossible for them to be the causes of our being rational, whether we assume their action to be natural or voluntary.

Fourth, since of the three faculties of the Soul, i.e., the rational, the passionate, and the appetitive, the latter two exist for the sake of the preservation or growth of the animal, whereas the first contributes to its perfection,[75] the heavenly bodies would only possess the rational faculty since, as stated above, they are not liable to growth or decay and are likewise free from desire.

Fifth, if we compare the circumference of the earth to that of the universe at large, and then compare the bulk of mankind to the bulk of the earth and the creatures that populate it, we will see how infinitesimal is the position of mankind in the universe at large. Now, if mankind were the only rational species in the universe as a whole, it would follow that the proportion of rational creatures to the rest of creation is almost infinitesimal, and this would be to detract from the power of God and His wisdom, since undoubtedly the rational creature is superior to the irrational. Therefore, God in the immensity of His power has "ordained that those creatures which are not subject to corruption, throughout the appointed term of their existence, will far surpass those which are subject to it."[76] He has also provided for the great diversity of creation by bringing into being simple as well as compound substances, animate as well as inanimate entities, rational as well as irrational, sensible as well as insensible, and conferred upon the whole creation the power of locomotion, whether rectilinear, as

[75] *Rasā'il*, I, 255; cf. Aristotle, *De Anima* III. 434^{b}24 and 435^{b}20, where all the faculties of the Soul higher than touch are said to be necessary for well being only.

[76] Abū Rīda, *Rasā'il*, I, 256 f.

in the case of terrestrial entities, or circular, as in the case of the heavenly bodies.[77]

When we ponder God's all-pervasive power and wisdom in ordering the universe so rationally and harmoniously, we are filled with awe, not so much at the sight of those huge and extraordinary creatures in the world that often compel our wonder, but rather at the nobility of those "higher entities" and at the manner in which he has made man the epitome of the whole creation. That is why the ancient philosophers describe man as the microcosm, as distinguished from the larger world or macrocosm—a teaching which, our philosopher is careful to note, is quite compatible with the teaching of Muḥammad.[78]

Now, considering the important role that heavenly bodies play in determining terrestrial happenings, the question would naturally arise as to how far al-Kindī was committed to popular astrology. On the one hand, he has gone down in ʿAbbāsid history as a great astrologer who served three caliphs in that capacity and wrote a whole series of astrological and astronomical works.[79] Yet, on the other, his repeated insistence on the all-pervasiveness of divine providence and God's role as the creator and superintendent of the world, coupled with his obvious Muʿtazilite sympathies, would appear to run counter to the thoroughgoing determinism of popular astrology. Without going to the extreme to which popular astrologers in the Islamic as well as the pagan worlds have gone, however, there can be little doubt that al-Kindī, who was careful to underscore the hazards of astrology, subscribed to some of its fundamental assumptions.

If the titles of his astrological works are any indication, we might safely infer that he believed astrology to be a genuine science; he appears to have drawn a clear-cut distinction between genuine and false astrologers and to have advocated the use of heavenly and meteorological phenomena, such as eclipses and planetary conjunctions, as clues to general as well as particular prognostics.[80] Moreover, his interest and the interest of his school in the beliefs of the Ḥarrānians, a

[77] Abū Rīda, *Rasā'il*, II, 45 f. [78] *Ibid.*, I, 260 f.

[79] Ibn al-Nadīm, *Kitāb al-Fihrist*, pp. 373–75.

[80] Cf. H. Ritter, "Schriften Jaʿqūb ibn Isḥāq al-Kindī's in Stambulen Bibliotheken," *Archiv Orientálni*, Vol. 4 (1932), p. 369; McCarthy, *al-Taṣānīf*, pp. 28, 50 et passim.

late Hellenistic island of star-worshipers in the midst of Islam,[81] points to a distinct dependence on Ḥarrānian astrological and philosophical sources and a certain sympathy with some of their views.

In his account of the Soul and the process of cognition in general, al-Kindī reveals an acute sense of criticism, despite his obvious eclecticism. The Soul, according to him, is affiliated with the incorruptible spheres, in so far as it is an incorporeal substance. His argument for the incorporeity of the Soul rests upon the Pythagorean-Platonic conception of the accidental and temporary union of Soul and body. The Soul is the principle of life, which supervenes upon the organic body for a given period and then relinquishes it without affecting its corporeity.

Moreover, since the Soul confers on the animate substance its very essence and definition, it must stand to it in the capacity of "rational form" or species. But the species of substance belongs obviously to the class of substances and is on that account incorporeal, since like all universals, the species is incorporeal. Otherwise, it could not inhere wholly in each particular member of the class to which it belongs. It follows then that the Soul is the incorporeal form or species of a living substance and *eo ipso* an incorporeal substance.[82]

In two of his very short psychological treatises, purporting to serve as an epitome of Aristotle's *De Anima*, supplemented by the views of Plato and the other philosophers, al-Kindī states in a distinctively Neo-Platonic fashion that "the Soul is a simple entity . . . , whose substance is analogous to the Creator's own substance, just as the light of the sun is analogous to the sun."[83] Being thus "divine and spiritual" in essence, the Soul is distinct from body and is in opposition to it. The passionate or appetitive faculties might move man to act vilely, but they are curbed by the Soul. This proves that the rational Soul, which holds them in check, is distinct from them. When it has left its temporary bodily dwelling, the Soul will rejoin the "real world," upon which shines the light of the Creator, and will be able to partake of all knowledge so that nothing will remain hidden from it, as Plato has shown.[84]

[81] Ibn al-Nadīm, *al-Fihrist*, pp. 456–60.

[82] Abū Rīda, *Rasā'il*, I, 265 f. [83] *Ibid.*, p. 273. [84] *Ibid.*, p. 274.

This noble destiny, however, is denied those who are engrossed in bodily pleasures; al-Kindī compares them to pigs because the appetitive faculty predominates in them. Others, in whom the passionate faculty is predominant, are compared to dogs, and those in whom Reason is master, to kings. Pythagoras, however, compares the Soul, once it has been cleansed of bodily desires, to a mirror in which external images are clearly reflected, for such a Soul is able to reflect the forms of all things and know all things.

Not every Soul, however, will rejoin the intelligible world beyond the spheres when it leaves the body. Some Souls will undergo purification in stages by abiding temporarily in the sphere of the moon and, subsequently, in that of Mercury and the spheres beyond it, until they become thoroughly cleansed and are fit to be ushered into the intelligible world.[85] This indeed is the burden of the philosophers' teachings, according to al-Kindī. Only through purification will the Soul be able, having shed its bodily frame, to join the intelligible or divine world. The lower world is but a bridge that leads our Souls into the higher world after death, where they will be able to partake of the intellectual vision of God.[86]

In his account of the faculties of the Soul, al-Kindī departs little from the Aristotelian tradition, with its distinction between the vegetative, sensitive, rational, and motive faculties, and with which the tripartite Platonic concept of the Soul is often fused without due discrimination.[87] He describes sensation as the act of abstracting the sensible form of the object of sense, by means of the sense organ. In this act, the sensible and the organ of sense are identified.[88] In the absence of the sensible object, the imagination, or representative faculty (*al-muṣawwirah*), conjures up the sensible image fully differentiated, whether in sleep or waking. The less the mind is distracted through the intrusion of particular sensibles, the keener the action of the imagination, as happens in intense concentration or sleep.[89] The representative faculty, being free from the action of external objects,

[85] Abū Rīda, *Rasā'il*, I, p. 278. Cf. the view of Poimandres in *Corpus Hermeticum*, ed. Nock and Festugière, I, 25 f.

[86] *Ibid.*, 277. [87] *Ibid.*, pp. 294 f., 258, 267, 273 f.

[88] *Ibid.*, pp. 301, 354 f.; cf. Aristotle, *De Anima* III. 429^a15. [89] *Ibid.*, 296 f.

is capable of producing composite images for which there are no counterparts in the realm of reality, such as horned men or talking beasts.[90] And this happens particularly in sleep. In that state, the Soul is sometimes so keen that it can even foretell the future by manipulating particular representations and making the necessary inferences from them. If, however, the Soul's faculty of inference is weak, its predictions are not borne out by future happenings and we say therefore that it has judged falsely.[91] The logical corollary of this proposition, which al-Kindī does not appear to draw and which al-Fārābī and others did not hesitate eventually to draw, is that the faculty of prophecy, which played such a decisive role in Islamic thought, is a function of the representative faculty developed to an extraordinary degree and conferred on the prophets as a divine favor.

Reason has a certain analogy to sensation, in so far as it also (1) abstracts the forms of intelligible objects, i.e., species and genera, and (2) becomes identical with its object in the act of thinking. The Soul, with its dual faculties of reason and sensation, might be called, as Plato had termed it, the "locus of forms."[92]

In his treatise on Reason, which played a major role in the history of the medieval discussions of the nature of the intellect both in Europe and the Near East, al-Kindī expounds the Aristotelian view of Reason, which he believes to be substantially the same as that of Plato. He distinguishes four senses of the term "Reason" (*'aql*), for the Stagirite: "The first is Reason which is always in act; the second is Reason which is in potentiality and is in the Soul; the third is the Reason which has passed from the state of potentiality in the Soul to that of actuality; and the fourth is the Reason which we call the manifest."[93] We will call these four aspects of Reason, for the sake of convenience, the active, the potential, the habitual, and the manifest,[94] respectively. When the Soul has apprehended the intelligible forms of the imagination, which are free from association with matter and

[90] Abū Rīda, *Rasā'il*, I, pp. 299 f. [91] *Ibid.*, pp. 303 ff.

[92] *Ibid.*, p. 302; cf. Aristotle, *De Anima* III. 429^{a}28. [93] *Ibid.*, 353 f.

[94] I read *al-bā'in*, which might also be rendered, as in the Latin version, demonstrative. McCarthy has recently suggested another reading: *al-nāti'* (emergent); see "Al-Kindī's Treatise on the Intellect," in *Islamic Studies*, III (June 1964), 119 f.

the representations, it becomes identified with them, and the subject matter of its cognition and Reason then passes from the state of potentiality to that of actuality. In this process of transition from potentiality to act, the intelligible forms play the role of efficient cause, since otherwise such a transition is not possible. But those intelligibles, considered in their actuality, are identical with active reason, since in the act of cognition the distinction between Reason and its object disappears completely. Viewed from the standpoint of the Soul, seeking to understand, these forms can be termed "acquired Reason" (*al-'aql al-mustafād*), in so far as the Soul acquires or receives them from the active reason itself. However, when the Soul has apprehended these forms, it can be conceived as capable of conjuring them up at will (while it is not actually occupied with such apprehension), in which case its cognition is *habitual*. Or it can be conceived as actually engaged in contemplating them or imparting them to others, in which case its cognitions would be *manifest*, both in the sense of being apprehended clearly and in that of being exhibited plainly to others.[95]

A great deal has been written, from medieval times to the present, in an attempt to untangle Aristotle's intricate view of Reason, especially in its active capacity. And, although al-Kindī is careful to emphasize that his account of Reason is that of Aristotle, "the foremost among the ancient philosophers," and that of his master Plato, who is in substantial agreement with him on this point, the question would naturally arise as to how far al-Kindī's account agrees with the statements of Stagirite in the *De Anima*. This question might simply be answered by saying, despite the extended controversy of scholars in recent times,[96] that al-Kindī appears to reaffirm here, with almost the same parsimony, the Aristotelian theory of the intellect in relation to his general theory of cognition without proceeding to exploit it, as the later Arab Neo-Platonists had done for any grand cosmological purpose. Where al-Kindī appears to differ from Aristotle is in his introduction of a fourth Reason; this might be an original addition of

[95] Abū Rīda, *Rasā'il*, I, 257 f.

[96] See especially Gilson, "Les sources gréco-arabes de l'augustinisme avicennisant," *Archives d'histoire doctrinale et littéraire du moyen âge*, 1929, pp. 5–27 and McCarthy, "Al-Kindī's Treatise," pp. 119 f.

his own or of Alexander[97] but is found on closer scrutiny to result from the eliciting of the two possible meanings of habitual reason or the *νοῦς καθ' ἕξιν* of *De Anima.* 429^b5, as referring either to the acquisition of the ability to think or the exercise of this ability. In relation to the bare potentiality of thought, the *habitus* is already a stage of actualization, corresponding in the Aristotelian scheme to the first actuality or *entelecheia*, as distinct from the exercise, corresponding to the *second* or higher stage of actuality, which Aristotle calls the second *entelecheia.*[98] When it is recalled that for Aristotle the three aspects of Reason, the potential, habitual, and actual, are so many phases in the complex process of cognition in its transition by degrees from potentiality to actuality, a final phase corresponding to what Aristotle calls the "second actuality" would appear to suggest itself quite naturally to an intelligent reader who wanted to probe deeply into his parsimonious but highly significant words.

The remaining treatises of al-Kindī that have come down to us deal with a variety of subjects from an Aristotelian point of view (broadly speaking), such as a treatise on the *Five Principles or Essences*, i.e., matter, space, form, motion, and time. Here he expounds succinctly the Aristotelian view of those five fundamental concepts of physics. In a second treatise purporting to show that the *Nature of the Sphere is Different from That of the Four Elements*, he argues that the heavenly bodies are incomposite and are not susceptible of the four primary qualities. They are made up, according to him, of a "fifth nature,"[99] which he does not explicitly name but can hardly be other than Aristotle's ether. The form of the four elements, as well as of the heavenly bodies beyond, is stated in another treatise to be spherical and to be ranged in concentric spheres or rings around the earth, the center of the universe.[100] Other treatises deal with the ancients' five geometrical figures of the elements, the cube, the pyramid, the

[97] See Gilson, "Les sources gréco-arabes," pp. 5–27.

[98] Cf. *De Anima*, II. 412^a6 and 15; III. 429^b7 f.

[99] See title of this treatise in Ibn al-Nadīm, *al-Fihrist*, pp. 258 f., and Abū Rīda, *Rasā'il*, II, 55.

[100] *Rasā'il*, II, 48 f.

octahedron, the duodecahedron, and the icosahedron[101]; the element that is susceptible of color and is the cause of color in other things, i.e., earth; the cause of the scarcity of rainfall in certain regions; the cause of the formation of clouds, of snow, lightning, sleet, and thunder; the cause of the coolness of the upper layers of the atmosphere and the warmth of the lower layers; the cause of the apparent azure of the celestial dome; the cause of the tides, etc. These treatises contain some subtle observations on the meteorological and cosmological phenomena discussed.

Of far greater significance for the history of philosophical ideas in Islam and the development of philosophical terminology among the Arabs is al-Kindī's *Definitions and Descriptions of Things*, the first link in a chain of similar treatises that emulated Aristotle's example in Book Delta of the *Metaphysics* in giving a list of technical terms and expounding them. At a time when philosophers were groping for a precise idiom, it is doubtless of great interest to see how they expressed themselves and how the subsequent development of a philosophical vocabulary modified, improved upon, or simply consecrated the original terminology. Many of the terms that al-Kindī uses bear the mark of a greater reliance on translation from Greek or Syriac, and it is not surprising that in the course of time such terms were dropped and others were substituted for them, acquiring in due course the character of classics. Such for instance are the terms "*jirm*" (body), "*ṭīnah*" (matter), "*al-tawahhum*" (imagination), "*al-tamām*" (end), "*al-ghalabiyah*" (passionate—of faculty), "*al-quniah*" (*habitus*),[102] and "*al-jāmi'ah*" (syllogism),[103] which were gradually replaced by the following terms, generally used by tenth- and eleventh-century writers: "*jism*," "*māddah*," "*al-takhayyul*," "*al-ghāyah*," "*al-ghaḍabiyah*," "*al-malakah*," and "*al-qiyās*," respectively. In some cases al-Kindī resorts to the use of unfamilar or archaic terms such as "*ais*" and "*lais*" to express the antithetic concepts of being and nonbeing, and even coins verbs, participles, and substantives from such terms. He creates even unlikelier terms still, such as "*hawwā*" and "*tahawwī*" (i.e., bring and

[101] Cf. Walzer and Kraus, *Galeni compendium Timaei Platonis*, p. 15 (translation, pp. 59 f.), and Taylor, *Commentary on the Timaeus*, pp. 369 ff.

[102] Abū Rīda, *Rasā'il*, I, 165 ff., *et passim*.

[103] *Ibid.*, p. 380, *et passim*.

bringing into being) from the third-person singular pronoun (*hua*), in an attempt to explain the concept of creation *ex nihilo*.[104]

Despite his inventiveness, however, it cannot be said that al-Kindī wrote with great grace or elegance. In general, his use of words is labored and tortuous, and his reasoning often long-winded and disrupted by parentheses or digressions. Sometimes he appears to resort deliberately to the use of far-fetched terms or idioms, in the manner of the great Arab rhetoricians, simply for their literary effect. One cannot help feeling in such instances that he was laboring under that sense of literary inferiority which the masters of the new learning must have felt at the strictures of the literary pundits[105] and sought to counter by being "literary" themselves.

His two favorite methods of proof were the *argumentum ad hominem* and the *reductio ad absurdum*, to which might be added the Platonic method of dichotomy. For instance, he used a combination of these three proofs to establish the proposition that the Eternal Being, or God, is incorruptible,[106] a technique he tends to employ to excess in most of his writings.

The contribution of al-Kindī to the development of philosophical terminology was by no means his only or even his major contribution to philosophical thought in the ninth century. Equally important was his active part in the introduction and diffusion of Greek philosophical ideas (of which we have already noted a number of instances), either as a patron of translations undertaken by other scholars or as reviser and expositor of philosophical texts. However, all this, coupled with the patronage of philosophy and science by the three caliphs with whom al-Kindī entered into such active association, would not have sufficed to insure the success of philosophy in establishing a firm foothold in the world of Islam had it not been for his singular zeal in pledging full allegiance to the cause of the nascent, though suspect, learning. Being committed to the fundamental tenets of Islamic

[104] Abū Rīda, *Rasā'il*, I, pp. 133, 162, 182, *et passim*.

[105] See for instance a debate between Mattā b. Yūnus and Abū Sa'īd al-Sīrāfi, said to have taken place in 320 A.H. (A.D. 932), in al-Tauḥīdi, *al-Muqābāsāt*, pp. 68 ff., and *infra*, pp. 207 f.

[106] See especially Abū Rīda, *Rasā'il*, I, 133 ff.

belief in the manner of the Mu'tazilite theologians, he ran a far less grave risk of public disapproval than the tenth- and eleventh-century Neo-Platonists who sought artfully to effect the impossible marriage of philosophy to Islamic belief. At the root of the difficulty was the reluctance of these Neo-Platonists to surrender any aspect of the former, or to attribute any mark of privilege or distinction to the latter by virtue of its supernatural or divine origin. For al-Kindī, however, the true vocation of philosophy was not to contest the truth of revelation or make impudent claims of superiority, or even parity, with it. Philosophy, he believed, should simply surrender its claims to be the highest pathway to truth and be willing to subordinate itself as an ancillary to revelation.

In an important treatise intended to serve as an introduction to the study of philosophy in general and Peripateticism in particular, and, like his lost *Protrepticus*,[107] to exhort the earnest searcher to embark on the arduous path of philosophy, al-Kindī classifies the treatises of the Corpus Aristotelicum in what appears to have been the late Greek, possibly Athenian fashion,[108] and the later Arab philosophers generally accepted this classification. First came the logical treatises in eight books, which included, according to the Arab syllabus, the *Rhetoric* and the *Poetics*.[109] Second came the physical treatises in seven books, from which the *Psychology* was excluded. Third came the psychological treatises, which included the *De Anima* and the *Parva Naturalia* in four books, dealing, according to al-Kindī, "with entities which do not require material bodies necessarily for their being or subsistence, but might nevertheless exist in conjunction with bodies."[110] Fourth came the *Metaphysics* in one book, which deals with entities that neither require matter nor exist in conjunction with matter. Fifth came the ethical treatises, which included the *Ethics to Nicomachus* in eleven books, addressed to his son, the *Ethics* (to Eudemus), "which he addressed to one of his friends" and is similar to the first, and finally

[107] See Ibn al-Nadīm, *al-Fihrist*, p. 372, i.e., *al-Ḥathth 'alā Ta'allum al-Falsafah*.

[108] Walzer, "New Studies on al-Kindī," in *Greek into Arabic*, p. 201.

[109] Rescher, "Al-Kindī's Sketch of Aristotle's Organon," *The New Scholasticism*, Jan. 1963, pp. 44 ff.

[110] Abū Rīda, *Rasā'il*, I, 368.

the *Magna Moralia*. The subject matter of these books might appear to resemble that of psychology, except that they are concerned with the cultivation of the virtues of the Soul, which is the ultimate goal of man in this life and the prelude to his well-being in the next.[111]

Mathematics is not included in this classification because, according to al-Kindī, its study does not form a part of the study of philosophy proper but serves as a preamble to its study. This introduction is so essential that, as al-Kindī asserts here and in a lost treatise,[112] it is impossible for one to attain proficiency in philosophy unless he first masters mathematics.[113] By mathematics he means the sciences of number, harmony, geometry, and astronomy; the principal or primary one is the science of number, i.e., arithmetic, for if number did not exist, nothing would.

The knowledge of quantity and quality is so crucial, believed al-Kindī, that without this knowledge which we acquire through sense perception no knowledge of primary substance is possible. And since we arrive at the knowledge of secondary substances (i.e., species and genera) by means of the latter, no knowledge of secondary substances is possible either. Thus without the knowledge of quantity and quality no knowledge is possible, at the human level at any rate, for it is not excluded that such knowledge might be possible at the superhuman, or divine level. Such, in fact, is the case with prophetic knowledge, reserved by God for his chosen emissaries or apostles, who can dispense altogether with the human process of rationalization and partake directly of a supernatural light, which God imparts to whomsoever he pleases. The mark of such knowledge is the extraordinary succinctness, lucidity, and comprehensiveness with which it is expressed, and which no human expression can possibly equal.[114]

As an instance of this superior, divine knowledge, al-Kindī cites a cluster of koranic verses in which an infidel, upon putting to Muḥammad the question "Who indeed will quicken the bones, once they have withered away?" is dramatically told: "Say, He, who originated them initially and is fully conversant with every creature, will quicken them,"[115] through his absolute fiat. For "He commands that a thing

[111] Abū Rīda, *Rasā'il*, I, p. 369. [112] See Ibn al-Nadīm, *al-Fihrist*, p. 371.
[113] Abū Rīda, *Rasā'il*, I, 376. [114] *Ibid.*, I, 373, and II, 93. [115] *Koran* 36, 78 f

be and it at once is." Here we have a masterly retort which surpasses in lucidity and concreteness any logical proof of which the keenest human intellect is capable.

Nor does the Koran stop at this point in its endeavor to demonstrate God's ability to create or recreate as He pleases. It goes on to state in the same passage that out of green wood God has caused fire to ignite, illustrating thereby how out of one contrary (green wood) another contrary (fire) is generated; that is, how fire arises from nonfire, or is made from that which it was not, which is precisely the meaning of creation *ex nihilo*.[116]

Against those who repudiate the possibility of such creation on the ground that, by analogy to human action, it would require a very protracted period, the Koran urges that God's action, far from being analogous to human action, is such that "whenever He desires anything, He commands it to be and it at once is," dispensing thereby with the two conditions of matter and time altogether, through His sovereign power.[117]

We need not concern ourselves here with the other aspects of al-Kindī's ventures into the domain of koranic exegesis. We might simply note that he, like the vast majority of Islamic theologians, is obsessed with the literary superiority of the Koran, whose arguments might differ from the stringent dialectical proofs of the philosophers but are often more effective and more concrete. Divine or revealed knowledge likewise surpasses human knowledge in so far as divine authority, which is its source, surpasses the human processes of knowing, which are ultimately rooted in sense perception. In this, as indeed in many other important respects, there can be little doubt that al-Kindī stands decidedly at the center of the Islamic theological tradition, and that his philosophical interests do not prejudice his unconditional adherence to the fundamental tenets of Islamic dogma. His fellow Muslim philosophers, from al-Fārābī on, were so carried away by their philosophical zeal that they were unable to perceive that, to have any significance, revealed truth could be neither equal nor inferior to philosophical truth, but must be superior to it, if the reality of its supernatural origin is to be safeguarded.

[116] Abū Rīda, *Rasā'il*, I, 374 f. [117] *Ibid.*, p. 375.

We cannot conclude this discussion without a final word about al-Kindī's only extant ethical treatise,[118] entitled the *Art of Dispelling Sorrow*.[119] In this work, which has numerous parallels in Arabic, the Stoic ideals of *apatheia*, moral fortitude, and abnegation are set out in noble philosophical terms. The prototype of moral excellence for al-Kindī, as indeed for many another philosopher from al-Rāzī to the Brethren of Purity, is Socrates, confused sometimes in the Arabic sources with another great moral teacher, Diogenes. As the earliest treatise of its kind in Arabic, this eloquent and very often moving disquisition on moral heroism has a special claim on the attention of the historian of ideas. We can only note in this survey its cardinal importance for the history of moral ideas in Islam.

II

THE RISE OF NATURALISM AND THE CHALLENGE TO ISLAMIC DOGMA: IBN AL-RĀWANDĪ AND AL-RĀZĪ

THE philosophical awakening, that followed in the wake of the introduction of Greek philosophy and was attended by the rise of a hitherto unknown spirit of free inquiry could not fail eventually to place in jeopardy some of the fundamental tenets of Islamic belief. The Mu'tazilite theologians, who initiated this current of free inquiry, were able on the whole to absorb the shock of Greek rationalism which generated this current. Some of the bolder spirits among them, however, like the great al-Naẓẓām (d. ca. 845), were driven by the sheer

[118] Except, that is, for his collection of the *Sayings of Socrates* preserved in *Koprülü* Ms No. 1608, which consists mostly of moral aphorisms ascribed to the Athenian sage. See Fakhry, "Al-Kindī and Socrates," *al-Abḥāth*, Vol. 12 (1963), pp. 28 ff.

[119] *Uno scritto morale inedito di al-Kindi*, ed. Ritter and Walzer; cf. Simon van Riet, "Joie et bonheur dans le traité d'al-Kindi," *Revue philosophique de Louvain*, Vol. 61 (1963), pp. 13–23.

force of abstract speculation to make a positive advance in the direction of naturalism without sacrificing their fundamental Islamic faith in the supernatural or questioning the concept of the validity of scripture.[120]

Of particular significance in this connection is the case of al-Kindī, whom we have just considered. As the earliest systematic protagonist of Hellenism, al-Kindī might be thought to have approached Muslim dogma, if not in a spirit of open skepticism, at least in one of guarded credulity. But such was not the case of this outstanding encyclopedist, whose interest in theology was no less than his interest in philosophy. Not only did his study of Greek thought leave intact his faith in such essential aspects of Islamic belief as the creation of the world in time, the resurrection of the body, the reality of God's all-pervasive providence, and the validity of prophetic revelation; but, what is more, he did not hesitate to place his philosophical insights fully at the service of his Islamic beliefs. Thus, unlike the subsequent proponents of Greek philosophy, he remained almost entirely impervious to the onslaught of religious skepticism.

Whether such a development was inherent in the new rationalism is difficult to determine. What might be asserted with relative confidence is that al-Kindī was historically a solitary and, in many ways, a heroic figure. Even within his own school the tide of doubt could not be stemmed or diverted for long, as illustrated by the case of his best-known disciple, Aḥmad b. al-Ṭayyib al-Sarakhsī, who was the tutor and boon companion (*nadīm*) of the ʿAbbāsid caliph al-Muʿtaḍid until his disgrace and execution in 899. Little is known about the life and thought of this successful and well-to-do[121] philosopher except that he seems to have followed in the footsteps of his better-known master and to have cultivated, like him, an interest in logic, theology, and astrology. In consequence of his success and the favors he enjoyed at court, al-Sarakhsī seems to have pushed the limits of familiarity with the caliph too far and to have taken the liberty of broaching heretical themes in his discourses with him. This circumstance, coupled with

[120] *Supra*, pp. 64 f.

[121] According to al-Masʿūdī (*Murūj*, VII, 179–80), when the caliph ordered his possessions to be confiscated, they were valued at 150,000 dinars. Even allowing for the natural tendency of Arab historians to exaggerate sums, this was doubtless a vast fortune.

his very preeminence at court,[122] appears to have finally induced the caliph to order his death. And if al-Bīrūnī's otherwise very great authority is to be credited, al-Sarakhsī did not confine his religious doubts to private discourses with the caliph, but embodied them in numerous treatises in which he attacked the prophets as charlatans.[123]

Al-Sarakhsī's Mu'tazilite sympathies, like those of his master al-Kindī, appear to be well founded.[124] And the rationalist preoccupations generated by these sympathies and his inquiries into philosophy apparently were at the basis of his religious doubts, and in particular his attacks on prophecy. The rationalist current unleashed by the Mu'tazilah did not fail ultimately to sweep away this concept.

Much more radical in his challenge to the whole edifice of theism, however, was the notorious free thinker Ibn al-Rāwandī (d. ca. 910), who under the compulsion of a seemingly genuine philosophical urge embarked on the hazardous path of religious skepticism with singular boldness. If we are to trust the undoubtedly hostile sources through which a very scant amount of information about Ibn al-Rāwandī's heterodox teaching has filtered down to us, this free thinker appears to have repudiated the grand supernatural themes of revelation and miracle, as well as the very possibility, according to one authority, of a satisfactory rational answer to the question of God's existence and the rationality of His ways.[125] (Like other suspect literature in Islam, the series of books expounding these ideas has not survived.) According to a less hostile source, Ibn al-Rāwandī denounced the whole fabric of revelation as superfluous. He is reported to have argued that human reason was sufficient to determine the knowledge of God and the distinction between good and evil, a view in keeping with the teachings of the majority of the Mu'tazilah to whom he was originally affiliated; revelation therefore was altogether unnecessary, and miracles, upon which the claims of prophecy are alleged to rest, were altogether absurd. The most important miracle from the Islamic point of view, that of the inimitable literary perfection of the Koran, is quite untenable, according to him, since it is not beyond reason that an Arab

122 Ibn al-Nadīm, *al-Fihrist*, p. 380.

123 Rosenthal, *Aḥmad b. aṭ-Ṭayyib as-Sarasḫī*, p. 132, *et passim*.

124 *Ibid.*, p. 35.

125 Al-Khayyāṭ, *Kitāb al-Intiṣār*, pp. 11–12.

(i.e., Muḥammad) should so excel all other Arabs in literary proficiency that his work would be unquestionably the best. Yet this excellence would not necessarily involve any extraordinary or miraculous character in his output. Nor can it be denied that this alleged literary miraculousness is hardly relevant, as probative evidence, in regard to foreigners to whom Arabic is an alien tongue.[126]

The other views ascribed to Ibn al-Rāwandī, such as the eternity of the world, the superiority of dualism (Manichaeanism) over monotheism, and the vanity of divine wisdom,[127] confirm the impression that this thinker, originally a very skilled and highly respected Mu'tazilite theologian, was later assailed by serious doubts born of an intense and searching spirit of inquiry, and that the stock answers and subtle formulas of the theologians could no longer satisfy him.

Despite his notoriety and incredible intellectual boldness, which reached such a point that he actually dared parody the Koran and ridicule Muḥammad,[128] Ibn al-Rāwandī is eclipsed in the history of free thought in Islam by a far greater contemporary fellow Persian, Abū Bakr Muḥammad b. Zakariyā al-Rāzī (the Rhazes of Latin sources), who was the greatest nonconformist in the whole history of Islam and undoubtedly the most celebrated medical authority in the tenth century. Al-Rāzī was born in Ray, in the province of Khurāsān, and is said by some authorities to have played the lute in his youth and by others to have been a money-changer before he turned to philosophy and medicine. He achieved such standing in the latter that he was made head of the hospital in his native town, apparently before he was thirty-two years of age, and later took charge of the hospital at Baghdad. He became generally recognized, in the words of one authority, as "the unsurpassed physician of Islam."[129] Little else is known of the particulars of his life or his personal traits except the fact that he dabbled in alchemy and was a man of great kindness,

[126] K. al-Zummurrud, in *Rivista degli Studi Orientali*, XIV (1934), 93–129, ed. and transl. Kraus. See also Ibn al-Nadīm, *al-Fihrist*, p. 255.

[127] Arnold, *al-Mu'tazilah*, p. 53; al-'Abbāsī, *Ma'āhid al-Tanṣīṣ*, Vol. 1, pp. 155 ff.; Nyberg in Brunschvig and Von Grunebaum, *Classicisme et déclin*, pp. 131 ff.

[128] *Ma'āhid al-Tanṣīṣ*, Vol. 1, pp. 155 ff.; Ibn al-Nadīm, *al-Fihrist*, p. 380.

[129] Ṣā'id, *Ṭabaqāt al-Umam*, pp. 52 f.; al-Qifṭī, *Tārīkh al-Ḥukamā'*, pp. 271 f.; Ibn Abī Uṣaybi'ah, *'Uyūn*, I, 313 f.

generosity, and industry. Possibly as a result of his exceptional studiousness, he developed a cataract shortly before his death but refused to have it removed because, as he judiciously observed, he had seen enough of the world to want to see any more;[130] he died probably in 925 or 932.[131]

Al-Rāzī's scientific and philosophical output apparently was voluminous. He himself claims in an autobiographical work that he composed no fewer than 200 works on the whole range of physical and metaphysical learning, with the exception of mathematics, which for some unknown reason he evidently avoided.[132] His greatest medical work was *al-Ḥāwī*, otherwise known as *al-Jāmiʿ*, or compendium of medicine, which was translated into Latin in 1279 under the title *Continens* and circulated widely in medical circles well into the sixteenth century. In addition to almost every aspect of medicine, his works concern philosophy, alchemy, astronomy, grammar, theology, logic, and other areas of learning, but it is naturally his philosophical writings that are particularly relevant here. The most important are listed below; unfortunately only a small number of these, and in some cases no more than a series of fragments, have come down to us.

1. A group of logical treatises dealing with the *Categories*, *Demonstration*, *Isagoge*, and with logic, as expressed in the idiom of Islamic *Kalām*.[133]
2. A group of treatises on metaphysics in general.
3. *Absolute and Particular Matter.*
4. *Plenum and Vacum, Fire and Space.*
5. *Physics.*
6. *That the World Has a Wise Creator.*
7. *On the Eternity and Noneternity of Bodies.*
8. *Refutation of Proclus.*
9. "*Plutarch's*" *Physical Opinions* (*Placita Philosophorum*).
10. *A Commentary on the Timaeus.*

[130] *Tārīkh al-Ḥukamā'*, pp. 271 f.; Ibn al-Nadīm, *Kitāb al-Fihrist*, p. 430.

[131] Kraus (ed.), *Epître de Béruni*, pp. 5 f.

[132] Cf. *al-Sīrah al-Falsafiyah* in Kraus (ed.), *Opera Philosophica*, p. 109, and *Epître de Béruni*, pp. 6 ff.

[133] Kraus, *Epître de Béruni*, p. 14.

11. *A Commentary on Plutarch's Commentary on the Timaeus.*
12. *A Treatise Showing That Bodies Move by Themselves and That Movement Belongs to Them Essentially.*
13. *The Spiritual Physic.*
14. *The Philosophical Way.*
15. *On the Soul.*
16. *On the Sayings of the Infallible Imām.*
17. *A Refutation of the Mu'tazilah.*
18. *Metaphysics according to Plato's Teaching.*
19. *Metaphysics according to Socrates' Teaching.*[134]

As might be supposed, the subject matter of al-Rāzī's thought can be only partially gleaned from the scant sources that have preserved his writings either in part or in full. Despite the haziness of the picture given in such sources, and the dense hostility through which he is viewed by later authors, however, al-Rāzī stands out as a towering figure in the history of metaphysical thought in Islam. At a time when the authority of Aristotle was being gradually established by such philosophers as al-Kindī and al-Fārābī, and the danger of religious heterodoxy and nonconformism had been dramatically highlighted by the repressive policies of many an 'Abbāsid caliph from al-Ma'mūn on, al-Rāzī had the courage to challenge some of the fundamental Islamic beliefs and to embark on a new philosophical path in a manner that brought censure from later authors. These critics berate him for departing from the beaten path of Aristotelianism, on the one hand, and for espousing the "views of ancient naturalists," or simply not grasping the finer points of Aristotelian philosophy, on the other.[135]

Despite the curious recurrent allegation that al-Rāzī derived his major metaphysical views, and in particular his central concept of the five co-eternal principles, from Ḥarrānean or Sabean sources,[136] there can be little doubt that the inspiration for his metaphysical thought is essentially Platonic, and that his ethical writings are imbued essentially

[134] Ibn al-Nadīm, *al-Fihrist*, pp. 430 f.; al-Qifṭī, *Tārīkh al-Ḥukamā'* pp. 273 f.; Pines, *Beiträge*, pp. 87 ff.; and Kraus, *Epître de Béruni*, pp. 11 ff.

[135] Ṣā'id, *Ṭabaqāt*, p. 33; al-Mas'ūdī, *al-Tanbīh wa'l-Ishrāf*, pp. 122, 162.

[136] See al-Rāzī, *al-Muḥaṣṣal*, pp. 85 f., and Kraus, *Opera Philosophica*, pp. 178 ff., for other authorities.

with Socratic ideas of morality. This seems quite natural considering al-Rāzī's preoccupation with Socratic, Platonic, and post-Platonic literature, as can be seen from the titles of his works such as a treatise on Plutarch's spurious *Physical Opinions* (as the Arabs called his *Placita Philosophorum*), a *Refutation of Proclus*, a commentary on *Plutarch's Commentary on the Timaeus*, as well as a *Commentary on the Timaeus* itself, and a treatise on *Metaphysics according to Plato's Doctrine*. Moreover, the examination of the internal evidence, as well as the substance of al-Rāzī's teaching as embodied in his extant writings, bears out fully this assumption.

Al-Rāzī's best-known ethical treatise, the *Spiritual Physic*, is a highly approving exposition of Plato's tripartite doctrine of the Soul as laid down in the *Republic*, and the role of music (which he calls the "spiritual physic") on the one hand, and gymnastics (which he calls the "bodily physic") on the other, in insuring the harmony and moderation that Plato teaches are the mark of the moral and spiritual rectitude of the soul.[137]

But before proceeding to elaborate al-Rāzī's concept of the five eternal principles in which his Platonism is most clearly revealed, we might examine his reaction to Aristotle. It is important to note in this context, however, that such a distinction between his acceptance of Plato and disagreement with Aristotle is simply a matter of convenience, since these two aspects of his thought are logically complementary.

To begin with, al-Rāzī rejects out of hand Aristotle's concept of the impossibility of the void as "the boundary of the containing body at which it is in contact with the contained body" (*Phys.* IV. 212^a5) and maintains, following what he thought was Plato's teaching, that the void is possible.[138]

In consonance with this view of the void, al-Rāzī considers motion an essential attribute of body, which, as the title of one of his treatises (No. 12, above) suggests, belongs to body essentially and is not, as

137 Kraus, *Opera Philosophica*, pp. 27 f.; cf. Fakhry, "A Tenth-Century Arabic Interpretation of Plato's Cosmology," *Journal of the History of Philosophy*, VI (1968), 15–22.

138 See Pines, *Beiträge*, pp. 45 ff. On Plato's doctrine of the void, see Taylor, *Commentary on the Timaeus*, pp. 384 f., 399, 559, 581. Cf. Aristotle, *De Gen. et Corrup.* I. 325^b34.

Aristotle had maintained, an attribute of nature conceived as a principle of change.[139] From this it follows that all bodies are impelled by their intrinsic motion to move downward, toward the center of the world, and not, as Aristotle had taught, either upward or downward depending on their natural locus or the predominant element entering into their composition.[140]

The analogy of this theory of motion and the void underlying it with Democritean doctrine is only too apparent. A critic of Aristotle, who had violently reacted against so many aspects of Democritean physics while highly praising Democritus' method of inquiry,[141] might naturally be drawn toward those very aspects of Democritus that Aristotle denounced. Thus, not only motion and the void, but the atomic composition of body was interpreted by al-Rāzī in Democritean terms. Matter, which he considered one of the five eternal principles, as will be shown shortly, is made up of indivisible parts or atoms, which are separated by the void. The density or sparsity of these atoms or the magnitude of the void separating them determine the primary qualities of objects, such as lightness or heaviness, hardness or softness.[142]

Much more startling from the standpoint of Aristotelianism, as well as Islamic teaching, was al-Rāzī's profession of the Pythagorean-Platonic doctrine of metempsychosis or the transmigration of the Soul. According to him, the Soul, which was originally living, was nonetheless impetuous and foolish. Becoming enamored of matter, it sought to be united to it and to endow it with form so that it might partake of bodily pleasures. In view of the recalcitrance of matter and its resistance to the in-forming activity of the Soul, however, God was compelled to come to its assistance and to create this world, with its material forms, in order to enable the Soul to satisfy its vile urge to partake of material pleasures for a while. In the same manner, God created man and imparted Reason to him from the "essence of His divinity," so that Reason might eventually rouse the Soul from its

139 *Phys.* II. 192^{b}. 140 *De Caelo*, IV. 308^{a}.

141 See, e.g., *De Gen. et Corrup.* I. 315^{a}32 f. and 324^{b}35 f.

142 See Pines, *Beiträge*, pp. 40 ff. and especially 76 f., for the relation of Democritus to al-Rāzī.

earthly slumber in man's body and remind it of its genuine destiny as a citizen of the higher (intelligible) world and of its duty to seek that world through the study of philosophy. To the extent that the Soul becomes addicted to this study it will be able to achieve its salvation and rejoin the intelligible world, whereby it will be released, as the old Pythagoreans put it, from the "wheel of birth." Such individual Souls as have not been purified by the study of philosophy, however, will continue to linger in this world until they discover the therapeutic virtue of philosophy and turn toward the intelligible world. When this ultimate goal has been reached, and the human Soul, guided by Reason, has been restored to its true abode, this "lower world" will cease, and matter, which had been forcibly chained to form, will return to its original condition of absolute formlessness and purity.[143]

In this conception of the Soul and its heavenly destiny, the sublime role of philosophy is set out in terms comparable in their dramatic ring to those of Socrates. Here al-Rāzī does not advance a bold and somewhat original theory of the Soul only, but an account of the creation of the world in time at the hand of the Demiurgus (*al-Bāri'*). The Pythagorean-Orphic conception of the cyclic return of the Soul and its eventual release from the "wheel of birth" are unequivocally set out, and the mystical therapeutic function of philosophy is highlighted.

In connection with his view of transmigration, we might consider here al-Rāzī's account in the *Philosophical Way* of the problem of animal slaughter and the grounds upon which it can be morally justified. Like other sensitive souls in the history of Islam, such as the Blind Poet of Ma'arra, Abu'l-'Alā' (d. 1057), al-Rāzī must have been disturbed by the problem of animal suffering, especially at the hands of men. The slaughter of wild animals, he observes, might be justified as safeguarding human life, but this obviously cannot apply to domestic animals. In the case of both wild and domestic animals, however, the ultimate justification, according to him, is that their slaughter is a means of liberating their Souls from the bondage of their bodies and thereby bringing them closer to their ultimate destiny, by enabling them to "dwell in other superior bodies,"[144] such as those of man.

[143] Kraus, *Opera Philosophica*, pp. 281 f.; Pines, *Beiträge*, pp. 59 f.
[144] *Opera Philosophica*, pp. 105, 174.

The Platonic element in al-Rāzī's thought, as we have already noted, is nowhere more apparent than in his central metaphysical conception of the five co-eternal principles. Although this concept is generally attributed to the mysterious Sabaean or Ḥarrānian sect, we can clearly discern a direct Platonic influence, emanating ultimately from Plato's great cosmological dialogue, the *Timaeaus*, which al-Rāzī studied obsessively. The five eternal principles that form the substance of al-Rāzī's metaphysical doctrine are matter, space, time, the Soul, and the Creator (*Bāri'* : Demiurgus). The eternity of matter is demonstrated in two ways. Creation, the act of "in-forming" matter, presupposes not only a Creator who has preceded it, but also a substratum or matter in which this act inheres. Moreover, the very concept of creation *ex nihilo* is logically untenable, for if God had been able to create *anything* out of nothing, He would have been bound in reason to create *everything* out of nothing, since this is the simplest and readiest mode of production. But since this is far from being the case, the world must be said to have been created out of a formless matter, which has preceded it since all time.[145]

Matter requires a locus in which to subsist, and this locus is the second eternal principle, space. Space is conceived by al-Rāzī as an abstract concept, which, unlike Aristotle's "place" (τόπος), is not logically inseparable from body. As a consequence, he draws a distinction between universal and particular place or space. Universal place (or space) is entirely distinct from body, so that the concept of the body occupying it need not enter into its definition, as is implicit in the Aristotelian concept of place, or "the innermost boundary of the body contained in it,"[146] and in this manner the possibility of the void is logically safeguarded. Being independent of body, and *eo ipso* of magnitude, this space is both infinite and eternal,[147] whereas for Aristotle, even in its universal capacity as *locus communis*, it is inseparable from the body of the universe at large and is on that account finite.[148]

Particular place, on the other hand, cannot be conceived separately

145 *Opera Philosophica*, pp. 224 f.; Pines, *Beiträge*, pp. 40 f.; Khusrū, *Zād al-Musāfirīn*, p. 76.
146 *Phys.* IV. 212ᵃ20. 147 Kraus, *Opera Philosophica*, pp. 258 f.
148 *Phys.* IV. 209ᵉ32 and 212ᵇ13 f.

from matter, which constitutes its very essence. In this way it differs from Aristotle's concept of place as the *locus* or *vehicle* of the particular or material objects contained in it, and it exhibits certain similarities with Plato's space, which, as Aristotle critically observes in *Physics* IV. $209^{b}11$, is represented in the *Timaeus* as the receptacle as well as the formless matter from which the Demiurgus fashions the particular objects of sense,[149] so that it is hardly distinguishable in its vehicular capacity, so to speak, from the material substratum occupying it.

In his view of time al-Rāzī also departs from Aristotle, who regarded time as a species of motion or the number thereof. Such a concept makes the reality of time logically dependent upon movement in general, and the movement of the heavens in particular; in al-Rāzī's view, however, motion does not *produce*, but simply *reveals* or exhibits time, which remains on that account essentially distinct from it.

Moreover, by analogy with space, al-Rāzī distinguishes between particular or determinate and absolute or universal time. The former he conceived to be measurable and finite, the latter to be immeasurable and infinite, and as such analogous to the Neo-Platonic *aeon* (*al-dahr*),[150] which is the measure of the duration of the intelligible world,[151] as distinct from the measure of the duration of the sensible world, called by Plato "the moving image of eternity."[152]

To conceive of absolute time, which is entirely independent of the created universe and its motion, al-Rāzī urges us to leave behind altogether the motions of the heavens and the setting and rising of the sun and the planets and to concentrate upon the bare concept of the "motion of eternity," which for him is synonymous with absolute time. Such a concept is no harder to grasp than the concept of an infinite void, which, like absolute time, can be intuitively conceived apart from the magnitude of the world or its duration.[153] In this respect, absolute time is to be identified with eternal recurrence, which precedes the genesis of particular time, and with the creation of the world and the movement of the heavens.

The eternity of the remaining two principles, the Creator and the Soul, is bound up in al-Rāzī's system with a bold attempt to grapple

[149] Cf. *Timaeus* 52 f. [150] Al-Bīrūnī, *Indica*, p. 163.
[151] Plotinus *Ennea*. III. 7, 11. [152] *Timaeus* 37c. [153] Pines, *Beiträge*, pp. 53 f.

with the crucial question of justifying the creation of the world, which had vexed philosophers since the time of Plato.[154] The problem he sets himself is not whether the world was created or not (since, like Plato, he believed it to be created in an eternal time), but rather the knottier problem that will echo through the polemical treatises of theology and philosophy, both in Islam and Christendom for centuries —whether God created the world, as the Latin Scholastics later put it, by a "necessity of nature," or by an act of free will? If "necessity of nature" is claimed, he argues, then the logical consequence would be that God, who created the world in time, is himself in time, since a natural product must ensue necessarily upon its natural agent in time. If, on the other hand, an act of free will is the answer, another question would at once arise: why did God choose to create the world at the particular time He created it rather than any other.[155]

The answer al-Rāzī proposes brings out vividly the Platonic and Neo-Platonic elements in his thought, as well as the ingenuity with which he sought to incorporate his five eternal principles into a coherent metaphysical system. The Soul, as we have seen, was co-eternal with God, matter, and time. In consequence of its infatuation with matter, God was compelled to bring about what, on its own, the Soul was incapable of achieving, namely, union with material forms. And it was with this union that the creation of this world, in which the Soul remains forever a stranger, was bound up. Thanks to the illumination of Reason, the Soul, which had been so engrossed with material forms and sensuous pleasures, is at last roused to an awareness of its true destiny and is made to seek its rehabilitation in the intelligible world, which is its true abode.[156]

It will be noted at once that al-Rāzī offers no proof for the eternity of either the Creator or the Soul. He clearly believed the world to be created in time and to be transient, unlike Plato, who believed it to be created, but everlasting. The eternity of the Soul and the Creator therefore must be asserted to have been advanced by al-Rāzī, in

[154] See particularly *Timaeus* 28 f.

[155] Khusru, *Zād al-Musāfirīn*, pp. 114 f.; Kraus, *Opera Philosophica*, pp. 290 f.; and Pines, *Beiträge*, pp. 58 f.

[156] *Supra*, p. 38.

emulation of Plato, as an axiomatic proposition. Not only the eternity of the Soul, both a *parte ante* and a *parte post*, but the role of philosophy as the only pathway to the Soul's purification and its release from the fetters of the body, reflect a distinct Platonic-Pythagorean influence, which ran counter to the Islamic concept of revelation and the cognate concept of prophecy. In fact, al-Rāzī, in perfect consonance with his rationalistic premises, had rejected outright the concept of revelation and the role of the prophets as mediators between God and man. He reasoned that prophecy was either superfluous, since the God-given light of Reason was sufficient for the knowledge of the truth; or obnoxious, since it has been the cause of so much bloodshed and warfare between the one people (presumably, the Arabs) who believed itself to be favored with divine revelation and the other less fortunate peoples.[157]

It was perhaps this aspect of his teaching—the rejection of prophecy (associated in Islamic sources with Brahmanism)—which caused al-Rāzī to be held in almost universal contempt as a schismatic and an infidel. Even in such heterodox circles as the Isma'īlī he found little favor, as witnessed by the virulent polemics leveled at him by the great Ismā'īlī *dā'ī* of the eleventh century, Nāṣir-i-Khusrū, and his own countryman and namesake, Abū Ḥātim al-Rāzī (d. 933), whose work has been a major source for reconstructing the elder's thought. The fact is, however, that those critics had far more in common with al-Rāzī than they would have been willing to admit; they had all received the impact of Pythagorean ideas, which set them apart from the main body of Orthodox Islam, as will appear in the next chapter.

[157] Kraus, *Opera Philosophica*, p. 295. Two anti-religious tracts, *On the Repudiation of Prophecy* and *On the Devices of False Prophets*, are attributed to him by al-Bīrūnī; see Kraus, *Epître de Béruni*, p. 20.

CHAPTER FOUR

The Further Development of Islamic Neo-Platonism

I

AL-FĀRĀBĪ

The Neo-Platonic tendencies implicit in the philosophy of al-Kindī and al-Rāzī came into full prominence in the work of al-Fārābī and Ibn Sīnā, the first two Muslim philosophers to construct an elaborate metaphysical system of great complexity. In the more eclectic thought of al-Kindī, an Aristotelian element predominates, whereas in the less encompassing work of al-Rāzī one notices a strong Platonic element. The first systematic exposition of Neo-Platonism in Arabic is undoubtedly the work of the first outstanding logician and metaphysician of Islam, Muḥammad b. Muḥammad b. Ṭarkhān al-Fārābī, better known in classical sources and among the Latins of the Middle Ages as Abū Naṣr (Latin: Abunaser).

Our authorities are unanimous in bestowing the highest praise on al-Fārābī, chiefly as the leading logician and expositor of Plato and Aristotle in his day. According to an early source, he studied logic with a Christian scholar, Yuḥannā b. Ḥailān in Baghdad, but soon outstripped all his Muslim contemporaries; he refined the study of logic and expanded and completed the subtler aspects that al-Kindī had overlooked.[1]

Of al-Fārābī's life we know only that he came from Fārāb in Transoxiana and that his father was a captain of Persian, or probably Turkish, origin. He is said to have grown up in Damascus, where he devoted himself to reading philosophical books at night by the "watchman's torch," while working as a garden keeper by day.[2] He was subsequently drawn to Baghdad, where he met the leading teachers of his day, such as Mattā and Yuḥannā, and they initiated him into the study of logic. After a journey into Egypt, he returned to Aleppo in northern Syria; shortly thereafter, in 950, he died at the age of eighty.[3]

His personal character and demeanor are hinted at in anecdotes about his association with the Ḥamdānī prince Saif al-Daula (918–967), a great patron of the arts and letters, whose capital was Aleppo. He is said to have had a great regard for al-Fārābī, but was exasperated on occasion by his outlandish attire and his boorish manner, as well as by the fact that, despite his ascetism and modesty, he frequently indulged in a certain degree of showmanship in the presence of his patron. This association, however, must have been rather short lived, and al-Fārābī, who shunned company, evidently did not avail himself of all the lucrative advantages of such princely favor.

His place in the history of philosophy is brought out in an interesting note on the development of that discipline preserved by a thirteenth-century historian of philosophy, Ibn Abī Uṣaybi'ah.[4] Al-Fārābī is reported by this historian to have written apparently in a lost work on the *Rise of Philosophy* that

> the study of philosophy became widespread during the reign of the Greek kings. However, following the death of Aristotle, it was cultivated at Alexandria until the end of Cleopatra's [literally, the woman's] reign. Teaching had remained unchanged, subsequent to Aristotle's death, throughout

[1] Ṣā'id, *Ṭabaqāt*, p. 53; and Ibn Abī Uṣaybi'ah, *'Uyūn*, II, 136. [2] *'Uyūn*, II, 134.

[3] Ibn Khallikān, *Wafayāt*, IV, 242. A reference to his violent death on the road to Ascalon is made in al-Bayhaqī, *Tārīkh Ḥukamā' al-Islām*, p. 34.

[4] Ibn Abī Uṣaybi'ah, *'Uyūn*, II, 134 f. See also Meyerhof, "Transmission of Science to the Arabs," *Islamic Culture*, XI (1937), 20; Steinschneider, *Al-Farabi* (*Al-pharabius*), *Des Arabischen Philosophen Leben und Schriften*, pp. 86 ff.; and Rescher, "Al-Fārābī on Logical Tradition," *Journal of the History of Ideas*, XXIV (1963), 127 ff.

the reign of the thirteen [Ptolemaic] kings. During their reign twelve teachers of philosophy succeeded one another, the last of whom being Andronicus. . . . When Augustus, the Roman Emperor, slew Cleopatra [literally, the woman] and consolidated his rule, he looked into the libraries and had their acquisitions catalogued. Among them, he found books written and transcribed in Aristotle's day, or that of Theophrastus, and observed that the teachers and philosophers had composed works on the subjects which Aristotle had dealt with. He ordered those books which had been transcribed during Aristotle's lifetime or that of his pupils to be reproduced and to serve as the basis of instruction, and the rest to be dropped. Andronicus was appointed as arbiter in these matters and was ordered to make copies to be carried with him to Rome, and others to be left at the School of Alexandria. He also ordered him to designate a teacher to succeed him at Alexandria, so that he might accompany him [i.e., the Emperor] to Rome. These two seats of learning existed side by side until the advent of Christianity.[5]

Subsequently Baghdad became the center of logical instruction. Al-Fārābī, himself, we are told by Ibn Abī Uṣaybi'ah, received instruction in logic from Yuḥannā b. Ḥailān. His study included the *Book of Demonstration* (i.e., *Analytica Posteriora*) and thus broke with the tradition inaugurated at Alexandria, which did not proceed beyond the *Analytica Priora.*[6]

Although this account of the successive schools of philosophy is too telescopic, it nevertheless shows clearly the state of instruction in al-Fārābī's day, and his own standing in a field in which Nestorian and Jacobite scholars such as Mattā, Quwayrī, and Yuḥannā apparently enjoyed exclusive preeminence until al-Fārābī's arrival. What enhances al-Fārābī's reputation in this regard appears to have been the fact that none of his Muslim predecessors, not even the great al-Kindī (who is expressly criticized for his perfunctory incursions into logic),[7] had achieved any fame. It is significant also that both al-Qifṭī and Ibn Abī Uṣaybi'ah eagerly point out that al-Fārābī, despite his youth, soon outstripped his chief rival, Mattā, who was the leading authority in logic "at Baghdad and throughout the Eastern Muslim world."[8]

[5] Ibn Abī Uṣaybi'ah, '*Uyūn*, II, 134 f.
[6] Ibn Abī Uṣaybi'ah, '*Uyūn*, II, 135; al-Qifṭī, *Tārīkh al-Ḥukamā'*, p. 277.
[7] *Supra*, p. 13.
[8] Al-Qifṭī, *Tārīkh al-Ḥukamā'*, pp. 278 f.; Ibn Abī Uṣaybi'ah, '*Uyūn*, II, 135.

Al-Fārābī's proficiency in logic can be gauged from the number and completeness of his commentaries and paraphrases of Aristotelian logic. Of his larger commentaries, enough has reached us to justify the high regard in which he was held by his contemporaries. The following are considered to be his chief logical works:[9] *Commentary on Analytica Posteria*, *Commentary on Analytica Priora*, *Commentary on the Isagoge*,[10] *Commentary on Topica* (Books II and VIII), *Commentary on Sophistica*, *Commentary on De Interpretatione*,[11] *Commentary on De Categoriae*, a treatise on *Necessary and Existential Premises*, and a treatise on the *Propositions and Syllogisms Employed in all the Sciences*.

Not only in logic, but also in physics, metaphysics, and politics, al-Fārābī's contribution entitles him to a position of undoubted pre-eminence among the philosophers of Islam. He is particularly commended by one of the earliest historiographers[12] for his masterly exposition of the philosophies of Plato and Aristotle. These two works, together with his *Enumeration of the Sciences*, are the most comprehensive general introduction to Aristotelianism and Platonism in Arabic, and they far surpass in quality and completeness any parallel works of that period.

In the first of these three works, entitled the *Philosophy of Plato, Its Parts and the Order of These Parts*,[13] al-Fārābī exhibits his vast knowledge of the Platonic corpus and illustrates the degree of the Muslims' acquaintance in the tenth century with this corpus. In this book he mentions by name not only all the *Dialogues* but the *Epistles* of Plato as well, and gives a succinct account of their subject matter. The measure of his acquaintance with this material is best demonstrated in his compendium of one of Plato's major works, *The Laws*, which is still extant; it is eloquent testimony to his profound understanding of and predilection for the moral and political philosophy of the "greatest [sage], the Divine Plato."[14]

The second work, entitled the *Philosophy of Aristotle*,[15] opens with a

[9] *'Uyūn*, II, 138; *Tārīkh al-Ḥukamā'*, p. 279.

[10] Ayasofia Ms No. 4839.

[11] Edited by W. Kutsch (Beirut, 1960).

[12] Ṣā'id, *Ṭabaqāt*, p. 53.

[13] *Alfarabius de Platonis philosophia*, ed. and transl. Rosenthal and Walzer; English translation by Mahdi in *Al farabi's Philosophy of Plato and Aristotle*.

[14] *Alfarabius compendium legum Platonis* (ed. and transl. Gabrieli), p. 43.

[15] *Al-Fârâbî's Philosophy of Aristotle*, edit. Mahdi.

discussion of the nature of human happiness and the manner in which "scientific knowledge" is a necessary part of the good life man must seek. It goes on to survey the whole range of Aristotelian philosophy, beginning with logic and ending with metaphysics. A noteworthy feature of al-Fārābī's analysis of Aristotle's philosophy is the close correlation between ethics or the theory of happiness (to which he devoted another treatise, the *Attainment of Happiness*), on the one hand, and the theory of knowledge (broached in this work) and his extant commentaries on the *Isagoge*, the *Categories*, and the *De Interpretatione*, on the other. The union of speculative and practical philosophy as being necessary for man's happiness in this life became a characteristic feature of subsequent Islamic thought. Religious and eschatological questions were of major importance, since man's life after death is considered to be an extension of his present one.

Another feature al-Fārābī delineated was the organic unity of the Aristotelian scheme of the sciences. The transition from logic to the philosophy of nature is seen as no less natural than the transition from logic to ethics. The *summa genera*, according to al-Fārābī, are considered in the *Categories* merely in their logical aspect, whereas in the *Physics* they are considered in their qualitative and quantitative aspects.[16] In the latter work, we are told, Aristotle begins by laying down the general principles upon which physics rests, such as the dualism of matter and form, the necessity of an efficient and a final cause of motion, etc. Then he proceeds to discuss the meaning of nature and the way in which the "physical inquiry" differs from other types of inquiry, the nature of magnitude, of the infinite, place, and time. Next, he discusses motion and the manner in which the series of particular movers must ultimately culminate in a first principle of motion, which is entirely nonphysical and immaterial, and the study of which consequently forms part of another inquiry,[17] i.e., the metaphysics.

The other physical and cosmological treatises mentioned by al-Fārābī are the *De Caelo*, the *Meteorologica*, the *Book of Minerals*,[18] the

[16] *Philosophy of Aristotle* pp. 85 ff. [17] *Ibid.*, p. 97.

[18] No mention of a book by this title is found in Diogenes Laertius's list or the Arabic list of Aristotle's works contained in al-Qifṭī, *Tārīkh al-Ḥukamā'*, p. 42.

De Plantis,[19] the *De Anima*, on *Health and Sickness*, *De Juventute et Senectute*, *De Longitudine et Brevitate Vitae*, *De Vita et Morte*, *De Sensu et Sensibilibus*, and *De Motu Animalium*. In these works, he observes, Aristotle discusses the role of the elements and their compounds in the composition of minerals, animals, and plants, and then touches on the processes of life and growth we associate with the animal kingdom. A brief account of the heavenly bodies and of meteorological phenomena is given, and the book closes with a rather lengthy discussion of psychology. According to al-Fārābī, Aristotle observes that the purely physical processes or functions which are common to man and the other animals do not account for man's nature, and that mind is the distinctive principle which sets him apart; it stands to the other faculties of the Soul in the same capacity as the Soul to nature, that is, as final principle or *telos*.[20] However, the mind which marks the perfection (or *entelecheia*) of man is merely a power or faculty of the Soul, which is subordinate to the activity or operation of Reason, as it lays hold of the intelligible forms of things. At the latter level, reason has become actual and has attained that ultimate stage of perfection to which all the preceding stages (the natural life of the organism as well as its other psychic functions) are subservient.[21] Considering its primacy in relation to nature and the Soul, Aristotle inquires into its role in its capacity as active reason, and in the generation and development of animate and inanimate bodies in the sublunary world. This inquiry leads him logically beyond physics into metaphysics and, for a reason which is not very clear, al-Fārābī's discussion breaks off at this point.

But the third of these works, entitled *The Enumeration of the Sciences* (which duplicates the former treatise in some respects), is perhaps the most crucial for the understanding of al-Fārābī's conception of philosophy in relation to the other sciences, as indeed of the conception of the whole Islamic philosophical school of the nature and interrelation of the Greek and the Islamic syllabus of the sciences, echoes of which still ring four centuries later in the writings of the anti-Hellenic encyclopedist and historiographer Ibn Khaldūn of Tūnis (d. 1406).

[19] The *De Plantis* is a Peripatetic work in two books, which in its present Greek form is a translation of the medieval Latin version of an Arabic version attributed to Isḥāq b. Ḥunain; cf. Badawi's edition, Cairo, 1954.

[20] *Philosophy of Aristotle*, p. 122.

[21] *Ibid.*, p. 126.

In this treatise, al-Fārābī surveys the whole range of the sciences known in his day. He classifies them under eight headings: the linguistic, the logical, the mathematical, the physical, the metaphysical, the political, the juridical, and the theological.[22] The linguistic sciences fall into two categories: those concerned with the use of language by any nation and those concerned with the rules governing such use respectively. This distinction, however, can be broadened to include the study of the rules governing single terms, propositions, penmanship, elocution, prosody, and their subdivisions.[23]

Logic differs from the linguistic sciences, particularly from grammar, in that it is concerned with concepts and the rules governing them, as well as with the means of guarding against error. Acquaintance with these rules and compliance with them are indispensable. It is not enough to entertain correct beliefs accidentally, as some maintain; it is also necessary to justify and defend them by reference to the "canon of proof" laid down in logic. If it is urged that practice might enable us to dispense with the knowledge of these rules, one might argue that by the same token the rules of grammar or prosody might be dispensed with as a result of the prolonged practice of grammatical speech or the writing of sound verse, which is far from being the case.

Moreover, unlike grammar, logic is concerned with the rules of "inner" and "outer" speech,[24] in so far as they apply universally to all the languages of mankind and are not on that account conventional like grammar. Logic's eight subdivisions are:

1. *The Categories*, which deals with the rules governing concepts and the use of the single terms corresponding to them.
2. *Peri Hermeneias*, which deals with simple statements or propositions, made up of two terms or more.
3. *Analytica Priora*, which deals with the rules of the syllogism used in the five types of argument, i.e., the demonstrative, the dialectical, the sophistical, the rhetorical, and the poetical.[25]

[22] *Iḥṣā' al-'Ulūm*, pp. 43 f. [23] *Ibid.*, pp. 58 f.

[24] The Arabic "*nuṭq*" corresponds to the Greek "*logos*," and bears like it this double connotation.

[25] *Iḥṣā' al-'Ulūm*, p. 64.

4. *Analytica Posteriora*, which deals with the rules of demonstrative proof and the nature of scientific knowledge.
5. *Topica*, which deals with dialectical questions and answers.
6. *Sophistica*, or the "false wisdom," which deals with sophistical arguments and the means to guard against them.
7. *Rhetorica*, which deals with types of persuasion and their impact on the auditor in oratory.
8. *Poetica*, which deals with the rules of verse-writing and the various types of poetical statements and their comparative excellence.[26]

The mathematical sciences include arithmetic, geometry, perspective, astronomy, music, dynamics, and mechanics. In each of these sciences there is a theoretical and a practical part, depending on whether the science in question is concerned with the abstract concepts or principles laid down in it or with their application in any art or trade.

Theoretical astronomy, for instance, deals with earthly and heavenly bodies in three respects: (1) their figures, masses, and relative distances; (2) their general, as well as their particular, motions, and their conjunctions; and (3) their positions in relation to the earth and its major zones.

Practical astronomy (or astrology), on the other hand, is concerned with the manner in which the movements of the planets serve as indices for prognosis and as clues to the understanding of past and present occurrences in the world.[27]

In an interesting treatise written at the request of an astrologer, Abū Isḥāq Ibrāhīm b. ʿAbdullah al-Baghdādī,[28] who appears to have been assailed by understandable doubts, al-Fārābī examines with considerable sobriety the claims of astrology to be a valid discipline. Events in the world, he observes, are either determined by certain particular causes, which can be ascertained, or they are simply fortuitous and therefore have no ascertainable causes. The heavenly bodies exert a certain causal influence upon earthly occurrences, but these fall into two categories: those which can be determined through astronomical computations, however difficult, such as the heating of certain regions

[26] *Iḥṣā al-ʿUlūm*, pp. 63 f. [27] *Ibid.*, pp. 84 f.
[28] On *Valid and Invalid Inference in Astrology*, in *Majmūʿ Rasāʾil*, pp. 76–89.

owing to their comparative proximity to the sun; and those which cannot. In the latter case, astrologers, dispensing with such computation, are simply content to resort to auguries and fanciful calculations, which are hardly credible. It is of course quite possible, considering the multiplicity of things and the diversity of their qualities and species, that such auguries might come true accidentally. The presumption of necessity would be unjustified here, and it would be folly at any rate to assume that such heavenly phenomena as the sun's eclipse, which results from the interposition of the moon between our vision and the sun, are occasions of prosperity or misfortune,[29] since by the same token the interposition of any object between our vision and the sun should also be the occasion of prosperity or misfortune. Further, notes al-Fārābī, the most illustrious among the astrologers are the least prone to manage their own affairs in the light of their own astrological findings; consequently we must assume that their prognosis is inspired by the quest for profit or is merely the result of ingrained habit.[30]

Physics and metaphysics occupy a central place in al-Fārābī's discussion of the sciences. Physics is defined as the investigation of "natural bodies and the accidents inherent in them." It deals with the material, formal, efficient, and final causes of things, and comprises eight major divisions, dealing with the accidents and the principles common to all physical substances (as in the *Physics* of Aristotle), with simple substances (as in *De Caelo*), with coming to be and passing away (as in *De Generatione*), with the affections of the elements (as in the first three books of *Meteorologica*), with the composite bodies arising from the elements (as in the fourth book of *Meteorologica*), with minerals (as in the *Book of Minerals*),[31] with plants (as in *De Plantis*), and finally with animals, including man (as in *De Historia Animalium* and *De Anima*).

Metaphysics, according to al-Fārābī, can be subdivided into three major parts:

1. A part dealing with the existence of beings, i.e., ontology.
2. A part dealing with immaterial substances, their nature, number, and the degrees of their excellence, culminating eventually in the study of "a perfect being nothing greater than which can be

[29] *On Valid and and Invalid Inference*, p. 86.
[30] *Ibid.*, pp. 88 f.
[31] *Supra*, p. 129, n. 18.

conceived,"[32] which is the ultimate principle of all things and from which everything else derives its being, i.e., theology.

3. A part dealing with the primary principles of demonstration underlying the special sciences.

The subject matter of this science, he says, is contained wholly in Aristotle's *Metaphysics*. In the analysis of this subject matter, however, al-Fārābī draws also upon the pseudo-*Theologia*, which he explicitly attributes to Aristotle in a similar context in the *Agreement of Plato and Aristotle*.[33]

With the discussion of metaphysics, the syllabus of the Hellenic sciences is complete except for politics, which for al-Fārābī and the older Peripatetic tradition comprises ethics and political science, and deals with the virtues and their relation to happiness, on the one hand, or the political regimes most suited to the preservation of these virtues, on the other. However, two more sciences, jurisprudence and scholastic theology, finally close the discussion. Jurisprudence is briefly described as the art of determining the right religious beliefs and practices, on which the lawgiver (God) was silent, by analogy to the express provisions of Scripture.[34] Theology, on the other hand, is described as the art of defending those beliefs and practices, as well as rebutting the arguments disputing their truth. The difference between the adept of jurisprudence and that of theology is that the former simply infers from Scriptural premises the corollaries thereof, whereas the theologian defends those premises by recourse either to the pronouncements of Scripture or to those general principles that are rooted in sense experience, tradition, or reason. Whenever such principles are found to conflict with the express statements of Scripture, the latter should be interpreted allegorically. Should this prove impossible, the alleged principles of tradition or reason should be dismissed as fallacious, so that the authority of Scripture might be vindicated without question. In this regard, the defenders of dogma should stop at nothing in their endeavor to confound their opponents, even if it requires falsehood, sophistry, or downright trickery.[35]

[32] *Iḥṣā' al-'Ulūm*, p. 100.
[33] *Al-Jam' bayna Ra'yai al-Ḥakīmayn*, pp. 101, 105, *et passim*.
[34] *Iḥṣā' al-'Ulūm*, p. 107. [35] *Ibid.*, pp. 111 f.

It is to be noted, however, that those radical views, as well as the view that the truth of revelation exceeds the powers of human reason and should consequently not be questioned at all, are presented by al-Fārābī as the views advanced by various protagonists, so that his own standpoint on this crucial question is left undetermined to some extent. Considering the role of reason in his general conception of the scheme of things, however, the inference is inescapable that it devolved upon reason, rather than revelation, to arbitrate in the conflict.

Al-Fārābī's account of the relation of Plato to Aristotle in an important treatise entitled the *Reconciliation of the Two Sages* reflects clearly the Neo-Platonic tradition associated with the names of Numenius, Plotinus, Simplicius, Syrianus, Porphyry, and others, whose various ideas had become blurred almost into one.[36] Against the background of the Islamic controversy which raged around the names of the two Greek sages and the opprobrium their alleged discord must have carried with it, al-Fārābī set out on the difficult task of reconciling the differences between them.[37]

The substantive thought of al-Fārābī, as distinct from the methodological and historical part on which we have dwelt, falls into two major divisions: metaphysics and politics. Considering that his profound Neo-Platonic and Stoic sympathies overlap to such an extent, we might look upon these as two aspects of the same science, which might be indifferently described as the pursuit of truth in so far as it conduces to happiness, or the pursuit of happiness in so far as it depends on truth. It is said that in the *Republic* Plato drew too graphic a parallel between the state and the individual and exploited it well in his portrayal of man as an individual, on the one hand, and as a social animal, on the other; similarly al-Fārābī might be said to have drawn an even more graphic parallel between man and the universe as a whole, which, as in Stoicism, does not only contain man within it as a part but also reflects and exhibits his nature on the grand scale.

This close association between metaphysics and politics in al-Fārābī's thought illustrates further the organic view of man in relation to God

[36] *Supra*, p. 44.

[37] See Fakhry, "Reconciliation of Plato and Aristotle," *Journal of the History of Ideas*, XXVI (Oct.–Sept. 1965), 469–78.

and the universe and to his fellow men, as embodied in the Islamic system of beliefs. On this view, politics and ethics are conceived as an extension or development of metaphysics or its highest manifestation, theology, i.e., the science of God. Thus al-Fārābī's major metaphysical work, the *Opinions of the Inhabitants of the Virtuous City* opens not with a discussion of justice and man's relation to the state, as in Plato's *Republic*, which was undoubtedly al-Fārābī's model,[38] but with the discussion of the First Being, or the One of Plotinus, his attributes and the manner in which he generated the whole multitude of existing things in the world, through the process of emanation. This One or "First," conceived by al-Fārābī as the First Cause of all things, is perfect, necessary, self-sufficient, eternal, uncaused, immaterial, without associate or contrary, and is not susceptible of being defined.[39] In addition to these attributes, the First possesses unity, wisdom, and life, not as distinct attributes superadded to his essence, but as part of his very essence. What sets him apart from other entities is logically the unity of his essence, by virtue of which he exists. And in so far as he is neither matter nor associated with matter, he must be essentially an intellect. Matter is what hinders form from being an intellect in act, so what is divested of matter altogether is essentially an intellect in act.

Similarly, the First is an object of Reason, since he requires no agency whereby he can conceive his essence, which he is engaged in contemplating eternally. Therefore, he is thought thinking itself, *intellectus intelligens intellectum*, as Aristotle and his medieval Latin interpreters have put it.[40]

Moreover, since by life is meant "the act of thinking the best object of knowledge, by the best faculty of knowledge,"[41] the attainment of the highest phase of perfection proper to the living entity, or its capacity for generating what belongs to it by nature to generate, it follows that the First is also life.

Despite its perfection, however, the First is far from being fully accessible to human reason. In fact, owing to its imperfection and its association with matter, human reason is dazzled by the beauty and

[38] *Supra*, p. 25.
[39] *Al-Madīnah al-Fāḍilah*, pp. 23 f.
[40] *Ibid.*, pp. 31 f.
[41] *Ibid.*, p. 32.

splendor of that perfect being, who is most manifest in himself but is only dimly perceived by us.[42]

Further, being beauty entire, by virtue of that perfection which belongs to him essentially and to the creation only accidentally, his contemplation of himself is attended by the greatest enjoyment possible: the enjoyment of the supremely beautiful being, himself, not only as an object of contemplation but also as an object of love.[43]

Next al-Fārābī gives an account of the emanation of things from the First Being in a very systematic, and from an Islamic standpoint a very heterodox way. The crux of the argument, which is reminiscent of Proclus',[44] is that the First—owing to the superabundance of his being and perfection—generates the whole order of being in the universe by a "necessity of nature," which is entirely independent of his choice or desire. The universe adds nothing to the perfection of the Supreme Being and does not determine him in any finalistic or teleological way, instead, it is the outcome of a spontaneous act of supererogatory generosity on his part.[45] Moreover, in this process of overflowing, the First requires no intermediary agency, accident, or instrument by means of which his grand creative purposes can be fulfilled. Nor, on the other hand, can an obstacle, internal or external, impede the everlasting unfolding of this process.

The first emanation from the First Being is the first intellect, which is capable of conceiving both its author and itself. By virtue of the former act of conception, the second intellect is generated, and by virtue of the latter, the outermost heaven. Next the second intellect conceives its author, giving rise to the third intellect, and conceives itself, giving rise thereby to the sphere of the fixed stars. This process goes on in successive stages, generating the fourth, fifth, sixth, seventh, eighth, ninth, and tenth intellects, as well as the corresponding spheres of Saturn, Jupiter, Mars, the Sun, Venus, Mercury, and the moon, respectively.[46] With the tenth, the series of cosmic intellects is completed, and with the moon that of the heavenly spheres, whose circular motions are determined by those cosmic intellects throughout all time.

Beneath the heavenly region lies the terrestrial, in which the process

[42] *Al-Madīnah al-Fāḍilah*, p. 34. [43] *Ibid.*, p. 37. [44] *Supra*, p. 43.
[45] *Al-Madīnah al-Fāḍilah*, p. 38. [46] *Ibid.*, pp. 44 f.

of development is reversed, so that from the imperfect the more perfect arises, from the simple the more complex, in accordance with a set cosmological pattern. At the lowest level lies prime matter, followed by the four elements, minerals, plants, animals, and finally man, who stands at the summit of this rising spiral of created objects in the terrestrial region.

The elements first combine to give rise to a variety of contrary bodies that are not very complex, and these combine in turn with one another, as well as with the elements, a second time, yielding a more complex class of bodies, possessing a variety of active and passive faculties. This process of combination, which is subject to the action of the heavenly bodies, goes on generating the higher and more complex entities in the sublunary world, until man emerges as a result of the final combination.[47]

Although it belongs to each of these terrestrial entities to endure, in so far as they are made up of matter and form, the supervention of a certain form upon the matter in question is no more necessary than its opposite. Consequently the perennial succession of the opposite forms upon this matter results in the alternation of generation and corruption in nature.

With the rise of man, who is an epitome of the cosmos, the hierarchical process of development is consummated. The first faculty of man to emerge in this process is the vegetative, followed successively by the sensitive, the appetitive, the representative,[48] and the rational. In each one of these faculties we might distinguish between a part that rules or orders and a part that subserves or obeys, and the same might be said about each of these faculties in relation to the faculty inferior to it. Considered collectively, all the faculties of the Soul are subservient to the rational, which rules or orders all the others. At the physiological level, however, the ruling element in each case has its seat in the heart, which is defined as the original source of animal heat.[49] Next in the order of preeminence, as well as the order of generation, comes the brain, which performs the all-important function of moderating the animal heat emanating from the heart and imparted to all the faculties

[47] *Al-Madīnah al-Fāḍilah*, pp. 49, 60 f.

[48] I.e., the imagination.

[49] *Al-Madīnah al-Fāḍilah*, pp. 75, 76.

of the Soul, insuring thereby that each faculty will function with the moderation necessary for excellence.[50] Next to the brain comes the liver, then the spleen, and finally the reproductive organs. Reproduction results from the action of the seminal fluid upon the blood circulating in the womb, in a manner analogous to the action of rennet upon milk as it turns into cheese.

The rational faculty in man is the repository of intelligible forms, which fall into two classes: those immaterial substances whose essence is to be both subjects and objects of intelligibility in act, and those which are only potentially intelligible because of their association with matter. Neither potential intelligibles nor the rational faculty as such are capable of effecting the transition from the state of potentiality to that of actuality without the intervention of an agency which actualizes their potentiality to know or to be known. This agency is stated by al-Fārābī to be "a substance whose essence is actual thought, and as such is separate from matter,"[51] i.e., is an actual intellect which stands to potential reason and its possible objects in the capacity of the sun to sight. The sun imparts both to potential sight and the potentially visible (colors) the light which makes them actually seeing and actually visible respectively. Likewise, potential reason receives from the active intellect that illumination which enables it to perceive (1) the active intellect which was the cause of this illumination, (2) this illumination itself, and finally (3) the intelligibles which have passed in the process from potentiality to act.[52]

The first group of intelligibles to result from this illumination which the active intellect imparts are the primary principles, which emanated originally from the sense faculty and were stored in the representative faculty and received subsequently the imprint of intelligibility in act. Those principles, universally accepted as true, fall into three categories: (1) the primary principles of geometrical knowledge, (2) the primary principles of ethical knowledge, and (3) the primary principles of metaphysical knowledge, by virtue of which the origins, ranks, and effects of the primary causes of things are known.[53]

We might pause here to consider at greater length this crucial

[50] *Al-Madīnah al-Fāḍilah*, p. 78. [51] *Ibid.*, p. 83. [52] *Ibid.*, pp. 83 f.
[53] *Ibid.*, p. 84.

problem of Reason, first broached among the Muslims by al-Kindī and to which al-Fārābī devoted a monograph, *Risālah fi'l-'Aql.* This work belongs to that long line of treatises stemming from Aristotle's *De Anima*, though formally initiated by Alexander's Περὶ Νοῦ.

In his monograph, the longest and most comprehensive treatise of its kind in Arabic, al-Fārābī distinguishes six types of Reason (Arabic: *'aql*):

1. The Reason which is generally predicated of the reasonable and virtuous in common parlance and which Aristotle calls *phronesis* (*al-ta'aqqul*).[54]

2. The Reason which the theologians posit as prescribing or proscribing certain general actions and which is in part identical with common sense.

3. The Reason which Aristotle describes in *Analytica Posteriora* as the faculty of perceiving the primary principles of demonstration, instinctively and intuitively.

4. The Reason, referred to in *Ethica* VI, as a *habitus*, and which is rooted in experience. This Reason enables us to judge infallibly, by some intuitive acumen, the principles of right and wrong.

5. The Reason referred to in *De Anima* III, and to which Aristotle has assigned four meanings: (*a*) The Reason which is in potentiality and which is "a Soul, a part of a Soul, or a faculty of the Soul," capable of abstracting the forms of existing entities with which it is ultimately identified, becoming thus: (*b*) The Reason in act, in which the intelligibles in act (or forms) acquire a new mode of being, to which the ten categories apply only partially and analogically. At this level, the intelligibles in act, which are identical with the intellect in act, might be said to have become the subjects of active thought and not merely its objects. If we imagine how active Reason possesses the knowledge of all the intelligible forms in act and becomes identified with them, we would appreciate how in this case the object of its apprehension is none other than Reason itself,[55] which is described at this stage as acquired Reason. (*c*) This acquired Reason stands to the preceding stage, i.e., Reason in act, in the capacity of form to matter, the agent of actualization to what is actualized. Moreover it differs from it in

[54] *Risālah fi'l-'Aql*, pp. 5 f.

[55] *Ibid.*, p. 19.

that the subject matter of its apprehension is the intelligible in act only. To this category belong intelligibles abstracted from matter by the former Reason, as well as the immaterial forms which this acquired Reason apprehends immediately, in the same way that it apprehends itself qua immaterial.[56] The acquired Reason, in which the highest degree of immateriality has been attained, might be viewed as the culmination of the intellectual process. As we have seen, however, this process has a cosmological counterpart in which the intelligibles in act (identified with the acquired intellect, as above) mark the uppermost limit. These two processes, the intellectual and the cosmological, are in direct interaction, so that one could either speak of the progressive ascent, at the intellectual level, from the perception of the material to that of the immaterial, or of the regressive descent, at the cosmological level, from the immaterial to the material. Thus there is a downward movement in this world, leading from the acquired intellect, through the Reason-in-act to the subordinate faculties of the Soul, nature, the forms of the four elements, and finally prime matter, which marks the lowest rung of the ladder of being in this world. In this respect, the acquired Reason, identified with the sum total of intelligible forms, might be regarded as the copestone of the terrestrial order. The ascent from the acquired Reason, on the other hand, leads beyond the terrestrial sphere, into the supramundane sphere, or that of the separate substances, of which the lowest is the active intellect. (*d*) This active intellect is an "immaterial form which neither inheres nor could inhere in matter"[57] and is in some respects analogous to the acquired Reason, which is in a sense a Reason in act. However, it is this agency which brings about the transition of reason from potentiality to act and renders the potential forms themselves actual, just as the sun makes it possible for sight to see and for colors to be seen.[58]

6. However, the action of this active intellect is neither continuous nor constant; it is not due to any passivity proper to it, but rather to the fact that the matter upon which it must operate is either wanting or is not sufficiently disposed to receive the forms emanating from it, due to some impediment or other. Hence two things are necessary for this purpose: (1) a material substratum and (2) the absence of all

[56] *Risālah fi'l-'Aql*, p. 20. [57] *Ibid.*, pp. 23 f. [58] *Ibid.*, pp. 25 f.

impediments to its action upon such a substratum, neither of which is within the power of this active intellect. This goes to show, argues the author, that it is far from being the First Principle of all things, for it depends for its own being on the First Principle, or God, on the one hand, and for the substrata upon which it acts, upon the heavenly bodies, on the other.[59]

The heavenly bodies themselves culminate in a prime mover, who generates the body of the first heaven, as well as the second mover, who causes the revolution of the sphere of the fixed stars. Both entities owe their being to the First Principle of all things, who is a being "nothing greater than which can be said to exist."[60] This principle is mentioned by Aristotle in Book Lambda of the *Metaphysics*, and is the sixth in the series of Reasons delineated at the beginning of the work.

It will be observed here how the theory of knowledge enabled al-Fārābī to rise gradually from the conception of Reason as a faculty of cognition in man, to Reason as an agency governing the sublunary region, and finally to the conception of Reason as the ultimate principle of all being, which Aristotle described as the actuality of thought thinking itself.[61] Reason is thus envisaged by al-Fārābī from three distinct, though closely interrelated, standpoints: the epistemological, the cosmological, and the metaphysical. But this is by no means the complete picture, for it can also just as legitimately be envisaged from the ethico-political standpoint.

From that point of view, Reason is represented by al-Fārābī as the ultimate pathway to happiness, which consists in the aspiration to attain the level of active Reason and to partake of its immateriality.[62] To attain this level, three types of action are required: voluntary, intellectual, and bodily, corresponding to the three types of virtue: the moral, the intellectual, and the artistic.[63] Intellectual virtue is the excellence of the faculty of cognition, which is concerned with the knowledge of the various types of being, culminating in the knowledge of the First Principle of all being, or God.[64] A subsidiary aspect of it is

[59] *Risālah fi'l-'Aql*, pp. 33 f. [60] *Ibid.*, p. 35. [61] *Met.* Lambda. 1074^{b}35.

[62] *Risālah fi'l-'Aql*, p. 85; see also *al-Siyāsāt al-Madaniyah*, pp. 3, 7; and *Fī Ithbāt al-Mufāriqāt*, p. 8.

[63] *Al-Madīnah*, p. 85; *Taḥṣīl al-Sa'ādah*, pp. 2 f. [64] *Taḥṣīl*, pp. 8 f.

the faculty of judgment, which is concerned with the determination of the useful and the good in any set of given circumstances. Unlike the former, therefore, the object of this faculty is the variable and the accidental, and its excellence consists in its proficiency in determining the means to the good of the state (as in political legislation), or a part of it (as in household economy), or that of the individual (as in the arts and crafts).[65]

In addition to determining what is good or useful, practical virtue is concerned with carrying these out. Here the will carries out the directions of judgment, which it might at first feel reluctant to do but will become habituated to do it. Since given natural dispositions or aptitudes differ, however, some people excel in some actions and their corresponding virtues, while others excel in other actions, and men are destined both by nature and by habit to be either rulers or ruled.[66]

It is through this diversity that various classes arise within the state, which is a necessary form of association answering man's basic needs, which he cannot gratify without the assistance of his fellow men.[67] Being analogous to the human body, the state requires a ruler, together with a series of subordinates, corresponding to the heart and the subordinate organs of the body respectively. This ruler must surpass all others in intellectual as well as practical virtue. In addition to the prophetic power bestowed upon him by God, he must possess, like Plato's philosopher-king, the following qualities: intelligence, good memory, keeness of mind, love of knowledge, moderation in matters of food, drink, and sex, love of truthfulness, magnanimity, frugality, love of justice, firmness or courage,[68] as well as physical fitness and eloquence, which Plato does not mention.

Al-Fārābī's analysis of justice, which was such a cardinal feature of Greek political thought, reflects to some extent the influence of Aristotle's *Ethics*, although here as elsewhere the predominant political motif is distinctly Platonic. The arguments of Thrasymachus and Polemarchus in the *Republic* are anonymously and incidentally given

[65] *Taḥṣīl*, pp. 22 f. [66] *Ibid.*, p. 29. [67] *Al-Madīnah*, pp. 96 f.

[68] *Al-Madīnah*, pp. 105 f.; cf. *Taḥṣīl*, pp. 44–45, where these qualities are expressly stated to be "the prerequisites which Plato mentioned in his *Republic*."

in the *Virtuous City*,[69] whereas in the *Fuṣūl* al-Fārābī's own viewpoint appears to be set forth. Here justice is said to concern either the distribution or the preservation of commonly cherished goods. These are stated expressly to be security, wealth, dignity, and material possessions generally.[70] As a corollary of this, justice is said to involve the restitution of dispossessed goods or their equivalent, as well as punishment commensurate with the injury or loss incurred in the process of dispossession.

A more general concept of justice concerns the "exercise of virtue in relation to one's fellow men, whatever this virtue might be." This concept is reminiscent of the Platonic definition of justice as a harmony of functions in the Soul and of classes in the state.[71] The exercise of this virtue presupposes division of labor within the state, made necessary by the diversity of natural aptitudes in the individuals or classes that make it up.

This view of justice is naturally at variance with what is called "natural justice" by those who make conquest or domination the ultimate goal of the state.[72] Al-Fārābī, reporting this view anonymously, argues that war might be justified if it is aimed at warding off invasion or serving some good purpose of the state, but not if conducted with a view to conquest or gain.[73]

States are classified by al-Fārābī according to rather abstract teleological principles. The virtuous city to which such frequent reference has been made is essentially one in which the good or happy life is pursued and in which the virtues proliferate. However, there might exist a state in which no goal beyond obtaining the necessities of life is envisaged.[74] In some states the king and his retainers might be content to seek glory or honor for themselves, either through virtue (as in aristocracy and timocracy), wealth (as in plutocracy), good breeding (as in hereditary monarchy), or conquest (as in tyranny). Finally, in some states (i.e., democracy) pleasure might be reckoned the ultimate goal of the state, whereas in others, with mixed forms of government, the goals of wealth, pleasure, and honor might be combined.[75]

[69] *Al-Madīnah*, pp. 132 f. [70] *Fuṣūl al-Madanī*, p. 142.
[71] *Republic* IV. 432. [72] *Al-Madīnah*, p. 132. [73] *Fuṣūl*, p. 146.
[74] *Al-Madīnah*, p. 132. [75] *Ibid.*, pp. 122 f.

In this descriptive account, states are distinguished from each other and from the virtuous state simply according to the goals they seek. However, it is possible to consider states normatively as well, in so far as they are naturally prone to degenerate into the various corrupt forms. In this respect, the corrupt forms are represented by al-Fārābī as "opposite" forms, in which the original harmony, the hallmark of the virtuous state, is disturbed and the "teleology of happiness," which was its guiding principle, is impaired or flouted.

Four such corrupt types of city are given: the city of ignorance, the wayward city, the renegade city, and the erring city.[76] The city of ignorance is defined as one whose inhabitants have not known real happiness and have not sought it, but were lured by the false pleasures of life, such as personal safety or self-preservation (as in the city of necessity), wealth (as in plutocracy, or as our author calls it, the city of meanness), pleasure (as in the city of ignominy), honor (as in timocracy), conquest (as in the predatory city or tyranny), or finally freedom and lawlessness (as in democracy or anarchy).[77]

The wayward city differs from the virtuous city in one important particular: although its inhabitants have apprehended the truth about God, the after-life, and the nature of true happiness, they have failed to live up to this truth. The renegade city, on the other hand, is one that conformed originally to this standard but departed from it in the course of time. The erring city is one that never achieved more than a false knowledge of God or of true happiness and was ruled by a false prophet, who resorted to deception and trickery in achieving his aims.

One final word might be said about the happiness or misery reserved for the Soul in the life to come. As we have noted, man's true happiness consists in partaking of the immaterial nature of active Reason, and the greater his share of virtue in this life, the more likely is his Soul to attain that condition of immateriality which is the token of ultimate bliss. The happiness which the Soul is destined to enjoy in the life to

[76] *Al-Madīnah*, pp. 109 f.; *al-Siyāsāt*, pp. 57 f.

[77] *Ibid.*, pp. 109 f. These corrupt forms of the city of ignorance correspond to Plato's timocracy, oligarchy (which includes plutocracy), democracy (which includes what al-Fārābī calls the city of ignonimy), and tyranny; cf. *Republic* VIII. 543 f. The necessary city is hinted at by Plato, but no name is given to it.

come is neither uniform nor definitive, however, as religious eschatology tacitly presupposes. For the nature of each Soul depends upon the body which served as its temporary abode, and it is clear that bodies differ in temperament and make-up. Consequently the fate of the Soul will depend upon the condition of the body with which it was associated during its earthly career, as will its portion of happiness or misery. This portion will increase, though, as successive generations of kindred Souls rejoin the intelligible world.[78]

This fate, however, is the one reserved individually to only the virtuous Souls and collectively to the inhabitants of the virtuous city. The inhabitants of the nonvirtuous cities, in so far as their happiness in life consisted in clinging to the gross pleasures of the body, will never be released from the bondage of the body. Instead their Souls will appear in one material condition, then another, either endlessly, if they are fated to be reincarnated in human form, or until such time as they have degenerated by degrees to the bestial level, whereupon they would simply perish.[79]

The misery of the life-to-come consists, on the other hand, in that tension or torment attendant upon the lingering pangs of yearning for bodily pleasures afflicting the wayward Souls. For, despite their theoretical partaking of virtue, these Souls are nevertheless dragged down by material cares, which bar them from living up to their intellectual vocation. Subsisting now in a disembodied state, they will suffer endlessly the desires which the pleasures of the senses had satisfied while they were united to the body, and their suffering will increase as they are joined by the throngs of fellow wayward Souls departing this world.

The general maxim which al-Fārābī lays down is that the knowledge of true happiness is not only the prerequisite of eternal bliss, but also that of bare survival after death. Hence the fate of the other cities, the renegade and the erring, will depend on the measure of their apprehension of true happiness. Whoever has been the cause of their deliberate perdition or degeneracy will suffer everlastingly. Their inhabitants, however, having lived in blissful ignorance, will meet the fate of the ignorant or nonvirtuous city, which is total annihilation.[80]

[78] *Al-Madīnah*, pp. 114 f. [79] *Ibid.*, p. 118. [80] *Ibid.*

From this it is plain how al-Fārābī solves the problem of immortality. Like Aristotle, he assigns immortality to the intellectual part of the Soul only, or, to put it more accurately, he makes it contingent upon the Soul's degree of intellectual apprehension. Unlike Aristotle, however, he recognizes variations in the mode of the survival of individual Souls. In keeping with his concept of the unique survival of active Reason as the universal principle of intellectuality common to the whole of mankind, Aristotle completely ruled out such variation. In this regard, and in his partial admission of the transmigration of the Soul or its endless progression through the cycle of rebirth, it is clear that al-Fārābī's view of individual immortality and of the ultimate destiny of the Soul is more akin to Plato's, though radically at variance with the Islamic doctrine of bodily resurrection and the indiscriminate survival of all Souls, ignorant and wise alike.

II

IBN SĪNĀ

Al-Fārābī, as we have seen, was the founder of Arab Neo-Platonism and the first major figure in the history of that philosophical movement since Proclus, who was its last great representative in the West. The greatest exponent of that philosophy in the East and the philosopher with whose name its whole cause was identified by subsequent writers, both in Europe and the East, was Abū 'Alī al-Ḥusain Ibn Sīnā, known to the Latin authors of the thirteenth century as Avicenna.

Ibn Sīnā's high standing in the history of Arab Neo-Platonism does not rest on his originality. An autobiographical tradition points out his debt to al-Fārābī, whose *Intentions of Aristotle's Metaphysics* unraveled for him the secrets of that work, which he read forty times and almost memorized, we are told, without grasping its sense.[81] His cosmology, his psychology, his theory of the intellect, his theory of

[81] Al-Qifṭī, *Tārīkh al-Ḥukamā'*, p. 416.

prophecy, etc., despite the refinements they make on al-Fārābī's parallel doctrines, are essentially variations on similar themes. However, Ibn Sīnā was a far more lucid and systematic writer than his predecessor, and the fluency of his style contributed greatly to the dissemination of his works among students of philosophy, historians of ideas, and others. And it is significant that despite al-Fārābī's standing as a logician and philosopher he had hardly any followers or commentators, whereas many of the more illustrious authors of the twelfth and thirteenth centuries, such as the doxographer al-Shahrastānī (d. 1153), the theologian Fakhr al-Dīn al-Rāzī (d. 1209), and the encyclopedist Nāṣir al-Ṭūsī (d. 1273), addressed themselves to expounding or commenting on Ibn Sīnā's writings. Even in Europe, as interest in Aristotelianism grew at this time thanks to translators like Michael the Scot, Hermann the German, Hispanus, and Gundissalinus, at first Avicenna and then Averroes were the chief Arab expositors of Aristotle who were translated into Latin.[82] The attack on Arab Neo-Platonism, which culminated in al-Ghazālī's classic onslaught in the *Tahāfut*, is chiefly leveled at Ibn Sīnā, whose name is tacitly identified with that philosophy.[83]

We know more about the life of Ibn Sīnā and his work than about any other philosopher yet mentioned, chiefly because he resorted to the unusual (and to Muslim writers somewhat reprehensible) expedient of composing a fairly detailed autobiography, which he dictated to his pupil Abū 'Ubaid al-Juzjānī.[84]

According to his own account, then, Ibn Sīnā was born in the village of Kharmaithān, not far from Bukhārā, in Transoxiana (northern Persia), where his father, a man of some culture, had settled with his family. Later on, the family moved to Bukhārā itself, where the young Ḥusain received private instruction in reading, writing, arithmetic, jurisprudence, and logic. Of his teachers only Abū 'Abdullah al-Nātilī and Ismā'īl the Ascetic are mentioned by name. However, he alludes to a grocer, apparently proficient in Indian arithmetic, as well as an Ismā'īlī propagandist who visited his father, already won over

[82] Bacon, *Opus Majus*, I, 55 f.; cf. Afnan, *Avicenna*, pp. 258 f.

[83] *Infra*, pp. 250 f.

[84] Al-Qifṭī, *Tārīkh al-Ḥukamā'*, pp. 413–18; cf. Afnan, *Avicenna*, pp. 57–75.

to the Ismāʿīlī cause. Ibn Sīnā's interest in philosophy appears to have developed from listening to their conversations, but his systematic study of logic, philosophy, and medicine started some time later.

It is noteworthy that Ibn Sīnā refers to his independent intellectual attainments without undue modesty. By the age of ten, he informs us, "I had completed the study of the Koran and a major part of Arabic letters [*adab*], so much so that people wondered at my attainments,"[85] and before long his teacher al-Nātilī could no longer vie with him in logical proficiency, so that he was compelled to fall back on his own resources. From logic, he turned to the study of physics, metaphysics, and medicine entirely on his own, and he attained such a standing in medicine that at the age of sixteen he had become the mentor of many a senior physician.

By the age of eighteen he had mastered logic, physics, and mathematics, so there was nothing left for him to learn except metaphysics. Having read the *Metaphysics* of Aristotle forty times, he was still unable to comprehend the intent of its author until he lighted accidentally on a copy of al-Fārābī's *Intentions of Aristotle's Metaphysics*, which at once illuminated for him Aristotle's meaning.

An unexpected turn in his career came as a result of being introduced to the Samānid Sultan of Bukhārā, Nūḥ b. Manṣūr, who was suffering from an incurable disease. This introduction brought him into contact with a succession of princes or viziers, who employed him as court physician or *aide*. But his association with such lords was often short-lived. He moved from the court of the Samānid sultan to that of the Buwayhids, from Bukhārā to Rayyand to Hamadān, reluctant to settle in one place because of perhaps simple restlessness or the fear of being persecuted for his Ismāʿīlī sympathies.[86]

In his association with the Buwayhid princes of the period, from Majd al-Daulah to Shams al-Daulah and 'Alā' al-Daulah, Ibn Sīnā did not escape his share of hardship or tribulation. His fate often hung on the good humor or ill health of his patrons, as well as on the good humor of their soldiers even. His own health eventually deteriorated as a result of over-indulgence in drink and sex. After repeated efforts to cure himself of colic by unorthodox methods, the greatest

[85] Al-Qifṭī, *Tārīkh al-Ḥukamā'*, p. 413. [86] See Afnan, *Avicenna*, pp. 77 f.

physician of his day ultimately failed. In 1037 he died at the age of fifty-eight.

The literary output of Ibn Sīnā was truly voluminous and his treatises far outstrip in comprehensiveness anything earlier philosophical authors such as al-Kindī and al-Rāzī ever produced. Moreover, he surpasses all his predecessors, even the great al-Fārābī, in the fluency of his style and the thoroughness with which he dealt with questions that often were only sketched perfunctorily by his predecessors. His fluency and thoroughness account perhaps for the fact that he soon superseded al-Fārābī, his acknowledged master, and became before long the champion of Islamic Neo-Platonism, which al-Fārābī had in fact founded, as mentioned above. He also contributed greatly to the development of a philosophical vocabulary both in Arabic, in which he wrote most of his works, and in Persian, in which he wrote the *Danish-Nāmeh*, the first philosophical book in post-Islamic Persian.[87] Following the eclipse of philosophy in the eleventh and twelfth centuries in the East, the tradition of Avicennian studies never really died, even at a time when al-Kindī's and al-Fārābī's names had almost been forgotten. The manuscript tradition bears this out. Of the extant works of al-Kindī only a single manuscript has been preserved at Istanbul;[88] of the works of al-Fārābī, a few imperfect copies exist; but scores of almost complete collections of Ibn Sīnā's works have been preserved. A Dominican scholar, Father G. C. Anawati, has drawn up an inventory of 276 of Ibn Sīnā's writings, in print and in manuscript.[89]

Ibn Sīnā's major philosophical treatise is *Kitāb al-Shifā'* or *Book of Healing*, known in Latin by the erroneous title of *Sufficientia*. It is an encyclopedia of Islamic-Greek learning in the eleventh century, ranging from logic to mathematics. Suspecting no doubt that the philosophical reader of the time, who had become accustomed to epitomes or even epitomes of epitomes, had no time for lengthy expositions, Ibn Sīnā made his own abridgment of this encyclopedic work. He called it *Kitāb al-Najāt*, or the *Book of Salvation*, which is much more widely read than *al-Shifā'*. His other major work is the

[87] See Afnan, *Avicenna*, p. 81. [88] Ayasofia Ms, No. 4832.
[89] Anawati, *Essai de bibliographie avicennienne.*

Book of Remarks and Admonitions (*Kitāb al-Ishārāt wa'l-Tanbīhāt*), one of his late books and the product of a more independent phase in his intellectual development. Next should be mentioned a treatise on *Definitions*, similar to al-Kindī's parallel treatise and patterned likewise on Book Delta of Aristotle's *Metaphysics*; then a treatise on the *Divisions of the Theoretical Sciences*, similar to al-Fārābī's *Enumeration of the Sciences*, though much sketchier; then a group of psychological, religious, and eschatological treatises that develop some aspects of his thought as embodied in *al-Shifā'* and the *Remarks* but add little to their substance. Finally, we should mention a group of mystical treatises,[90] which like the foregoing *Remarks* shows distinct progress in the direction of what Ibn Sīnā designated the "Oriental Philosophy" or "Illumination." His biographer says he devoted a volume to this subject,[91] and it may very well be the *Oriental Philosophy*, with which we can conclude our list.[92] We are not concerned here with his numerous medical, linguistic, and astronomical works.

Apart from the works of Aristotle and his Greek commentators, the two chief formative influences on Ibn Sīnā's thought appear to have been the *Epistles of the Brethren of Purity* and the writings of al-Fārābī. Although he may have been anxious to stress in his autobiography his own attainments rather than his debt to his masters, and to disassociate himself from Ismā'īlism, he nonetheless does refer to the fact that his initiation in philosophy came from listening to discussions between Ismā'īlī visitors and his father and brother, as mentioned earlier. It is significant that the twelfth-century historian al-Bayhaqī makes a point of the fact that like his father Ibn Sīnā was in the habit of reading the *Epistles of the Brethren of Purity*.[93]

We have already noted his frank acknowledgment of his debt to al-Fārābī, who had enabled him to understand Aristotle's *Metaphysics*.

[90] Mehren, *Traités mystiques d'Avicenne*, and the Bibliography at the end of this book.

[91] Al-Qifṭī, *Tārīkh al-Ḥukamā'*, p. 418.

[92] The "Oriental Philosophy" of Ibn Sīnā has been the subject of considerable controversy among scholars. A book entitled *Oriental Philosophy* exists in manuscript form (see, e.g., Ayasofia Ms, No. 2403, and Oxford, Pococke 181) but differs little in content or arrangement from his other conventional works.

[93] Al-Bayhaqī, *Muntakhab Ṣuwān al-Ḥikmah*, p. 40; Afnan, *Avicenna*, p. 58; al-Qifṭī, *Tārīkh al-Ḥukamā'*, p. 413.

A late bibliographer, Hājjī Khalīfah (d. 1657), even states that Ibn Sīnā's major work, *al-Shifā'*, is based on a similar book of al-Fārābī's, with the probable title of the *Second Teaching* (*al-Ta'līm al-Thānī*),[94] which has not been preserved. The debt of Ibn Sīnā to al-Fārābī, however, is borne out by more than these external indications. Almost all the major themes of his metaphysics and cosmology are implicit in al-Fārābī. His own contribution is often a matter of greater systematic elaboration. In his account of the division of the sciences, for instance, he adds very little to the subject-matter of al-Fārābī's *Enumeration of the Sciences*.

In the introduction to *al-Shifā'*, which surveys the whole range of Greco-Arab learning, Ibn Sīnā raises a methodological difficulty of the first importance. His aim in this book, he says, is to give the gist of the philosophical sciences attributed to the ancients without omitting anything of value. Since his purpose is purely expository, however, Ibn Sīnā is careful to observe that one should not seek in this book the substance of his own thought; this, he maintains, is to be found in his *Oriental Philosophy*. Whether he actually wrote that book in full is a question which cannot be easily settled. Extant manuscripts of a book that goes by the name of "Oriental Philosophy" do not bear out the alleged bipolarity of his thought,[95] but in a work purporting to constitute the logical part of the *Oriental Philosophy* Ibn Sīnā reasserts the dual character of his thought. Having observed that scholars of his day were particularly devoted to the Peripatetics, he found no cause to break with the Peripatetic tradition in his popular works. In the minds of the vulgar, Peripateticism was the superior philosophy and was to be preferred to any other. However, having written *al-Shifā'* and its commentary (*al-Lawāḥiq*) in that spirit, and even made good the deficiencies of Peripateticism in it, Ibn Sīnā felt compelled to write a further book "embodying the fundamentals of the true science," which was not to be divulged except "to ourselves—and those who are akin to ourselves," in accordance with their understanding and love for truth.[96]

[94] *Kashf al-Ẓunūn*, III, 98. Al-Fārābī is referred to in the Arabic sources as the "Second Teacher," in contradistinction to Aristotle, the First Teacher.

[95] *Supra*, p. 151, n. 92.

[96] Ibn Sīnā, *Manṭiq al-Mashriqiyīn*, pp. 2 f.

Without dwelling on this controversial issue, most of the evidence, both internal and external, appears to conflict with the claim of this alleged bipolarity in Ibn Sīnā's thought. First, both in *Manṭiq al-Mashriqiyīn* or the *Oriental Philosophy* and the book of *Remarks and Admonitions*, one of his latest and presumably maturest works, the departure from Peripateticism is often purely verbal. Secondly, his disciples and successors, such as Ibn al-Marzubān, al-Shahrastānī, and al-Ṭūsī, present a uniform picture of Ibn Sīnā's philosophy as an avowed Neo-Platonism of the conventional Islamic type. And even his sharpest critics, such as al-Ghazālī and Ibn Rushd, whose fairness in reporting his views cannot be questioned, betray no acquaintance with this alleged bipolarity.

The continuity and homogeneity of Ibn Sīnā's thought can be seen in his illuminationist (or *Ishrāqī*) tendency, which is the finishing touch of the conventional Neo-Platonism he had made his own. Like al-Fārābī, Ibn Sīnā builds upon an Aristotelian-Ptolemaic cosmological substructure a Neo-Platonic edifice, in which the emanationist scale of being has been thoroughly incorporated. Although essentially similar to al-Fārābī's, this scale of being is more complete and the treatises embodying it more comprehensive. If we take his abridgment of *al-Shifā'* as an instance, we find that he starts off with a succinct account of logic in which Aristotelian, Neo-Platonic, and Stoic elements are intermingled. After a short introduction in which the whole subject matter of logic is divided into what is an object of conception and what is an object of judgment, Ibn Sīnā discusses the five terms of Porphyry's *Isagoge*, then proceeds to classify the propositions in the traditional manner. Next, modality is discussed at length, and the views of Theophrastus, Themistius, and Alexander are set forth and appraised.

With this preliminary discussion as a background, Ibn Sīnā turns to demonstration and the syllogism generally. For him, the possibility of all demonstration depends on the existence of certain indemonstrable principles which are directly apprehended, such as the objects of sense, empirical maxims, beliefs accepted on authority, possible or probable opinions universally believed, and finally those primary principles of knowledge on which all proof rests and which are intuitively certain.[97]

[97] Ibn Sīnā, *al-Najāt*, pp. 60 ff.

Demonstration (*al-burhān*) is defined as an argument consisting of indubitable premises resulting in indubitable conclusions. The absolute form of demonstration is the argument from the fact and the argument from the reason of the fact.[98] In the former, the fact, and in the latter the cause, serve as the mediating principles of demonstration.[99]

All proof requires three essential elements: postulates, premises, and problems. Postulates are matters presupposed in any science, the essential attributes of which constitute the subject matter of that science, e.g., number in relation to arithmetic, mass in relation to physics, and being in relation to metaphysics. Premises are propositions upon which the proof rests. Problems are those specific questions or doubts (*aporiae*), upon whose solution the proof turns.

In addition to these elements, as we have said, demonstration presupposes certain primary principles, the knowledge of which must precede the demonstration proper. These principles consist of definitions, hypotheses, and axioms. Hypotheses are propositions, which, though not self-evident, are either received from other disciplines, where their truth has been established, or become evident in the process of demonstration itself.[100] Axioms, on the other hand, are self-evident propositions that are either of general import, such as the proposition that every statement is either affirmative or negative, or of more restricted import, such as the proposition that two sums equal to the same sum are equal to each other.

Definitions, Ibn Sīnā next argues, are propositions, which though indispensable for demonstration, cannot be arrived at either through demonstration or division (dichotomy). For all demonstration presupposes a middle term that is elicited either by definition or by description[101] or is simply an attribute (elicited, presumably, by induction). If elicited by definition, then it either requires proof involving another middle term, which in turn involves another middle term and so on ad infinitum, or it is apprehended directly. If by description or induction, the inference is that an accidental feature on which description or

[98] Cf. *Anal. Post.* I. 13. [99] Ibn Sīnā, *al-Najāt*, p. 6. [100] *Ibid.*, p. 72.

[101] Description (*rasm*) differs from definition in that it rests on an accidental attribute of the *definiendum*, unlike the definition (*ḥadd*) proper, which rests on an essential attribute thereof.

induction bears can be more relevant to the proof than the essential feature on which definition bears, which is absurd.

Nor can the definition be arrived at through dichotomy, because the contrary aspects of a division or disjunction are either presupposed, in which case they do not naturally result from division, or are equally obvious, in which case they do not contribute to eliciting the *definiendum*. It remains therefore that the definition is formed by the process of subsuming the *definiendum* under its proper genus and determining what its specific attribute (or *differentia*) is. Once the two are linked together in thought, the definition results.[102]

The section on logic closes, as was customary in Islamic discussions of this type, with a survey of fallacies. Fallacies are either a matter of form or of substance, according to Ibn Sīnā, and are either intentional or unintentional. In formal fallacies (*in dictionem*), the error might be due to equivocation, or syntactical, grammatical, or other faults to which the terms that make up the proposition are liable. In material fallacies, the error might result from circularity, petition of principle, causal misinterpretation (*non causa pro causa*), or confusion of the issue, etc.[103]

Ibn Sīnā begins his discussion of physics with an inquiry into the subject matter of natural science, stated to be "bodies, in so far as they are liable to change."[104] And although the existence of its subject matter is postulated by physics, the demonstration of the principles upon which it rests is left to a higher science, i.e., metaphysics or the universal science, from which these principles are received as axiomatic, since it is not necessary in any of the special sciences to demonstrate the postulates or presuppositions upon which they rest.

Of these principles or presuppositions, Ibn Sīnā mentions the maxim that physical bodies are compounded of matter and form, and that by reason of their matter they are liable to spatial determinations, whereas by reason of their form they are liable to certain substantial or accidental attributes. To these two physical principles is added a nonphysical principle, the active intellect, upon which they depend for both their matter and form. The investigation of this intellect, as

[102] Ibn Sīnā, *al-Najāt*, p. 78. [103] *Ibid.*, pp. 89 f. [104] *Ibid.*, p. 98.

such, is not the proper object of the science of physics. In addition, this principle contributes to the preservation of the primary and secondary perfections (singular: *kamāl*; *entelecheia*) of physical entities, through the intermediary of those primary physical powers with which they are endowed, and which generate in their turn the secondary powers of such entities. The actions of bodies are among the secondary perfections emanating from these powers, which are of three kinds: (1) Inanimate powers, which preserve bodies and their derivatives in their natural state of motion and rest in a necessary manner. (2) Animate powers, which preserve such bodies through certain vital organs, sometimes in a voluntary, sometimes in an involuntary way, such as the Soul in its vegetative, animal, or rational capacities. (3) Celestial powers (or Souls),[105] which determine the voluntary motions of the planets according to an unalterable pattern.

The forms of physical bodies are also divided into those which are never separable from these bodies and those which are. The latter supervene upon them in alternation, giving rise thereby to the generation and corruption of physical objects. This alternation, however, presupposes in addition to the forms which succeed one another and the matter in which they inhere, a third factor, privation, which is the necessary condition of generation and corruption, though only *per accidens*. Thus the occurrence of a given state (A) is possible only through the corresponding privation (not-A), which implies, according to the author, that events follow a logical sequence and are ordered according to a "rational providence" in which there is no room for contingency or chance.[106]

On the classic question of the divisibility of substance, Ibn Sīnā takes a distinctly antiatomistic stand. Whether we accept the atomistic view of Democritus or the quasi-atomistic view of Anaxagoras, who spoke of homogeneous particles (*homoeomera*), the theory is logically untenable. If bodies are assumed to consist, as in the former case, of indivisible particles, then such particles are either in contact with other

[105] Ibn Sīnā, *al-Najāt*, p. 100. The celestial souls cause the particular motions of the planets through an act of deliberation; hence they are described as voluntary, as distinct from natural or involuntary, powers.

[106] *Ibid.*, p. 102.

particles adjoining them, in which case they are not indivisible, or they are in contact by interpenetration or overlapping, in which case they could not give rise to larger masses.[107]

The second chapter dealing with physics takes up the concomitants of body, i.e., motion and rest, space and the void, finitude and infinity, contact, conjunction, succession, etc. In general, the discussion shows very little originality and is a mere exposition of these concepts along Aristotelian lines.

Motion is defined as the "first actuality or perfection of that which is in potentiality in that respect in which it is potential."[108] As such, motion presupposes a substratum which is susceptible of the progressive transition from potentiality to act and is predicable of all the categories, with the exception of substance. For "the coming to be and the passing away of substance are not forms of motion, since they are processes which take place instantly."[109]

Motion, however, is not a generic attribute of body, and accordingly presupposes a cause distinct from the movable body. When it inheres in the body, it is said to be self-moved, otherwise it is moved by an extraneous agent of motion. When it is self-moved, the motion is either intermittent and is called voluntary, or continuous and is called natural. Natural motion is nevertheless of two kinds, voluntary and involuntary; the ultimate cause of the latter is nature, that of the former is the celestial Soul.[110]

But beyond both nature and the celestial Soul, there is a primary principle of all motion in the universe, which is the single, eternal, and circular motion of the outermost heaven. Such a motion, being unending, must be numerically one and circular, since it is impossible for rectilinear motion, whose nature is to turn back or to be succeeded by rest, to be endless.

This primary motion is described by Ibn Sīnā as creative (*ibdāʿī*), as distinct from the other forms of motion in the world of generation and corruption, which are noncreative. The power generating this creative motion must be infinite, or else its action would not be everlasting,

[107] Ibn Sīnā, *al-Nājāt*, pp. 102 f.

[108] *Ibid.*, p. 105; cf. Aristotle's *Physics* III. 201ᵃ10.

[109] *Ibid.*, p. 105. [110] *Ibid.*, p. 109.

and it must be incorporeal or else it would not be infinite. But, being incorporeal, it must act through a corporeal power or Soul naturally disposed to receive the incorporeal action.

Before considering the nature of this incorporeal agency that acts upon the heavenly bodies and the world of generation and corruption as well through the agency of the celestial Souls, Ibn Sīnā turns to the constituent parts of that world, which is the proper subject matter of physics.

"Generable bodies," he observes, arise through the combination of two or more of the four elements, which are differentiated by the four contrary qualities, i.e., hot and cold, dry and moist. Two of these qualities are active and two are passive. For a body to be capable of cohesion, on the one hand, and disintegration, on the other, it must consist of at least one active and one passive quality. Of the various views purporting to determine the nature of these qualities, Ibn Sīnā's is that they are concomitant attributes of the "substantial forms" of physical objects rather than *differentiae* thereof. For either these qualities or their effects are always naturally manifested through those bodies, either in the form of coldness or heat, moistness or dryness, or motion or rest. The only exception to this general rule is the heavenly bodies, which are incomposite, and accordingly are not liable either to generation, corruption, or any of the "natural" motions of the elements,[111] their only motion being the "creative" circular motion already mentioned.

The heavenly bodies begin with the sphere of the moon. What characterizes them, in addition to simplicity and motion in a circle, is the fact that they are neither light nor heavy, nor liable to any of the contrary qualities. Moreover, they are endowed with Soul (i.e., are animate).[112]

The creative action of these heavenly bodies is manifested in diverse ways. First, although not liable to any of the four contrary qualities themselves, they nevertheless can cause such qualities in material objects, as can be seen from the cooling effect of opium and the burning

[111] I.e., the upward and downward movements.
[112] Ibn Sīnā, *al-Nājāt*, pp. 144 f.

effect of some plants, etc.[113] Moreover they can cause diverse meteorological phenomena through their action upon the elements in the sublunary world, or they can generate the phenomenon of life in them when these elements are combined in due proportion. What sets the lowest manifestation of life in plants apart from inanimate matter are the powers of nutrition, growth, and reproduction. As the proportion increases, the disposition of the compound to receive the higher manifestations of life increases also. Thus animal and human life arise by virtue of the action of these heavenly bodies. But the Soul, as the principle of life, is an emanation from the lowest of the "separate intelligences" or active intellect, the true agent of generation and corruption in the sublunary world and "giver of forms" (*wāhib al-ṣuwar*) in it.[114]

The general definition of the Soul is "the first perfection of an organic body," either in so far as it is generated, grows, and is nourished (as in the case of the vegetable Soul), or in so far as it apprehends particulars and is moved by will (as in the case of the animal Soul), or in so far as it apprehends universals and acts by deliberation (as in the case of the human Soul).

Despite its unity, the Soul possesses a series of faculties at each of its three levels, as shown in the diagram on page 160.

As will be noticed from the diagram, the interest of Ibn Sīnā's theory of the Soul and its diverse faculties is not purely psychological. A considerable part of this theory bears directly on epistemological questions and leads ultimately beyond epistemology into cosmology and metaphysics. This, as we have noted in the case of al-Fārābī, is part of the complex role assigned in Arab Neo-Platonism to the Soul in general and to Reason in particular.

If we consider the cognitive aspect of this theory, we see at once how Reason marks the crowning of the psychic process, which begins with the vegetative functions and rises by degrees from the sensuous to the imaginative-retentive functions, culminating finally in the rational. A refinement on Aristotle's theory of sensation is the distinction in the faculty of touch of four subsidiary functions corresponding

[113] Ibn Sīnā, *al-Najāt*, pp. 150 f. [114] *Ibid.*, pp. 184, 278 ff.

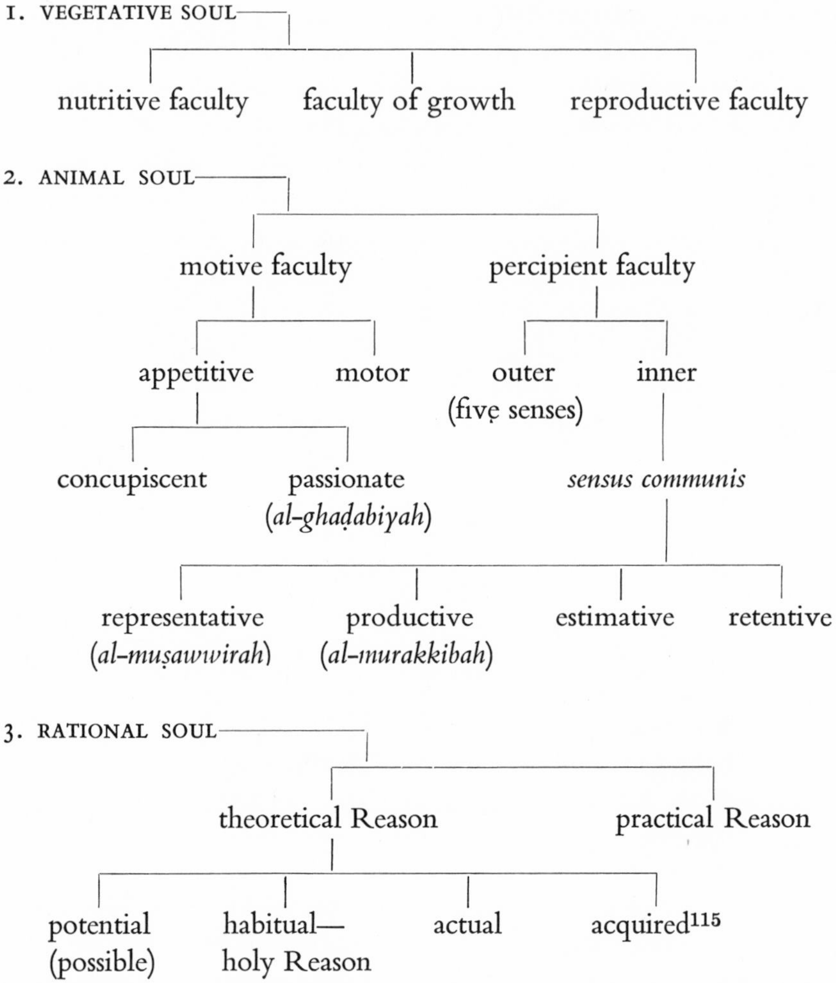

to the perception of hot and cold, moist and dry, hard and soft, rough and smooth, hinted at by Aristotle but not clearly delineated.[116]

Another refinement is the close correlation between the *sensus communis* and the imaginative faculty (*phantasia*) and the introduction of a separate inner faculty, which he calls the estimative (*al-wāhimah*), whereby the animal discriminates instinctively between what is

[115] Ibn Sīnā, *al-Najāt*, pp. 158 f.; Rahman, *Avicenna's Psychology*, pp. 34 f.
[116] *De Anima* II. 422b25.

desirable and what is repugnant.[117] Such perceptions are stored in the retentive faculty, analogous in this respect to the imaginative, in which the ordinary sensible perceptions are stored away.

When we come to the rational faculty, we find that it has two essential divisions, the practical and the theoretical. The practical is the source of motion and operation in those types of action that involve deliberation, and it is related to the appetitive faculty, the imaginative-estimative faculty, and to itself. In the first two cases it cooperates with those faculties in initiating or hastening the action or directing and coordinating it, as in the human arts and crafts. In the latter case it gives rise, in conjunction with theoretical reason, to the general maxims of morality and exerts a moderating influence on the bodily functions, thereby insuring their conformity with the norms of virtue.[118]

The objects of the theoretical faculty, on the other hand, are the universal forms, which either exist in an immaterial condition already or are reduced to the condition of immateriality by the abstractive powers of Reason itself. In the first case they are actually intelligible, in the second only potentially so. Likewise, the theoretical faculty might, in relation to them, be either actually or potentially susceptible of apprehension. However, potentiality is used in three different senses: (1) It might refer to the pure ability or aptitude of the agent, as in the case of the child's ability to write prior to instruction. Or (2), it may refer to that ability, in so far as it has been determined to some extent; as, for example, with the child who has become acquainted with the alphabet and the tools of writing. Or finally (3), it may refer to the fulfillment of that ability in a concrete way, as with the calligrapher who has mastered the art of writing in such a way that he can exercise it at will. The first is designated by Ibn Sīnā as absolute or "material" power, the second as a possible power, and the third as a habitus (*malakah*) or the "perfection of power."

[117] Ibn Sīnā, *al-Nājāt*, p. 163; cf. Aristotle's "sensitive imagination," *De Anima* III. 434^{a}5. The identification of imagination and *sensus communis* is tacitly assumed by Aristotle in *De Anima* III. 429^{a}1, where he states that "imagination [*phantasia*] must be a movement resulting from an actual exercise of a power of sense," identified in *De Mem.* 450^{a}12 as the *sensus communis*, which Aristotle calls here "the primary faculty of perception."

[118] *Ibid.*, p. 164.

In keeping with this threefold meaning of potentiality, Reason is designated material (or *hylic*), possible or habitual. Reason may be called "material" either in the pure sense, by analogy with pure matter, which in itself is entirely formless but is the substratum of all possible forms; or in the qualified sense, in so far as it is the bearer of the "primary intelligibles," i.e., the primary principles of demonstration which are apprehended intuitively and upon which the "secondary intelligibles" are based.[119]

Habitual Reason, on the other hand, might be viewed as partly actual and partly potential. It is actual in relation to that higher stage of actuality which it attains as it apprehends universals and apprehends this apprehension as well, whereby it is called actual Reason or Reason in act. Or it is actual in relation to that unconditional stage of actuality, at which its apprehension of the universals is no longer dependent on the natural process but stems from that supernatural or supermundane agency which governs all the processes of generation and corruption, including the process of cognition, in this world, i.e., the active intellect. At that stage it is designated as acquired Reason.

With acquired Reason, it might be said, man attains the perfection for which he is destined and approximates the higher beings of the supermundane world.[120] This "contact" with active Reason is not for Ibn Sīnā the key to human destiny only, but also the key to the whole process of cognition. For as the depository of all intelligibles or universals, the active Reason imparts to human reason, as it reaches that stage of readiness we call acquired Reason, the acquired forms that make up its stock of knowledge. This "acquisition," however, is far from being uniform in all men. In some, the aptitude for it is so great that they require hardly any instruction, since they are able to apprehend universals at once by virtue of an inborn power, which the author calls "holy Reason" and which is reserved as a divine favor for the very few.[121] Its chief characteristic is the ability to apprehend the middle term directly and thereby to be able to dispense altogether with learning or reflection.[122]

The order of the rational powers of the Soul is described by Ibn

[119] Ibn Sīnā, *al-Nājāt*, p. 166. [120] *Ibid.*, p. 160. [121] *Ibid.*, p. 167.
[122] Ibn Sīnā, *al-Ishārāt wa'l Tanbīhāt*, pt. 2, p. 370.

Sīnā in terms of subordination or subservience. To holy Reason, which stands at the top of the scale, is subordinated Reason-in-act, followed in descending order by habitual Reason, material Reason, practical Reason, the estimative faculty, memory, the imagination, and so on, until we come to the lowest faculties of the Soul, the nutritive.[123]

An important implication of Ibn Sīnā's concept of holy Reason should be noted here. This is its bearing on his theory of prophecy. Al-Fārābī, it will be recalled, had ascribed prophecy to an exceptional perfection of the imaginative faculty. Ibn Sīnā, however, conscious perhaps of the derogation from the prophetic office which this theory implies, assigns prophecy to this holy Reason, described as the highest stage which human Reason can attain. And although this view was, in the nature of the case, much more consistent with the dignity of the prophetic office in Islam, it raised at least one question that Ibn Sīnā does not flinch from. This is the question of prophetic knowledge in so far as it bears on particulars rather than universals.

The ultimate cause of generation and corruption in the world, he argues, is the heavenly bodies. Being particular, the motions of those heavenly bodies must be induced by the particular perception of the separate agencies that operate on them, that is, the celestial Souls, which act by means of physical powers, as all Souls must. Now since these motions are dependent on determined chains of causes, the celestial Souls must be conversant with the whole series of possible events in the future. And although these events are objects of transcendent foreknowledge regarding their heavenly movers, they are nevertheless unknown to us, as a rule, owing to the deficiency of our powers, but are not on that account unknowable in themselves.[124] Consequently, "contact" with them is not impossible, either for practical Reason assisted by the imagination, where particular motions or events are concerned, on the one hand; or for theoretical Reason, where their universal intelligible forms are concerned, on the other. This possibility, as has already been pointed out, is bound up with the diversity of intellectual aptitudes meted out to various people, especially where the apprehension of particulars through contact with celestial Souls is

[123] *Al-Nājāt*, p. 168. [124] Ibn Sīnā, *Aḥwāl al-Nafs*, pp. 114 ff.

concerned. In some people, this aptitude is rather weak, due to the weakness of their imaginative faculty, whereas in others it may attain such a degree of acuteness that it is no longer in need of the assistance of the senses on which it normally depends, but is able to assist the rational faculty in achieving "contact" with the immaterial agencies that impart prophetic knowledge of particulars to it, and even in forming audible and visible representations of the revealed conceptions, analogous to dream images.[125]

In the theoretical faculty, there also are degrees of excellence commensurate with the excellence of the intuitive faculty, which apprehends the primary principles of cognition upon which all knowledge ultimately depends. Since the degrees of this apprehension vary radically, the intuitive power in some people may certainly be so feeble as to be almost nonexistent, whereas in others it might reach extraordinary proportions. "A person's Soul might then attain such a degree of lucidity or susceptibility for contact with [higher] intellectual agencies that he will burst forth with intuition: I mean the ability to receive the enlightenment of the active intellect in all matters."[126] When he attains that level, the intelligible forms stored in the active intellect will appear to him instantaneously and thus he will apprehend without effort or discourse matters that others apprehend only discursively, through the assistance of a teacher. To bear this supposition out, it is enough to note the kinship between the intelligible forms and the human Soul, both equally immaterial in nature and yet capable of some manner of association with matter. The Soul, which normally acts upon the body as its circumscribed province, might nevertheless go beyond that province and act upon the remoter regions of matter, causing motion or rest, heating or cooling, hardening or softening in them, as well as the consequent phenomena of lightning, earthquakes, rain, wind, etc. These are the phenomena that we designate as miraculous or extraordinary.[127]

In the light of this theory of prophecy and miracle-making, Ibn Sīnā divides men into four classes: those whose theoretical faculty has reached such a degree of refinement that they require no human teacher, whereas their practical faculty has reached such a pitch that by virtue

[125] Ibn Sīnā, *Aḥwāl al-Nafs*, pp. 118 f. [126] *Ibid.*, p. 123. [127] *Ibid.*, p. 125.

of their acute imaginative faculty they partake directly of the knowledge of present and future happenings and are able to effect miraculous deeds in the world of nature. Next come those who possess the perfection of the intuitive power, but not the imaginative. Then there are those in whom the theoretical power is perfect, but not the practical. Finally there are those who surpass their fellow men only in the acuteness of their practical power. To the first class belongs the function of rulership, since they partake of citizenship in the intelligible world by virtue of their Reason, in the subordinate world of Souls by virtue of their Souls, and in the world of nature, upon which they can exercise effective control as well. To the members of the second class belongs subordinate political authority, followed by the third class, to whom the bulk of the aristocracy belongs. Those, however, who do not possess any of those extraordinary powers but are nevertheless active in the pursuit of practical virtue are distinct from the common run of men but do not belong to any of the three superior classes.[128]

On the crucial question of survival after death, Ibn Sīnā's position is not entirely free from ambiguity. The resurrection of the body and the pleasures or miseries attendant upon it in the life to come have been clearly set down in Scripture and cannot for that reason be questioned by the philosopher. "Spiritual resurrection" and the fate of the Soul in the life to come, on the other hand, are the province of philosophy and, though alluded to in Scripture, are to some extent a matter of rational discourse.

It is the latter aspect of the question of resurrection that is of particular interest to the "metaphysical philosophers," who yearn for the spiritual pleasures in the life-to-come and would partake of the corporeal pleasures, if they must, only reluctantly. For the happiness they seek consists in that "approximation to truth" which is bound up with the freeing of their Souls, especially in their rational part, from any dependence upon or attachment to the body. This happiness, which consists in the perfection of the highest faculty of the Soul, namely the rational, is in the nature of the case superior to the happiness or perfection of the lower, namely corporeal, faculties.

"The perfection proper to the Soul is to become identified with the

[128] Ibn Sīnā, *Aḥwāl al-Nafs*, p. 127.

intelligible world in which the form of the whole, its rational order, and the good overflowing from it are inscribed."[129] This world is presided over by the First Principle of all things, beneath which are the immaterial substances, the spiritual substances which have a certain relation to matter, and finally the heavenly bodies. When it has achieved this perfection the Soul becomes in effect a replica of the intelligible world and is united to the absolute good and absolute beauty, wherein its highest bliss lies. So long as it is barred from such union through the body and its cares, however, it can only partake of that bliss occasionally and, as it were, furtively, as happens when it sometimes shakes loose from the appetities or passions and desires the pleasures of the mind. But such bliss is achieved only after it has been freed altogether, through death, from the bondage of the body.[130] Those Souls which have fallen short of this stage of yearning after intellectual perfection (which Ibn Sīnā suggests is a matter of personal initiative or endeavor) will suffer the misery consequent upon unwanted separation from the body. This condition is brought about either through sluggishness in the quest for excellence or through obduracy in clinging to false beliefs.[131]

The point at which the Soul crosses the borderline between the earth-bound condition of the wretched and the heaven-bound condition of the blessed can only be surmised, according to Ibn Sīnā. Briefly, this point appears to coincide with the full apprehension of the intelligible world, in its orderliness, beauty, and dependence upon its sovereign Ruler. The greater that apprehension in this life, the greater the Soul's readiness for the other-worldly bliss consequent upon it. It is as though man were not to be released from attachment to the material world until his yearning for the intelligible world had reached the pitch of passionate love (*'ishq*).[132]

Even in death, this disassociation from the body and its cares may prove very hard, if not impossible, for the Soul. Weighed down by yearning for the body and its pleasures, the Soul will continue in death to partake of a condition of corporeality analogous to the one it partook of in life, but will be visited by added hardships, because of

[129] Ibn Sīnā, *Aḥwāl al-Nafs*, p. 130. [130] *Ibid.*, p. 133 [131] *Ibid.*, p. 134
[132] *Ibid.*, p. 135.

the futility of such yearning. And yet neither the hardship nor the concomitant suffering is everlasting, since it rests upon an accidental correlation of the Soul with the body. When this correlation ceases, the Soul will be entirely cleansed of any association with matter and will enter the state of bliss which essentially belongs to it.

Since yearning for its intellectual destiny is the condition of the Soul's final liberation, the ignorant Souls that in life did not attain even that stage will pass, unless they have contracted certain evil traits, into a condition of passivity similar to Dante's Limbo. Otherwise they will partake of those miseries that are a result of their yearning after the body, from which they have now been weaned.[133]

With the discussion of the Soul and its destiny in the after-life, the stage is set for transition into the higher realm of metaphysics. Metaphysics (*ilāhiyāt*: *theologia*) deals with "entities which are separable from matter, both in reality and in definition," or, otherwise stated, the "primary causes of both physical and mathematical reality, as well as the Cause of all causes or the Principle of all principles, namely God."[134]

Whether the Supreme Being is to be viewed as the proper object of metaphysics—designated by Ibn Sīnā as the divine science, first philosophy, or absolute wisdom—raises a major methodological question. The proper objects of a science, according to Ibn Sīnā, are matters whose existence, as we have seen in the case of physics, is either already established or, alternatively, is self-evident or intuitively certain. The existence of God and the other primary causes, however, is demonstrated in this science, rather than any other,[135] so it would be more appropriate to speak of God as one of the objectives sought in metaphysics, rather than its proper object. This object is in fact stated explicitly to be being qua being, since only being as such is common to all the categories with which the particular sciences are severally concerned. Thus "the primary object of this science is being qua being, and the questions on which it turns are the entities which are predicated of it in so far as it is, unconditionally."[136] Of these objects some stand to it in the capacity of species, such as substance, quality,

[133] Ibn Sīnā, *Aḥwāl al-Nafs*, p. 138. [134] Ibn Sīnā, *al-Shifā'* (*Ilāhiyāt*), Pt. I, p. 4.
[135] *Ibid.*, pp. 7 f. [136] *Ibid.*, p. 13.

or quantity; others in that of specific attributes, such as one and many, action and passivity, particular and universal, possible and actual.

On the basis of these preliminary distinctions, the "universal science" might be subdivided into three distinct parts: (1) A part which is concerned with the ultimate causes of being in general, and God as the First Cause, in particular; we might call this part etiology. (2) A part which is concerned with the fundamental attributes or determinations of being; we will call it ontology. (3) A part which is concerned with the fundamental principles upon which the particular sciences rest, and which we might call the metaphysical foundations of knowledge.[137]

The concept "being," like other "transcendental" concepts, such as the one, the thing and necessary, is apprehended directly by the mind, since it is the most primary concept and therefore cannot be referred to, or defined in terms of, some other concept. Indeed this concept is so pervasive that even its antithesis, not-being, can be apprehended only through some oblique reference to it.[138]

Being is divisible into essential being, or being per se, on the one hand, and accidental or derivative being, on the other. Of the two, the former is the primary meaning and is reducible to that of substance, conceived both as the subject of all predication and the bearer of all accidents.

The essential divisions of substance are the material and the immaterial. In the latter case, substance either stands in some relation to body, as an attribute or mover thereof, or in no relation whatsoever to it, and belongs accordingly to the classes of Soul and Reason respectively.

Material substance or body is essentially characterized by unity and continuity. The definition of body as a substance susceptible of length, breadth, and depth that is advanced by some theologians[139] mistakes

[137] Ibn Sīnā, *al-Shifā'*, p. 14; cf. al-Fārābī, *supra*, p. 133 f. The discussion of the "primary principles of demonstration" forms an integral part of Aristotle's *Metaphysics*, embodied chiefly in Book IV. However, in his delineation of the scope of metaphysics in *Met. I.* 983[a–f], IV. 1003[a]-20[f], and VI. 1025[b], Aristotle does not explicitly state this to be part of the inquiry in question.

[138] *Ibid.*, pp. 32, 36.

[139] This view is ascribed by al-Ash'arī to al-Naẓẓām (d. 845), a naturalist of the ninth century; see al-Ash'arī, *Maqālāt*, pp. 3, 4.

the accidental (namely, spatial) determinations of the *definiendum* for essential ones, and consequently is not a definition in the strict sense.

The two components of body are matter and form. Body is a potential, form is an actual principle. What is common to all bodies, both terrestrial or heavenly, is susceptibility to one or the other of the ultimate or primary contrary qualities of body—hot and cold, moist and dry.

The relation of matter to form is discussed at some length in *al-Shifā'*. Matter can never be divested of form, for if it were it would be neither divisible nor indivisible and would have no locus. Material bodies, however, can be shown to differ from mathematical entities and immaterial entities, in respect of both divisibility and location in space.

However, corporeal matter owes its actual being to form, not in the sense of correlation but rather in that of dependence. For the existence of matter depends on form in the same way an effect depends on the cause, so if the latter is removed, the former would be removed also. From this it would follow that form enjoys a certain ontological priority in relation to matter, since whereas matter depends on form for its existence in the concrete and cannot exist separately from it, form can, as is the case with immaterial substances.[140]

The priority of actuality to potentiality, or form to matter, is both logical and ontological. Only in the succession of particulars does the potential precede the actual, namely, chronologically. In universals, this is ruled out on the ground that eternal entities are always in actuality and the potential always depends for its actualization on a preceding actual entity; so, absolutely and in an unqualified sense, actuality is prior to potentiality, both in being and rank. Generally speaking, then, one might say that potentiality corresponds to a defect, actuality to a perfection, in any process involving both terms, and that wherever there is imperfection or defect, there also is potentiality. This imperfection is sometimes identified with evil. However, to the extent a thing exists, it is good, since evil is the privation of an actual state or feature only.[141]

The relation of cause, and ultimately the First Cause, to being, which

[140] Ibn Sīnā, *al-Shifā'*, pp. 83 f.

[141] *Ibid.*, pp. 181 f.

is the chief subject matter of metaphysics, is discussed next. Of the four Aristotelian causes, the *efficient* stands in a decisive relation to *being*. It imparts being to an entity which did not possess it, in so far as it did not possess it while remaining distinct from it. However, the former aspect of the process is not contributed by the agent, but rather by the patient, since it is only in so far as it did not exist previously that the patient now comes to exist. From this it would follow that the time determination (*ḥudūth*) is independent of the action of the efficient cause, which contributes being per se to the patient. Otherwise the agent's role in the production of the patient would be confined to its coming-into-being *after* it was not; so once it is, it is no longer dependent on the agent.[142]

The advocates of this view illustrate it by the fact that the effect, e.g., a building or offspring, continues to exist after the activity of the builder or father ends, and they infer from this that the agent was merely responsible for the initial act of bringing that effect into being. They forget, however, that in such a process the agent in question is not the real cause, but merely the cause of certain effects supervening upon the entity in question. Once its action upon it ceases, those particular effects cease also.[143] Rather than precede the effect, the real cause is always contemporaneous to and coextensive with it, so that the more enduring the action upon the effect, the more perfect the agent. From this it follows that the eternal agent is preeminent and prior to the temporal agent, since "it bars not-being absolutely and confers being entire upon the entity in question,"[144] and this is what the philosophers understand by creation *ex nihilo*.

The theological implications of this subtle distinction between the coming-to-be (*ḥudūth*) and production, as applied to the world as a whole, are not far to seek. The Muslim theologians, following the lead of John Philoponus, as we have seen, rested their case for the existence of God on the temporal determination of the world—on the fact that, prior to its creation, the world was not. Emphasizing the incoherence of this view, Ibn Sīnā observes that not only is this circumstance far from surprising, since a thing could not come into being unless it had not been previously, but, what is more, the action of the

[142] Ibn Sīnā, *al-Shifā'*, p. 261. [143] *Ibid.*, p. 264. [144] *Ibid.*, 266.

agent (God) upon the world would, on this assumption, cease as soon as the world came into being. Likewise, the fact that its being was preceded by not-being is only an accident, consequent upon its nature as a created object rather than upon the activity of its Creator, and it is obvious that the Creator can "operate on the being, which the patient derives from it, rather than the not-being preceding it."[145] Indeed, the agent can have no influence whatsoever upon the former, and whether eternal or not, that is, whether it has a beginning in time or not, the world would still depend on its author for the being belonging to it. If noneternal, then it would depend upon an author for its inception as well as its perdurance.

Between the efficient cause and its effect, argues Ibn Sīnā, there must be a certain correspondence or porportion. Thus, to the action issuing from the agent there must correspond a disposition or susceptibility in the patient for the reception of the action, and the two together—the action and the susceptibility—will determine the degree as well as the mode of the action in question. However, a fundamental difference between the effect and the cause should be noted. This is the dependence upon its own cause of the effect for the being of which it is susceptible. Such being does not belong to the effect per se, or else it would not stand in need of the agency of the cause at all, would not be an effect or caused entity either. The cause, on the other hand, might be either possible or necessary, but in neither case does it depend on its own effect. From this it would follow that the cause is ontologically prior to the effect, and as such is more preeminent in the degree of reality. Hence, if absolute being is predicated of an entity, such an entity would be tantamount to the most real being (*ens realissimum*). In so far as it imparts reality to other things, such an entity would be the truth per se, and the science concerned with investigating its nature would be the science of absolute truth or, alternatively, the absolutely true science.[146]

The consideration of the remaining three causes forms part of this "absolute science" as well. The material cause, with its diverse connotations ranging from the prime matter in relation to form in general, to the unit in relation to number, or wood in relation to the bed, etc.,

[145] Ibn Sīnā, *al-Nājāt*, p. 213. [146] Ibn Sīnā, *al-Shifā'*, p. 278.

is reducible to the principle of potentiality or receptivity, proximate or ultimate. Form, on the other hand, corresponds to the principle of actuality or fulfillment. Material forms inhere in matter and impart actual being to it. Immaterial forms are entirely divested of matter. Accidents, motions, species, genera, *differentiae*, as well as the figures of artifacts, are designated as forms as well.[147] Even art, in so far as it inheres in the mind of the artisan, may be referred to as form, in relation to its object.

The final cause is defined as "that for the sake of which" the action is done. As such, it might be predicated of the agent, the patient, or something different from both.

Ibn Sīnā observes that some have denied the reality of final causes, either on the ground that every such cause must have a cause, or that what happens in the world happens purely fortuitously. Chance events, however, are not fully undetermined and caprice in voluntary actions involves purpose, which may be identified either with the imagined or rational good toward which the will of the agent tends, or with something objective outside the agent.

The infinity of the series of final causes, on the other hand, does not prejudice their reality. For in final causation we should distinguish between the existence of the individual and the possible progression of the series ad infinitum, as a condition thereof. In the universal teleology of nature, the existence of the individual is purely fortuitous or accidental, but not the fulfillment of the grand designs of nature, which may depend on an infinite series of conditions, but only accidentally. Since the real purpose of nature is the survival of the species, the succession of individuals might go on forever while remaining incidental to that purpose.[148]

Although analogous to the other three causes, the final cause enjoys a certain preeminence. In the conception of the agent, it is prior to the other causes, since they are conceived subsequently to it. It is also prior in point of definition, since it enters into the definition of the other causes.[149]

The problems of unity and plurality in their Pythagorean-Platonic context and the Aristotelian concept of the convertibility of being and

[147] Ibn Sīnā, *al-Shifā'*, p. 282. [148] *Ibid.*, p. 290. [149] *Ibid.*, p. 293.

unity are next discussed at some length. Ibn Sīnā, however, is critical of the Platonic doctrine of Ideas as the *summa genera* of things, which subsist on their own eternally and which are the prototypes of particulars. The chief fallacy of this doctrine, according to him, consists in the contention that whatever can be conceived (namely, the universal) apart from its concomitants (namely, the particular embodiments of it) can exist apart from them, whereas only through abstraction from such concomitants do we arrive at the concept of their prototype.[150] Moreover, when we predicate unity of the universal, we do not mean that it actually inheres in all particulars which partake of it, but rather that it has the potentiality to inhere in numerous substrata disposed to receive it; while remaining numerically one, therefore, it is potentially multiple.[151]

The discussion of the problem of unity and plurality leads logically to the discussion of the First Principle of Being, who is supremely one. Aristotle had made of this "principle upon which the heavens and the world of nature depend,"[152] the supreme object of metaphysical thought. Plotinus had raised it so far above the planes of thought and being that it is portrayed in his system as the sidereal center from which all light shines forth and all being emanates. In the koranic view of God, an immense gulf separates the Being "unto whom nothing is like" and the multiplicity of creatures He has, by his sheer fiat, brought forth.

For Ibn Sīnā, the essential characteristic of this Being, who rises above the world of contingent entities, is necessity. The proof of its existence is logically bound up with this characteristic, since however long the series of contingent entities in the world might be it must terminate ultimately in a necessary principle upon which this series depends. Otherwise it would not be a contingent series.[153]

In this proof, Ibn Sīnā observes, we are concerned with the first, efficient cause of the series, who stands to it in an essential, generic relation rather than an accidental or individual one. Otherwise it would be possible for the series to go on ad infinitum, both in the past and into the future. Thus the generation of an individual son by an

150 Ibn Sīnā, *al-Shifā'*, p. 315. 151 *Ibid.* 152 *Met.* XII. 1072b14.
153 Ibn Sīnā, *al-Shifā'*, pp. 327 f.; *al-Nājāt*, pp. 235 ff.

individual father, or a series of particular motions succeeding one another, can go on ad infinitum. Where the relation is one of essential dependence, it cannot.[154]

Nevertheless, the same reasoning can be applied, according to Ibn Sīnā, both to the formal and the final causes of such a series. The infinite regress would nullify the meaning of the very concept of a *final* cause, as the entity who determines that series teleologically and gives it completeness. And the unity and order of the *formal* cause, as the pattern of the development or growth of an entity, would be radically jeopardized.[155]

Although necessity is the chief mark of the Supreme Being, it is not, according to Ibn Sīnā, its only distinguishing mark. Its second major characteristic is absolute unity. Such a unity excludes every mode of composition, including the composition of essence (*māhiyah*: *quidditas*) and existence, since only entities which are contingent can admit of such composition, in so far as existence belongs to them by virtue of their dependence upon their cause, rather than by virtue of their own essence. Hence such entities are at once caused, composite, and contingent; the attribute of being therefore belongs to them not essentially or per se, but rather *per accidens*. The Necessary Being, on the other hand, does not depend on any other agent or being. Its existence is part of its very essence or definition.[156]

Having no distinct essence, the Necessary Being has also no genus and no *differentia*. Now an entity of this kind is indefinable and indemonstrable[157] and neither its being nor its action can be an object of discursive thought, since it is without cause, quality, position, or time. Furthermore, it is without equal. For only if it were assumed to share in some quality or perfection pertaining to other entities as well, could it be said to bear some similitude to other beings. This is ruled out,

[154] *Al-Shifā'*, p. 331. [155] *Ibid.*, p. 341. [156] *Ibid.*, p. 346.

[157] *Ibid.*, p. 348. In the sequel, the author states that "it admits of no apodeictic proof, since it is the proof of all things and is manifested clearly in so many ways" (*ibid.*, p. 354). This statement is at variance with the express attempt to demonstrate it, as just outlined, and with the view expressed earlier that the existence of the Necessary Being is not the object of metaphysics, but one of its primary *problems*, in so far as metaphysics, rather than any other science, is concerned with establishing this existence (*ibid.*, p. 6, and *infra*, p. 324 for Ibn Rushd's Critique).

however, by its simplicity, namely, the impossibility of any composition in it, including that of subject and predicate. In short, concludes Ibn Sīnā, apart from existence (*al-anniyah*) the Necessary Being should be characterized negatively, through the exclusion of all similitude to other beings, and positively through the assertion of all relations pertaining to them: "For everything derives from it, but does not share with it [in anything], and it is the source of all things, without being any one of the things posterior to it."[158]

The last statement brings out clearly the Plotinian character of this conception of the Supreme Being, to whom all perfection belongs, but who, like the One of the *Enneads* and the Demiurgus of the *Timaeus*, is the fount of all being and goodness in the world and is indeed being and goodness entire. For since being or the perfection of being is what is universally desired, the Necessary Being to whom being belongs essentially and who is not susceptible of any privation or not-being, will not only be good, but will be the absolute good as well.[159]

From another standpoint, the Necessary Being can be shown to be pure reason. Whatever is free from imperfection, especially the imperfection of potentiality or materiality, must be a pure form. For matter is the bar to "formal" or "intelligible" being, namely, "the being which once it is predicated of anything, this being becomes a reason,"[160] either in a potential or in an actual sense. In the latter case such a being is both the subject and object of its own cognition, since there is no material bar to its becoming an object of thought. Consequently the Necessary Being is at one and the same time the act, subject, and object of thought or the substance, act, and object of Reason.

The act of self-cognition, observes Ibn Sīnā, need not introduce any duality into the nature of this absolutely unique being. In thought, whatever is pure or immaterial is both agent and patient, since it is not hindered by any material impediment. Nor does it require an extraneous agency to bring about that condition of immateriality or abstractness which is the sign of both intellectuality and intelligibility.[161]

The mode and object of the divine cognition, however, raises a difficulty that loomed large in the philosophical and theological

158 *Al-Shifā*, p. 354. 159 *Ibid.*, pp. 355 f. 160 *Ibid.*, p. 356.
161 *Ibid.*, p. 358.

controversies of the tenth and eleventh centuries. Like Ibn Sīnā, Aristotle had identified the object of divine thought with the divine essence and had reduced the supreme act of divine thought to one of self-contemplation. Driven by the force of the dialectic of divine perfection, he was compelled to rule out the possibility of any intellectual commerce on the part of the Supreme Being either with the imperfect world of generation and corruption, or with the supermundane world of the heavens. "For there are even some things which it is better not to see than to see,"[162] he states with a melancholy sense of finality, in his desire to spare this Being the indignity of vulgar curiosity.

For the Muslim philosopher, such a conception, so radically at variance with the koranic view of an omniscient and omnipresent God, could hardly be endorsed without qualification. Ibn Sīnā's Necessary Being, however, is only partially released from the fetters of this rigid solipsism or narcissism. Despite its total independence of anything outside it or other than it, it apprehends, in the very act of self-apprehension, whatever has emanated from it, namely the "higher entities" of the heavenly sphere and the lower entities of the sublunary world. The mode of this apprehension is explicitly stated to be universal, since it does not befit the Necessary Being to partake, without prejudice to its perfection, of that particular mode of cognition which belongs to finite knowers.

What this universal mode of cognition involves specifically is the cognition of the primary causes of particulars, as Ibn Rushd was later to demonstrate. For, since particulars result from their cause necessarily, "the First Being, who knows these causes as well as their consequences, will know necessarily what results from them, so that He would apprehend particulars, in so far as they are universal."[163]

The origination of the universe is described as an eternal procession, or emanation. It is impossible that any change, whether it be an act of willing, intention, or capacity, should supervene upon it without prejudice to its immutability and perfection; and even a new relationship to an entity previously nonexistent, such as the creation of the world at a given moment, would involve change in its essence.[164]

[162] *Met.* XII. 1074^{b}32. [163] Ibn Sīnā, *al-Shifā'*, p. 360. [164] *Ibid.*, p. 380.

This process of emanation is bound up with the act of self-apprehension previously outlined. In so far as it apprehends itself both as the pure act of thought and the origin of all contingent entities in the world, the Supreme Being without any intermediary whatsoever generates the whole Creation and the order that permeates it. Neither will, intention, or any other form of passion or affection is involved in this process of generation, but only the act of apprehending itself as the cause and origin of all things.[165] This necessary correlation between thinking and doing is a unique prerogative of this Being, and therein lies its ability to dispense with all the other conditions, including the condition of time, without which neither voluntary nor natural agents can generate any of their effects.

The first entity to result from this act of generation is the first intellect, who moves the outermost heavenly sphere and is, like its author, numerically one. Unlike this author, however, it is multiple, in so far as the act of its own apprehension involves a certain duality. For it apprehends itself in so far as it is contingent in itself, and in so far as, through its author, it is necessary.

In addition to this act of self-apprehension, however, the first intellect is also engaged in the contemplation of its supreme author or principle. In apprehending itself as necessary through this author, it generates the Soul of the outermost heaven. In apprehending itself as contingent in itself, it generates the body of this heaven, and in apprehending its author it generates the second intellectual substance in the series. This process is then repeated until we come to the tenth intellect, which concludes the series and dominates the nethermost sphere, namely, that of the sublunary world in which we live.

The four elements that make up the generable and corruptible entities of this netherworld result from a common matter, which is differentiated through the action of the heavenly bodies. The substantial forms of these entities, however, are derived from of the last the intellectual substances or active intellect (*al-ʿaql al-faʿʿāl*), once their matter has become disposed for their reception, either through the natural processes of motion or growth in the world, or through the supernatural processes upon which the heavenly bodies preside.[166]

[165] Ibn Sīnā, *al-Shifāʾ*, p. 403. [166] *Ibid.*, pp. 410 f.

A mystical strain in Ibn Sīnā's thought, which had remained latent in his earlier and more speculative writings, appears in *al-Ishārāt* and a group of highly pictorial treatises, such as *Ḥayy b. Yaqẓān*, *The Bird*, *On Love*, *On Prayer*, and *On Fate*.[167] These works shed considerable light on this important aspect of his philosophy. Whatever the difficulties his so-called Oriental philosophy raises, we have in these treatises and in a famous *Ode on the Soul* a dramatic instance of the intricate texture of the Greek, Hellenistic, Islamic, and Persian ideas that make up the fabric of the thought of this encyclopedic genius.

Perhaps the most striking feature of Ibn Sīnā's mysticism, whatever its relationship to his general theory, is the sudden change in idiom and tone that sets it apart from his other Peripatetic writings. Even the extant logical part of the *Oriental Philosophy* bears this out to some extent. The allegorical idiom of some of these treatises and the *Ode on the Soul* reveal an obvious preoccupation with the problem of philosophical expression, which Plato himself betrays in the highest flights of his philosophical fancy. This preoccupation, both in Plato and Ibn Sīnā, involves more than the special problem of the use of allegory or myth. It is the outward expression of a spirit of dissatisfaction with the discursive forms of philosophic exposition and the urge to transcend or bypass them by evolving a new idiom that is more consonant with the Soul's vision or aspiration because it is more elusive and less direct.

In the allegory of *The Bird* he graphically portrays the destiny of the Soul, in its quest for truth, caught up in the meshes of sense (symbolized by a net).[168] In some of its aspects, the symbolism of this allegory is reminiscent of Plato's, whether in the allegory of the cave or the sevenfold ladder of love. It is difficult, however, to determine whether the imitation is deliberate or not.

In another mystical work, however, the *Ode on the Soul*, we can see an unmistakable influence of the *Phaedrus* on Ibn Sīnā's conception of the descent of the Soul into the "wilderness" of the body and its eventual release from its fetters through knowledge. Having been ensnared by a group of hunters and locked up in a cage, the Souls of mortals, like a swarm of captive birds, refuse to accept fate and struggle

[167] Mehren, *Traités mystiques d'Avicenne*.

[168] *Ibid.*, pp. 42–48.

for release. Only a few of them, however, are fortunate enough to escape, with parts of their shackles still clinging to their claws. The others are left behind but are eventually rescued by their companions. They set out together in search of safety on the top of the eight-story Mountain of God. As they reach the seventh story they settle down to rest in the midst of green pastures and flowing streams. They are soon roused to a new sense of urgency and head for the eighth story, where they come upon a species of bird the like of which, in beauty, sweetness, and affability, they had never seen before. Before long, the bonds of friendship between them have grown so strong that the hosts are only too glad now to lead their guests to the city of the Great King, before whom they would lay their burdens. But as soon as their eyes fall on the radiant countenance of the King, they are infatuated. As they enumerate their grievances, the Great King listens sympathetically, promises them complete restitution of liberty, and bids them go in peace. And so they go, with the most vivid impression of that vision of beauty whose enjoyment brings supreme happiness, and the conviction that never again will they be able to feel quite at home in that "vale of sorrow" from which they originally came.

The same mystical note is struck in a treatise dealing more specifically with the favorite mystical theme of love, or *'ishq*,[169] and consisting (significantly enough from the standpoint of Platonic symbolism) of seven chapters. In the first three chapters the author dwells on the all-pervasive character of love, described as the urge to seek the good and cling to it, and to shun the evil of nothingness and materiality at every cost.[170] Even at the most elementary levels of material existence we encounter "an instinctive impulse which can never be disassociated from [love], since it is the cause of its coming into being."[171] In pure matter, this urge manifests itself in the persistence of its search for form and its desire to possess it. This is why we notice that, as soon as matter is divested of one form, it at once proceeds to acquire another, owing to the dread of nothingness with which it is continually seized.

At the higher levels of vegetable and animal life we observe that all the faculties of the animate entity are directed toward an activity or

[169] Mehren, *Traités mystiques d'Avicenne*, pp. 1–27. [170] *Ibid.*, p. 2.
[171] *Ibid.*, p. 6.

function determined by the same "instinctive love impulse." For all such functions are directed toward the preservation or propagation of the vegetable or the animal. In the beast, this love impulse is blind and all-compelling, whereas in man a certain element of discrimination is present, so that passion is subordinated to the higher pursuits of virtue, honor, or prosperity. The truly rational manifestation of human love, however, is to be found in the love of the pure forms. This love is the prerogative of the "divine Soul," as well as the separate intelligences or angels. The highest object of this love is God, the chief good, or, as previously designated, the Great King, who, in the abundance of his grace, freely reciprocates this love.[172]

In the third of this cycle of mystical treatises, *Ḥayy b. Yaqẓān*, which became, in the philosophical and mystical tradition, the prototype of the "solitary," the extramundane aspirations of the Soul are allegorically set out. Ḥayy, who is presented as a mystical globe-trotter, unburdens himself of a secret wisdom passed on by his father. The substance of this wisdom is an invitation to the earth-bound Soul to turn away from the gross pleasures of the body and to fix its gaze upon that ultimate source of beauty and light whose dazzling brilliance has shut it from view, so that its "beauty had become the veil which conceals its beauty—and like the sun, which is amply manifest only when it sets,"[173] can be only dimly perceived while it shines with such magnificence.

Despite his transcendence, however, this King communicates his beauty and splendor to his subordinates and accords them the privilege of communing with him. He is most gracious and good, and, once a glimpse of his beauty is caught, the beholder can never be parted from him.

In this allegory it will be noticed that the light imagery, a favorite of Neo-Platonism and mysticism, is used to illustrate the doctrine of emanation. The category of goodness as a predicate of the Supreme Being, so radically emphasized in Ibn Sīnā's writings on metaphysics, is relegated to some extent to the category of beauty, which plays such a central role in the mystical-speculative attempts to describe figuratively the ineffable reality toward which the Soul tends. The passion,

[172] Mehren, *Traités mystiques d'Avicenne*, p. 26. [173] *Ibid.*, p. 21.

which moves it to seek union with this reality, is assimilated to human love (*'ishq*).

To this light imagery, which is probably of hermetic and gnostic origin,[174] should be added the equally rich symbolism of the East, home of light, and the West, home of darkness. The mentor of Ḥayy depicts in glowing colors the glory of the East, in which the Soul, a "stranger" in this "wilderness" of generation and corruption, finds its liberation or salvation and invites Ḥayy to turn away from this world and "follow him if he would."

Apart from the mystical allegories, the Oriental philosophy of Ibn Sīnā is embodied in the *Book of Allusions and Admonitions* (*Kitāb al-Ishārāt*) and the fragments from his lost work, *al-Inṣāf*, commenting on the treatise known as Aristotle's *Theologia*. In the former book, Ibn Sīnā's more mature personal thought is laid out better than in any other extant work. Even the idiom in which his thought is expressed differs to some extent from the more conventional language of *al-Shifā'* and the other Peripatetic works. The subject matter does not differ essentially from that of the latter writings except for what is added to it. Thus it falls into the categories of logic, physics, and metaphysics, together with a supplement dealing with the "disembodied" condition of the Soul and its destiny after death, the ranks of mystics, and the possibility of supernatural or preternatural phenomena such as divination, miracles, and sorcery.[175]

Of particular interest is Ibn Sīnā's account in the psychological part of *al-Ishārāt* of the persistence of the Soul's consciousness of itself and its identity throughout the changing cycle of psychic conditions and states, from dreaming to intoxication and sleep. This persistence is such that even if the Soul is supposed to have been suspended in the air, upon its creation, without any contact with the body or the external world, it would still be fully "unconscious of anything else except the fact of its existence."[176] In this act of self-awareness, the Soul apprehends its existence and its identity at once, without intermediaries. For it is not through sense or anything associated with sense, such as

[174] Corbin, *Avicenne et le récit visionnaire*, Tome I, pp. 19 f., 144 f., *et passim*.
[175] Ibn Sīnā, *al-Ishārāt wa'l-Tanbīhāt*, Pt. 4, pp. 882 f.; cf. *Fi'l Fi'l wa'l-Infi'āl*.
[176] *Ibid.*, Pt. 2, p. 320.

bodily motion or affection of any kind, that the Soul achieves this self-awareness. Instead, the Soul itself is the ground of all the motive, cognitive, or vital functions we associate with it, and as such is logically prior to all these functions. Hence "this entity which remains one and the same is truly you" and is diversified through the various functions of the body which attest to its existence.[177]

The similarity of this concept of the identity and unity of the Soul to the Cartesian *cogito* has been noted by many scholars. Some have even gone so far as to assert a historical link between Descartes and Ibn Sīnā.[178] Be this as it may, the Aristotelian and Neo-Platonic basis of the concept is unmistakable. Both Aristotle and Plotinus had insisted on the unity or identity of the Soul and the fact that, in its inner and outer functions, motive and cognitive, it is diversified purely accidentally. This is particularly apparent in the Arabic recension of parts of Plotinus' *Enneads* designated as the *Theologia* of Aristotle, in which this diversification is ascribed to the Soul's association with the body.[179] Plurality belongs essentially to the body, unity to the Soul. In so far as during its earthly career the Soul stands in dire need of the body, which is its instrument, it has become diversified through the diversity of the bodily functions or faculties, indispensable to its actualization or self-fulfillment.[180] But it does not on that account lose the essential character of unity, which belongs to it.

In *al-Ishārāt* a certain stress is placed on the problem of intuitive knowledge, of which the act of self-awareness is an instance. Discursive thought is described as the process of arriving mediately (through the intermediary of the middle term or its equivalent) at the knowledge of matters not previously known to us. Intuitive thought, on the other hand, is described as the act of apprehending this middle term at once, whether as a result of prolonged search or not, together with its relation to the minor and major terms in a syllogism.[181] The capacity for intuitive thought, like the capacity for reflection, varies from person

177 Ibn Sīnā, *al-Ishārāt wa'l-Tanbīhāt*, pt. 2, p. 332; cf. *al-Shifā'*, Physics, Pt. 1, p. 281.

178 See, e.g., Furlani, "Avicenna e il Cogito Ergo Sum di Cartesio," *Islamica*, Vol. 3 (1927), pp. 53 ff.

179 See *supra*, p. 35; Henry, *plotini opera*, II, 63 f.; Aristotle, *De Anima* I. 411^{a}–24^{f}.

180 Commentary on the Theologia in *Arisṭū 'ind al-'Arab* (ed. Badawi), I, p. 54.

181 Ibn Sīnā, *al-Ishārāt*, Pt. 2, pp. 368 f.

to person. The acuteness of this power is ultimately bound up with the ability to apprehend the intelligible forms, which are the proper objects of knowledge.

These intelligible forms, which inhere in the particular objects of sense prior to their apprehension through the process of abstraction, have an extrasensuous and extramundane locus, i.e., the active intellect. In so far as this intellect is entirely separate from body, its apprehension is not susceptible to change or decay, to which the subordinate faculties of memory, imagination, and estimation (*al-wahm*) are subject. These faculties simply abstract the "material forms" from their particular substrata and store them away until such time as they are conjured up by one or the other of the cognitive faculties of memory, imagination, or reflection. The active intellect, as the store of these forms, overflows with the appropriate forms as soon as the Soul has become prepared for their reception through the foregoing process.

Described as emanation in relation to the active intellect, this process of intellectual discovery or enlightenment may be understood as "contact" (*ittiṣāl*), in relation to the individual Souls seeking to achieve it.[182] The "ultimate agency" which initiates this process in man is called by Ibn Sīnā the material intellect, which is to the active intellect what prime matter is to the pure form, or pure potentiality to the Pure Act. The "proximate agency," on the other hand, is the habitual intellect, which differs from the former in that it has attained the stage of partial actualization at the behest of the Soul as it turns toward the "source of illumination" (*ishrāq*),[183] or active intellect. When this stage has been attained, the Soul would have passed beyond the world of generation and corruption and entered upon that supermundane career with which its ultimate bliss is bound up, and which consists in the contemplation of and love for the First Principle of all things, who enjoys the everlasting bliss of self-contemplation.[184] The active intellect as an emanation from this First Principle serves in this process simply as a subordinate link in the chain of being, linking man to his Maker and Goal.

[182] Ibn Sīnā, *al-Ishārāt*, Pt. 2, p. 375.
[183] *Ibid.*, p. 377; Pt. 3, p. 674.
[184] *Ibid.*, Pt. 4, pp. 782 f., 810 f.

CHAPTER FIVE

Neo-Pythagoreanism and the Popularization of the Philosophical Sciences

I

PHILOSOPHY, THE HANDMAID OF POLITICS

THE interest of the Arabs in Pythagoreanism was the direct product of the Alexandrian or Hellenistic influences already discussed.[1] However, the obsession of Muslim thinkers with the problem of unity contributed in large measure to their progressive adoption of the Pythagorean metaphysics of number, in so far as it reserved to the One, like Neo-Platonism, a preeminent status at the apex of reality. Mathematical and astronomico-astrological considerations, on the one hand, and moral religious preoccupations, on the other, contributed likewise to the diffusion of Pythagoreanism in philosophical circles. Even metempsychosis, the boldest feature of Pythagoreanism, was professed by such outstanding philosophers as al-Rāzī.

[1] *Supra*, p. 32 f.

In general, the peculiar blend of mysticism and science so characteristic of Pythagoreanism made a decisive impact upon a large section of opinion in Islam that had come under the influence of Hellenic and Hellenistic thought. This blend satisfied the bipolarity in Muslim thought, torn as it was between Greece and the Orient, and pointed the way to the resolution of the intellectual and spiritual tensions this bipolarity generated.

Moreover, the esoteric character of Pythagoreanism harmonized with the Oriental spirit of withdrawal from the world, as well as the urge to seek security in the inner fort of the Soul during this era of severe political and social upheavals. The tenth century, it will be recalled, witnessed not only the most brilliant intellectual and scientific achievements in the history of Islam, but also the gradual breakup of the political unity of the Muslim empire and the eclipse of that splendor that was characteristic of the reign of the early Baghdad caliphs. The vast expanse of territory that was once the exclusive domain of a single and sovereign caliph whose decrees ran from the Indus to the Atlantic was now dotted with small principalities governed by various rulers: the Ṣaffarids in Persia (867–908), the Samānids in Transoxiania and Persia (874–979), the Ghaznawids in Afghanistan and the Punjab (962–1186), and the Buwayhids (946–1055), who for the first time insured the hegemony of the Shī'ite element in Islam, and the Turkish Saljūks (1055–1194), who superseded them and, through their policy of religious intolerance, ushered in the Crusades in 1096.[2] In Egypt and Spain, the authority of the Baghdad caliphate had been so successfully challenged that two rivals, the Fāṭimids of Egypt (909–1171) and the Umayyads of Spain (912–1031), were set up by the beginning of the tenth century.

It was during the reign of the Buwayhids that a secret philosophico-religious society who styled themselves the Brethren of Purity (*Ikhwān al-Ṣafā*) arose at Baṣrah. Issuing from the ranks of the Ismā'īlī, heterodox Shī'ite subsect who had been engaged in secret political propaganda ever since the death of their *Imām*, Ismā'īl, in 760, the Brethren of Purity continued the secret propagandist activity of the early

[2] Hitti, *History of the Arabs*, pp. 461 f.

Ismā'īlī, and especially Qarmaṭian, *dā'īs*,[3] but injected into it a new scientific and philosophical spirit.

According to the oldest Arabic tradition, contained in al-Sijistānī's *Vessel of Wisdom* (*Ṣuwān al-Ḥikmah*) (tenth century) and reproduced by later authors,[4] the active core of the Brethren of Purity, who are responsible for fifty-two philosophical epistles and a compendium, consisted of Abū Sulaymān al-Bustī (known as al-Muqaddasī), Abu'l-Ḥasan al-Zanjānī, Abū Aḥmad al-Nahrajūrī (alias al-Mihrajānī), al-'Aufī, and Zaid b. Rifā'a. According to al-Sijistānī, these formed "a group of scholars who met and composed the *Epistles* of the Brethren of Purity, the actual words being al-Muqaddasī's."[5]

Those epistles formed an encyclopedia of the philosophical sciences current among the Arabs in the tenth century, in which mathematics and astrology occupied a primary position. Before long, apparently, they circulated throughout the whole Muslim world, and the Spanish astronomer al-Majrīṭī (d. ca. 1008) or his disciple al-Kirmānī (d. 1066) is said to have been responsible for importing them into Spain from the East, together with other Arabic and Greek manuscripts.[6]

The composition and aims of this politico-religious society may be gathered from the account contained in Epistle 44, entitled "The Creed of the Brethren of Purity," where it is stated that the Brethren are a group of fellow-seekers after truth, who are held together by their contempt for the world and its allurements and their devotion to truth, whatever its origin; and that theology, or the "divine science," is their primary concern.

Their organization is described as communal or fraternal. The initiates of this society are urged to cling to each other through thick or thin, to assist and support each other in worldly as well as spiritual matters, and to be on their guard against association with unworthy

[3] Hitti, *History of the Arabs*, pp. 444 f., and *Encyclopaedia of Islam*, art. Qarmaṭians.

[4] Koprülü Ms., No. 902, Fol. 129, and al-Bayhaqī, *Tārīkh Ḥukamā' al-Islām*, pp. 35 f. Also al-Qifṭī, *Tārīkh al-Ḥukamā'*, pp. 83 f., quoting Abu Ḥayyān al-Tauḥīdī (d. 1023), who invokes in turn the authority of the writer of *Ṣuwān al-Ḥikmah*; and 'Awa, *L'esprit critique des Frères de la Pureté*, pp. 23 f.

[5] Al-Bayhaqī, *Tārīkh Ḥukamā'*, pp. 35 f.

[6] Al-Qifṭī, *Tārīkh al-Ḥukamā'*, p. 243; 'Awa, *L'esprit critique*, pp. 19 f.; *Encyclopaedia of Islam*, art. al-Majrīṭī, and Istanbul (Raghip Pasha) Ms., No. 965, foll. 47–139 (1–92), where al-Majrīṭī claims explicitly to have composed the *Epistles of the Brethren*.

fellows. The membership of the society should be drawn chiefly from the ranks of the young, who are still fresh and eager and whose minds can be more readily formed, rather than from the old and decrepit, who are averse to all change or reform.[7] However, four grades or ranks are recognized as forming the progressive stages along the path of illumination upon which the Brethren are engaged:

1. The rank of the novitiate, open to those who have reached the age of fifteen and show keenness of understanding and purity of heart.

2. The rank of leadership, open to those who at the age of thirty have learned kindliness, shrewdness, and practical prudence in the management of public affairs.

3. The rank of magistracy or kingship, which belongs to those who are called upon to demand obedience, and, at forty, are assisted by the Divine Law.

4. The prophetic or "angelic" rank, which all the Brethren are called upon to seek at fifty and which is attended by the "visual perception of the truth" and the privileges of ascending to the "kingdom of heaven" and propinquity to God.[8]

To insure secrecy, the Brethren are urged to meet in a "private lodge" at "appointed times"—or, as it is laid down elsewhere, once every twelve days, wherever they can,[9] in order to engage in their cherished pursuit, i.e., the discussion of questions of psychology, mathematics, physics, astronomy, and especially theology and cognate subjects. In this endeavor, their motto is

> to shun no science, scorn any book, or to cling fanatically to no single creed. For [their] own creed encompasses all the others and comprehends all the sciences generally. This creed is the consideration of all existing things, both sensible and intelligible, from beginning to end, whether hidden or overt, manifest or obscure . . . in so far as they all derive from a single principle, a single cause, a single world, and a single Soul.[10]

[7] Ikhwān al-Ṣafā, *Rasā'il*, IV, 52. [8] *Ibid.*, pp. 57 f.

[9] Ikhwān al-Ṣafā, *al-Risālah al-Jāmi'ah*, II, 395.

[10] Ikhwān al-Ṣafā, *Rasā'il*, IV, 42.

II

THE MATHEMATICO-PHILOSOPHICAL PRESUPPOSITIONS OF THE BRETHREN

THE fifty-two epistles of the Brethren embody a peculiar Neo-Pythagorean, Neo-Platonic blend of physico-mathematical ideas. These ideas form the groundwork for an eclectic metaphysics of the most complex type, which they expounded in a more popular idiom than that of the professional philosophers.

These epistles fall into four groups: the mathematical (or didactic),[11] the physical, the psychological-intellectual, and the theological-juridical. The first of the fourteen mathematical epistles is said by the author to deal with number, its essence, quantity, and quality,[12] and to serve as a means of training in philosophy and a prelude to the study of the more advanced aspects of that science. For, he says, "the science of number is the root of the other sciences, the fount of wisdom, the starting point of all knowledge, and the origin of all concepts."[13]

The second epistle deals with geometry, the third with astronomy, the fourth with music, the fifth with geography (considered as a branch of mathematics), the sixth with "numerical, geometric, and harmonic ratios," the seventh and eighth with the theoretical and practical arts, and the ninth with the diversity of morals and its causes. Epistles ten through fourteen deal with the five divisions of Aristotelian logic, corresponding to the five treatises of logic that circulated among the Arabs: i.e., *Isagoge*, *De Categoriae*, *Peri Hermeneias*, *Analytica Priora*, and *Analytica Posteriora*. These epistles give the most cursory account of the subject matter of Aristotle's works, and, with the exception of a sixth term, the individual (*al-shakhṣ*),[14] which they add

[11] From Greek: *μανθάνω*. [12] Ikhwān al-Ṣafā, *Rasā'il*, I, 21. [13] *Ibid.*, p. 22.
[14] *Ibid.*, p. 395.

to Porphyry's five and which they may have borrowed from al-Kindī,[15] they make no original contribution to the analysis of logical concepts.

Not only the science of number but all the mathematical and alleged mathematical epistles (including ethical, artistic, and logical subjects) are represented as subservient to the higher practical and theoretical aims of philosophy and metaphysics.

The subject matter of the second, or physical, group (consisting of seventeen treatises) corresponds roughly to the physical treatises of Aristotle: *Physica* or *De Auditu* (*Samʿ al-Kiyān*), *De Caelo et Mundo*,[16] *De Generatione et Corruptione*, *Meteorologica*, *De Partibus*, and *De Sensu*, and includes such titles as the essence of nature (Epistle 6), mineralogy (5), botany (7), the nature of life and death (15), the nature of pleasure and pain (16), and even the transmigration and resurrection of the soul (14), the limits of man's cognitive ability (14), and the causes of the diversity of languages in the world (17).

The psychological-intellectual group opens with a treatise dealing with "the mental principles" according to the Pythagoreans (Epistle 1) and the Brethren (2). Next is broached the problem of the intellect (4), the nature of love, especially mystical love (6), the nature of resurrection (7), the number and variety of movements (8), of causes and effects (9), and of definitions and descriptions (10).

The juridical-theological group comprises eleven epistles, dealing with such questions as beliefs and creeds (1), the means of achieving communion with God through moral and spiritual purification (2), the creed of the Brethren and their common association (3 and 4), prophecy and its conditions (6), the actions of spiritual entities, jinnees, angels, and demons (8), the number of political constitutions (9), the providence or ordering of the world (10), magic, talismans, and finally the nature of angels, jinnees, and demons (11).

This summary of the philosophical sciences, as known to the Arabs

[15] Abū Rīda, *Rasā'il al-Kindī*, I, 126.

[16] The *De Mundo* is an apocryphal compilation of the first century A.D. which owes much to the Stoic Posidonius of Apamea, but which the Arabs took for a genuine Aristotelian work. See Ross, *Aristotle*, p. 11. In the Arabic tradition it is normally appended to the genuine *De Caelo*.

in the tenth century, is likened by the author to a garden of untold splendor,[17] whose "wise and generous owner" bids everyone to step in and help himself to its fruits and enjoy its "green shade." Few would indeed avail themselves of this opportunity, however, because of their skepticism or ignorance. In order to dispel their doubts, the owner displays samples of the garden's fruits and vegetables and so lures passers-by into coming in and partaking of the pleasures of the garden.

The *Epistles* are thus presented simply as a specimen of a hidden, and presumably richer and fuller, wisdom that should be disclosed to worthy neophytes only in part, so that once their appetite is whetted they might be introduced to the deeper and more secret instruction reserved for those who have already crossed the threshold of the garden. This partial disclosure of the secret wisdom of the Brethren displayed in the *Epistles*, could be construed as just an invitation to judge the splendor of what remains undisclosed, rather than the unwarranted divulging of occult knowledge.

As an illustration of the Pythagorean or Neo-Pythagorean sympathies of the Brethren, we might examine here some of their mathematico-philosophical presuppositions and, in particular, their ontological conception of number, in which they claim to follow Nicomachus[18] and Pythagoras, a "monotheistic sage who hailed from Ḥarrān."[19]

The "real one," which is synonymous with thing (*res*) as the most general or comprehensive term, is defined by the author of the *Epistles* as "that which has no parts at all, and being indivisible, is one in so far as it is indivisible."[20] The "figurative one," on the other hand, refers to any sum or collection of things that is spoken of as a unit, e.g., one hundred, one heap.

Number or multiplicity arises from the progressive addition of one,

[17] The simile of the garden is of some historical interest, since one of the Ismāʿīlī groups, the Assassins of Alamūt, later resorted to a similar expedient in their desire to lure initiates (Hitti, *History of the Arabs*, pp. 446 f.).

[18] Nicomachus of Gerasa (first century A.D.), like Jamblichus, developed the theological implications of Pythagoreanism, in a treatise entitled *Θεῶλογουμενα της ἄριθμητικης* (Sarton, *History of Science*, Vol. I), p. 360. An Arabic version ascribed to Thābit b. Qurra of his *Introduction to Arithmetic* (*'Αριθμητικη εἴσαγωγή*) has reached us; see W. Kutsch's edition (Beirut, 1959).

[19] Ikhwān al-Ṣafā, *Rasā'il*, III, 200. [20] *Ibid.*, p. 53.

which is said on that account to be the "first principle of number." Of the original integers, number four occupies a place all its own, not only in mathematics or arithmetic but also in the composition of the universe as a whole. For "most natural things have been created by God in fours," such as the four elements, the four primary qualities, the four humors, the four seasons, the four corners of the earth, etc. The reason for this is that God desired that natural entities should reflect or imitate supernatural entities, equally constituting a group of four entities: God, universal Reason, the universal Soul, primary matter.[21] Moreover, the relation of God to the multiplicity of particulars in the world corresponds to the relation of one to number in general, that of Reason to that of two, that of the Soul to that of three, and that of matter to that of four.

In order to appreciate this, it is necessary to consider how God first created, "from the light of His uniqueness," a simple substance called the active intellect, as he had created two from one by repetition, and then created the "universal and celestial Soul" from the "light of Reason"; matter from the "movement of the Soul"; and finally the multiplicity of things in the world from matter, through the intermediacy of Reason and Soul, in the same manner in which He created the first four integers by the repetition of one.[22] In this respect, God might be said to be the first principle of things, in exactly the same way as one is the first principle of number.

Next, the author of the *Epistles* expounds the specific properties of the various numbers. The property of one, as has just been said, is that it is the principle of number, of two is that it is strictly the first number and is the common denominator of all even numbers. The property of three is that it is the first odd number and the common denominator of one-third of all numbers, both odd and even. Four is the first square number, five the first circular or round, six the first complete, seven the first perfect, eight the first cubic, nine the first odd and the last integer, ten the first decade, and so on.[23]

[21] Ikhwān al-Ṣafā, *Rasā'il*, III, 53.

[22] *Ibid.*, pp. 54, 181, *et passim*. In the latter passage the writer speaks more explicitly in terms of creation, whereas in the former the terms "creation" and "production" are used.

[23] *Ibid.*, p. 56 f.

We need not concern ourselves here with the other properties of number. Suffice it to note that the author develops at great length Pythagorean and pseudo-Pythagorean conceptions bearing on the properties of numbers taken singly or in combination, in a manner which illustrates how these properties were viewed as essential or substantial characteristics of things. These characteristics arise not from our conception of number or our procedure in ordering it, but from the very nature of things to which number can be applied. As an instance of the arbitrariness with which such properties were evolved, we note that seven is called the perfect number because it arises from the addition of odd and even, since it is the total of the addition of the first odd number (3), to an even number (4), as well as the first even number (2) to an odd (5), and the principle of all number (1) to the "complete" number (6). Eight, on the other hand, is called cubic, because if its root, which is two, is multiplied by its square, which is four, the product is eight. It is also called the first solid number, because the solid is the product of a number of planes and the plane the product of a number of lines. For the simplest line consists of two parts, the smallest body of two planes, so that the smallest body (or solid) will consist of eight parts, one of which is the line, which consists of two parts. If we multiply the line by itself, this will give rise to the plane, which consists of four parts. If, on the other hand, we multiply the plane by one of its two sides, this will give rise to depth, so that the total will be eight.[24]

Despite this obsession with number and its properties, the author is careful to observe that the aim of the Brethren in the discussion of number is to demonstrate how the properties of number are the prototype of the properties of things, so that "whoever comprehends number, its laws, its nature, its kinds, species, and properties will comprehend the quantity of the various kinds of things and their species and the wisdom underlying their specific quantities and the reason why they are neither more nor less."[25] For God, the Creator of all things, being actually one in all respects, did not see fit to make all things either wholly one or wholly multiple, but decreed that they should be one, in respect of matter, multiple in respect of form. Moreover, He did not

[24] Ikhwān al-Ṣafā, *Rasā'il*, III, 58–59. [25] *Ibid.*, pp. 178–79.

deem it fit that all things should exist either in dyads or triads or decades, etc., but rather that they should correspond numerically to, and possess the properties of, the whole gamut of number to which they actually correspond.[26]

The other primary reason for this discussion of number is to provide a prelude to the knowledge of the Soul. For the study of number will inevitably reveal that the various numbers are so many accidents inhering in the Soul in the manner in which accidents inhere in substance generally. This knowledge of the Soul should prepare the ground for the highest knowledge of which philosophy is capable, i.e., the knowledge of God, since it is from the knowledge of the Soul, its origin, and its destiny in the life-to-come that the mind ascends to the knowledge of God, as it has been said:[27] "He who knows himself [his Soul], knows his Creator," or "He who knows himself best knows his Creator best."[28]

III

THE COSMOLOGY AND METAPHYSICS OF THE BRETHREN

THE interest of the Brethren of Purity in the mathematical sciences, in which they included arithmetic, geometry, astronomy, geography, music, logic, and even the arts and crafts, has been shown to be purely pragmatic. At every stage in the discussion the author of the *Epistles* reiterates the thesis that the study of mathematics is conducive to moral edification as well as intellectual insight, and that it serves primarily as a clue to the knowledge of the self, which is the pathway to the highest knowledge, i.e., the knowledge of God.

26 Ikhwān al-Ṣafā, *Rasā'il*, III, 178–79; see also I, 75 f.

27 By Muḥammad or 'Ali, the fourth caliph. This statement is especially underlined by the later mystics of Islam.

28 Ikhwān al-Ṣafā, *Rasā'il*, I, 76.

In the astronomical epistles, the author describes astronomy as the study of the heavenly bodies, which consist, according to him, of 1,029 "large bodies." Seven of these (i.e., the planets) are in constant motion and revolve in their respective spheres, which are described as "round, concave, and transparent bodies,"[29] arranged round each other like the layers of an onion, with the earth at the center. The lowest of these planets and the nearest to earth is that of the moon, whereas the farthest is that of Mercury, beyond which two more spheres are found: the sphere of the fixed stars (or firmament) and that of the Empyrean.

The diurnal motion of the empyrean from East to West, and again from West to East, accounts for the succession of day and night. This sphere is divided into twelve sections, which are the twelve signs of the Zodiac, and each sign is divided into thirty degrees. The succession of the seasons is bound up with the position of the sun in relation to these signs.

The sun lies halfway between the outermost sphere of the empyrean and the earth, which lies at the center of the universe. For "in so far as the sun is to the heavens what the king is to his kingdom, and the planets are to it what soldiers, auxiliaries, and subjects generally are to the king, and the spheres are like regions and the constellations like countries and the degrees and minutes like towns, it was enjoined by divine wisdom that it should be located at the center of the universe."[30] Altogether there are eleven spheres, which in consecutive order are: the empyrean, the firmament, the spheres of Jupiter, Saturn, Mars, the sun, Venus, Mercury, the moon, the atmosphere, and the earth.[31]

The diameter of the earth is estimated at 2,176 parasangs or 7,372 miles, that of the hollow sphere of the moon at 370922.5 parasangs, that of the sun at 200 times the diameter of the earth, that of Jupiter at 11,054 times as much, and that of the firmament at approximately 2,400 times.[32] The movement of these concentric spheres is ultimately induced by the all-enveloping movement of the empyrean heaven,

[29] Ikhwān al-Ṣafā, *Rasā'il*, I, 115. [30] *Ibid.*, II, 30.

[31] In the traditional cosmology of the Arab Neo-Platonists (e.g., Avicenna's), four spheres or, more accurately, balls or rings (singular: *kurah*), corresponding to the four elements, are interposed between the spheres of the moon and the earth as follows: fire, air, water, and earth.

[32] Ikhwān al-Ṣafā, *Rasā'il*, II, 31.

which derives its motion from the universal Soul, called on that account the Prime Mover. However, the movement of the spheres is not uniform, since their orbits are uneven. The fastest motion is that of the outermost sphere, which is completed in 24 hours, the slowest that of the moon, completed in $24\frac{6}{7}$ hours.[33]

The substance of the heavenly bodies is described by the *Epistles* as a "fifth nature" or quintessence, which sets them apart from other entities in the world of generation and corruption. Some characteristics pertaining to body are common to both, such as length, breadth, depth, cohesion, motion, shape, transparency, etc. Others, such as weight, moistness, change, rectilinear motion, belong to physical objects in the sublunary world only. The reason why those heavenly bodies are divested of weight or gravity is that they have been created by God from the beginning and made to cling to their proper places, whereas gravity is an attribute of objects that have been forced out of their natural places and are seeking to rejoin them.[34] In short, heavenly bodies are said by the "philosophers," according to the *Epistles*, to consist of a "fifth nature," simply in the sense that their motion is circular and that they are not, like physical objects, susceptible of generation and corruption, increase or decrease.

Physical objects are made up of the four elements, which give rise through the agency of the four primary qualities to the composite objects in this world, i.e., minerals, plants, and animals. Everything in the world, however, is ultimately reducible to two original substances, vapor and slime. When the sun and the planets cause water to evaporate, it turns into vapor or mist, and those two are converted in turn into cloud, which turns into rain; and the rain, upon mixing with earth, turns into slime or mud, which forms finally the substratum of minerals, plants, and animals.

At the lowest rung of creation we encounter the mineral kingdom, the highest strata of which are in contact with the vegetable kingdom, which is in contact likewise with the animal kingdom, culminating in man, who stands at the boundary between the angelic and animal orders and is God's vicegerent on earth. Minerals arise from the four elements by composition; plants on the other hand arise by assimilation,

[33] Ikhwān al-Ṣafā, *Rasā'il*, II, 35. [34] *Ibid.*, p. 47.

whereby they are capable of growth, like animals, which further have the capacity for sensation and locomotion, and, in the case of man, of speech and discrimination as well.[35]

Thus the three kingdoms are hierarchically ordered in such a way that the superior kind always presupposes and rises above the inferior. But, according to the Brethren, there is in addition a certain chronological order which they follow, amounting almost to an anticipation of Darwinian evolution. Thus plants precede animals in the order of their appearance in the world, since they are to them what matter is to form. Similarly the lower animals "have preceded the more perfect, at the beginning of creation, in so far as they take a shorter time to develop, compared with the more perfect, which take a longer time.... Moreover, sea animals have preceded land animals by a long stretch, because water came before earth, and the sea before dry land, at the beginning of creation."[36] The appearance of animals generally upon the globe must therefore have come after minerals, and prepared the ground for the appearance of man, for whose sake not only the animal kingdom but everything else beneath it were created.

Not only the various species, but also the organs of the more advanced animals are ordered hierarchically: each inferior organ is subordinated to the organ above it and contributes to its preservation or perfection. Thus the brain is the sovereign organ in man and the seat of thought, sensation, and memory. The heart, as the junction from which blood vessels branch out and the fount of vital heat in the animal, is the brain's subordinate or its auxiliary and is itself assisted by three subordinate organs, the liver, blood vessels, and the lungs.[37]

As one might expect from the Brethren, the multiplicity and diversity of such organs, as indeed of every feature of reality, are determined by the same universal law of number that governs everything in the world. The frame of the more advanced animals was divided by God into right and left, for example, in order to correspond to the first number (2) and to dual entities in the world at large. Similarly, it was made to possess two extremities and an intermediary part, in order to correspond to the first odd number (3) and to those things which are likewise constituted in three parts. The four humors, which determine

[35] Ikhwān al-Ṣafā, *Rasā'il*, II, 180. [36] *Ibid.*, p. 181. [37] *Ibid.*, pp. 189–90.

human character and temperament, correspond to the first square number, as well as to the four primary qualities and the four elements; the five senses to the first circular number (5) and the four elements plus the quintessence of the heavenly bodies. The twelve orifices of the body correspond to the twelve signs of the Zodiac, and so on.[38]

To carry this parallelism further the Brethren follow the Stoics in describing man as a microcosm. The body of man epitomized for them the universe as a whole. To the nine spheres that constitute the world correspond the nine organic substances forming the human body: bone, marrow, flesh, veins, blood, nerves, skin, hair, and nails; and these are arranged like the nine concentric spheres. To the twelve signs of the Zodiac, as we have seen, correspond the twelve orifices of the body: two eyes, two ears, two nostrils, two nipples, the mouth, the navel and the two eliminative canals. To the physical and spiritual powers of the seven planets there also correspond seven physical powers: attraction, grasping, digestion, impulsion, nutrition, growth, and representation; and seven spiritual powers: sight, hearing, taste, smell, touch, speech, and thought, each of which corresponds to one of the planets. To the four elements, i.e., fire, air, water, and earth, correspond the head, the breast, the stomach, and the belly, in view of the association between each one of those parts of the body and the corresponding element. Even the configurations of the globe as well as meteorological phenomena have a certain analogy to man's body; his bones are similar to mountains, his marrow to metal ores, his belly to the sea, his intestines to rivers, his veins to streams, his flesh to earth, his hair to plants, his breathing to the wind, his speech to thunder, his laughter to daylight, his tears to rain, his sleep to death, and his waking to rebirth.[39]

The other fundamental concepts upon which the physics of the Brethren rests are chiefly Aristotelian. The discussion of matter, form, place, and motion, with occasional refinements or subtleties, follows a familiar Aristotelian pattern. The existence of the void is ruled out on the well-known Aristotelian ground that the void, conceived as a place in which nothing is placed, involves a logical contradiction. Beyond the world as a whole, there is nothing either void or full,

[38] Ikhwān al-Ṣafā, *Rasā'il*, II, 197. [39] *Ibid.*, pp. 456–67.

contrary to the illusory representations of the imagination, which deludes us into positing another body beyond the outermost regions of the heavens. Whoever denies, in opposition to the truth attested by philosophy and revelation alike, that every created body is finite and that no physical body can exist beyond the world must bear the burden of the proof.[40]

IV

THE PSYCHOLOGY AND THE EPISTEMOLOGY OF THE BRETHREN

The problem of the formation and development of the embryo, and the influence of the heavenly conjunctions upon this process, was of especial interest to the Brethren. Here a good deal of astrological information is set forth, which appears to have been drawn from the astrological lore of tenth-century Islam.[41]

The growth of the infant culminates in the attainment of the age of Reason. If born under the sign of good fortune, its Soul eventually will discover its true vocation as an immaterial substance and will seek to rejoin its heavenly abode, "through the pursuit of wisdom in the Socratic manner, and the practice of asceticism in the Christian manner, coupled with devotion to the Muslim faith."[42] In this way, the cleansing of the Soul from the material accretions that may attach to it during its confinement in the body will be achieved, and it will consequently be able to perceive "those spiritual forms and luminous entities" which the purified Soul alone is able to perceive. So long as it is weighed down by the body and engrossed in its desires and pleasures, it will be unable to "ascend to the spheres and contemplate directly what lies there," or partake of that bliss which Hermes

[40] Ikhwān al-Ṣafā, *Rasā'il*, II, 28, 12 ff.

[41] *Ibid.*, pp. 417–55; III, 336–454; I, 147–53. [42] *Ibid.*, III, 8.

Trismegistus partook of and Aristotle,[43] Pythagoras, Christ, and Muḥammad bore witness to.[44] Likewise, upon quitting the body, it will be unable to be freed from its yoke or join "the angelic host" in heaven. Instead, it will remain hovering in the sky until the Day of Judgment and will be eventually dragged down by the "evil spirits" attending it back to the world of generation and corruption (which the author identifies with hell) and the "captivity of bodily existence."[45] Thus the author of the *Epistles* can adopt much of the Pythagorean doctrine of metempsychosis, couched in the pious language of mysticism and illustrated freely by koranic citations, without arousing the suspicions of his more orthodox co-religionists.

Man's chief clue to the knowledge of the world must be the knowledge of himself. Such knowledge is so undeniably prior to any other knowledge that seeking to know the world outside before mastering the knowledge of the world within is as foolhardy for a man as attempting to carry a thousand pounds while yet unable to carry a hundred, or to attempt to run while still unable to walk.[46] Psychology thus becomes for the Brethren the prelude to metaphysics and cosmology, as indeed to all learning. For man's consideration of his condition in the world will reveal to him, as Pascal later put it, that he falls in an intermediary position between the infinitesimally small and the infinitely large; his body is neither too large nor too small, the span of his life neither too long nor too short, his appearance upon the earth neither too early nor too late, his rank in the hierarchy of Creation neither too low nor too lofty, falling as he does halfway between the angels and the beasts,[47] his knowledge being intermediate between the total ignorance of the latter and the total apprehension of the former. Even in point of subject matter, his powers are neither infinite nor infinitesimal. For he can neither grasp the infinite in quantity, nor the infinitesimal in bulk,[48] nor perceive extremely dazzling colors, extremely sharp sounds, on the one hand, or the extremely dim or faint, on the other.

[43] Here the author quotes the *Theologia*. [44] Ikhwān al-Ṣafā, *Rasā'il*, I, 137 f.

[45] *Ibid.*, III, 7 f., 79 f., *et passim*. [46] *Ibid.*, p. 20. [47] *Ibid.*

[48] The negative does not appear in the text, but since the context requires one I have supplied it, assuming it has been lost from the original.

As one might expect, the author is not content to note those features of human knowledge, but draws from them the inevitable agnostic inference which Pascal also drew. Man's reason cannot encompass such vast concepts as God's majesty or His essence, the form of the universe as a whole, or the pure forms which have been divested from matter, because of their dazzling lucidity and purity.

Moreover, even less lofty truths are inaccessible to human intelligence. Thus man's senses can grasp the qualities of things in the state of completion but not in the process of development. For instance, man cannot grasp the origin of the universe or the cause of its coming-to-be, or account for the specific qualities and quantities of the myriads of objects both in the heavenly and the sublunary worlds, although he can easily comprehend those objects as they are actually given or presented to his senses. In such sublime matters, where man's reason or his senses are powerless to enlighten him, his only recourse is to defer to the prophets, who are the oracles of God, and to assent to their instruction unquestioningly, as they themselves have assented to the instruction of the angels, who are their mentors.[49]

It should not be inferred from this however, as some narrow-minded and reactionary theologians have claimed, according to the author, that the teaching of the prophets as embodied in the Holy Law (*al-Sharīʿah*) is necessarily incompatible with the subject matter of rational knowledge embodied in science and philosophy. The ultimate aim of philosophy and the Law alike is the "emulation of the Divinity, in proportion to human capacity,"[50] through the pursuit of knowledge and the practice of virtue, whereby the Soul can attain perfection and gain everlasting bliss.

Any differences that might arise between religion and philosophy are differences in method or approach, corresponding to the diversity of temperament or disposition proper to each Soul.[51] The more purified and unencumbered of its bodily attachments the Soul becomes, the more it will perceive the hidden meaning underlying Scripture, and its conformity with the data of rational knowledge in philosophy. Conversely, the Soul that is too engrossed in the body and its pleasures will be unable to rise above the literal or "overt" meaning of Scripture;

[49] Ikhwān al-Ṣafā, *Rasāʾil*, III, 23. [50] *Ibid.*, p. 30. [51] *Ibid.*

in consequence it will see in the pleasures and pains of hell and paradise, as depicted in the Koran, nothing but the gross bodily pleasures and pains of which it partook in the world. But this in effect is the "essence of that disbelief [*kufr*], error, ignorance, and blindness" which afflict those who are content with the outward or literal connotation of Scripture and who are unable to plumb its hidden or "covert" meaning.[52]

For the author of the *Epistles*, hell is understood as the "world of generation and corruption, which lies beneath the sphere of the moon," and paradise is "the abode of the spirits and the vast expanse of the heavens."[53] Once the Soul has attained the heavenly sphere, it will partake of everlasting bliss and will be forever rid of the tribulations and hardships to which the flesh is heir.

In fact, even before its dissassociation from the body, the Soul can partake of those moral and intellectual pleasures that are the portents of heavenly bliss beyond the grave, as well as those tribulations reserved for the Soul which has become a prey to the bestial desires of the flesh or has been swayed by false beliefs about God and the Last Day. As instances of those false beliefs which will lead to perdition, the author cites the (Christian) belief that God was killed at the hands of the Jews, the (Jewish) belief that He is a jealous and angry God, and the (Muslim) belief that He will order his angels on the Day of Judgment to cast the sinners and the infidels into a "ditch of fire" in which they will roast forever and will invite the pious to indulge in such gross bodily pleasures as the deflowering of virgins, the drinking of wine, the eating of flesh, etc.[54]

What justifies the use of the gross sensuous representations of hell and paradise in the Koran, according to the author, is the fact that the vulgar to whom it is addressed cannot be induced to seek the one and shun the other unless they are described in terms they can comprehend. Nevertheless, the Koran has not omitted altogether the use of abstract or spiritual representations of heaven and hell, which its more refined readers can grasp. In this manner the Koran caters to all classes, the vulgar, the less vulgar, and the elect. The Gospels, on the

[52] Ikhwān al-Ṣafā, *Rasā'il*, III, 62, 63.
[53] *Ibid., et passim*; cf. *al-Risālah al-Jāmi'ah*, I, 689 f.
[54] *Ibid.*, pp. 71 f.

other hand, speak of the blessedness of the life to come in purely incorporeal terms, because Christ addressed himself therein to a people whose intellects and characters had been refined by the reading of the writings of the prophets and the philosophers, unlike the Arabs, whom Muḥammad was addressing and who were untouched by the refinements of culture or revelation.[55]

V

CONCLUSION

THE perceptive reader will see that this remarkable philosophico-religious society of the tenth century was sympathetic to Shīʿite ideas and was disaffected from and discontented with the established political order.[56] And, like many Shīʿite theological groups, it subscribed to the Muʿtazilite view of free will and sought to moderate the claims of the more orthodox theologians who advocated an astringent predestinarianism, which left no scope for human initiative whatever. In so doing, however, it inadvertently flouted the cosmological presuppositions upon which its view of the world rested. These revolved round the concept of an all-embracing celestial providence in which earthly happenings were wholly dominated by superior forces emanating from the stars.[57]

Of particular interest to the historian of ideas is the attitude which the Brethren assumed toward other religious groups. At a time when doctrinal bigotry was so rife that each religious sect was convinced of its unquestioned monopoly on truth, those encyclopedists argued that religious differences stemmed from the accidental factors of race, habitat, or epoch, and in some cases even of personal temperament and make-up,[58] but did not necessarily affect the unity and universality of truth, which remains unmarred by such particularities or differences.

[55] Ikhwān al-Ṣafā, *Rasā'il*, III, 76 f. [56] *Ibid.*, IV, 33; III, 165, 308.
[57] *Ibid.*, III, 165 f., 498 f. [58] *Ibid.*, pp. 486 f., 431.

An illustration of this religious liberalism can be found in their approach to Christianity and their estimate of the validity of the Gospels. This validity, as is well known, is usually discounted by Muslim writers on the ground that the Koran, as the consummate embodiment of God's word, had rendered any other revelation superfluous. And although the Brethren follow most Muslim writers in representing Christ as the paragon of piety and holiness, they go one step further by quoting the canonical Gospels at length with tacit approval. Thus the crucifixion and resurrection of Christ, which the Koran declared to be an illusion, are alluded to in clearly affirmative terms, and Christ's travels and miracles as given in the canonical Gospels rather than the Koran are recounted at length and the appropriate spiritual lessons drawn from them.[59]

The philosophical world-view of the Brethren presented fundamentally the same character of emanationism and eclecticism that marked the other teaching of the Arab Neo-Platonists with a pronounced Neo-Pythagoreanism. The Plotinian tetrad of God, Reason, Soul, and Matter forms the metaphysical base upon which they erected the world and corresponds to the numerical tetrad from which all numbers and their properties are derived.[60] The universal Soul, however, plays a far more decisive role in their metaphysics than in the other Arab Neo-Platonic systems, which assign to Reason a primordial role as the agent or instrument through which God's creative designs are carried out. Despite their regard for Pythagoras, "the Sage," whom they do not tire of praising or paraphrasing, the Brethren are not loath to glean their teaching from every possible quarter, since their motto is to not leave any source of knowledge untapped and to encompass in their doctrine the positive aspects of all creeds.[61] Accordingly, not only Greek philosophy, but Persian and Indian scientific and literary lore, Jewish and Christian Scripture, both canonical and apocryphal, Ptolemaic and post-Ptolemaic astronomy, as well as a fair sprinkling of astrological and magical legends, are brought together in this massive, though often ill-organized, verbose, and repetitious compendium of Arabic learning in the tenth century. A puzzling feature of this

[59] Ikhwān al-Ṣafā, *Rasā'il*, IV, 28 f., 53, 74, 117, *et passim*; but compare III, 72.
[60] *Ibid.*, III, 203 f. [61] *Ibid.*, IV, 42, and *supra*.

compendium is that, despite the undoubted reliance of its writers on other Islamic philosophers and theologians, hardly any of them are mentioned by name, possibly in deference to the spirit of anonymity in which it was written. Thus al-Rāzī, who reflected definite Pythagorean sympathies; al-Kindī, whose concept of the creation of the world in time they made their own,[62] despite the fact that it was ill-suited to their Neo-Platonic purposes; the Mu'tazilah, whose view of free will they adopted, notwithstanding its obvious incompatibility with their astrological belief in the influence of the stars on earthly phenomena, etc., are not explicitly mentioned by the author or authors of this compendium.

Once all this has been said, however, it must be noted that the Brethren occupy a unique position in the history of Islamic thought. Unlike the professional philosophers, from al-Kindī to Ibn Rushd, or the theologians, from Wāṣil to al-Ash'arī, the Brethren sought earnestly to break down the barrier between philosophy and dogma and to bring metaphysics and science from the inaccessible heights of pure speculation down to the market place of active, practical concern. It was their view that there were three classes of beliefs: those fit for the elect, those fit for the masses, and those fit for both. The third of these, however, was the most commendable, according to them, since it was rooted in reason, supported by Scripture, and accordingly was accessible to all classes of seekers after truth.[63]

[62] Ikhwān al-Ṣafā, *Rasā'il*, III, 461, 452, *et passim*.

[63] *Ibid.*, pp. 452 f.

CHAPTER SIX

The Diffusion of Philosophical Culture in the Tenth Century

I

ABŪ ḤAYYĀN AL-TAUḤĪDĪ

ALTHOUGH the towering reputations of al-Fārābī and Ibn Sīnā tend to eclipse minor, although still significant, exponents of Neo-Platonism in the tenth and early eleventh centuries, a few disciples of Ibn Sīnā should be noted. Ibn al-Marzubān (Bahmaniyār), one of his better-known followers, wrote a three-part compendium of his master's philosophy called *al-Taḥṣīl*,[1] dealing with logic, physics, and metaphysics. It lacks originality, however, and despite its lucidity it holds little interest for the student of philosophical ideas in Islam. A peculiarity of this treatise is the unconventional arrangement of its topics, as illustrated by the relegation of physics to metaphysics. Other disciples of Ibn Sīnā, such as al-Kirmānī, al-Maʿṣūmī, and Ibn Zaila, left no written works or else their works have disappeared, so we can do no more than just mention their names.

[1] Koprülü Ms. 863; Vatican, Arab Ms. 1411, and Cairo edition, 1329 A.H.

Of the more important authors of the period was the erudite litterateur Abū Ḥayyān al-Tauḥīdī (d. ca. 1023), who had considerable influence in literary and philosophical circles in the latter part of the tenth century. He was a disciple and friend of another important figure, Abū Sulaymān al-Sijistānī (d. 1000), whose Greek learning was vast, judging from the recension of his history of Greek-Islamic philosophy, *Ṣuwān al-Ḥikmah*, which al-Bayhaqī (d. 1070) made in the eleventh century.[2] Nicknamed the logician, al-Sijistānī is said to have written numerous commentaries on Aristotelian logic and related subjects,[3] but unfortunately none of these works has come down to us. In fact, with the exception of al-Tauḥīdī's account of his philosophical and logical views, we have no other clue to his thought except the cursory, if complimentary, references to him by the later historians of philosophy.[4]

Al-Tauḥīdī, who has already been mentioned in connection with the Brethren of Purity,[5] is better known for a group of literary-philosophical works; the most important, from a historical point of view, is *Kitāb al-Imtā'*, a series of nightly discourses on almost every literary and philosophical theme. This book, which has been described as a kind of philosophical *Arabian Nights*, is written in a more leisurely and ornate style than was customary among the philosophers, but was much less uncommon among the litterateurs of the tenth century.

Melancholy and bitter reflections on life in general, and the author's personal plight and miseries in particular, are typical of this literary-philosophical *genre* and indeed have their place in *Kitāb al-Imtā'*, but we are not concerned here with that portion of the work. What is particularly striking in this and other writings of al-Tauḥīdī is that, though far from being a systematic philosopher, he was remarkably well informed about philosophy. His comments on his contemporaries tend to be biting and sometimes even malicious, but are frequently quite pertinent and informative. His general estimate of many of them, from the translator Ibn Zur'a to the philosopher Miskawayh, who was his associate, is that they are either mercenary or hedonistic.[6]

[2] *Muntakhab Ṣuwān al-Ḥikmah*, Koprülü Ms. 902, etc.

[3] Al-Tauḥīdī, *al-Muqābasāt*, pp. 149 f. *et passim*.

[4] E.g., al-Qifṭī, *Tārīkh al-Ḥukamā'*, pp. 82 f.

[5] *Supra*, p. 186, Cf. *al-Imtā'*, II, 4–5.

[6] Al-Tauḥīdī, *al-Imtā'*, I, 33 f. *et passim*.

An instructive debate between Abū Bishr Mattā, the leading logician of his day, and Abū Sa'īd al-Sīrāfī, a grammarian and jurist of some standing at Baghdad, is recorded by al-Tauḥīdī and forms part of the proceedings of the Eighth Night. This debate was conducted in the presence of the vizier Ibn al-Furāt in the year 326 A.H. (A.D. 932) and was recorded by the author from an oral report.[7] Echoes of this debate can be heard in al-Fārābī's account of the relation of logic to grammar, which was discussed above.[8] The debate is charged with emotion, however, owing to the racial and religious tensions involved in the controversy. Abū Bishr is chided for his Greek bias, despite his ignorance of Greek (his logical translations were done wholly from Syriac), and he is reproached for his imperfect knowledge of Arabic. He does not counter this criticism; he is content to reply that, whereas grammar is concerned with words, logic is concerned with concepts, and these are unaffected by translation. "I am content to know enough of *your* language," he says, "to attain those objectives which Greece has refined."[9]

Mattā's major thesis that logic is a tool (*organon*) for distinguishing correct from incorrect usage is then countered by al-Sīrāfī's claim that this distinction is the prerogative of grammar. How could logic, invented by a Greek (namely, Aristotle), he asks, guard a Turk, an Indian, or an Arab against incorrect usage? Mattā's retort is that logic is concerned with the concepts underlying linguistic usage, and differences between ethnic groups are irrelevant on this score. Two plus two, for instance, equals four everywhere. Al-Sīrāfī observes, however, that the analogy between logic and this instance from arithmetic is misleading, for logical assertions do not attain the same degree of astringency as arithmetic. Moreover, the logician can never dispense with language altogether, so it would seem that one could not master grammar unless one masters the language in which logic was originally conceived, i.e., Greek. And this is a language of which his interlocutor was ignorant.[10]

[7] Al-Tauḥīdī, *al-Imtā'*, pp. 170 ff.; cf. *al-Muqābasāt*, pp. 68 f., and Margoliouth, "The Discussion between Abū Bishr Mattā and Abū Sa'īd al-Sīrāfī," in *Journal of the Royal Asiatic Society*, 1905, pp. 79–129.

[8] *Supra*, p. 131. [9] Al-Tauḥīdī, *al-Imtā'*, I, 115. [10] *Ibid.*, p. 111.

Al-Sīrāfī next proceeds to ask Mattā a series of grammatical questions, which he is unable to answer. He thus scores a rather hollow victory on an adversary whose ignorance of the intricacies of a notoriously complex language had been readily conceded earlier in the discussion. The more Mattā is unable to meet these linguistic challenges, the more self-assured al-Sīrāfī becomes. On one occasion, Mattā reminds his adversary that if he were subjected to the same cross-examination in logic, he would surely be as hopelessly confused as he himself had been in language. But al-Sīrāfī will not relent. Mattā and his fellow-logicians, he charges, have mutilated and corrupted the Arabic language by introducing terms and locutions entirely alien to that language. In addition, their exposition of logic is never complete or exhaustive, and their art, despite its lofty claims to be the arbiter of truth, has never settled any dialectical differences.

Needless to say, not only the vizier but also the audience felt exultant at the victory of the grammarian over the logician. Not only the Nestorian Mattā, but a fellow-Muslim philosopher of undoubted orthodoxy, al-Kindī, is finally drowned in the flood of ridicule with which the whole debate closes. The anti-Hellenic, antiphilosophical bias no doubt ran very high at this time, and linguistic, racial, religious, and political factors added to the vehemence with which issues of this kind were debated in public. This was, as we soon shall see, the period that witnessed the rise of the anti-Mu'tazilite school in theology, the Ash'arite, which was destined to dominate the theological scene for a long time to come.

The proceedings of the Seventeenth Night bear on another major controversy of the period, the relation of philosophy to Muslim dogma. In this connection, al-Tauḥīdī simply narrates the views of his master, al-Sijistānī, on a topical issue: the *Epistles of the Brethren of Purity*, which had just appeared.[11] Al-Sijistānī's, and, we may safely surmise, al-Tauḥīdī's, estimate of the attempts of the Brethren of Purity to combine Greek philosophy and Islamic dogma is that they are doomed to failure. Others more competent than the Brethren had attempted this reconciliation without much success, he notes. Religious belief is a matter of divine revelation and requires none of the skills of

[11] *Supra*, p. 186.

philosophers, logicians, or astrologers. Had these skills been essential to religion, Scripture would have exhorted us to cultivate them; instead, it has admonished us to avoid these pursuits. And despite the differences which have divided the Muslims in matters of belief or practice, none of the theological or juridical schools has appealed to philosophy to arbitrate their conflicts. Even Christians and Magians (fire-worshipers) never appeal to philosophy in their dialectical disputes.[12]

The philosopher is subordinated to the prophet, as reason is subordinated to revelation. Revelation is God's means of addressing mankind, including the philosophers themselves. Furthermore, were reason able to discover the truth alone, faith would be superfluous. But reason, as the common possession of mankind, is not evenly distributed among all men, so in the absence of revelation the truth would remain forever inaccessible to some.[13]

II

MISKAWAYH

Two other important contemporaries of al-Tauḥīdī figure among the chief luminaries of the period: Yaḥia b. ʿAdī, already referred to among the translators, and Miskawayh, treasurer of the Buwayhid sultan ʿAḍud al-Daulah. The latter moved in the same literary and philosophical circles as al-Tauḥīdī, and despite al-Tauḥīdī's poor opinion of Miskawayh's intellectual attainments (shared incidentally by Ibn Sīnā) and his contempt for his avarice and his vain alchemical pursuits,[14] al-Tauḥīdī nevertheless provides us with the fullest record extant of his views on literary and philosophical matters in another major work of his, *al-Hawāmil wa'l-Shawāmil.*

Miskawayh, like al-Tauḥīdī and al-Sijistānī, should be reckoned chiefly among the litterateurs and polymaths of the period. His

[12] Al-Tauḥīdī, *al-Imtāʿ*, II, 9. [13] *Ibid.*, p. 10. [14] *Ibid.*, I, 35.

learning ranged from history to psychology to ethics. Of his writings, we have a world history, *Tajārib al-Umam*; a collection of Greco-Persian-Arab maxims, *Jawidān Khirad*, already discussed;[15] an ethical treatise, *Tahdhīb al-Akhlāq*; and psychological tracts.[16] Works on pharmaceutical and culinary subjects are also ascribed to him by ancient authorities.[17]

In one of his chief works, *al-Fauz al-Aṣghar*, Miskawayh gives a succinct account of Neo-Platonism, which antedates Ibn Sīnā's parallel work, *al-Najāt*. There are striking differences in method and subject matter between the two works. The order of the philosophical sciences is given by Miskawayh as mathematics, logic, physics, and metaphysics, whereas in the Arab Neo-Platonic tradition as represented by al-Fārābī and Ibn Sīnā logic usually was the propaedeutic to the study of the other philosophical sciences. Miskawayh states that the existence of God and his unity were universally upheld by all the "ancient" philosophers, whose position on this question agreed fully with the teaching of the prophets.[18] His favorite argument for the existence of God, unlike the rest of philosophers of Islam, is the Aristotelian argument from motion, "which is the most manifest and the most susceptible to proving the existence of the Creator." This Creator or Unmoved Mover is unchanging and entirely different from any other entity, hence the impossibility of describing him rationally in any but negative terms. Since it is necessary to ascribe to him the highest perfections, however, we ought to be guided in that matter by the pronouncements of Scripture and the consensus of the community.[19]

The derivation of things from God is described by Miskawayh as a process of emanation. The first entity to emanate from this primeval source of being is the first Reason, which he calls the active intellect

[15] *Supra*, p. 48.

[16] Excerpts from tracts on *Pleasure*, on *Nature*, on the *Essence of the Soul*, on *Reason*, and the *Soul* are contained in an Istanbul manuscript (Raghip Pasha 1463, foll. 57–86) dated 545 A.H.

[17] Al-Qifṭī, *Tārīkh al-Ḥukamā'*, pp. 331 f.

[18] *Al-Fauz al-Aṣghar*, ch. 2; cf. Iqbāl, *The Development of Metaphysical Thought in Persia*, pp. 23 ff.

[19] *Al-Fauz al-Aṣghar*, chs. 7, 8.

(in contradistinction to the Arab Neo-Platonists, who gave this name to the tenth intellect). The second emanation is the Soul and the third the heavens. And, as though unaware of the incompatibility of the emanationist and creationist theses, he proceeds to add that God has created everything from nothing.

In his discussion of the Soul he complains of the brevity of Aristotle's account and the differences between his commentators, especially Alexander of Aphrodisias and Themistius; but he informs us that he was greatly assisted in his psychological studies by the writings of al-Ḥasan b. Suwār (alias Ibn al-Khammār), the best-known disciple of Yaḥia b. 'Adī, whom we will consider shortly. The substantiality of the Soul, he says, follows from its ability to receive contrary forms at the same time. Its cognitions encompass everything near or remote, sensible or intelligible. As to the mode of this cognition, he follows Aristotle in stating that, despite the diversity of its faculties, the apprehension of the Soul is nevertheless wholly one, since otherwise it would not be able to distinguish between its diverse forms of apprehension, such as the sensible and the intelligible.

The book closes with a discussion of prophecy and divination, in which Neo-Platonic, Islamic, and possibly Persian elements intermingle. After demonstrating the Soul's survival after death, he dwells on its destiny in the life-to-come and the happiness which both in this life and the life to come had been its object.

More important perhaps than this conventional exposition of Neo-Platonism is Miskawayh's contribution to ethical theory, contained in one of the few systematic ethical treatises in Arabic, *Tahdhīb al-Akhlāq* (*Cultivation of Morals*). The aim of this work, as the author states in the introduction, is to cultivate in us those moral traits that render the performance of virtuous actions congenial or spontaneous.[20] In doing so, it is necessary to inquire first into the nature, perfection, power, and end of the Soul as laid down in psychology.

The Soul, as previously mentioned, is a substance entirely different from the body, and as such is capable of apprehending contrary forms, whether sensible or intelligible, near or remote, large or small. Of the different parts of the Soul, the rational differs from the sensuous in that

[20] *Tahdhīb al-Akhlāq*, p. 1.

it alone can judge of truth or falsity and apprehend not only its own apprehensions but also the proper objects of these apprehensions. Its virtue or excellence consists in the pursuit of knowledge, its essential function, as well as the contempt for whatever is bodily or material. This virtue, then, may be measured by the extent of the cultivation of what naturally belongs to it and the eschewing of all that belongs to the body.

What sets man apart from the other animals is more specifically stated to be the capacity for voluntary actions resulting from reflection and deliberation. Such actions are divided into good and bad, or virtuous and evil. Virtuous actions are defined as those "which ensue upon man's will and initiative, in those matters for which he was destined by the Creator," and evil actions are defined as those voluntarily undertaken, "but [which] hinder him from attaining those desirable ends."[21]

In the light of this teleological account of good and evil, it can be shown that to the extent that man is able to live up to the precepts of his nature, as a rational animal, he would be assured of happiness both in this life and the next. Considering, however, that the ends which man must seek are numerous and his individual abilities limited, association is the indispensable condition of the good life. Association enables men to assist each other in their pursuits and to love each other "in so far as each finds in the other his own complement or perfection."[22]

The division of the faculties of the Soul that underlies this theory of virtue is essentially Platonic. The Soul possesses, according to Miskawayh, three faculties: (1) the rational or angelic, lodged in the brain; (2) the appetitive or bestial, lodged in the liver; and (3) the passionate or leonine,[23] lodged in the heart.

From this division it follows that the virtues, like their parallel vices, are divisible into three corresponding groups. Thus when the rational part of the Soul is moderate and yearns for genuine knowledge, which is its true object, its virtue, which is science or wisdom, would ensue. When the appetitive faculty seeks its own object in moderation and

[21] *Tahdhīb al-Akhlāq*, p. 11. [22] *Ibid.*, p. 15.

[23] The Arabic "*al-sab ʿiyah*" refers to those wild animals, such as the lion, which are superior to the others.

complies with the directions of reason, its virtue, which is temperance and its concomitant, liberality, would ensue. Finally, when the passionate faculty is ruled by the rational, self-control and its concomitant virtue, courage, would result. From the conjunction of these virtues will ultimately result the virtue of justice, which is the excellence or perfection of the other three, in so far as they are related to one another and are exercised in due proportion. That is why the principal virtues are deemed by the philosophers to consist in these four only: wisdom, temperance, courage, and justice; and their corresponding vices are designated as ignorance, incontinence, cowardice, and injustice.[24]

Subsidiary virtues can be subsumed under these cardinal ones. Thus under wisdom the following virtues are given: intelligence, memory, prudence, keenness, and teachability. Under temperance are modesty, meekness, forbearance, liberality, integrity, contentedness, good-nature, self-discipline, docility, peacefulness, dignity, and piety. Under courage are magnanimity, courage, valor, steadfastness, composure, single-mindedness, nobility, and adroitness. Finally, under justice are friendship, gregariousness, kindness to one's kin, gratitude, good companionship, fairness, affability, and worship.

This remarkable blend of Platonic and Aristotelian concepts of virtue appears to continue the Stoic and Neo-Platonic tradition that sought to reconcile the ethical teachings of Plato and Aristotle, and in which a lost commentary on the *Nicomachean Ethics* by Porphyry, known only from an Arab bibliographical tradition, may have been the link.[25] Miskawayh uses a Platonic substructure for not only his scheme of the virtues and their corresponding vices, but for the Aristotelian doctrine of the mean as well, and he exploits them for the purpose of determining the nature of virtue. Like Aristotle, he observes in this regard that virtue, as the mean between two extremes, cannot always be determined,[26] and that we ought to understand by the mean, not the mean in general, but rather the mean in relation to us, i.e., in relation to the particular agent in a particular context; hence the difficulty of

[24] Miskawayh, *Tahdhīb al-Akhlāq*, pp. 16 f.; cf. Plato's *Republic* IV. 427 ff.
[25] Cf. Walzer, *Greek into Arabic*, pp. 220 ff., 240.
[26] Miskawayh, *Tahdhīb*, p. 25; *Nicomachean Ethics* II. 1107^{b}2.

discovering this mean. It is much easier to light upon the extremes, which are numerous, than on the mean, which in principle is one.

Miskawayh's account of happiness considers the earthly and spiritual separately. Man's earthly happiness consists in establishing his dominion in this world of which he is a part and ordering it in accordance with the precepts of practical wisdom, as his nature is partly bestial or carnal, partly angelic or spiritual. His supermundane happiness consists in that spiritual bliss of which he will partake in the after-life in the company of the angels and the blessed. The former is a type of happiness far inferior to the latter, which marks the climax of all our moral and spiritual endeavors. In it we partake of that self-sufficiency which is characteristic of the divine life. In support of this view, Miskawayh quotes, in the translation of Abū 'Uthmān al-Dimashqī, a passage which purports to come from an Aristotelian treatise on the *Virtues of the Soul*, but is undoubtedly a modified version of *Ethica Nicomachaea* X, 6 and 7.[27] Here Aristotle describes the contemplative life as a way of partaking in the divine life, toward which the whole of human nature essentially tends.[28]

However, like Aristotle, Miskawayh is careful not to disparage the life of action, which cannot be realized without the external goods of life and the assistance of friends. Human friendship is for him an essential complement of the good life, as are external goods sought in moderation. The urge to seek and enjoy the company of friends is described in terms of that gregariousness in which Aristotle had found, in the *Politics*, the essential characteristic of man, who is "neither a god nor a beast."[29] The various forms of love other than friendship, such as the love of spouse or offspring, the devotion to the wise and the virtuous and ultimately the love of God, are discussed, and directions for the conduct of life, both in relation to our fellow men and ourselves, are set out. In this regard, two distinct problems face the virtuous man and the moral teacher alike: the preservation of moral "health," once achieved, and its restoration, once lost, so that we might speak of a

[27] See Pines, "Un texte inconnu d'Aristote en version Arabe," *Archives d'histoire doctrinale et littérairre du moyen âge*, 1956, pp. 5–43.

[28] Miskawayh, *Tahdhīb al-Akhlāq*, pp. 86 f. and 170.

[29] *Politics* I, 1253^{a}29.

preventive as well as a therapeutic function of moral philosophy, just as we do in medicine.[30]

The moral ill that is to be particularly condemned, of all those which afflict the Soul and cause it undue anxiety, is fear, particularly the fear of death. It is this fear which preys on the minds of the ignorant and the vulgar, who do not apprehend the true nature of death but believe that with the disintegration of their bodies they would altogether cease to exist. Death, however, is simply the process whereby the Soul, upon leaving the body, which had been its instrument during its earthly career, passes on to another and higher stage of purity and bliss. Being a simple substance, the Soul is not susceptible of decay or disintegration, but only of transformation. The philosopher who apprehends this truth about the Soul will be prone no longer to that anxiety which the fear of death or even of worldly hardships brings. Indeed the true philosopher is one who has achieved the condition of "voluntary death," which no pain, imaginary or real, will disturb. This voluntary death, as distinct from physical death, consists in the mortification of the body and the atrophy of emotions, which the philosophers, particularly Plato, have recommended.[31]

Should the fear of death be provoked by the fear of suffering, believed to be associated with death, however, one should be reminded of the fact that suffering can only affect the living. The dead, whose Souls have departed from their bodies, are past all suffering because they are past all feeling. Should one claim nevertheless that we fear death on account of the punishment consequent upon death, then clearly the object of our apprehension is not death but punishment, which the wise will avert by avoiding the sins that occasion it.[32]

The other most grievous moral ill which afflicts the Soul and of which philosophy is the best cure is sorrow. Like the fear of death, sorrow results from ignorance, whether it be the ignorance of our ephemeral condition in this life, the ignorance of what constitutes our genuine happiness, or the futility of that solicitude for earthly possessions which is the token of our misery. With this diagnosis of sorrow

[30] Miskawayh, *Tahdhīb al-Akhlāq*, pp. 175 f. This analogy with medicine recurs in later ethical writers.

[31] *Ibid.*, p. 212. [32] *Ibid.*, p. 213.

and its essential nature as a background, Miskawayh then concludes his ethics with a meditation, impregnated with a Socratic and cynical spirit, upon the art of dispelling sorrow, with which many Muslim philosophers, such as al-Kindī and al-Rāzī, as we have seen, were wont to conclude their ethical writings.

III

YAḤIA B. 'ADĪ

Another major tenth-century figure who belonged to this active core of philosophers and logicians was Yaḥia b. 'Adī, the Jacobite scholar whom we mentioned earlier as a leading figure in the translation movement of the period.[33] He was far more than a simple dragoman of Syriac-Greek learning and deserves a place all his own in the narrative of philosophical and theological controversy during the tenth century. His vast erudition is shown by numerous accounts that credit him with preserving and disseminating, very often in his own handwriting, some of the more important philosophical or logical texts prized so highly by scholars and patrons of learning. Such, for instance, is the tradition naming him as the translator of the whole *Metaphysics* of Aristotle, whose translation is generally ascribed to others.[34]

Yaḥia's standing in logic is illustrated by his voluminous writings[35] as well as by the fact that he is singled out by our authorities as the chief logician of his day. This title came to him as he succeeded the two leading logicians of their day at Baghdad, al-Fārābī and Abū Bishr Mattā, both of whom were his masters.[36]

To his logical writings should be added numerous philosophical and ethical works which are lost, with the exception of an important

[33] *Supra*, p. 28 f.

[34] Ibn al-'Ibrī, *Mukhtaṣar Tārīkh al-Umam*, p. 56, and *supra*, p. 28.

[35] *Supra*, p. 28.

[36] Al-Qifṭī, *Tārīkh al-Ḥukāma'*, p. 361; Ibn al-Nadīm, *al-Fihrist*, pp. 361 f.; Rescher, *The Development of Arabic Logic*, pp. 34 f.

ethical treatise, *Tahdhīb al-Akhlāq*. Noteworthy among these original works are a treatise on the relation of logic to grammar, which belongs to that cycle of tracts or debates in which, as we have already noted, the relation of Greek logic to Arabic grammar was hotly debated at Baghdad; and treatises on the nature of the continuous, the infinite, atomism, the nature of the possible, etc.[37]

His *Tahdhīb al-Akhlāq*, which probably antedates Miskawayh's parallel work by five decades, is one of the few ethical treatises in Arabic to have come down to us. Man's natural tendency, according to this treatise, is to follow the evil propensities of his bestial nature; however, education can check this tendency to a certain extent. In certain cases, though, only forceful restraint will deter the wicked, unless their depravity is such that they are past all reform.[38]

Yaḥia attributes the fundamental differences in ethical traits, as does Miskawayh, to the disharmony that may result from the stresses and strains that set the three powers of the Soul, the appetitive, the passionate, and the rational, one against the other. Thus, when the appetitive power takes a firm hold upon a person, he will become more akin to beasts than humans, will shun the company of his fellow men, and will give free rein to his natural impulses and desires. When a person becomes irrevocably lost it is the duty of the state to chastise him by barring him from the society of his fellows, lest he should corrupt their morals by his example. When the passionate (or irascible) power takes hold of him, on the other hand, he will become aggressive or vindictive and will end up by engaging in belligerent action with his fellow men.[39]

As to the rational power, which alone sets man apart from the beasts, man's excellence is bound up with its domination over the two other powers. The virtues proper to this power are the assimilation of knowledge, the right conduct of one's private and public affairs, friendliness, charity, forbearance, and temperance. Its vices are cunning, hypocrisy, and jealousy, which obviously result from the ill use to which it is put. The cultivation of the rational virtues is the ground of virtue in general, since the man in whom these virtues are forceful will be equipped to

[37] *Supra*, p. 29; al-Qifṭī, *Tārīkh al-Ḥukamā'*, pp. 362 f.
[38] *Tahdhīb al-Akhlāq*, p. 15. [39] *Ibid.*, pp. 18 f.

moderate his appetitive and irascible powers and bring them into harmony with each other.[40]

The cardinal virtues include, according to Yaḥia, temperance, moderation, dignity, patience, decorum, friendliness, mercy, loyalty, humility, and generosity. To these virtues correspond a whole class of vices, such as concupiscence, immodesty, levity, excitability, callousness, pride, bad faith, lying, and avarice.

In his account of these virtues, which are clearly of Aristotelian-Stoic extraction, Yaḥia does not explicitly invoke the doctrine or the mean. This doctrine, however, is implicit in his analysis, and in keeping with this doctrine he recognizes with Aristotle that certain actions or traits are virtuous in relation to some people, but vicious in relation to others. Of the latter type is the avidity for praise, which in an exaggerated form is reprehensible, particularly in the old; frugality, which is commendable in clerics, scholars, and the like, but not in kings or rulers; outward pomp, which is proper to the latter, but unworthy of the former.[41]

The virtues and the vices reviewed above are evenly distributed among people, so that no man is entirely free from vice or fully endowed with virtue. Virtue, however, is the true mark of excellence and not, as is commonly supposed, riches or social standing, which are simply the indices of a person's external estate in life. It is nonetheless true, that if the external goods of life are added to virtue, their conjunction is the guarantee of greater happiness, but only if he who possesses them is a virtuous and charitable person. In the ignorant and vicious, riches often conduce to greater depravity, in so far as they provide the rich with the means to indulgence and vice. Moreover, the possession of riches is transient, and once the rich have lost their worldly possessions, they become the equals of their less fortunate fellows, and consequently lose the esteem in which their money, rather than their persons, were originally held.[42]

As to the acquisition of virtue, which can be achieved only progressively or through habituation, the first step is the subjection of the appetitive and irascible powers of the Soul to the authority of reason.

[40] *Tahdhīb al-Akhlāq*, pp. 21 f. [41] *Ibid.*, pp. 35 ff. [42] *Ibid.*, p. 39.

Thus in taming the appetites, one should try to divert the impulse from the base object toward which it might tend, to a more worthy object of the same type. If, at first, the impulse should prove recalcitrant, he should not give up, but should keep trying, until the Soul is coaxed into obedience. In this undertaking, it is particularly helpful to seek the company of ascetics, monks, pious and learned people, and to avoid the company of the wicked and the profligate.[43]

The worst company which one can keep is that of drunkards. For drink stimulates the appetites, and, although taken in moderation it is not essentially evil, taken in the company of boon companions it is bound to lead to intoxication and abuse, especially when accompanied with music and song, performed by "painted women."[44]

He who seeks to tame his irascible power should consider the ludicrous demeanor or manner of the irate, their precipitancy and their irrational outbursts. This should deter him from emulating their example whenever he is provoked, and incline him instead to moderate his anger. He should also refrain from associating with the violent and the unruly and avoid strong drink, as well as those occasions which might give rise to anger.

The general rule in the matter of moral education, as the author observes, is the subordination of both the appetitive and irascible powers to the rational. To the extent that this power is in control of the other two powers, the Soul is safe from temptation and vice.[45] Accordingly, the primary aim of moral education is the cultivation of this power, through study and the meditation upon the more difficult or abstruse rational matters. This study should begin with the study of ethics and politics, and move on to the more speculative or abstract disciplines.

Once the Soul is truly submissive to the rational power, it will find much less difficulty in discriminating between what is good or bad, useful or harmful, and it will live according to the directions of that power. In particular, the Soul will realize how futile are evil deeds or thoughts, and how much greater the harm which they bring upon agent and patient alike, than the advantage expected from them.

[43] *Tahdhīb al-Akhlāq*, p. 40. [44] *Ibid.*, p. 41. [45] *Ibid.*, p. 45.

The qualities of the truly virtuous person are:

1. He must possess all the virtues and be free from all the vices. But admittedly this condition is beyond man's reach and if he is presumed to attain it, he will be more akin to the angels than to men.[46]

2. He must also aspire to the highest rank and yet deem that rank no more than a stage in his journey toward moral perfection.

3. He must strive to study the sciences and proceed then to the study of ethics and politics.

4. He must seek the company of the learned and the pious and shun the company of the profligate and aggressive.

5. He must lay down a "canon of moderation" by which he would regulate his everyday life in matters of food, drink, and pleasure.

6. He must despise wealth, which is purely a means to the noble pursuits of life, and he must not hoard it, or begrudge spending it in a good cause when the occasion arises.

7. He must accustom himself to love all men and be merciful to them. For in reason, which is man's essence, men form a single family or clan. Unless he is dominated by his irascible faculty and the urge to dominate others, he will see in all men his brothers and friends.[47] The more he examines the matter rationally, the more he will realize that men are either virtuous, and deserving of his love, or vicious and deserving of his mercy or compassion. This quality is particularly desirable in the king or ruler, who is to his subjects what the master is to his household.[48]

The theological interests of Yaḥia, however, appear to have been as great as his logico-philosophical interests, and his standing in the history of Islamic theological thought is such that he is one of the few Christian scholars of the period to have taken an active part in theological debates with his Muslim contemporaries. Of particular significance in this regard is his refutation of an anti-Trinitarian tract, written by the ninth-century philosopher al-Kindī, which has been preserved in Yaḥia's rebuttal only. Moreover, he is one of the few Christian authors whose theological views are quoted or discussed by subsequent Muslim authors, and the twelfth-century Jewish philosopher

[46] *Tahdhīb al-Akhlāq*, p. 49. [47] *Ibid.*, p. 55. [48] *Ibid.*, p. 56.

Maimonides credits him with being the first to introduce the Muslims to the methods of scholastic theology (*kalām*).[49]

His theological works, of which numerous manuscripts are still extant at the Vatican or in Paris,[50] can be divided into two groups, expository and polemical. Some of his polemical writings that have not survived appear to have been directed against the nascent Ash'arite school, which many Muslim philosophers and theologians had also attacked. Thus the *Refutation of the Arguments of Those Who Claim That* [*Human*] *Acts Are Created by God and Acquired by the Servants*, as well as a similar treatise that may be identical with this one and deals with creation of the acts of man by God, is obviously directed at the Ash'arite concept of acquisition (*kasb*), which we will consider below. A treatise decrying the error of those who believe that God knows contingent events before their occurrence and another treatise on the reality of the possible appear to have dealt with a question which exercised Muslim theologians of the rival Mu'tazilite and Ash'arite schools, namely, whether or not an entity had any mode of being prior to its actual creation. The Ash'arites answered in the negative, and the Mu'tazilites in the affirmative, urging, as their expression went, that "not-being was also a thing [*shay'*]."

His treatise on the unity of God was no doubt designed to vindicate the Christian belief in monotheism, which Muslim theologians as well as the masses have always approached with a certain degree of skepticism. And a treatise written by his disciple Ibn al-Khammār, on the agreement of the philosophers and the Christians, obviously reflected the preoccupation of Yaḥia and his school with the problem of reconciling philosophy and dogma—a concern indeed of the whole philosophical school of Islam from al-Kindī to Ibn Rushd.

Of particular interest to the student of Christian-Islamic polemics is Yaḥia's previously mentioned refutation of al-Kindī's *Critique of the Trinity*.[51] Although the critique has disappeared, al-Kindī's arguments

[49] *Guide des égarés*, Vol. I, Ch. 71, pp. 95b and 97b. Maimonides' claim, however, should not be taken uncritically. Kalām, as we have seen, was already well developed by Yaḥia's time.

[50] Some of these treatises have been published by A. Périer; see *Petits traités apologétiques de Yaḥia ben 'Adī*.

[51] *Revue de l'Orient Chrétien*, Vol. 22 (Tome II, XXII), 1920, pp. 4–14.

can be reconstructed from Yaḥia's rebuttal with a certain degree of completeness. Al-Kindī apparently argued that the concepts of a single substance (*jauhar*) in three persons (singular: *uqnūm*), upon which the whole trinitarian doctrine rested, involved composition, since the "notion of substance" is common to the three persons, whereas each one of them differs from the other two through some specific property. Being composite, the three persons will thus be caused (*ma'lūl*) and cannot *eo ipso* be eternal.

In his rebuttal, Yaḥia admits the first premise that the "notion of substance" is common to the three persons of the Trinity, but denies the second, according to which each person is distinct from the other two by virtue of some specific *differentia*. For the Christians, he argues, the three persons are in fact three distinct properties or attributes, in terms of which the single substance of the Godhead is determined as good, wise, and powerful, goodness being called the Father, wisdom the Son, power the Holy Ghost. Consequently each of the three persons is endowed with one quality which it shares with the other two, and with one by which it is differentiated from them, and this circumstance involves no plurality or composition in the essence of God. The opponent (i.e., al-Kindī) must admit that the Creator is one, good, as well as substance (in the Aristotelian sense of that which is not predicable of a subject), and, however he might conceive it, each one of these terms will designate a "notion" distinct from the other two and is nonetheless eternal.[52]

The second argument of al-Kindī appears to have been that, according to Porphyry's *Isagoge*, if the three persons of the Trinity are said to be three genera, there would be three species of individual gods, since the genus is made up of the species subsumed under it. Nor would the Supreme Being be eternal on that assumption, for the genus consists of the essence of the individual plus the accidents thereof.[53] Being composite, it will be caused and what is caused cannot be eternal.

Yaḥia counters this argument by stating that, according to the Christian view, the three persons of the Trinity are neither three genera nor three species. Al-Kindī's premise that what is caused cannot

[52] *Revue de l'Orient Chrétien*, Vol. 22 (Tome II, XXII), p. 8.
[53] *Isagoge* (Arabic), p. 70.

be eternal need not be accepted without question. We distinguish in efficient causes between that which is responsible for the supervention of the form upon the matter and that which causes the being of the form rather than its mere supervention. Only in the former case is the cause prior to its effect in time. In the latter, however, the cause is always contemporaneous with its effect. Now the relation of the Father, as cause, to the Son and Holy Spirit, as its effects, is of the latter type,[54] of which we find many analogies in the world of experience, for instance, the rising of the sun in relation to daylight, the collision of hard bodies in relation to sound, etc.

Finally, al-Kindī argued, still basing his case on Porphyry's *Isagoge*, that the three persons, if not wholly genera, are either common accidents, specific accidents (or properties), or partly genera, partly *differentiae*, partly species.[55] In his retort, Yaḥia challenges this argument on the ground that none of these alternatives tallies with the Christian view of the three persons of the Trinity. The Christian view is that each of the divine persons is to be distinguished from the other two, not that they form a real aggregate. In other words, the distinction between these persons, according to Yaḥia, is conceptual rather than real.

Throughout this phase of the argument, as we have noted, al-Kindī draws on the *Isagoge*, "with which children and beginners" are conversant and which is to be found in the "homes of most of them" (the Christians). Next he invokes the authority of Aristotle, who in *Topica* I,[56] states that "one" may refer to the numerical, the specific, or the generic one. If the Trinity is understood in the first sense, there would be three gods, if in the second and third, there would be three composite persons, as has been previously shown.

In his rebuttal Yaḥia observes that this threefold distinction between the various meanings to "one" is not exhaustive, it leaves out the sense of "one" in respect of relation. Thus we say that the relation of

[54] In the Nicene Creed, the relation of the Father to the Son is described as "begetting," that of the Holy Spirit to the Father and the Son as "procession," rather than causation. It is clear, however, that this is what Yaḥia means by the second type of causation, and his analogies are significantly drawn from emanationism.

[55] Porphyry's *Isagoge* dealt with the five voices or terms: i.e., species, genus, *differentia*, property, and accident.

[56] *Topica* I, 103^{e} 5^{f}.

the tributaries to the river and the arteries to the heart, or the relation of two and four to twenty and forty is one (i.e., the same). Furthermore, even in the numerical "one" we should distinguish between the continuous or homogeneous. In the latter case, we describe an entity as one if its essence (or definition) is one, which is precisely how the Christians understand the unity of God. For by the trinity of persons they understand goodness, wisdom, and power, which though predicated of God are nevertheless distinct one from the other.

The problem of the Trinity appears to have been one of the chief philosophical and theological preoccupations of this Jacobite scholar, who worked in such close association with the leading Muslim logicians and philosophers of his day. Not only in his refutation of al-Kindī, but in numerous other works, Yaḥia undertook to vindicate the doctrine of the Trinity against its detractors. Thus in a treatise on the *Validity of the Belief of Christians*[57] he reaffirms the thesis that the Creator is to be understood as a single substance, possessing three distinct attributes. The Father is the cause of the Son and Holy Spirit, which together proceed from the Father while remaining wholly identical with Him. In this way, the three persons, though distinct, are nevertheless identical with one another, like reflections in two juxtaposed mirrors, or like thought in the act of thinking itself. For in so far as it thinks itself, it is agent or subject, in so far as it is thought, it is patient or object, whereas in itself it is an intellectual subtance (*ʿaql*).[58]

If it is now asked whether or not the three persons differ among themselves, the answer should be that, though identical in point of substance and what is a concomitant of substance, such as eternity, self-subsistence, etc., they differ one from the other in their specific nature (or proper being), so that, in fact, the three persons are neither similar in all respects nor dissimilar in all respects.[59]

Briefly stated, the view of Yaḥia thus appears to be that God is a unity in one sense, a trinity in another. Per se, or in so far as He is the subject of qualification (*mauṣūf*), He is one, but correlatively, i.e., in so far as he possesses the three attributes of goodness, wisdom, and power,[60] He is three. What his argument demonstrates, in this and

[57] Périer, *Petits traités*, pp. 11 ff. [58] *Ibid.*, p. 18.
[59] *Ibid.*, p. 38. [60] *Ibid.*, p. 67 *et passim*.

similar treatises, is not a trinity of persons, but rather a trinity of specific or essential attributes. It is doubtful whether any theologian of note, not excepting Muslim theologians, would have deemed it necessary to challenge this view. Perhaps in his attempt to rationalize the doctrine of the Trinity and make it at the same time more readily acceptable to his adversaries, this Monophysite theologian had ended up by emptying the whole doctrine of any element of mystery, on the one hand, and had conceptualized it to such an extent, on the other, that what was left was no longer a *real* trinity of persons, but a *conceptual* trinity of attributes. The latter proposition is not only at variance with the Nicene formula and the pronouncements of Scripture, but is at variance also with the concept of God's unique status as the being in whom the unity of substance is not incompatible with the plurality of persons. As regards the plurality of attributes, predicable of a single entity or substance, it is obvious that every entity can lay a perfectly legitimate claim to such a plurality, which does not compromise its unity in the least.

Two other fundamental theological problems are broached by Yaḥia in an equally stimulating way: the Creation and the Incarnation. In a treatise on the Incarnation (*ta'annus*), he argues that God in his infinite goodness was driven to communicate his essence, just as fire and the other active elements communicate their essences to other things, or just as the mind, in apprehending an entity, assumes the form of that entity or appropriates it and in so doing becomes identified with it. Thus God has assumed the human form in Christ, without thereby forsaking his identity or his Godhead, and Christ, as the Son of Man, has become identified with God without destroying His unity.[61]

Here the Monophysite sympathies of Yaḥia are clearly brought out. Although he speaks of this quasi-mystical or intellectual union of Christ with God, as well as of God's self-manifestation in His creation, he stops short of admitting the "self-humiliation" of God involved in his "becoming flesh" and in his assuming the form of human nature, which is precisely what the concept of the real humanity of Christ implied. In answer to a question, Yaḥia replied that "the claim that

61 Périer, *Petits traités*, pp. 82 f.

the Creator (may He be exalted . . .) has passed through the womb of a woman, was born, grew up, ate and drank, was persecuted by the Jews, donned the crown of thorns and the purple, was crucified, died and was buried is a *false* claim because no Christian has ever believed such a thing."[62] This error, according to Yaḥia, stems from the fact that since in Christ there are two natures, the divine and the human, we tend to predicate the term God of both and also impute to the divine what must be imputed to human nature, such as suffering or death.[63] In short, the attribution of human qualities and affections does not become the Supreme Being, according to this Jacobite scholar, who like many of his contemporaries persists in ignoring the Nicene formula of the Christ who is fully man and fully God, as well as the logical, if "scandalous," implications of this formula.

On the question of creation, Yaḥia, unlike his Muslim Neo-Platonic master, al-Fārābī, stands unequivocally behind the protagonists of creation *ex nihilo*. God, according to him, brought the whole universe forth entirely out of nothing, through sheer creative fiat. God's creative act was completely free, so that if He had so desired He could have refrained from creating the universe altogether. Consequently, no compulsion of any kind could have determined this creative act, or else God would have been subservient to a power higher than Himself and therefore no longer truly the First or Supreme Being. Even the claim (fostered by the Neo-Platonists, especially al-Fārābī) that God's action in creating the world was determined by a "necessity of nature" inherent in his self-communicative goodness would entail that the universe must have existed since all eternity, since God's nature is immutable or eternal.[64] Creation nevertheless manifests the Creator, in so far as it exhibits that order and harmony which are the tokens of His wisdom and power.

As their creator, God must be assumed to know the particulars of which the universe is made and which the Arab Neo-Platonists tended to place outside the pale of divine omniscience. The proof of God's knowledge of particulars is the consideration of the visible signs of the intelligent workmanship that has gone into the innumerable particulars

[62] Périer, *Petits traités*, p. 93. [63] *Ibid.*, p. 96 f.
[64] Périer, *Yaḥia b. 'Adī*, pp. 138 f.

making up the universe, and especially the way in which each part is ordered toward the end for which it was designed.

Finally, even those who maintain, like al-Fārābī, that God knows only universals must admit that He knows particulars, since the former enter into the definition of particulars,[65] and apart from them they cannot possibly be known.

[65] Périer, *Yaḥia b. ʿAdī*, p. 142.

CHAPTER SEVEN

The Interaction of Philosophy and Dogma

I

THE ECLIPSE OF THEOLOGICAL RATIONALISM

As we mentioned earlier, the rise of Scholastic theology in the middle of the eighth century was the outcome of a new spirit of inquiry, which the introduction of Greek philosophy in the Muslim world had sparked. In some cases, however, the interaction of philosophy and dogma resulted in a gradual cleavage between the two. The systematic philosophers, like al-Fārābī and Ibn Sīnā, tried hard to lessen the effect of such cleavage by emphasizing the areas of agreement and the common concerns of philosophy and dogma. Some, such as al-Kindī, went so far as to espouse the cause of dogma almost unconditionally and sought to erect a compact intellectual edifice on the foundation of dogma.

A gradual reaction to rationalism in theology, championed originally by the Muʿtazilah, was to set in less than a century after the death of the founder of that school, Wāṣil b. ʿAtā'. We have already discussed the role which the great theologian and jurist Aḥmad b. Ḥanbal, as well as the 'Abbāsid caliph al-Mutawakkil, played in the reversal of the pro-Mu'tazilite policies of al-Ma'mūn in the middle of the ninth century.[1] However, the theological influence of the Mu'tazilah did not cease altogether as a result of al-Mutawakkil's policy of repression. Despite the virtual triumph of the Ḥanbalī and Traditionist party, the spirit of theological inquiry was not completely snuffed out. In its pure form, the primitive traditionalism of the early jurists and exegetes was gone forever. The new Traditionism or orthodoxy was a qualified one that stemmed from the Mu'tazilite movement itself. Its rise is associated with the name of Abu'l-Ḥasan al-Ash'arī (d. 935), who, according to the traditional account, studied theology with al-Jubā'ī, head of the Basra branch of the Mu'tazilite school but broke away from that school at the age of forty.[2] The Prophet appeared to him in a dream and urged him to "take charge" of the Muslim community, whereupon al-Ash'arī ascended the pulpit at the mosque of Basra and proclaimed his recantation and his determination to make public "the scandals and follies" of the Mu'tazilah.

A debate with his master, al-Jubā'ī, concerning God's justice and man's worthiness brings out vividly his original anti-Mu'tazilite sympathies.[3] Whether historical or not, this debate is significant in so far as it illustrates one of the cardinal issues on which al-Ash'arī broke with the Mu'tazilah. The pupil asks his master: What will be the fate in the after-life of three brothers, one of whom dies in a state of grace, one in a state of sin, and one in a state of innocence (i.e., before he comes of age)? The righteous brother, answers al-Jubā'ī, will be consigned to paradise, the sinner to hell, and the third to an intermediate position.[4] Al-Ash'arī then asks: What if the third brother were to ask to be allowed to join his more fortunate brother? This privilege, replies al-Jubā'ī, would be denied him on the ground that the first brother was admitted to paradise on the strength of his good works. If the third brother were to protest that if he had been given a long life he would have lived righteously, God would have replied: I foresaw that you would not and therefore chose to spare you

[1] *Supra*, p. 79. [2] See Ibn 'Asākir, *Tabyīn Kadhib al-Muftarī*, pp. 38 f.
[3] Ibn Khallikān, *Wafayāt*, Vol. 3, p. 398.
[4] See the teaching of the Mu'tazilah on the "intermediate position," *supra*, p. 59.

everlasting damnation in hell. At this, the brother who had died in sin exclaims: Surely, Lord, you foresaw my own plight, as well. Why, then, did you not deal with me as mercifully as you have dealt with my other brother?

We are told that al-Jubā'ī was unable to say what God's possible answer to such protestations might be, on the Mu'tazilite assumption of the unqualified justice of God. The corollaries drawn by al-Ash'arī constitute the substance of his view of God's absolute omnipotence and sovereignty in the world and the finality of his moral and religious decrees. These decrees are entirely independent of any conditions, moral or other, apart from God's absolute fiat. To Him it belongs to order human life as He pleases, and to the "servant" to obey without question. Contrary to the contention of the Mu'tazilah, the human agent plays no part in the drama of choosing or doing and reaps none of the moral or religious fruits accruing from such initiative. In their desire to stress man's moral freedom and responsibility, the Mu'tazilah had described him, somewhat extravagantly, as "the creator of his deeds." To al-Ash'arī, such blasphemous language was tantamount to the denial of God's uniqueness as the sole Creator and Sovereign of the world, and consequently implied the recognition of two creators, in the manner of the Manichaeans (*Majūs*).[5]

The vindication of God's absolute power and sovereignty in the world had certain moral implications, which al-Ash'arī was quick to draw. To deny man's role in the drama of moral action and decision and to impute the responsibility for his deeds and volitions to God involved the repudiation of God's justice. However, the claim that man's deeds are the result of God's "decree and preordination" did not necessarily imply, according to him, the nullification of His justice. Injustice can only denote the transgression of what has been prescribed by a superior, or the perpetration of what falls outside the domain of the doer. In both cases, injustice cannot be imputed to God, who is the undisputed master and lawgiver of the universe and who owes no allegiance to anyone whatsoever.[6]

On the question of the attributes of God and the creation of the Koran, the position of al-Ash'arī was equally at variance with that of

[5] Al-Ash'arī, *Al-Ibānah*, pp. 6 f. [6] *Al-Luma'*, in *Theology of Al-Ash'arī*, p. 70.

his Mu'tazilite master, on the one hand, and that of the crude anthropomorphists or literalists, on the other. Moved by the desire to retain the concept of the full-blooded Creator-God of the Koran, he opposed the Mu'tazilite tendency to divest God of His positive attributes, and argued, according to a twelfth-century historiographer and fellow-Ash'arite, al-Shahrastānī, that the essential divine attributes of knowledge, power, and life are eternal and subsist in God's essence.[7] They cannot, however, be said to be either identical with this essence, as the Mu'tazilah claimed, or not identical with it. For this would mean that God's knowledge, power, or life is the same as God, so that one could address one's petitions to God's knowledge, power, or life instead of to God Himself,[8] which is absurd.

The rationalization of the inherence of the attributes in God which the Mu'tazilah attempted is not fully worked out by al-Ash'arī or his followers. *How* these attributes are to be distinguished from God's essence, in which they inhere and yet introduce no plurality into it, al-Ash'arī just refused to say. In this respect he is content to revert to the position of the early Traditionists, such as Mālik b. Anas, who is reported to have argued, in the matter of God's "sitting upon the throne," that the "sitting is known, whereas its mode is unknown. Belief in its truth is a duty, and its questioning a heresy."[9]

In his polemical works, however, al-Ash'arī is as concerned to refute the views of the "negators of the attributes," i.e., the Mu'tazilah, as he is to refute the position of the literalists and anthropomorphists. In their deference to Scripture, the latter had gone so far as to attribute corporeity to God, chiefly on the ground that the text of the Koran undeniably stipulated it. Thus Koran 75, 22–23 speak of the ability of the faithful to perceive God on the Last Day, and 7,54, and 20,5 speak of His sitting upon the throne. The anthropomorphists, such as Hishām b. al-Ḥakam, 'Abdullah b. Karrām, and their followers in the ninth century, had not hesitated to draw from such koranic passages their full logical consequences and to conceive of God, as Ibn Rushd will say later, simply as an "eternal man" endowed with gross corporeal qualities.

[7] *Al-Milal*, p. 67. [8] Al-Ash'arī, *al-Ibānah*, p. 54.
[9] Al-Shahrastānī, *al-Milal*, pp. 65, 76.

The use of logical argument in matters of theology, and its permissibility, should first be justified satisfactorily, however. Al-Ash'arī's position, though reactionary by the standards of the philosophers and thoroughgoing rationalists, is certainly *nuancé*. Against the literalists and Traditionists, who questioned the permissibility of deduction or analogy, al-Ash'arī invokes the authority of the Koran, which recognizes the principle of analogy and employs it effectively in numerous passages.[10] In a tract devoted to the systematic discussion of this question and entitled *Vindication of the Use of Theological Proof* (*Kalām*), this ex-Mu'tazilite doctor's anti-Traditionist views on an issue which split the ranks of tenth-century theologians are clearly exhibited. The use of analogy, as indeed the whole method of dialectic or deduction, is repudiated by the Traditionists on the ground that the Prophet, who had dealt with every aspect of religion or morals essential to salvation, has not touched on the question of dialectic (*Kalām*) at all. Hence recourse to it constitutes an heretical departure (*bid'ah*) from what is traditionally and authoritatively received.

This argument from silence is artfully turned by al-Ash'arī against the Traditionists, who, by the same token, are just as heretical themselves, since their claim has no basis in the pronouncements or sayings of the Prophet either. More important still is the fact that the Prophet was fully conversant with the questions of motion and rest, accident and body, divine attributes, and so on, with which theology is concerned. However, they are referred to in the Traditions and the Koran in general terms only, and it is on such references that the whole of theology is based.[11]

Finally, the silence of the Koran and the Traditions on those questions that subsequently were dealt with by the theologians or the jurists is easily justified. The Muslim community was not faced with the difficulties or doubts which eventually led to them, or else the Prophet would have laid down explicitly the principles for solving them. As a result, the jurists and theologians in attempting to solve them had no other recourse than to draw analogies with what was explicitly laid down in Scripture. For it is the duty of every "reasonable Muslim" in

[10] Al-Ash'arī, *al-Luma'* in McCarthy, *Theology of al-Ash'arī*, p. 9.
[11] *Istiḥsān al-Khauḍ fī 'Ilm al-Kalām*, in *Theology of al-Ash'arī*, pp. 88 f.

such matters, al-Ash'arī argues, "to refer them to the body of principles consecrated by reason, sense-experience, and common sense."[12]

In applying this qualified rationalism to the cardinal questions debated in theological circles at the time, al-Ash'arī, though in fundamental disagreement with the Mu'tazilah, is nonetheless anxious to justify his opposition to them on rational grounds. The result is that his *method* is analogous to that of the Mu'tazilah, whereas his *doctrine* is substantially a restatement of Traditionist or Ḥanbalī theses.

If we take the Mu'tazilite concept of free will as an instance, this dichotomy is clearly brought out. In the *Ibānah*, al-Ash'arī describes the arbitrary power of God in terms that leave hardly any scope for human initiative:

We believe that God has created everything, by simply bidding it: Be, as He says [in Koran 16, 42]: "Verily, when we will a thing, our only utterance is: 'Be' and it is"; and that there is nothing good or evil on earth, except what God has preordained. We hold that everything is through God's will and that no one can do a thing before he actually does it, or do it without God's assistance, or escape God's knowledge. We hold that there is no Creator but God, and that the deeds of the creature are created and preordained by God, as He said [in Koran 37, 94]: "He has created you and what you make" . . . we hold that God helps the faithful to obey Him, favors them, is gracious to them, reforms and guides them; whereas He has led the unfaithful astray, did not guide or favor them with signs, as the impious heretics claim. However, were He to favor and reform them, they would have been righteous, and had He guided them they would have been rightly guided. . . . But it was His will that they should be ungodly [singular: *kāfir*], as He foresaw. Accordingly He abandoned them and sealed their hearts. We believe that good and evil are the outcome of God's decree and preordination [*qaḍā' wa qadar*]: good or evil, sweet or bitter, and we know that what has missed us could not have hit us, or what has hit us could not have missed us, and that creatures are unable to profit or injure themselves, without God.[13]

In this vindication of the omnipotence of God and the powerlessness of the creature, al-Ash'arī simply reaffirms the koranic concept of the God-Despot, whose decrees are both irreversible and inscrutable.

[12] *Istiḥān al-Khauḍ fī 'Ilm al-Kalām*, in *Theology of al-Ash'arī*, p. 95.
[13] *Al-Ibānah*, pp. 7 f.; cf. McCarthy, *Theology of al-Ash'arī*, pp. 238 f.

At the back of this polemic, however, is the view of the Mu'tazilah that man is the "creator of his deeds," and consequently a fully free and responsible agent. The concept of a co-creator with God, according to al-Ash'arī, amounts to polytheism and involves a radical curtailing of God's absolute power. Despite these strictures, he does not concur with the Traditionists in their claim that man does not play any part whatsoever in the drama of moral activity. In his doctrine of *al-kasb*, or acquisition of the merit or demerit for the deed done, al-Ash'arī seeks a way out of the moral dilemma of responsibility, without sacrificing the omnipotence of God. Voluntary actions, in his view, are created by God, but acquired by the human agent or imputed to him. Creation differs from acquisition in that the former is the outcome of "eternal power," whereas the latter is the outcome of the "created power" of the agent, so that the same action is said to be created by the one and acquired by the other. Stated differently, man acquires the credit or discredit for the deed created by God, since it is impossible that God should acquire it in time, while He is its author eternally.[14] In this subtle verbal distinction between what is acquired in time and what is created or predestined eternally, lies, according to al-Ash'arī, the distinction between voluntary and involuntary action, and also that between the merit or demerit which attaches to the latter. Man, as the locus or bearer of "acquired" action, becomes responsible for such action, whereas for involuntary action, such as trembling or falling, etc., he is totally irresponsible. The fundamental difference between the two forms of action, according to al-Ash'arī and his followers, is that man is intuitively conscious of the difference between the one action and the other. Thus, rather than restore to man the freedom of which the extreme determinists (*al-Jabriyah*) had robbed him, al-Ash'arī is content to restore to him the consciousness of his subjection to the "eternal power." Through this subtle distinction, the predestinarian presuppositions of the Traditionists and determinists are not repudiated, but their linguistic sting is removed without surrendering the substance of the predestinarian thesis. The elaboration of this peculiar ethical position, as well as the occasionalist world-view on which it rested, should perhaps be left to a subsequent section,

[14] *Al-Luma'*, pp. 39 f.

because of the part which the successors of al-Ash'arī played in developing or refining it.

The historical significance of al-Ash'arī's "reform" lies not in the elaborateness of his solutions of the theological problems raised by the Mu'tazilah, but rather in his willingness to exploit their dialectical method, and, *ipso facto*, to moderate the claims of the Traditionists and antirationalists to whom he was temperamentally drawn. If his theological position, expressed in the classic formula of *bilā kaifa* (ask not how) must be described as agnostic, it is nonetheless to be clearly distinguished from the blind agnosticism of the religious bigot who will entertain no questions whatsoever. For his was the qualified agnosticism of the earnest seeker who ends up by asserting, rightly or wrongly, the inability of reason to plumb the mystery of man in relation to God, or of God in relation to man.

II

THE ASH'ARITE SCHOOL AND THE FORMULATION OF THE OCCASIONALIST METAPHYSICS OF ATOMS AND ACCIDENTS

The elaboration of the implications of al-Ash'arī's new theological outlook was left chiefly to his successors in the tenth and the eleventh centuries. Apart from the substance of their anti-Mu'tazilite creed, their attention was now centered on two fundamental questions: (1) the nature and limits of rational knowledge in relation to religious truth ('*aql* vs. *sam'*), and (2) the metaphysical framework in which the concept of God's sovereignty and omnipotence should be expressed. Neither of these questions appears to have been discussed with any thoroughness by the founder of the Ash'arite movement himself.

The first major figure in the history of the Ash'arite school was Abū Bakr al-Bāqillānī (d. 1013), who belongs to the second generation of Ash'arite doctors. This theologian, who is credited by later authors with refining the methods of Kalām,[15] gives in his *al-Tamhīd* the first systematic statement of the Ash'arite doctrine and its metaphysical framework.

The book opens with a discussion of the nature of knowledge or science (*'ilm*), in a manner which sets the pattern for similar Ash'arite treatises such as al-Baghdādī's *Uṣūl al-Dīn* and al-Juwaynī's *al-Irshād*, but it has a distinctly modern ring. Thus, science is defined by the author as 'the knowledge of the object, as it really is."[16] The object in question is then shown to include both that which is and that which is not (*al-ma'dūm*), which the Mu'tazilah but not the Ash'arites had declared to be a thing (*shay'*). Such science falls into two major categories: the eternal knowledge of God and the temporal or created knowledge of creatures capable of cognition, such as men, angels, jinn, etc. The latter knowledge is subdivided in turn into necessary (or intuitive) and discursive.

Necessary knowledge is knowledge which cannot be doubted. A subsidiary meaning of necessary, however, is that which cannot be dispensed with, i.e., needful.[17] Discursive knowledge, on the other hand, is knowledge which is the result of prolonged reflection, or, stated differently, knowledge which rests on necessary or empirical knowledge.

Such necessary knowledge is acquired through one or the other of the five senses and is essentially indubitable. However, there is a type of necessary knowledge which is not a matter of sensation, but is the result of the immediate apprehension of the mind, for instance man's knowledge of his own existence and his inner states or affections, such as pleasure or pain, love or hate, knowledge or ignorance. To this should also be added the knowledge of the truth or falsity of indicative statements, as well as the second-intention type of knowledge, such as the knowledge of what makes shame shameful, fear fearful, etc.[18]

The third type of necessary knowledge includes, significantly enough,

[15] Ibn Khaldūn, *al-Muqaddimah*, p. 465. [16] Al-Bāqillānī, *al-Tamhīd*, p. 6.
[17] *Ibid.*, p. 8. [18] *Ibid.*, p. 10.

the authoritative accounts of events or facts which are geographically or historically remote, such as the existence of other countries, of historical personages, and of ancient kingdoms. To this type of knowledge belongs a supernatural or extraordinary variety, which God infuses directly into the Soul, without the help of intermediaries or sense organs, which are the normal channels of this type of knowledge.[19]

The distinction between rational and authoritative knowledge was first broached by the Mu'tazilah,[20] who sought to extend the domain of reason well into regions which so far had been considered the exclusive preserve of revelation or faith. The Ash'arite doctors, as illustrated in al-Bāqillānī's case, recognized the validity of rational knowledge but reacted instinctively against the Mu'tazilite infringement on the domain of faith. On two fundamental questions of "natural theology," namely, whether God can be known rationally, independently of revelation, and whether the knowledge of good and evil is possible prior to revelation, the Ash'arite theologians took a qualified anti-Mu'tazilite stand. The existence of God and His unity can be known rationally from the consideration of the createdness (*ḥudūth*) of the world and the logical necessity of a creator (*muḥdith*).

To demonstrate this necessity, Ash'arite doctors argued that the world, which they defined as everything other than God,[21] was composed of atoms and accidents. Now accidents cannot endure for two successive moments, but are continually created by God, who produces and annihilates them at will.[22] Similarly, the atoms in which these accidents inhere are continually created by God and can only endure by virtue of the accident of duration created in them by God.[23] It follows from this premise that the world, being created, must necessarily have a creator.[24]

Al-Bāqillānī's version of this argument differs little from the general Ash'arite argument. He does, however, strengthen this argument by two others in which the "middle term" is different, but not the

[19] Al-Bāqillānī, *al-Tamhīd*, p. 11. [20] *Supra*, p. 34.

[21] Al-Baghdādī, *Uṣūl al-Dīn*, p. 33.

[22] Al-Bāqillānī, *al-Tamhīd*, p. 18. [23] Al-Baghdādī, *Uṣūl al-Dīn*, p. 56.

[24] Fakhry, "The Classical Islamic Arguments for the Existence of God," *Muslim World*, XLVII (1957), 139 f.

dialectical structure of the reasoning. In the first, he argues that the priority of certain things in time requires an "agent who made them prior," who is God. In the second, he introduces the concept of contingency and argues that things, considered in themselves, are susceptible of various forms or qualities. The fact that they actually possess certain forms and no others presupposes a "determinant" who decrees that they should receive these forms and no others, and this determinant is God.[25]

The last argument, or argument *a contingentia mundi*, is more fully developed by later authors, particularly al-Juwaynī (d. 1086) in his *al-Risālah al-Niẓāmiyah*, and is the argument which, as we have seen,[26] Ibn Sīnā fully exploited in his *Metaphysics*. It is noteworthy, however, that the generality of the Ash'arite theologians showed a distinct predilection for the argument *a novitate mundi* (*ḥudūth*) in so far as it harmonized with their concept of a world created in time by an omnipotent God.[27]

On the other major issue of moral theology, the distinction between good and evil, the Ash'arite doctors were equally in disagreement with the Mu'tazilah. For, whereas the latter held that man can determine rationally what is good and evil, prior to revelation, the Ash'arites adhered to a strict voluntarist ethics. Good is what God has prescribed, evil what He has prohibited. In keeping with this voluntarist thesis, they were reluctant to admit that any merit attached to that type of rational knowledge which is attainable through unaided reason.[28] God's power and sovereignty are such that the very meaning of justice and injustice is bound up with His arbitary decrees. Apart from those decrees, justice and injustice, good and evil, have no meaning whatsoever. Thus God is not compelled, as the Mu'tazilah had argued, to take note of what is "fitting" in regard to His creatures and to safeguard their moral or religious interests, so to speak, but is entirely free to punish the innocent and remit the sins of the wicked. And had He so desired, He could have created a universe entirely different from the

[25] Al-Bāqillānī, *al-Tamhīd*, pp. 23 f. [26] *Supra*, p. 173.

[27] Fakhry, "The Classical Islamic Arguments for the Existence of God," *Muslim World*, XLVII (1957), 139 f.

[28] Al-Baghdādī, *Uṣūl al-Dīn*, p. 26.

one which He has in fact created, or refrained from creating this universe or any part of it altogether.[29]

The metaphysical implementation of the theological and ethical outlook we have just outlined was the other major philosophical task the Ash'arite school set itself. In this regard the differences between its major representatives, from al-Bāqillānī to al-Shahrastānī, are minor. Al-Bāqillānī, however, played a pioneering role in elaborating the metaphysical groundwork of Ash'arism. Significantly, later authors credit him with the introduction of atomism, which served as the metaphysical prop of Ash'arite theology.

The introduction of atomism certainly antedates the rise of the Ash'arite school itself, despite the statement of Ibn Khaldūn that al-Bāqillānī was responsible for the "introduction of the rational premises on which proofs or theories depend, such as the existence of atoms, the void, and the proposition that an accident does not endure for two moments."[30] From the accounts of Islamic atomism contained in the earliest treatise on Islamic "schisms and heresies," *Maqālāt al-Islāmiyīn*, written by the founder of the Ash'arite school himself, it appears that atomism had become firmly established in theological circles by the middle of the ninth century. Thus Ḍirār b. 'Amr, a contemporary of Wāṣil b. 'Atā' (d. 748) and one of the earliest Mu'tazilite doctors of Basra, seems to have been the first theologian to challenge the generally accepted dualism of substance and accident. Al-Ash'arī reports that Ḍirār held that "body is an aggregate of accidents, which once constituted, becomes the bearer of accidents."[31] Similarly a thoroughgoing Shī'ite materialist who professed an anthropomorphic view of God of the crudest type, Hishām b. al-Ḥakam, challenged, as we have seen,[32] this orthodox dualism and reduced everything to the notion of body, which according to him was divisible ad infinitum[33] and consequently was not made up of atoms.

By the ninth century, the atomic theory of Kalām began to take definite shape. From al-Ash'arī's account, we can infer that

[29] Al-Baghdādī, *Uṣūl al-Dīn*, pp. 150 f. [30] Ibn Khaldūn, *al-Muqaddimah*, p. 645.

[31] Al-Ash'arī, *Maqālāt*, pp. 305, 281; see also al-Baghdādī, *Uṣūl al-Dīn*, p. 46.

[32] *Supra*, p. 68.

[33] Al-Ash'arī, *Maqālāt*, pp. 343, 59; cf. Fakhry, *Islamic Occasionalism*, p. 33.

Abu'l-Hudhail (d. 841 or 849), al-Iskāfī (d. 854–855), al-Jubā'ī (d. 915), al-Ash'arī's own master, Mu'ammar, a contemporary of Abu'l-Hudhail, as well as two contemporaries of his, Hishām al-Fuwaṭī and 'Abbād b. Sulaymān, accepted the atomic theory in one form or another.[34] To take al-Jubā'ī as an instance, this doctor defined substance or the atom as the bearer or substratum of accidents, which, he added, "was such in itself, and can be conceived as substance prior to its coming-to-be,"[35] presumably in some disembodied Platonic state.

The metaphysical speculation on substance and accident, initiated by the Mu'tazilah in the eighth century, was continued and refined by post-Mu'tazilite doctors. The Ash'arites, engrossed as they were with God's omnipotence and sovereignty in the world, found in atomism a convenient device for bolstering their theological claims. An Aristotelian world-view, dominated by causal processes that unfolded themselves almost mechanically, was ill-suited to their declared purpose of affirming God's prerogative to act freely and imperiously in the world. A collocation of atoms which depended, like the accidents inhering in them, on God's good pleasure, both for their creation and their duration, was more compatible in their view with the notion of God's arbitrary power.

Against the negators of the accidents, these doctors urged that the motion of a body subsequent to its rest is either due to the body itself or to something other than the body. The first alternative is absurd, since the body remains the same throughout the two successive states of motion and rest. Consequently it can only be due to something other than the body, which we call the accident.[36] Similarly, the existence of a number of strokes inflicted by an agent on a patient, for instance, is distinct from the agent, the patient, or the instrument of striking. Therefore, the number of strokes is something distinct from all those factors, and that is what we understand by accident.

The number of the accidents which the orthodox recognized totals thirty. In a general way, they may be divided into primary and

34 Al-Ash'arī, *Maqālāt*, pp. 301 ff.

35 *Ibid.*, pp. 307, 161. This view was also held by al-Khayyāt and possibly his pupil al-Ka'bī; see al-Shahrastānī, *al-Milal*, p. 53.

36 Al-Baghdādī, *Uṣūl al-Dīn*, p. 37, and al-Juwaynī, *Kitāb al-Irshād*, pp. 10–11.

secondary accidents, depending on whether they accompany substance necessarily or not. The first of the primary accidents are the essential *modi* or states (singular: *kaun*) such as motion, rest, composition, location. Then come the accidents of color, heat, cold, etc.[37] Al-Ash'arī is reported by al-Baghdādī as holding that eight of the accidents accompany substance necessarily: motion, color, taste, smell, heat or its opposite, dampness or its opposite, life or its opposite, and finally duration.[38]

The most peculiar variations on the theme of accidents are ascribed to Mu'tazilite and Ash'arite doctors. Thus the Mu'tazilite al-Ka'bī and his followers are said to have held that substance can be divested of all these "primary accidents" save color; and Abū Hāshim, al-Jubā'ī's son, held that upon its coming into being, an atom can be divested of all accidents save the accident of being (*kaun*). Another Mu'tazilite, al-Ṣāliḥī, went a step further and argued that an atom could exist without any accidents whatsoever.[39]

It is characteristic of these accidents, as al-Baghdādī relates, that they are not susceptible by themselves of any composition, contact, or transmission, since these are characteristics of the body alone. In this regard they were obviously analogous to the atoms, which were said by some theologians to be incapable by themselves of any composition, contact, or motion. However, the two are distinguished somehow, but theoretical difficulties persisted. Thus the Ash'arite and, to some extent, the Mu'tazilite doctors found the phenomena of motion quite baffling, and they resorted to the most far-fetched devices in attempting to explain motion rationally. Al-Naẓẓām, for instance, reduced every accident or quality, including human actions, to the universal category of motion, and even explained rest as a "motion of intention."[40] Therefore, he argued, when a body is said to be static at a certain point, this can only mean that it had "moved in it twice." To account for the possibility of covering a certain distance, which consisted to him of an infinite number of points or particles, al-Naẓẓām introduced the

[37] Fakhry, *Islamic Occasionalism*, pp. 37 f.
[38] Al-Baghdādī, *Uṣūl al-Dīn*, pp. 42 and 56 f.
[39] *Ibid.*, pp. 56 f.; al-Ash'arī, *Maqālāt*, pp. 310, 570.
[40] Al-Baghdādī, *Farq*, p. 121, and *Maqālāt*, pp. 324 f.

concept of the leap (*ṭafrah*), or the view that a body could move from point A to point C without passing by the intermediary point B.[41]

The Ash'arites, who subscribed to an even more extreme concept of discontinuous or discrete being, solved the difficulty in another way. They argued that motion and rest are two primary states or *modi* of substance, as has been noted. A substance which moves from one point to the other is at rest in relation to the second point, but in motion in relation to the first. Only al-Qalānisī, a somewhat dissident Ash'arite, is reported by al-Baghdādī as holding that rest consisted of two successive states of being in the same place, whereas motion consisted of two successive states in the first and the second places necessarily.[42]

The most characteristic feature of the atoms of *Kalām*, as we have seen,[43] was their perishable nature, which the Ash'arites, adhered to almost without exception. Not only al-Bāqillānī but the founder of the Ash'arite school himself believed the accidents to be perishable by nature and to belong to the class of "transient things" (*a'rāḍ*) of this world, referred to in the Koran (8,67 and 46,24).[44]

In demonstrating the perishability of accidents, al-Baghdādī argues that the "thesis of the durability of accidents entails their indestructibility. For if an accident is said to endure by itself . . . then it could persist in being until an opposite, necessitating its destruction, should come into being. However, there is no sufficient reason why such an opposite should arise and thereby counter its tendency to resist such an incursion."[45]

Thus the duration of substances was made contingent upon the inherence in them of the accident of duration (*baqā'*). Since, however, this accident is not capable of duration per se, it followed that either the durability of substance is to be referred to other accidents of duration indefinitely, or else another principle of durability had to be introduced. This principle the Ash'arites identified with God's own decree to preserve in being or destroy at will the atoms or ultimate

[41] Al-Shahrastānī, *al-Milal*, pp. 38 f.; al-Ash'arī, *Maqālāt*, p. 321.
[42] Al-Baghdādī, *Uṣūl al-Dīn*, p. 40. [43] *Supra*, p. 237.
[44] Al-Bāqillānī, *al-Tamhīd*, p. 18; al-Ash'arī, *Maqālāt*, p. 370.
[45] Al-Baghdādī, *Uṣūl al-Dīn*, p. 51.

components of physical objects in the world. Both the accidents and the atoms in which they inhere depended for their duration in this way on God's decree to repeat the process of their recreation as long as He pleased. Notwithstanding this circumstance, some Ash'arite doctors found it necessary to give a rational account of a body's eventual corruption or cessation. Thus al-Bāqillānī described annihilation (*fanā'*) as the act of withholding the two accidents of color and mode (*kaun*) from the body. Inasmuch as a body can never be divested of these two accidents, such an action necessarily entailed, according to him, the annihilation of the body.[46] Such annihilation did not depend therefore on the inherence of the accident of corruption in the body, a thesis which, despite its strangeness, had at least one exponent. Al-Qalānisī argued that when God wishes to destroy a certain body, He creates *in it* the accident of corruption, which results in its destruction forthwith.[47]

The contribution of late Ash'arite doctors, such as al-Juwaynī and al-Shahrastānī, consists chiefly in elaborating or defending the concepts and methods to which the school as a whole was committed. The former, known also as Imām al-Ḥaramayn, developed some of the epistemological and theological implications of Ash'arite doctrine in *al-Shāmil*, of which an abridgement, *al-Irshād*, was made by the author. Al-Shahrastānī, an author of encyclopedic learning, wrote one of the best known and most comprehensive "heresiographies" in Arabic, *K. al-Milal wa'l-Niḥal.* The second part of it is an invaluable source for the reconstruction of the Islamic picture of Greek philosophy, and we have drawn freely upon it in an earlier chapter.[48] In addition, al-Shahrastānī wrote a compendium of theology, *Nihāyat al-Iqdām*, which surpasses many of the earlier treatises in its thoroughness and logical coherence, although it adds little to our knowledge of the scholastic tradition in theology.

[46] Al-Baghdādī, *Uṣūl al-Dīn*, p. 45. [47] *Ibid.*, pp. 67, 45. [48] *Supra*, pp. 56 f.

III

THE SYSTEMATIC REFUTATION OF NEO-PLATONISM: AL-GHAZĀLĪ

The greatest figure in the history of the Islamic reaction to Neo-Platonism is al-Ghazālī, jurist, theologian, philosopher, and mystic. Born in Ṭūs (Khurāsān) in 1058, al-Ghazālī addressed himself at an early age to the study of jurisprudence (*fiqh*) with a certain Rādhkānī, then moved on to Jurjān, where he continued his studies with Abu'l-Qāsim al-Ismā'īlī. His greatest teacher, however, was al-Juwaynī, the outstanding Ash'arite theologian of the period. Al-Juwāynī initiated his brilliant pupil into the study of *Kalām*, philosophy, and logic. His introduction to the theory and practice of mysticism was due to al-Fārmadhī (d. 1084), a renowned *Ṣūfī* of the period.

Al-Ghazālī's fortunes took a decisive turn as a result of meeting Niẓām al-Mulk, vizier of the Saljūk sultan Malikshah. This able but doctrinaire vizier was fired by an intense zeal for the defense of Sunnite orthodoxy, and he consequently attacked the Shī'ite (Ismā'īlī) heterodoxy of the rival Fāṭimid caliphate at Cairo. The latter had so successfully wielded the double weapon of propaganda and political assassination throughout the Muslim world that the Saljūks felt compelled to reply in kind. To this end, Niẓām al-Mulk set up a series of theological schools or seminaries, named after him, throughout the eastern part of the empire, where the study of Shāfi'ī *fiqh* and Ash'arite theology were actively pursued. Al-Juwaynī had been the head of the Niẓāmiyah of Nishapūr until his death in 1085. It now devolved upon his disciple to serve the cause of Sunnite orthodoxy.[49]

For five years (1091 to 1095), then, al-Ghazālī, as head of the Niẓāmiyah of Baghdad, pursued his teaching in jurisprudence and theology

[49] See al-Subkī, *Ṭabaqāt al-Shāfi'iyah al-Kubra*, IV, 101 f., and Jabre," La biographie et l'œuvre de Ghazali considérés à la lumière des *Ṭabaqāts* de Subki," *Mélanges de l'Institut Dominicain d'Etudes Orientales du Caire*, 1954, pp. 83 f.

with great success. The troubled political situation of the times and the violent death of Niẓām al-Mulk in 1092 at the hand of an Ismā'īlī assassin, followed shortly after by the death of the sultan Malikshah, appear to have contributed to his gradual disillusionment with teaching. His initiation into the practice of the *Ṣūfī* way, between 1093 and 1094, no doubt added to his sense of the futility of a career that was not dedicated to the disinterested quest of truth or the service of God.

In a moving autobiographical work, *al-Munqidh*, which has been compared to St. Augustine's *Confessions*, al-Ghazālī tells the dramatic story of his spiritual and intellectual anxiety and doubt; his renunciation, at the height of his fame, of his teaching career at Baghdad in 1095; his peregrinations throughout Syria, Palestine, and Ḥijāz; and his eventual resumption of teaching, eleven years later, at Nishapūr.[50] This second term of instruction, however, was short lived. Five years later, in 1111, his eventful and active life as a scholar and mystic came to an untimely end.

Al-Ghazālī's autobiography introduces us, almost from the very first line, to the intellectual and spiritual problems with which he had to contend throughout his whole life, and particularly during the period of tribulation which followed his resignation from the Niẓāmiyah school at Baghdad. Even before he was twenty, al-Ghazālī tells us, he had been seized by an ardent desire for truth and had been distressed at the spectacle of conflicting beliefs and creeds and the passivity and credulity of the common run of mankind who defer blindly to the authority of their elders. Accordingly, he resolved to search for "certain knowledge," which he defines as "that knowledge in which the object is known in a manner which is not open to doubt at all,"[51] so that if its truth were to be challenged by a miracle-maker, it would withstand that challenge. When he proceeded to inquire whether he was actually in possession of such knowledge, he was led to conclude that the only knowledge which tallied with this description was sense knowledge and the knowledge of self-evident propositions. In order to pursue the process of doubt to its logical consequence, however, he felt he had to satisfy himself that such knowledge was

[50] For al-Ghazālī's itinerary see *ibid.*, pp. 94 ff.
[51] *Al-Munqidh mina'l-Ḍalāl*, p. 11.

indeed certain. At the end of a painful process of doubt, he found that in fact it was not. For, in the case of the former, our senses often judge that the object is such and such, but their judgment is soon subverted by reason. For instance, we look at a shadow and infer that it is stationary, but soon after we are compelled to admit that it was not. Or we look at a remote object, such as the planet, which appears to our senses to be the size of a coin, whereas astronomical evidence compels us to believe that it is many times larger than the earth.[52]

If sense experience is not to be trusted, then by analogy the knowledge of necessary propositions or axioms is not to be trusted either. For, as the senses at once reminded al-Ghazālī: What right had he to think that his confidence in the necessary propositions of reason differed from his confidence in sensible knowledge? The latter had been shown by reason to be doubtful; might it not then be that there "exists beyond reason a higher authority, which would, upon its manifestation, show the judgment of reason to be invalid, just as the authority of reason had shown the judgment of sense to be invalid?"[53] The analogy of dream is instructive here. Very often in dreams we are confident of the reality of our experiences but this confidence is dispelled as soon as we wake up. Might it not be, then, that our waking life is no better, as the Prophet has said, than dreaming, in comparison with the life after death?

These doubts, al-Ghazālī tells us, continued to afflict him like a real sickness for almost two months. Eventually he recovered his intellectual health, not through his own efforts, but rather through a "light which God infused into his heart, which indeed is the key to most species of knowledge."[54] This light, he now realized, was not a matter of discourse or argument, but of divine grace, which the Prophet had described as "the dilation of the heart, whereby it becomes prone to the reception of Islam."[55] The signs attendant upon it are the renunciation of this world of illusion and the turning toward the world of reality.

Much has been written about al-Ghazālī's sincerity and the significance of his use of the method of doubt. Whether or not the account given in *al-Munqidh* is a factual record of his spiritual and intellectual

[52] *Al-Munqidh mina'l-Ḍalāl*, p. 12. [53] *Ibid.*, p. 13. [54] *Ibid.*
[55] Koran, 6,125.

experience is a purely academic question. What is of particular significance is the profound earnestness with which he depicts in this work the "states of his own soul" as it was assailed by doubt, recovered faith through the outpouring of divine light, and how finally he consented to champion publicly the cause of orthodoxy against the sectarians of heresy and deceit.

Of these sectarians he singles out four groups that might be presumed to be in possession of the (Islamic) truth in the eleventh century; if none of them was in possession of such truth, the quest for certainty would be entirely futile. These four are the theologians, the Ismā'īlīs (or Bāṭinīs), the philosophers, and the *Ṣūfīs*.

The aim of theology (*Kalām*), which he had first studied, was the defense of orthodoxy and the repulsion of the heretics' attacks on it. In this defense, the theologians start with some premises that are not certain in themselves but must be accepted on the authority of Scripture or the consensus of the community. Hence, this branch of learning, though useful, does not lead per se to that indubitable certainty which al-Ghazālī was seeking.[56]

The Ismā'īlī doctrine, known as *Ta'līm* (instruction) during this period, did not quench his thirst for truth either. For the substance of Ismā'īlī doctrine is that the knowledge of truth is not possible without a teacher, and the only teacher whose teaching cannot be doubted is an infallible teacher, or, as he was called by the Ismā'īlīs, the *Imām*. Here, however, the question arises: What are the marks of such an infallible *Imām* and where is he to be found? Muslims have an infallible teacher, namely, the Prophet. The Ismā'īlīs who recognize the authority of the Prophet argue nevertheless that he is dead. In reply to this argument it can be urged that the *Imām*, though not dead, is equally inaccessible, since he is said to be in temporary concealment (*ghā'ib*).[57]

Despite the vehemence with which al-Ghazālī inveighs against the Ismā'īlīs and their splinter groups in his works,[58] his polemics against

[56] *Al-Munqidh*, pp. 16 f.

[57] *Ibid.*, pp. 29 f. The seventh *Imām* in Ismā'īlī and the twelfth in Imāmī doctrine are both believed to be in "temporary concealment" but will reappear at the end of the millennium.

[58] The most detailed critique of the Ismā'īlīs is in *Faḍāi'ḥ al-Bāṭiniyah* (*The Scandals of the Baṭīnīs*).

the Arab Neo-Platonists are by far the most sustained and the most searching. And it is naturally these polemics that are particularly interesting to us here. The suppressed, almost instinctive, reaction against rationalism in general and Greek philosophy in particular, which had been a characteristic mark of orthodoxy heretofore, bursts forth in al-Ghazālī's attacks on the Muslim Neo-Platonists, particularly al-Fārābī and Ibn Sīnā. Earlier orthodox writers had been content to challenge rationalism or to reproach the philosophically inclined, on grounds either of piety or of xenophobia. Al-Ghazālī, who agreed with the general sentiment of the orthodox, felt nonetheless that "only one who has mastered the science [of philosophy] to such a degree that he can vie with the most proficient in that science"[59] and even excel them will be qualified to show the incoherence of their doctrine. Since no one had accomplished this difficult task before him, al-Ghazālī felt compelled to grapple with this problem with all his might. He therefore turned to the study of philosophy in his spare time, since he was occupied during this period with teaching religious subjects to no fewer than 300 students at the Niẓāmiyah of Baghdad. Although he does not mention this in his autobiography, he had, as we have seen, already made a start in that direction as a student of al-Juwaynī in Nishapūr.[60] Presumably, his study of philosophy in a systematic way was made during this second period. In three years, he was able, according to his own account, "through God's assistance," to master the philosophical sciences completely. The fruit of these years of philosophical initiation was a work entitled the *Intentions of the Philosophers*, in which he states that his express purpose is to expound the doctrines of the philosophers, as a prelude to refuting them in a subsequent work.[61] This exposition of the tenets of Arab Neo-Platonism is so skillfully written that a careless reader would conclude that it is the work of a conventional Neo-Platonist, as indeed the thirteenth-century Scholastic doctors had concluded when it appeared in the Latin version of Dominicus Gundissalinus, entitled *Logica et Philosophia Algazelis Arabis*. This circumstance was at the root of the widespread belief in

[59] *Al-Munqidh*, p. 18.
[60] *Supra*, p. 244, and Jabre, "La biographie," pp. 78 f.
[61] *Maqāṣid al-Falāsifah*, pp. 31 ff., 385.

the later Middle Ages that Algazel was a genuine Neo-Platonist of the stamp of Avicenna and others.[62]

Other fruits of al-Ghazālī's philosophical initiation are to be found in an important manual of Aristotelian logic, *Mi'yār al-'Ilm* (*The Criterion of Science*). This work, and the *Intentions* and *Tahāfut*, form a philosophical trilogy of the utmost significance for the study of the history of the struggle between the theologians and the philosophers of Islam.

We are not, however, concerned here with al-Ghazālī's contribution to the dissemination of Neo-Platonism, since his professed aim was not its advancement but rather its rebuttal. Indeed, al-Fārābī and Ibn Sīnā, the two major targets of his attack, had by their thoroughness rendered any further creative contribution in that domain almost impossible. The chief contribution of al-Ghazālī lay instead in his identification with the antiphilosophical party, and his attempt to prove the incoherence of the philosophers on *philosophical* grounds; hence his importance in the history of philosophical thought in Islam.

Al-Ghazālī's motive in writing his *Tahāfut* (or *Collapse of the Philosophers*) is stated explicitly to be religious. What prompted him to write this work, he tells us, was the way in which a small group of free-thinkers had been led to repudiate Islamic beliefs and neglect the ritual basis of worship as unworthy of their intellectual attainments. They were confirmed in this by the widespread adulation reserved for the ancient philosophers, from Socrates to Aristotle, who were erroneously supposed to partake of their irreligion. However, had they taken the trouble to examine the teaching of these philosophers, they would have discovered that "every one worthy of note among the ancients and the moderns"[63] subscribed to the two fundamentals of religious belief, i.e., the existence of God and the reality of the Day of Judgment. Differences among them affect only incidentally the substance of their belief.

In substantiating the latter claim, al-Ghazālī draws a distinction between those philosophical sciences such as mathematics and logic, which are completely innocuous from a religious point of view, and

[62] Salman, "Algazel et les Latins," *Archives d'histoire doctrinale et littéraire du moyen âge*, 1935–36, pp. 103–27.

[63] *Tahāfut al-Falāsifah*, p. 6.

those which, like physics and metaphysics, contain the bulk of the heresies or errors of the philosophers.[64] Three of those philosophers deserve special mention: Aristotle, who organized and perfected the philosophical sciences; and al-Fārābī and Ibn Sīnā, who are the two most authoritative and trustworthy expositors of Aristotelian philosophy in Islam.[65] The rebuttal of the view of these three should enable the critic of philosophy to dispense with the rebuttal of lesser figures.

Al-Ghazālī's attack is thus judiciously leveled directly at the two leading Muslim Neo-Platonists, and indirectly at Aristotle, their master. Altogether, he enumerates sixteen metaphysical and four physical propositions that have an obvious religious relevance and against which the unguarded believer must be warned. Of these propositions, three are particularly obnoxious from a religious point of view, and consequently those who uphold them must be declared renegades, liable to the religious sanctions against renegades in Islam. These propositions are the eternity of the world *a parte ante*, God's knowledge of universals only, and the denial of the resurrection of the body.[66] The remaining seventeen propositions do not, in al-Ghazālī's opinion, justify the charge of irreligion (*kufr*), but simply that of heresy (*bid'ah*). Many of them are professed by other sectarians of Muslim heresy, such as the Mu'tazilah, and should not on that account be regarded as equivalent to apostasy except on a very narrow-minded or bigoted interpretation, which al-Ghazālī is careful to disallow.

The first proposition of the *Tahāfut* bears on the eternity of the world as professed by the Islamic Neo-Platonists and Aristotle. In their espousal of the emanationist world-view, as we have seen, the latter had disassociated themselves from the main body of orthodox Islam. As early as al-Ash'arī, the heterodox implications of the thesis of eternity had been clearly discerned by the theologians, but with the exception of Ibn Ḥazm[67] (d. 1064) no systematic exposition and refutation of these implications had been attempted before al-Ghazālī's time. Implicit in the polemic of the theologians against this thesis is the claim that it militated against the Koranic concept of creation *ex nihilo*, and as a corollary involved an arbitrary limitation of God's absolute power.

[64] *Tahāfut al-Falāsifah*, p. 6; cf. *al-Munqidh*, pp. 20 f.
[65] *Tahāfut al-Falāsifah*, p. 9.
[66] *Ibid.*, p. 376, and *al-Munqidh*, pp. 23 f.
[67] *Al-Fiṣal*, Bk. I, pp. 3 f.

The views of the philosophers on the question of the eternity of the world are stated by al-Ghazālī to be three: (1) the view of the vast majority, ancient and modern, who believed it to be eternal; (2) the view of Plato, who held that it was created in time;[68] and (3) the view of Galen, who suspended judgment on this issue.[69]

In his rebuttal of the eternalist thesis, al-Ghazālī asserts that the world was created in time, through an eternal decree of God. He rejects in this connection the claim that the lapse of time which separates the eternal decree of God and the creation of the world involves the supposition that God could not accomplish the creation at once. This claim, he argues, does not rest on any demonstrative grounds but is simply a dogmatic assertion.[70]

A mathematical argument is then advanced against the Neo-Platonists. The eternity of the world entails logically that an infinite number of revolutions of the heavens have already elapsed. We know, however, that these revolutions can serve as the basis of mathematical computations. For instance, the sphere of the sun completes a single revolution in a year, that of Saturn in 30, that of Jupiter in 12, and that of the firmament in 36,000 years. A finite ratio between the revolutions of the sun and the other spheres can be given as follows: 1/30, 1/12, 1/36,000 respectively, which would contradict the assumption that these revolutions are infinite and occur in an infinite time.[71]

Moreover, these revolutions are either odd or even, and must consequently be finite. For the infinite is neither odd nor even, since it can be increased by one indefinitely, while remaining infinite. To top it all, the Neo-Platonists assert the possibility of an infinite number

[68] *Tahāfut al-Falāsifah*, pp. 21 f. Plato's view is reported with the proviso that some have questioned that he actually believed this to be the case. Of the Greek interpreters of Plato, Aristotle (*Physics* 251^{b}17; *De Caelo* 280^{a}30), understood Plato to mean in *Timaeus* 38B, that both the universe and time were created together. Xenocrates, on the other hand, followed by the Platonists and the Neo-Platonists, generally understood Plato to imply the eternity of the universe, but to use the metaphorical language of temporal production. See Taylor, *Plato*, pp. 442 f.

[69] Galen's view is said to have been given in his work *What Galen Believed*; cf. *Tahāfut*, p. 21, and F. D. al-Rāzī, *al-Muḥaṣṣal*, p. 86.

[70] *Tahāfut al-Falāsifah*, pp. 29 f.

[71] *Ibid.*, pp. 31 f. This argument appears to derive ultimately from John Philoponus and is quoted by Simplicius in his commentary on *Physica* (Diels, 1179, 15–27). Cf. *Averroes' Tahāfut al-Tahāfut*, II, 7.

of Souls, existing in a disembodied condition, as Ibn Sīnā held,[72] despite the logical contradiction which the concept of an actual infinite involves.

In his rebuttal of the Avicennian arguments that God is prior to the world in essence, rather than in time, al-Ghazālī takes an unequivocal stand in support of the creation of time. When we say that God is prior to the world, we simply mean, according to him, that God existed while the world was not, and continued to exist together with the world. What these two propositions assert is the existence of an entity (God) concurrently with the nonexistence of both entities together.[73] The representation of a *tertium quid* (time) is a trick of the imagination, which compels us to represent both entities as linked together, through this *tertium quid*.

As for the view that prior to its creation the world was obviously possible, it does not necessarily entail, as the Neo-Platonists contend, an eternal substratum in which possibility inheres. For, on this view, not only the possible but its two contraries, the impossible and the necessary, would also require such a substratum, and this is clearly absurd. The possible, the impossible, and the necessary, as indeed all other common qualities, have only a conceptual reality. What exists is simply the entity of which they are predicated.[74]

The second question of the *Tahāfut* deals with perpetuity or eternity *a parte post*. But, neither in itself nor for al-Ghazālī, does this question raise the same crucial theological issues as that of pre-eternity, of which post-eternity is explicitly stated to be a logical offshoot. A whole group of questions (3 to 11) deals next with God and His attributes. In Question 3, the fundamental issue is raised whether, in the context of Neo-Platonism, God could be rightly described as the Creator or Maker of the world. For, according to the Neo-Platonists, the world emanates from God (or the First, as they call Him) necessarily, just as the effect emanates from the cause or the light from the sun. Now a genuine agent must be conscious and free, so that God can only be designated by these philosophers as the Maker (*Ṣāni'*) of the world metaphorically.

[72] For a discussion of this question, see Marmura, "Avicenna and the Problem of the Infinite Number of Souls," *Mediaeval Studies*, XXII (1960), 232 ff.

[73] *Tahāfut al-Falāsifah*, p. 53.

[74] *Ibid.*, pp. 70 f.

Moreover the world, being eternal, according to them, can hardly be said to be created. For creation or making denotes the act of bringing an entity forth into being, out of nothing, and the eternal is forever in being.[75] Likewise the Neo-Platonists hold that out of one only one can come (*ex uno non fit nisi unum*), but since God is one and the world multiple, there can be no sense in saying that He is its Maker. Indeed, from their premises it would follow that only a series of ones or simple entities could emanate from the "First." As to the multiple or composite entities which make up the world, none of the arguments of the Neo-Platonists can account for their production.

What is more, the Neo-Platonists are unable to prove the existence of God either (Question 4). All their arguments rest on the impossibility of an infinite regress and the necessity of positing ultimately an Uncaused Cause of the series of effects. However, (a) bodies are eternal, according to them, and require, in consequence, no cause, and (b) an infinite series is not impossible since it follows from their thesis of the eternity of the world that an infinite series of effects has come and gone heretofore. Some of them, as we have seen in the case of Ibn Sīnā, even admit that an infinite number of Souls can exist in a disembodied condition.[76]

Al-Ghazālī next turns to the question of divine attributes. The Neo-Platonists are unable to prove the unity of God (Question 5). The substance of their proof is that if we posit two necessary beings, necessity would not belong to each of them essentially, but through a cause, so that the Necessary Being would be caused, which is absurd. This proof is not valid because their distinction between the necessary-in-itself and the necessary-through-a-cause, upon which this proof rests, is unfounded. The Neo-Platonists, in fact, deny the divine attributes altogether (Question 6). Such attributes are, according to them, accidents of the essence and, as such, involve plurality and contingency in the subject. God, they claim, cannot be the bearer of any attributes, but they admit at the same time that He is nonetheless knowing (*'ālim*), which obviously implies that He possesses the attribute of knowledge, however we might interpret it.[77]

[75] *Tahāfut al-Falāsifah*, pp. 103 f.

[76] *Ibid.*, pp. 136 f., and *supra*, p. 252.

[77] *Ibid.*, pp. 172 f.

The question of divine knowledge is the second issue on which al-Ghazālī denounces the Neo-Platonists. We might pause therefore to consider his objections at length. In Question 11 he introduces the discussion by expounding the Islamic (Ash'arite) view of divine knowledge. Since the act of willing implies the knowledge of what is willed, and the whole world has been willed by God, it follows that the whole world is known to Him and is caused by this double act of knowing and willing.[78] But to be capable of knowledge and will is to be alive. Therefore God must be alive and, as such, capable of knowing everything which emanates from Him, together with Himself, as its source. The Neo-Platonists, who have stripped God of all essential attributes, have been led to conclude that "the Lord of Lords and the Cause of Causes has no knowledge whatsoever of anything which happens in the world. [One might ask them, therefore] what difference is there between Him and the dead, except in regard of His self-knowledge [which they admit], and what excellence does this self-knowledge involve, when coupled with ignorance of everything else?"[79]

The philosophers, having thus denied that God has will, are unable to prove that He has knowledge either. The substance of the argument of Ibn Sīnā on this score, for instance, is that the First, being entirely immaterial, must be a pure intellect ('*aql*), and must accordingly know all things, since the only bar to such knowledge is matter.[80] However, Ibn Sīnā and his fellow Neo-Platonists are unable to substantiate their claim that God is an intellect, but simply infer it from the premise that He is *not* a material entity. However, all that can be inferred from the proposition that the First is not a material object, nor an accident of a material object, is that He is self-subsistent. To argue that He is in consequence an intellect, since He knows Himself or knows other things, is to beg the question. Only on the assumption that He knows Himself, as well as other things, can it be asserted that He is a pure intellect, which is precisely the point at issue.[81]

It may be objected that the philosophers do not deny that the world is the product of God's action, but only that He has willed it in time.

[78] *Tahāfut al-Falāsifah*, pp. 210 f. [79] *Ibid.*, p. 182. [80] *Ibid.*, p. 211.
[81] *Ibid.*, p. 212.

For they do not question the general proposition that the agent is necessarily conscious of his action. God, who has produced the "whole," must in consequence be conscious of His production.[82]

Al-Ghazālī counters this objection on three grounds. (1) The world is said by the Neo-Platonists to emanate from God by a "necessity of nature," analogous to the emanation of light from the sun. Obviously, such an emanation does not involve either willing or thinking on the part of the agent. (2) Some (e.g., Ibn Sīnā) claim that the emanation of the "whole" from God is the result of His knowledge of this "whole" and this knowledge is identical with the essence of God. This claim, however, is disputed by other philosophers, who describe emanation in terms of natural necessity, as in (1). (3) Even if the latter version of emanation is accepted, the only corollary thereof is that God knows only the first entity to result from His action, i.e., the first intellect, which in turn knows what results from it, and so on down the scale of subsequent emanations. God cannot, according to this version, know the "whole" either.[83]

Indeed, it does not follow from the premises of the philosophers that God knows Himself either (Question 12), for we infer the knowledge of self from the fact of life, which in turn is inferred from knowledge and will. The philosophers, in denying that God is capable of willing, as we have seen, are unable to prove that He knows Himself or anything that follows from Him either. To be consistent, the philosophers must deny that God is capable of knowing, seeing, or hearing (attributed to Him by the generality of Muslims), since these attributes denote, according to them, imperfections rightly predicated of the creature but not of God.[84]

Perhaps the most crucial aspect of the problem of divine knowledge, from the Islamic point of view, is the denial of God's knowledge of particulars. The Koran states explicitly (e.g., 34,3) that nothing escapes God's knowledge, not even "the smallest particle in heaven or on earth." Philosophers who admit, like Ibn Sīnā, that God knows things other than Himself, have argued nevertheless that the mode of His knowledge is "universal." It is not subject, like "particular" knowledge, to the limitations of time or place. Thus God knows an

[82] *Tahāfut al-Falāsifah*, p. 214. [83] *Ibid.*, p. 216. [84] *Ibid.*, pp. 221 f.

event (say, the eclipse of the sun) prior to its occurrence or subsequently thereto, in the same instantaneous manner. For He knows a priori the series of causes from which it will ultimately result. Similarly, He knows an individual man, for instance Zaid or 'Amr, in so far as He knows the "absolute man," i.e., independently of the conditions of time or place. The particular or accidental qualities, or the spatio-temporal determinations, which set such an individual apart from other individuals, are objects of sense experience of which God cannot possibly partake.[85]

In his rebuttal al-Ghazālī argues that God's knowledge is indeed independent of the conditions of time and space. It does not, on that account, exclude relation to particulars, which are subject to such conditions. The changes to which the mode of this knowledge is liable do not involve change in the essence of the knower, but rather in the relationship of his knowledge to the object, which is continually changing.

If it is maintained nonetheless that such relations enter into the definition of the object, so that change in the latter will involve change in the knower necessarily, one might retort that, if this were true, even the knowledge of universals would involve change in the knower, in so far as such knowledge involves different relationships to the knower. And since these universals are infinite in number, it is not clear how, on the argument of the philosophers, the unity of God's knowledge can be safeguarded, unless we assume that the change or plurality in the object does not necessarily affect the knower.[86]

Nor does it follow from the premises of the Neo-Platonists that the Eternal Being (God) is not subject to change. They posit that the world (which according to them is eternal) is nevertheless subject to change. As to the detraction from the perfection of God which the dependence of His knowledge upon the changing object must involve, we can only observe that there can be no greater detraction from this perfection than the claim of the philosophers that everything emanates from God by way of natural necessity, without His knowledge or preordination.[87]

In the "physical" part of the *Tahāfut*, al-Ghazālī considers two major questions: the repudiation of the necessity of the causal nexus and the

[85] *Tahāfut al-Falāsifah*, p. 227. [86] *Ibid.*, pp. 232 f [87] *Ibid.*, p. 237.

resurrection of the body. The former (Question 17) had been one of the major issues which more than two centuries earlier had set the theologians against the philosophers in general and the Peripatetics in particular. The tendency of the latter to ascribe to "secondary causes" a certain degree of efficacy in the natural order was frowned upon by the theologians on the ground that it militated against the koranic concept of an omnipotent Deity who carried out His grand cosmic designs imperiously and directly and who, in consequence, had no need of any mediator.[88] The occasionalist metaphysics of atoms and accidents, which as we have seen was developed by the theologians of the ninth century, was designed precisely to safeguard God's absolute independence from any conditions or limitations, natural or other. With the exception of a few Mu'tazilite theologians who introduced the concept of generation (*tawallud*) as a theoretical device for retaining the efficacy of natural agents,[89] the Muslim theologians rejected "secondary causation" as incompatible with God's uniqueness and sovereignty in the world. Al-Ghazālī, however, was the first theologian to undertake a systematic refutation of the concept of a necessary causal nexus. In this, he appears to have been influenced by the Greek skeptics of the Pyrrhonian school.[90]

The discussion of causality opens with the statement that the correlation between the so-called cause and effect is not necessary, for only where logical implication is involved can a necessary correlation be admitted. It is plain, however, that between two distinct conditions or events, such as eating and satiety, contact with fire and burning, decapitation and dying, no such correlation can be asserted. The observed correlation between concomitant events in medicine, astronomy, and the arts is due merely to God's action in joining them constantly. It is logically possible, however, for this conjunction to be infringed and the so-called effects be produced *ab initio*, without their concomitant causes, as indeed happens in what Muslims universally regard as miracles.[91]

88 Fakhry, *Islamic Occasionalism*, pp. 56 ff., and *supra*, p. 233.

89 Fakhry, "Some Paradoxical Implications of the Mu'tazilite View of Free Will," *Muslim World*, XLIII (1953), pp. 98 ff.

90 Van den Bergh, *Averroes' Tahāfut al-Tahāfut*, Vol. I, Introduction, pp. xxix *et seq.*; Vol. II, *passim*.

91 Al-Ghazālī, *Tahāfut al-Falāsifah*, pp. 276 f.

Take the case of fire in relation to cotton. The philosophers claim that fire causes the burning of the cotton, whereas we maintain, says al-Ghazālī, that the real agent in this process is God, acting either directly by Himself, or indirectly through an angel. For fire is inanimate, and cannot therefore be said to cause anything whatsoever. The only proof that the philosophers can advance is that we observe burning to occur upon contact with fire, but observation simply proves that the burning follows upon contact with fire, not that it is due to it, or that it is in fact the only possible cause of burning.

Or take the case of life and growth, in relation to the animal. It is plain that life, as well as the cognitive and motive faculties which inhere in the sperm of the animal, are not the effects of the four primary qualities.[92] Nor is the father, who deposits the sperm in the mother's womb, the cause of the infant's life, hearing, or seeing, etc. This cause is the First Being. In fact, the major philosophers admit that the accidents or events which result from the conjunction of natural causes and effects are ultimately due to the "Giver of Forms," who is an angel or a separate substance,[93] from whom the "substantial forms" of natural objects emanate, once matter has become sufficiently disposed to receive them.

However, the philosophers might admit that the ultimate causes of natural processes are supermundane, and yet ascribe to the action of natural causes or agents the disposition or aptitude for receiving their action. Accordingly, if we posit that fire is of a certain nature and cotton is of a certain nature also, it is impossible that fire should sometimes burn cotton and sometimes not, unless the nature of fire or that of cotton has changed in the interval.[94]

Al-Ghazālī's solution of this difficulty is that the supermundane principles or agents, particularly God, do not act by way of causal necessity, as the philosophers claim, but rather by way of will. Consequently, it is quite possible logically for God to cause burning in some

[92] I.e., moist and dry, hot and cold.

[93] *Tahāfut al-Falāsifah*, p. 281; cf. Ibn Sīnā, *al-Najāt*, pp. 283 *et passim*; *al-Shifā'* (*Ilāhiyāt*), pp. 410 ff. The Giver of Forms is explicitly stated by Ibn Sīnā to be the active intellect, or the last of the separate intelligences emanating from the One; see *supra*, p. 177.

[94] Al-Ghazālī, *Tahāfut al-Falāsifah*, p. 283.

instances but not in others. One might object that, on this supposition, everything becomes possible and nothing will be known with certainty, except where God wished at the same time to impart directly the knowledge corresponding to the action. For instance, we may imagine a man looking out on a strange scene: fire burning, lions roaring, soldiers marching, without beholding any part of it, because God did not create in him the corresponding perception of this scene at the time. Or we may leave a book behind and, on returning home, find that the book has changed into a lad or a beast, or the lad has turned into a dog, etc. God could thus create whatever He pleases, in any order He pleases, since He is not bound by any order, causal or other.[95]

In his retort, al-Ghazālī states that these absurdities would result only if we assume that God will not create in us the knowledge corresponding to the events or to the fact that they are possible. But God has created in us the knowledge that these events are merely possible, not that they are actual. They could just as well occur as not occur. Their repetitiveness "establishes firmly in our minds [the notion] of their occurrence according to the past habitual course."[96] But it is possible for a prophet or an ordinary man with prophetic or acute intuitive powers to foresee that such events will happen in a manner which does not conform with the normal course of events in nature. In such situations God simply creates in the mind of the knower the corresponding knowledge and thereby the alleged difficulty vanishes.

The knowledge of the sequence of such events is normally dependent on their actual occurrence. Without denying that certain elements, e.g., fire, are endowed with certain properties, such as the power to burn cotton, however, it is not logically excluded that God or His angels may cause this power to be checked in such a way that it will not cause burning in the cotton; or He may create in the cotton the power to resist the action of burning. Such miracles, reported in the Koran, as [Christ's] resurrecting the dead or [Moses'] turning a stick into a serpent could thus be explained in a perfectly rational manner. Or it may be possible for God to effect His miraculous designs without violence to the natural process of events, but rather through what might be called telescoping or abridging this process. Thus matter, according

[95] Al-Ghazālī, *Tahāfut al-Falāsifah*, pp. 284 f. [96] *Ibid.*, p. 285.

to the Peripatetic philosophers, is susceptible of many contrary qualities. The generation of animals, in their view, results from a series of permutations culminating in the animal in question. Earth turns into a vegetable, which upon being consumed by the animal parent turns into blood, which in turn is converted inside the body into the seminal fluid, which eventually develops into an individual offspring. *Habitually*, this process takes a fairly long time, but it is not logically excluded that God could bring these permutations about in a shorter period than is His wont, and then in progressively shorter periods until we come to a period so short as to be instantaneous. And this is what we denote as a miracle.[97]

Indeed the philosophers allow that the generation of animals or vegetables is bound up with the ability of matter, as it becomes disposed through the influence of the heavenly conjunctions and their diverse motions, to receive the forms which emanate from the active intellect or Giver of Forms, as we have seen. On this supposition, the most extraordinary occurrences in the world become possible, and extraordinary events or miracles perfectly intelligible.

The final three "physical" questions of the *Tahāfut* deal with the nature of the Soul and its immortality, according to Neo-Platonic doctrine. In Question 18, al-Ghazālī sets forth the arguments of those philosophers for the immateriality and simplicity of the Soul and shows that they are simply inconclusive. Nor are their arguments for its immortality conclusive either, for these rest on the simplicity and the immateriality of the Soul, which they are unable to establish (Question 19).

Since none of these arguments is conclusive, the only recourse left is the authority of Scripture or revelation (*al-shar'*),[98] which asserts immortality in an undoubted manner and expatiates on the state of the Soul in the after-life. Much of what the philosophers say concerning the noncorporeal or spiritual pleasures reserved to the Soul in the after-life is in conformity with the teaching of Scripture. What we question, al-Ghazālī argues, is that their knowledge of the immortality of the Soul and the spiritual pleasures or pains of the after-life are known through unaided reason, and that they are the only types of pleasure or

[97] Al-Ghazālī, *Tahāfut al-Falāsifah*, p. 288. [98] *Ibid.*, p. 354.

pain which man can experience after death. There is no logical absurdity involved in positing both types of pleasure or pain, i.e., the spiritual and the bodily, as well as the bodily resurrection laid down in Scripture. The claim of the philosophers that sensuous pleasures and pains, as depicted in the Koran, are no more than allegories intended for the edification of the masses is very tenuous, and the analogy between the passages in the Koran that describe them and the passages that refer to God in anthropomorphic terms is not a sound analogy. The latter can and ought to be interpreted allegorically, but not the former. For, whereas it is logically impossible that God should be described in corporeal terms and as possessing physical members or occupying space, the bodily rewards and punishments alluded to in the Koran are not logically impossible, as has been shown under the general heading of miracle and the miraculous.[99] God could thus restore the Soul on the Day of Judgment to a body either identical with or analogous to its original body, and thereby enable it to partake of both bodily and nonbodily pleasure. In fact, it is with the possibility of such a dual enjoyment that its complete happiness is bound up.

[99] Al-Ghazālī, *Tahāfut al-Falāsifah*, pp. 356 ff.

CHAPTER EIGHT

The Rise and Development of Islamic Mysticism (Ṣūfism)

I

ASCETIC ORIGINS

MYSTICISM, defined as the attempt to reach out to the infinite and to be identified with it either through some kind of connaturality, as in Christianity, or through the total destruction of personal identity and the reversion to the primordial condition of undifferentiated unity, as in Hinduism and Buddhism,[1] is discouraged by many teachings of the Islamic religion. First, the concept of the absolute transcendence of God "unto Him nothing is like," as the Koran[2] expresses it, militates against the spirit of close or intimate relationship with God. Second, the ritual basis of the cult, with its rigid stipulations and forms, excludes the possibility of the unfettered reaching out to a reality beyond without conditions or restrictions. Third, the Islamic concept of the unity or continuity of man's life in this world and the next makes the "divorce"

[1] Zaehner, *Hindu and Muslim Mysticism*, pp. 6 f. [2] Koran 42, 11.

between finite and infinite existence in the form of withdrawal from the world much more difficult. The Muslim believer is called upon to accept this world of transient existence (*dār fanā'*) and cling to it, almost as much as he is called upon to seek the everlasting kingdom (*dār baqā'*) beyond and cling to it.[3]

However, the Koran and the Traditions present another picture of the God-man relationship and the life-to-come which is very different from the one just outlined. Thus God is represented in this perspective as closer to the believer than "his jugular vein" (Koran 50, 15), and is so omnipresent and omniscient as to witness man's every deed and read his every thought.[4] The ephemeral goods of this life are said to be utterly worthless in comparison with the everlasting goods of the life-to-come.[5]

Moreover the spectacle of God's final judgment is drawn in such graphic and awe-inspiring terms, particularly in the early Meccan *Sūrahs*, that the reader is overwhelmed with the sense of the futility and wretchedness of man's estate in this life. Fear (*al-khauf*) not unnaturally became the chief expression of piety (*wara'*, *taqwā*)[6] and the token of a genuine religious vocation in the early centuries of Islam. And although the strict monastic ideal (*al-rahbāniyah*) has been proscribed, we hear of many an early pious Muslim, such as Abū Dharr al-Ghifārī (d. 652) and Ḥudhayfa (d. 657), both companions of the Prophet,[7] who chose the hard ascetic life at a time when most of their contemporaries had chosen the softer life of the world.

Perhaps the most important figure in the history of early Muslim asceticism is a venerable divine of the first century of the Muslim era whom we have already met. Al-Ḥasan al-Baṣrī (d. 728) lived through one of the most momentous periods in the history of Islam. The "war of succession," which split the ranks of Islam following the assassination of the third caliph, Uthmān, in 656, pitted the Umayyads against the 'Alid party and set the stage for almost a whole century of political and

[3] See Koran 7, 30; 2, 181; 22, 77. [4] Koran 33, 37, etc.

[5] Koran 6, 99; 10, 25; 13, 18, etc.

[6] It is noteworthy that these two terms and many others denoting piety derive from roots that signify fear in Arabic.

[7] Anawati and Gardet, *Mystique musulmane*, pp. 23 f. and Smith, *Studies in Early Mysticism in the Near and Middle East*, pp. 153 f.

theological strife. The theological controversies over the status of the grave sinner and other cognate questions of free will and predestination grew out of this strife and led to the rise of the first theological movement in Islam, whose champion, Wāṣil b. ʿAtā', had been a disciple of al-Ḥasan al-Baṣrī.[8]

Al-Baṣrī's concept of the religious life was essentially an ascetic one, of which piety, poverty, and contempt for worldly goods were the primary ingredients. The method he proposed consisted of reflection (*fikr*), self-examination (*muḥāsabah*), and total submission to God's will, resulting ultimately in a state of inner contentment (*riḍā*). In this state, the tension between the divine and the human will is finally resolved.[9]

Al-Baṣrī's influence on the subsequent history of theology and mysticism, transmitted by a long series of disciples, was very great. The new current of poverty and devotional piety started at Basra, and drew many followers. The greatest female mystic of Islam, Rābiʿah al-ʿAdawiyah (d. 801), spent all her life at Basra and cultivated the same ideals of poverty, celibacy, and other-worldliness which al-Baṣrī had identified with a true mystical calling. She introduced for the first time in the history of Islamic mysticism, however, the concept of divine love (*al-ḥubb*).[10] Earlier mystics had spoken of yearning (*shauq*) or friendship (*khullah*), but Rābiʿah went far beyond them by speaking in passionate terms of the believer's love of God. In this regard she ran counter to the whole religious tradition in Islam, in which man dare not approach God except in a spirit of devotion, piety, or awe. Asked once whether she loved God and hated the devil, she replied, "My love of God has barred me from occupying myself with the hate of satan." On another occasion the Prophet appeared to her in a dream and asked, "O Rābiʿah, do you love me?" Her answer was, "O Apostle of God, is there any one who does not love you? However, my love of God Almighty has filled my heart so completely that there is no room left in it for the love or hate of anybody else."[11] Her most graphic description of this love is given in these well-known lines:

[8] See Hitti, *History of the Arabs*, pp. 178 ff., and *supra*, p. 59.
[9] Massignon, *Essai sur les origines du lexique téchnique de la mystique musulmane*, pp. 168 f.
[10] *Ibid.*, pp. 194 f.
[11] See Badawī, *Shahīdat al-ʿIshq al-Ilāhī*, p. 251.

I love thee with two loves: a love of passion and a love prompted by Thine worthiness as an object of love. As for the love of passion, it is indeed the reiteration of Thine name, to the exclusion of anything else. As to the love of worthiness, it is the love in which Thou removest the veil, so that I can see Thee. However, mine is not the praise for this or that. But Thine is the praise for this and that.[12]

The center of mystical activity shifted from Basra to Baghdad, which had become the political and religious capital of the whole empire after al-Manṣūr founded it in 762. Of the first mystics of Baghdad, the most noteworthy are Ma'rūf al-Karkhī (d. 815), Manṣūr b. 'Ammār (d. 839), Bishr b. al-Ḥāfī (d. 842), and Ibn Abi'l-Dunia (d. 894).[13] The two greatest *Ṣūfīs* that the school of Baghdad produced, however, were without doubt al-Muḥāsibī (d. 857) and al-Junayd (d. 910). Born at Basra, al-Muḥāsibī later moved to Baghdad, where he soon came into conflict with the Ḥanbalis for his willingness to use the methods of scholastic theology in his religious disquisitions. His mysticism rests on two pillars: self-examination (*al-muḥāsabah*), hence his own nickname, and readiness to suffer the worst tribulations in the service of God, the Beloved.[14] The touchstone of genuine piety, according to him, is death, and the token of the great virtue of fortitude (*al-ṣabr*) is readiness to suffer. Without rejecting the validity of the ritual basis of worship, al-Muḥāsibī insisted on the inward aspect of belief, which yields, when imbued with the spirit of obedience or devotion, a spiritual condition (*ḥāl*) commensurate with the purity of that belief.[15]

Abu'l-Qāsim al-Junayd is regarded in the *Ṣūfī* tradition as one of the foremost pioneers and is universally venerated by orthodox and heterodox doctors alike, from al-Sarrāj and al-Qushayrī to al-Ḥallāj and Sa'īd b. Abi'l-Khayr.[16] His teachers included al-Muḥāsibī, al-Saqaṭī (d. 870), and Abū Ḥafs al-Ḥaddād (d. 873) and, despite his moderation, he venerated al-Bisṭāmī (d. 874), the extravagant votary of

[12] See Badawī, *Shahīdat al-'Ishq al-Ilāhī*, p. 123; cf. Eng. trans., Smith, *Studies in Early Mysticism*, p. 223.

[13] Massignon, *Essai*, pp. 206 f., and Anawati and Gardet, *Mystique musulmane*, p. 28.

[14] Anawati and Gardet, *Mystique musulmane*, p. 29; Massignon, *Essai*, p. 217.

[15] Massignon, *Essai*, pp. 221 f.

[16] See Massignon, *La passion d'al-Ḥallāj*, II, 34; Abdel-Kader, *The Life, Personality and Writings of al-Junayd*, pp. 34 f.; al-Qushayrī, *Risālah*, p. 18.

divine union, who will be discussed later. His influence on the subsequent development of *Ṣūfism* was very great. And, although he was diffident and dispassionate by nature, his profound sense of the unity and transcendence of God reached its culmination in the most exuberant expression of passion for union with God, of which al-Ḥallāj (d. 922) eventually became the symbol. It is noteworthy that his disciples included, in addition to this extravagant lover of divine union, some of the most orthodox adepts of theology and *Ṣūfism*, such as al-Ghazālī, who singles him out as one of his chief spiritual masters.[17]

Conscious of the hazards inherent in mysticism, al-Junayd declared mystical knowledge to be circumscribed by the Koran and the Traditions.[18] This did not bar him, however, from defining clearly the conditions of mystical union, which he fully understood though he never experienced.[19] The starting point of his mysticism is the divine covenant (*mīthāq*) God concluded with man (Koran 7, 171) before creating him. Man's intellectual and mystical vocation consists in the progressive apprehension of his essence as an idea in the divine mind prior to his creation in time, and the abysmal difference between his essence and God's. This isolation of the eternal from the temporal (*ifrād*)[20] is for al-Junayd the token of the genuine recognition of God's unity (*tauḥīd*), as indeed of any genuine knowledge of God. However, such knowledge is not by itself capable of bringing man to his final goal whereby he is lifted above the precepts of the law and brought so close to God that "he is reduced to dust, killed, buried, and later, if it pleases Him, resuscitated."[21] Once this isolation of the temporal from the eternal has been completed and the creature has been reduced to his primordial condition as an idea in the mind of God, man becomes dead unto himself and alive unto God and this, as al-Junayd has put it, is the essence of the mystical experience.[22]

Those two concepts of isolating the human from the divine and the reduction of man to his original condition of not-being or preexistence

[17] See *al-Munqidh*, p. 35.

[18] Al-Qushayrī, *Risālah*, p. 19, and Abdel-Kader, *The Life, Personality and Writings of al-Junayd*, pp. 67, 86 f.

[19] Massignon, *Essai*, pp. 275 f., and Abdel-Kader, *al-Junayd*, pp. 76 f.

[20] Al-Qushayrī, *Risālah*, p. 3.

[21] Massignon, *La passion d'al-Ḥallāj*, I, 36.

[22] Al-Qushayrī, *Risālah*, p. 126; cf. Zaehner, *Hindu and Muslim Mysticism*, p. 141.

in the mind of God are symptomatic of the gradual maturation and sophistication of *Ṣūfism*. Having grown out of the ascetic ideal and the need to inject a new sense of inwardness into the ritualism of worship, *Ṣūfism* now felt the urge to break loose completely, to soar aloft into the vast spaces of spiritual experience. The extent of foreign influence could not, prior to this point, be determined. With the rise of this bold concept of self-destruction and the reabsorption of the human in the divine, the possible influence of foreign ideas can be fruitfully explored.

In Yoga mysticism (*vineka-jnāna* or "knowledge of difference" [*ifrād*]), as expounded for instance by Shankara, the aim of the Yogi sage is not union with God, but rather the isolation of the Soul and the realization of an eternal mode of being outside space and time.[23] This "isolation" amounts in fact to the destruction of particular existence, which is the ultimate goal of *Sāmkhia-Yoga*, as indeed of all Hinduism. Likewise, the ultimate goal of the mystic, according to al-Junayd, is to achieve this condition of self-destruction (*fanā'*) as the prelude to its restoration to its original condition of eternity (*baqā'*), from which creation in time has robbed it.[24]

The other *Ṣūfīs* of this formative period included a number of outstanding figures. Dhu'l-Nūn al-Miṣrī (d. 859), an Egyptian of Coptic stock, is almost a legendary character in the annals of *Ṣūfism*. Like the more legendary Shī'ite Jābir b. Ḥayyān (d. 776), who is said to have been his master,[25] he is reported to have been a mystic, an alchemist, and a philosopher. Despite the literary exuberance of his language, al-Miṣrī remains the prototype of the moderate or balanced mystic. The aim of the *Ṣūfī*, according to him, is fellowship with God. Beyond the "vision of God's countenance," no grace is reserved for the blessed save the privilege of hearing the voices of angelic spirits.[26] The mystical path consisted for him in a series of stations (*maqāmāt*) which the mystic must travel, and a corresponding series of states (*aḥwāl*) with which God might favor him. This distinction between stations and states, the one earned through human endeavor, the other conferred on him by

[23] Zaehner, *Hindu and Muslim Mysticism*, pp. 9, 135 f.

[24] *Ibid.*, pp. 146 f., and Appendix B, II; cf. Abdel-Kader, *The Life, Personality and Writings of al-Junayd*, Arabic text.

[25] Ibn al-Nadīm, *al-Fihrist*, pp. 358, 355.

[26] Smith, *Studies in Early Mysticism*, p. 235, and Massignon, *Essai*, p. 187.

God, became subsequently a key distinction in the *Ṣūfī* tradition. Without dwelling unduly on the privileged aspect of the *Ṣūfī* life, al-Miṣrī was careful to emphasize the purgatory character of ritual and mental prayer, as well as the practice of self-mortification. Once the Soul has become cleansed of its sins, it becomes fit to receive its Lord and to hold spiritual converse with Him in intimate fellowship. Thereby the Soul is restored to its primordial condition of preexistence in God.[27]

A major condition of this fellowship is love. The true love of God consists in shutting out all other emotions so that nothing but God remains in the heart. Moreover, like the higher love spoken of by Rābi'ah, whom al-Miṣrī reportedly met,[28] this love of God must be absolutely disinterested and have no object other than God Himself.[29]

An earlier *Ṣūfī*, Ibrāhīm b. Adham (d. 776), is often quoted by later authors and recognized as a model of piety and other-worldliness. A legend reflecting that of Gutama Buddha makes him a prince who became disillusioned with worldly pleasures. As he was out hunting, a voice spoke to him twice: "Is this what you were born for?" Repenting from his worldly life, he dismounted, traded his horse for the woolen tunic of a shepherd, wandered in the desert, and visited Mecca, where he is supposed to have met Rābi'ah.[30] Legend has it that it took him forty years to reach his destination, since with every step he would perform two genuflections. "Others," he mused, "make the journey on their feet, whereas I make it on my head [i.e., forehead],"[31] alluding to the Muslim practice of touching the ground with the forehead with every genuflection (*rak'ah*). When he finally arrived in Mecca, however, he could not find the *Ka'bah*, the Sacred Shrine which was the object of his pilgrimage, because, as a voice told him, the *Ka'bah*, had gone to meet Rābi'ah. As he saw her coming, he reprimanded her gently, saying: "What is this uproar you cause in the world? Everybody is saying: the *Ka'bah* has gone out to meet Rābi'ah." She replied: "What about the uproar you cause yourself,

[27] Smith, *Studies in Early Mysticism*, pp. 232 f.
[28] Badawī, *Shahīdat al-'Ishq al-Ilāhī*, p. 162.
[29] Smith, *Studies in Early Mysticism*, p. 234.
[30] Al-Qushayrī, *Risālah*, p. 8; cf. Smith, *Studies in Early Mysticism*, pp. 179 f.
[31] Badawī, *Shahīdat al-'Ishq al-Ilāhī*, p. 145.

by spending forty years to get here? Everybody says that Ibrāhīm stops to perform two genuflections at every step he takes."[32] The most characteristic commentary on Rābi'ah's response to this divine favor, however, is contained in another legend. When she saw the *Ka'bah* coming her way, she exclaimed: "It is not the *Ka'bah*, but its Lord that I want. For what use is the *Ka'bah* to me?"[33]

Ibrāhīm's exalted concept of the love of God is best expressed in a fragment which al-Muḥāsibī has preserved in his *Kitāb al-Muḥāsabah*. Ibrāhīm states to one of his brethren: "If you wish to be the friend of God or to be loved by Him, renounce this world and the next. Do not desire either of them; empty yourself of those two worlds and turn your face toward God. Then God will turn His face toward you and overwhelm you with His grace. For I have learned that God revealed the following to John, son of Zakariyah [John the Baptist]: O, John, I have pledged that none of My servants will love Me (I who know his secret intentions), without being the sight with which he sees, the tongue with which he speaks, and the heart through which he understands.[34] Once this is done, I will make him shun occupying himself with anything other than Myself . . . and will be present to him day and night. He will come closer to Me and I will come closer to him, in order to hear his voice, out of love for his humility. By My glory and majesty, I will invest him with a mission, which even the prophets will envy."[35]

[32] Badawī, *Shahīdat al-'Ishq al-Ilāhī*, pp. 145 f. [33] *Ibid.*

[34] This is a variation on a *qudsī* tradition allegedly dictated to Muḥammad by God; see al-Qushayrī, *Risālah*, p. 143.

[35] Quoted in Massignon, *Essai*, pp. 226–27.

II

PANTHEISTIC TENDENCIES: AL-BASṬĀMĪ (OR AL-BISṬĀMĪ), AL-ḤALLĀJ, AND OTHERS

THE Islamic origin of *Ṣūfīsm* has been asserted by some scholars, such as Massignon,[36] and questioned by others, such as Nicholson and Zaehner.[37] Our survey has shown that there is little in the early *Ṣūfī* ideal of life for which a basis cannot be found in the Koran and the Traditions, and Massignon is probably right in asserting that "from the Koran continually recited, meditated upon and practiced, Islamic mysticism proceeds in its origins and its development."[38] The concepts of religious poverty (*faqr*), meditation (*fikr*, *dhikr*), fortitude (*ṣabr*), renunciation (*zuhd*), and even the love of God and His contemplation can be shown to be a logical development from that other-worldly strain in the Koran to which we have already referred. What may be rightly regarded as a non-Islamic component of *Ṣūfīsm* is the tendency in the writings and practices of the earliest *Ṣūfīs* to go beyond the ritual aspect of the religious law (*al-Sharī'ah*) and to reach out to a reality (*Ḥaqīqah*) that thoroughly transcends it. It signifies that in this process of reaching out, not only the law, but even Muḥammad, as the vehicle of divine revelation, are dispensed with and the believer desires a direct fellowship or communion with God.

An important instance of the tendency to discount or bypass the religious law is the practice of celibacy and the admonition against marriage as an obstacle to the realization of the mystical ideal of piety or holiness. Ḥasan al-Baṣrī, Rābi'ah, and other early *Ṣūfīs* not only

[36] *Essai*, pp. 84 f., 116 f.

[37] Zaehner, *Hindu and Muslim Mysticism*, pp. 111 f., and Nicholson, *Mystics of Islam*, pp. 10 f.

[38] *Essai*, p. 84. We should distinguish here between the origins of mysticism and its ultimate development.

shunned marriage, but inveighed against it. Some apparently forged Traditions were even ascribed to the Prophet to justify celibacy as early as the first two centuries of the Muslim era.[39] A clear recognition of an insoluble antithesis between marriage and the ascetic life was growing within *Ṣūfī* circles, but Muḥammad's example made it necessary to resort to the strange view that the prohibition of celibacy (*rahbāniyah*) had been lifted by Muḥammad himself subsequent to the end of the second century.

If Muḥammad's example in the matter of matrimony could thus be flouted or reinterpreted, a more serious difficulty arose in connection with his role as the major link between man and God. Some early *Ṣūfīs*, without going to the length to which later *Ṣūfīs* did, clearly regarded Muḥammad's role as mediator between God and man as somewhat secondary. Asked by the Prophet in a dream, "Do you love me?," Rābi'ah is said to have replied, "O, Apostle of God, is there anyone who does not love thee? My love of God Almighty, however, has filled my heart to such an extent that there is no room left in it for the love or hate of anyone else."[40] Possibly conscious of this difficulty, later *Ṣūfīs* such as Ibn 'Arabī (d. 1240) refer to the "reality of Muḥammad" as an archetypal nature, preexisting all time, rather than to Muḥammad as a historical personality discharging a divine function in the context of space and time.[41]

Despite those inherent tendencies, the early mystics remained generally firm in their adherence to orthodoxy. Even al-Junayd, who had sown the seeds of a unitary mysticism conditioned by Hindu concepts of the self, did not draw all the possible logical consequences that later and bolder spirits were to draw.

Of these bolder men who became so "intoxicated" with divine love that they could not help taking the final step across the pantheistic abyss, the two best known in the ninth century are al-Bisṭāmī (al-Basṭāmī) and al-Ḥallāj. Others, such as Sa'īd b. Abi'l-Khayr (d. 1049),[42] friend and correspondent of Ibn Sīnā, and al-Shiblī (d. 945), followed in their wake in the next two centuries and gave expression in their

[39] See Badawī, *Shahīdat al-'Ishq al-Ilāhī*, pp. 53 f.
[40] *Ibid.*, p. 151. See *supra*.
[41] See *al-Futūḥāt al-Makkiyah*, Pt. 2, p. 97; and *Fuṣuṣ al-Ḥikam*, pp. 319 f.
[42] See Nicholson, *Studies in Islamic Mysticism*, pp. 1 ff.

life and thought to other features of extravagant mysticism, such as affected eccentricity or madness.

Abū Yazīd al-Basṭāmī was born in Basṭām in western Khurāsān and was introduced to mysticism by an Indian convert to Islam, Abū 'Alī al-Sindī, who taught al-Basṭāmī the doctrine of "extinction in unity" (*al-fanā' fi'l-tauḥīd*).[43] Much more than any other *Ṣūfī* mentioned heretofore, al-Basṭāmī subjected himself to the most rigorous austerities so that, as he himself put it, he might be completely stripped of his human condition and encounter God face-to-face.[44] Whatever the constructions that have been put upon them by later scholars, al-Basṭāmī's "extravagances" (*shaṭaḥāt*) bear on the general mystical themes of ecstasy or union with God and imply a clear presupposition of self-deification. Thus in one of those "extravagant utterances" reported by a late *Ṣūfī* author al-Basṭāmī says: "Once [God] lifted me up and placed me before Him and said to me: O, Abū Yazīd, my creation desires to see thee. And I said: Adorn me with Thy unity and clothe me in Thine I-ness and raise me up unto Thy oneness, so that when Thy creatures see me they may say: We have seen Thee [i.e., God] and Thou art that. Yet I [Abū Yazīd] will not be there."[45] In another utterance probably his best known, he exclaims, "Glory be to me, how great is my worth." But despite the unquestionable pantheistic implications of these utterances, the culmination of the mystical experience remains for him somewhat negative and hollow, since the Soul remains suspended, as it does in some forms of Hindu mysticism (e.g., Patanjali) between the I and the Thou, the Self and the Absolute, which have both been annihilated.[46] A statement ascribed to him speaks of the station of nonbeing (*laisiyah*) which he reached and continued to hover in for ten years until, he says, "I could pass from the No (*lais*) to the No, through the No."[47]

The Hindu influence on this type of mysticism has been shown by Zaehner to be unmistakable. There is a clear link to Vedantic metaphysics not only in the case of al-Basṭāmī's Indian master, al-Sindī,

[43] Zaehner, *Hindu and Muslim Mysticism*, pp. 93 f.
[44] Massignon, *Essai*, p. 246.
[45] Zaehner, *Hindu and Muslim Mysticism*, p. 76.
[46] Massignon, *Essai*, p. 255. [47] *Ibid.*, p. 248.

who taught him some "ultimate truths," but also in the very complexion of his thought and its "nihilistic" implications. Al-Basṭāmī lived at a time in which the revival and systematization of Vedantic thought itself was being actively pursued by Shankara (d. 820) and his school.[48] His ecstatic utterances, such as the already quoted "Glory be to me" (*Subḥānī*) or "I am Thou" or "I am I," all purport to assert his total self-identification with the divine and have numerous parallels in the *Upanishads* and the *Vedanta*.[49] Perhaps the wildest of all his utterances is the one in which he speaks of his search for God: he could not find God and therefore took His place on the Throne. "I plunged into the ocean of *malakūt* [the realm of Ideas], and the veils of divinity [*lāhūt*]," he writes, "until I reached the Throne and lo! it was empty; so I cast myself upon it and said: 'Master, where shall I seek Thee? and the veils were lifted up and I saw that I am I, yea I am I. I turned back into what I sought, and it was I and no other, into which I was going."[50]

How a Muslim could make such extravagant claims that placed him almost above God and yet go unscathed in the ninth century is truly surprising. However, a note made by later authors gives us the clue to this problem. When al-Basṭāmī was accused of laxity in the performance of his ritual duties, we are told, he resorted to the expedient which other *Ṣūfīs* also employed: affected madness. This device apparently saved his life as well as the life of numerous fellow *Ṣūfīs*.

There was one ninth-century *Ṣūfī*, however, who was not willing to resort to this dodge, and the price he paid for his extravagances was very dear. Al-Ḥusain b. Manṣūr al-Ḥallāj was born around 858 in a small town called al-Bayḍā, not far from the eastern shores of the Persian Gulf. His *Ṣūfī* teachers included al-Makkī (d. 909), al-Tustarī (d. 986), al-Shiblī (d. 945), and al-Junayd,[51] four of the greatest figures in the whole history of *Ṣūfism*. It was apparently al-Junayd who induced al-Ḥallāj to wear the woolen garment (*ṣūf*). He served as his spiritual director for twenty years but was aware of the hyperbolic strain in his character and eventually broke with him because of his arrogance, we are told.

[48] See Zaehner, *Hindu and Muslim Mysticism*, p. 111.

[49] *Ibid.*, pp. 112 f. [50] Al-Salḥajī, *Manāqib al-Bisṭāmī*, p. 111.

[51] Massignon, *La passion d'al-Ḥallāj*, I, 24 f.; Ibn Khallikān, *Wafayāt*, Wustenfeld ed. (Gottingen, 1935), p. 186.

Al-Ḥallāj's first pilgrimage to Mecca and his early ascetic bouts illustrate this strain very well. During that first pilgrimage he remained immobile for a whole year in the hall of the mosque. Visitors who watched him as he later sat down at high noon on a rock outside Mecca, with sweat streaming down his body, were amazed at his pig-headedness rather than his piety. "This man in his folly," some mused, "is out to rival God in his capacity for endurance."[52] One of his disciples states that he never lay down to sleep, but slept standing up or squatting for no more than one hour at a time.[53] Back in Baghdad he sought the company of al-Junayd once more. The latter reproached him for his misunderstanding of the nature of mystical intoxication (*sukr*), his dispensing with Scripture or ritual, but especially for his presumption to be God.[54]

The break with al-Junayd coincided with the gradual disassociation of al-Ḥallāj from the established *Ṣūfī* orders. From the somewhat monastic life of these orders, he now embarked on a public career of preaching, full of hazards. He associated with all manner of men—philosophers such as al-Rāzī, statesmen such as the Prince of Ṭāliqān—and professed a variety of creeds which completely confused his contemporaries and increased the roster of his enemies. In particular, he appears to have identified himself at one stage with the Shī'ite or 'Alid cause,[55] a political step which radically compromised him.

Following a third pilgrimage to Mecca, al-Ḥallāj returned to Baghdad "completely changed," as his son Ḥamd put it. The change appears to have been marked by a clearer and firmer sense of his identification with God, with whom he now entered into a more intimate personal converse, as it were. This condition of personal communion with the I-Thou is what he called the "essence of union" (*'ain al-jam'*), in which all the actions, thoughts, and aspirations of the mystic are wholly permeated by God. But, according to him, this union did not result, as it had in the case of al-Basṭāmī, in the total destruction or nullification of the self, but rather in its elevation to joyful and intimate communion with the Beloved.[56]

[52] Massignon, *La passion d'al-Ḥallāj*, I, 55.
[53] *Ibid.*, p. 69. [54] *Ibid.*, pp. 60 f. [55] *Ibid.*, p. 76. [56] *Ibid.*, pp. 116 f.

The impact of his preaching on the Baghdadī public was mixed. Some hailed him as a savior, others as a miracle-worker or simply a pious practitioner of the religious way. His reverence for the memory of Ibn Ḥanbal, the great Traditionist and anti-Muʿtazilite doctor, appears to have enhanced his prestige with the masses. But there were many who looked upon him as a charlatan and a heretic deserving death. In one of his sermons at the mosque of al-Manṣūr in Baghdad, he himself appears to have recognized that his execution was prescribed by the Holy Law.[57] Eventually proceedings against him were instituted by the vizier, ʿAlī b. al-Furāt in 909, but he was actually arrested and brought before an extraordinary tribunal at Baghdad four years later, during the vizierate of ʿAlī b. ʿĪsa. He was publicly exposed as a Qarmaṭian agent and then jailed for nine years. Despite a certain favor which he enjoyed for a while with the caliph, thanks to the good offices of the chamberlain, who was sympathetic to his case, he was finally convicted on the charge of blasphemy by decree of a canonical jury, which invoked the koranic sanction against the heretics (Koran 5, 32) and was countersigned by the caliph.[58]

Although the official charge against al-Ḥallāj was his claim to be God and to have the authority to free the pious of the ritual prescriptions of the Islamic law, political sedition was a decisive factor in his final torture and execution. As regards the charge of self-deification, it is noteworthy that when confronted with statements he had made and in which he spoke on behalf of God in the first person, he defended himself on the ground that this practice was perfectly compatible with the *Ṣūfī* doctrine of "essence of union," a mystical condition in which it is God who writes or speaks through the mystic, who is simply His instrument.[59] But his accusers, especially the vizier Ḥāmid, would not hear of such theological subtlety, and although he had been ordered to be whipped and decapitated by the caliph, in an excess of zeal the vizier ordered him to be whipped, mutilated, crucified, decapitated, cremated, and his remains scattered to the four winds.[60] Nothing like this had ever happened in the whole history of Muslim piety.

[57] Massignon, *La passion d'al-Ḥallāj*, I, 129 f.
[58] *Ibid.*, pp. 274 f.
[59] *Ibid.*, p. 260.
[60] *Ibid.*, pp. 289, 305; cf. Ibn Khallikān, *Wafayāt*, p. 186.

III

SYNTHESIS AND SYSTEMATIZATION —AL-GHAZĀLĪ AND IBN 'ARABĪ

THE extraordinary teaching and martyrdom of al-Ḥallāj illustrate very well the excesses latent in mysticism and its tendency to explode all the conventional forms in which religious devotion or reflection is expressed. Its lasting value in the history of Islamic religious thought, however, lay precisely in the spirit of exhilaration and uninhibited freedom it infused into an otherwise arid cult. A sympathetic appraisal of *Ṣūfism* would regard its excesses as instances of the urge of the religious spirit to assert itself and thereby to be released from the rigid ritual forms into which it was sometimes forced. Thus the concept of divine love, the suffering and joy such love generates, the other-worldliness and disregard for the morrow which burst out in mysticism like a tree in full bloom gave Islam an added spiritual dimension of incalculable value.

This radical development was not, however, without hazards. And if the price al-Ḥallāj and many of his disciples had to pay was very high, the sense of total freedom, of direct encounter with the divine, was bound to breed a certain spiritual presumption from which only God could save His elects. Perhaps the most tragic commentary on the fate of al-Ḥallāj is this account of a divine apparition, reported by his son Ḥamd, in which one of his father's disciples told Ḥamd: "I saw the God of Majesty in a dream. I thought I stood face-to-face with Him and so I said: God, what has Ḥusain b. Manṣūr al-Ḥallāj done [to deserve such a fate]?—I revealed to him the Reality, but he called men to God on his own account and so I inflicted on him the punishment which you have seen."[61]

The other practitioners of this extravagant unitary mysticism require little discussion. Al-Shiblī, whose concept of union was identical with

[61] Massignon, *La passion d'al-Ḥallāj*, I, 10, 318.

that of al-Ḥallāj, lacked the courage and single-mindedness of the latter. Not only did he disassociate himself publicly from al-Ḥallāj's doctrine, but he came forward at his trial to denounce him as a madman. There was probably no malice in this denunciation, since he himself affected madness when his own life was threatened and he admitted later that, whereas his madness had saved him, al-Ḥallāj's sanity had led to his doom.

Al-Ḥallāj's martyrdom was the most eloquent commentary on his key doctrine of *'ain al-jam'* (essence of union). Misunderstood, misrepresented, and bitterly criticized, it marked a turning point in the history of mysticism and served as a stern warning against the dangers with which mysticism is fraught. The great figures in the history of post-Ḥallājian mysticism, such as al-Ghazālī and Ibn 'Arabī, addressed themselves primarily to the task of systematization or synthesis. Al-Ghazālī, whose reaction against Neo-Platonism has already been discussed,[62] found in *Ṣūfism* the answer to his own intellectual and spiritual quest. His chief masters in that field were al-Junayd, al-Makkī, al-Basṭāmī, and al-Shiblī. A man of greater learning and intellectual earnestness than any of these masters, he pledged his full support to orthodoxy and bent his efforts to bringing everything he cherished into harmony with it. Three elements contributed radically to his success in formulating a mystical creed essentially compatible with orthodoxy: (1) The koranic concept of a Supreme Being, wholly other than the world, which He created by an unconditioned act of free will (*al-amr*); (2) the Neo-Platonic hierarchy of being, in which Reason serves as the link between God and His Creation; and (3) The Ḥallājian concept of God dwelling in the Soul and using it as an instrument (*'ain al-jam'*).

In a history of philosophy it is perhaps the second element that is of particular interest. Whether or not al-Ghazālī is guilty of duplicity in his polemics against the Neo-Platonists, as Ibn Rushd charged,[63] it is clear that in two of his major mystical treatises, *Mishkāt al-Anwār* and *al-Risālah al-Laduniyah*, the Neo-Platonic hierarchy of being serves as the metaphysical groundwork of his whole mysticism. The *Mishkāt* is a commentary on a koranic verse (Koran 24, 34) which speaks of

[62] *Supra*, pp. 244. [63] See *Faṣl al-Maqāl*, p. 18.

God as the light of heaven and earth and which, like the Illuminationists of the twelfth century, al-Ghazālī, interprets in distinctly mystical terms.

The name "light," he argues, applies to God primarily, and to other luminous objects figuratively or derivatively. We speak of sight and Reason as a light because they make objects manifest or discernible. Reason, however, is more appropriately spoken of as a light, since in addition to manifesting objects it is able to manifest itself and is not circumscribed by the conditions of space and time. Consequently it has a greater analogy to God, who created Adam, the prototype of rational nature, in His own likeness.

The visible world (*'ālam al-shahādah*) is an inferior replica or shadow of the intelligible world (*'ālam al-malakūt*), which may also be called the spiritual and luminous world, of which the Koran and other revealed scriptures are the expression.[64]

The hierarchy of luminous entities is determined by the degree of their proximity to the Supreme Light or God. Thus Isrāfīl precedes Gabriel, who is followed by other subordinate spirits, who, together with the multitude of corporeal entities beneath them, receive their being from the Supreme Light. Consequently, their being is purely derivative in relation to their Author, who alone possesses the character of essential being. Indeed nothing else has being, apart from Him. Thus the mystics or seers, writes al-Ghazālī, having attained the pinnacle of reality and risen above the "plane of metaphor"

> are able to see visually that there is no being in the world other than God and that the face of everything is perishable, save His face (Koran 28, 88), not in the sense that it perishes at some time or other, but rather in the sense that it is perishing eternally and everlastingly and cannot be conceived to be otherwise. Indeed, everything other than He, considered in itself, is pure nonbeing, and, considered from the standpoint of the being which it receives from the First Reality, has being not in itself but in regard to the face of its Maker, so that the only thing which truly is is God's face. Therefore, nothing is except God Almighty and His face, and consequently everything is perishable eternally and everlastingly, save God's face.[65]

[64] *Mishkāt al-Anwār*, p. 51. The traditional emanationist terminology is used in this context.

[65] *Ibid.*, pp. 55 f.; cf. Fakhry, *Islamic Occasionalism*, pp. 7 f.

Man occupies a unique position in this hierarchy. Not only did God create him in His likeness, but He has made him a "compendium" of the whole universe. The divine image in him has been inscribed by God Himself, hence only he who knows himself can attain to a knowledge of his Lord, as a *Ṣūfī*, tradition has it. However, this image is merely that of God the Merciful (*al-Raḥmān*), not God the Lord, since the latter can never be portrayed or expressed in created terms. This is the divine mystery, which, al-Ghazālī insists, can only be expressed metaphorically or figuratively.[66]

The human powers of apprehension start with sense and culminate in Reason, which through inference and synthesis increases the scope of knowledge indefinitely. However, to the prophets and saints a special faculty called the holy, prophetic spirit is given. Through it they are able to obtain knowledge concerning the future, the life-to-come, and things supernatural or divine. Those who doubt the existence of such a faculty are like those who lack a poetic or musical sense and therefore cannot comprehend these forms of art. Let them at least believe in its possibility.[67]

The highest type of knowledge, argues al-Ghazālī, is not that of Reason or that of faith, but that of direct experience. Thus the genuine knowledge of God belongs to this "experiential" order. Some are so engrossed in the pleasures and cares of this world that they are unable to perceive the light of God. Others know God merely as He is related to the world, namely, as the Prime Mover of the heavens. To safeguard His unity some among them have recognized Him as the Mover of the outermost sphere only, whereas others assign this function to a subordinate agent or spirit who simply carries out the orders of his Lord (*al-Muṭā'*).[68]

In all these cases of divine knowledge, God is divinely perceived through a "veil of light" that conceals His true nature. A fourth category of knowers, *al-wāṣilūn* (those who have arrived), recognize, however, that this *al-Muṭā'* lacks the attribute of absolute unity and perfection, and they consequently look beyond it to the ineffable

[66] *Mishkāt al-Anwār*, pp. 71 f. [67] *Ibid.*, p. 78.

[68] This *Muṭā'* is identified in *al-Risālah al-Laduniyah* with the 'universal intellect' of Neo-Platonism; see *al-Jawāhir al-Ghawālī*, p. 25.

Creator of heaven and earth, to whom *al-Muṭāʿ*, the mover of the outermost sphere, and the movers of the remaining spheres are all subordinated.[69] The most privileged are those who, having attained this stage, are completely annihilated or absorbed in the Supreme One and consequently see neither themselves nor any other being but only God's face. This mystical condition may be called annihilation (*fanā'*) or the annihilation of annihilation, since in it the mystic is dead to himself as well as to his own death. In their excess of zeal some[70] have become so intoxicated that they believed that they had become God. In reality, the condition they attained is no more than the recognition of God's unity (*tauḥīd*), i.e., the consciousness of the fact that there is no real being in the world other than He.[71] But this is entirely different from identity with Him (*ittiḥād*).

Without divorcing himself explicitly from the extravagant *Ṣūfīs* referred to earlier, and whom he sometimes reproaches for divulging what ought to have remained secret, al-Ghazālī like his master al-Junayd artfully skirts the pantheistic abyss without falling into it. His mysticism might then be looked upon as an attempt to give the monotheistic ideal of Islam a greater degree of metaphysical cogency. As Wensinck has written: "Ghazālī does not see in existence anything save the Unique Being, who for some unknown reason has at one moment of eternity figured out and realized a world which possesses in itself neither existence, nor the power to act. . . . According to pantheism, God does not exist except through the universe. According to Ghazālī the universe does not exist at all. The doctrine of Ghazālī is Semitic monotheism seen through the prism of Neo-Platonism."[72]

The boldest and most radical attempt to express the mystical version of reality in Neo-Platonic terms, however, is without doubt that of Ibn ʿArabī. Born in Murcia (Spain) in 1165, he traveled extensively throughout Spain, North Africa, and the Near East and settled eventually in Damascus, where he died in 1240. His initiation to *Ṣūfism*

[69] *Mishkāt al-Anwār*, pp. 91 f.

[70] Namely, al-Shiblī and al-Basṭāmī, who are mentioned by name (*ibid.*, pp. 5 f.).

[71] See *Iḥyā'*, Pt. IV, p. 243; cf. the parallel doctrine of al-Junayd in Abdel-Kader, *The Life, Personality and Writings of al-Junayd*, pp. 73 f.

[72] Wensinck, *La pensée de Ghazali*, p. 9; cf. Zaehner, *Hindu and Muslim Mysticism*, pp. 162 f., for Hindu parallels of this doctrine.

appears to have started at Almeira, where the school of Ibn Masarrah (d. 931), philosopher and *Ṣūfī*, flourished.[73] In addition to Ibn Masarrah, his precursors included al-Tirmidhī (d. 898), al-Wāsiṭī (d. 942), and Ibn al-'Ārif (d. 1141). He was enjoined in a vision to journey east, and so visited Mecca in 1201. There he was "commanded" to begin the writing of his voluminous work, *al-Futūḥāt al-Makkiyah* (*The Meccan Revelations*), and met the girl who was to become his wife, a Persian *Ṣūfī*. From Mecca he traveled throughout the Near East, visiting Mosul, Conia, Baghdad, Cairo, and finally Damascus, which he made his home in 1223 and where he spent the last years of his life.

According to the latest research, no fewer than 846 works are attributed to Ibn 'Arabī, of which 550 have come down to us. Out of this vast number, almost 400 appear to be genuine.[74] In many of these Ibn 'Arabī states explicitly that in writing them he was prompted directly by God or commanded by the Prophet.[75] We have already seen, in the case of al-Ḥallāj, the claim that God uses the mystic as His mouthpiece or instrument.

Ibn 'Arabī's doctrine, as embodied in his two major works, *al-Futuḥāt al-Makkiyah* and *Fuṣūṣ al-Ḥikam* (*The Gems of Wisdom*), centers around the concept of the unity of being (*waḥdat al-wujūd*). The starting point of his speculation, however, is the theory of the Logos. According to him, to every prophet corresponds a reality, which he calls a Logos (*Kalimah*) and which is an aspect of the unique Divine Being. But for the self-manifestation of the divine in these *Logoi* or prophetic epiphanies, which start with Adam and culminate in Muḥammad, the nature of the Supreme Being would have remained forever hidden. As the fount of all reality, this Being is essentially undivided, eternal, and immutable. Ibn 'Arabī distinguishes between the hidden aspect of this Being, which can neither be known nor described and is the aspect of unity (*aḥadiyah*), and the aspect of lordship (*rubūbiyah*), through which God enters into relationship with the world and becomes an object of worship, as Lord and Creator. In the first aspect there is no plurality or opposition and no determination of

[73] Asin Palacios, *Ibn Masarra y su escuela*, pp. 94 f.; but compare Affifi, *The Mystical Philosophy of Ibnu'l-'Arabi*, pp. 178 f.

[74] See Yaḥia, *Histoire et classification de l'œuvre d'Ibn 'Arabī*, I, 73 f.

[75] See *Fuṣūṣ al-Ḥikam*, pp. 47 f., *et passim*.

any kind. Hence God is spoken of in this respect as the pure light, the pure good, or simply the Blindness (*al-ʻAmā'*). In the second there is multiplicity and differentiation, in so far as God is both the Creator and the multitude of created objects.[76]

God is multiplied only through His attributes or modifications. Considered in Himself, He is the Real (*al-Ḥaqq*). Considered in relation to His attributes as manifested in the multiplicity of possible entities, He is the Creation (*al-Khalq*). The two, however—the one and the many, the first and the last, the eternal and the temporal, the necessary and the contingent—are essentially one and the same reality.[77]

The creation existed originally in the divine mind, as a series of archetypes, called by Ibn ʻArabī "fixed entities" (*aʻyān thābitah*). But God, who had remained hidden, desired to manifest Himself visually, so to speak, and thus called forth the whole creation into being by His divine fiat (*al-amr*), which is to Him what a mirror is to the image, the shadow to the figure, and number to the unit. His motive in this act of bringing the world into being out of nothing is love, as expressed in the Tradition "I was a hidden treasure and I wished [Arabic: loved] to be known."[78]

The highest manifestation or epiphany of the divine is the human prototype, identified by Ibn ʻArabī with Adam and called the Adamic Logos or perfect man.[79] Indeed the existence of this perfect man is the very warrant of the preservation of the world and the *raison d'être* of its existence.

This concept of the perfect man, who was created in God's image and likeness, goes back to al-Ḥallāj and has played an important part in the *Ṣūfī* attempt to rationalize the God-man relationship. According to Ibn ʻArabī, divinity and humanity are not two distinct natures, but rather two aspects which find their expression at every level of creation. Divinity corresponds to the hidden or inward (*bāṭin*) aspect of any reality, humanity to the external or outward (*ẓāhir*). In philosophical terminology, the first corresponds to substance, the second to accident.

[76] *Fuṣūṣ al-Ḥikam*, pp. 38 f., 63.

[77] *Ibid.*, pp. 76 f. and commentary; cf. Affifi, *The Mystical Philosophy of Ibnu'l-ʻArabi*, pp. 10 f.

[78] *Ibid.*, p. 203, and Affifi, *The Mystical Philosophy of Ibnu'l-Arabi*, p. 82.

[79] *Ibid.*, pp. 48 f., 75 f.

The manifestation of reality reaches its consummation in man.[80] Man is thus the microcosm or compendium of the whole creation, who embodies in himself all the perfections of the macrocosm as well as that of the divine nature itself. It was for this reason that he was designated (in the Koran) as God's vicegerent on earth (*khalīfah*).

Although Ibn 'Arabī speaks of the human race or Adam's progeny as a whole in terms of such superlative praise, he reserves to the prophets and saints a position of undoubted preeminence among the rest of mankind and to Muḥammad the title of the truly "perfect man." As the fullest manifestation of God, the perfect man corresponds to the prophetic Logos, of which the "reality of Muḥammad" is the expression. By this is to be understood, not the historical personality of Muḥammad, but rather his eternal spirit or essence as the bearer of the highest and final revelation of God's word. This reality is identified by Ibn 'Arabī with the first intellect or universal Reason of Neo-Platonic cosmology. The general class of "perfect men" or prophets are direct manifestations of this intellect of which Muḥammad is the highest, whereas other prophets are so many inferior or subordinate manifestations.[81] Not only is the reality of Muḥammad the primary Logos through which God's will is revealed to mankind, but it is the creative principle through which the world is created. In this respect it is clearly analogous to the Christian Logos, through which, as St. John has put it, "everything was made which was made." Moreover, it is analogous to the Shī'ite concept of the *Imām*, represented as God's vicegerent on earth and the pivot of the whole creation and its very *raison d'être*.[82]

Man is thus for Ibn 'Arabī the embodiment of universal Reason and the being in whom all the attributes or perfections of God are reflected. In addition, it belongs to man alone to know God fully. The angels know Him as a transcendent or spiritual reality only, whereas man knows Him in His dual character as essential reality (*Ḥaqq*), on the one hand, and the manifestation of this reality in the phenomenal world (*Khalq*), on the other.

[80] *Fuṣūṣ al-Ḥikam*, pp. 35 f.
[81] Affifi, *The Mystical Philosophy of Ibnu'l-'Arabi*, pp. 71
[82] Nicholson, *Studies in Islamic Mysticism*, pp. vi, 138 f.

The human or rational Soul is distinguished by Ibn 'Arabī from the animal or bestial. Like Aristotle he identifies the latter with the vital principle in the animal, but like Plotinus he holds it to be part of the universal Soul. However, this Soul is material, permeates the body, and has its seat in the heart. The rational Soul, on the other hand, is immaterial and indestructible. Unlike Ibn Rushd and the Arab Neo-Platonists generally, he does not believe in its eventual reunion with the universal Reason, of which it forms a part. Instead God will create a vehicle for the Soul, similar to this world, to which it will go upon leaving the body.[83]

This rational Soul or spirit (*rūḥ*) is diametrically opposed to the body, which is its temporary abode in this world. Hence it cannot be either a part of, nor a power in, the body, but is a simple substance which dominates all the subordinate powers of the animal Soul and is a member of the "world of command" or spiritual realm.[84]

What the rational Soul actually knows, at the highest level of mystical experience, is ultimately the unity of the whole and its own identity with it. When the Soul has achieved this condition, it is no longer conscious of itself as a separate entity and may therefore be said to have attained the mystical stage of annihilation (*fanā'*) of which *Ṣūfīs* from al-Junayd down had become accustomed to speak. Such a Soul becomes dead, not only to itself, but also to the world as a whole, and is conscious of no entity, quality, or activity in the world other than God.[85] In attaining this stage, the Soul would have attained the final goal of all human endeavor and realized intuitively and experientially the absolute unity of all things. This final stage of mystical awareness might be called, as al-Ghazālī had called it, the stage of annihilation or extinction in unity (*al-fanā' fi'l-tauḥīd*).[86]

The subsequent course of *Ṣūfism* is of minor interest to the historian of Islamic ideas. With Ibn 'Arabī *Ṣūfism* had attained the zenith of its development and its creative energy had been spent. Ibn 'Arabī combined in his grandiose system the urge of the early *Ṣūfīs* to cut themselves off from the world, on the one hand, and to achieve a sense of the unity of all things, on the other. In addition, like Rābi'ah and

[83] Affifi, *The Mystical Philosophy of Ibnu'l-'Arabi*, p. 121.
[84] *Ibid.*, p. 123. [85] *Ibid.*, pp. 143 f. [86] *Supra*, p. 280.

similar ascetics, he raised love, particularly the love of God, to the level of a ritual religious creed.

Three of Ibn 'Arabī's contemporaries or successors, Ibnu'l-Fāriḍ (d. 1235), 'Aṭṭār (d. 1229), and Jalāl al-Dīn Rūmī (d. 1273), gave the most moving expression in verse of the profound emotions of wonder, love, elation, and sheer incomprehension attendant upon the mystical experience, which other mystics had tried to express in more sober philosophical terms.

Ibn Sab'īn (d. 1270), a countryman and follower of Ibn 'Arabī, expressed his version of unity of being in terms of the Aristotelian concept of the form and reacted violently against Muslim Neo-Platonism.[87] A century or so later 'Abd al-Karīm al-Jīlī (d. 1428), the last great *Ṣūfī* and poet, continued the speculation of Ibn 'Arabī on the themes of the perfect man, the reality of Muḥammad and emanation, and exploited some of them, especially that of the perfect man, to the full.[88]

On the popular religious plane, the trend *Ṣūfism* followed was the more practical or social one of fraternities. Thus the al-Qādiriyah order, founded by 'Abd al-Qādir al-Kīlānī (or Jīlānī) (d. 1166) in Baghdad, spread in the nineteenth century throughout the Muslim world, from India to Morocco, and claims an active following in the Western Sudan today. Another order, al-Rifā'iyah, was founded by Aḥmad al-Rifā'ī (d. 1175) and differs from the former in the greater degree of fanaticism or superstition characteristic of its practices. Another order founded in Egypt during the invasion of St. Louis by Aḥmad al-Badawī (d. 1276) (hence its name Aḥmadiyah or Badawiyah) has its center today in Ṭanṭa in lower Egypt.[89]

Both in Western Asia and in North Africa *Ṣūfī* orders became deeply entrenched in popular life. During the reign of Almohades, *Ṣūfism* received the official recognition and support of the state, probably for the first time in the history of Islam. A characteristic feature of North African *Ṣūfism* is its *maraboutisme* or cult of saints. The *Maraboute* sects spread south as far as the Niger and west as far as Egypt. Their success

[87] Anawati and Gardet, *Mystique musulmane*, p. 65.
[88] Nicholson, *Studies in Islamic Mysticism*, pp. 76 f.
[89] Anawati and Gardet, *Mystique musulmane*, p. 69.

was due in part to the fact that they found a fertile soil in the vestiges of animism and magic among the Berbers of North Africa.[90]

One of the best-known *Ṣūfī* orders of all time is the Shādhiliyah. Founded by the disciples of Shādhilī (d. 1256) in Tūnis, it spread throughout North Africa, and its offshoots (such as al-Tījāniyah and al-Raḥmāniyah) continue to have some influence in Morocco and Algeria up to the present day.

Despite the tendency of this popular type of mysticism to degenerate into a corporation of those who merely seek ecstasy through the mechanical repetition of the divine name Allah, *Ṣūfism* has repeatedly reasserted its vitality in modern times. We might mention here the remarkable case of Ben 'Aliwa (d. 1934), who founded at the turn of the century a *Ṣūfī* order that enjoyed great popularity at one time, even among European intellectuals, chiefly in France and Switzerland. The monism of Ben 'Aliwa was even more radical than that of Ibn 'Arabī, and his doctrine was marked by a greater degree of syncretism. In general, however, both this order and the other more ancient orders are continually battered in the Muslim world today by the most diverse forces: secularism, nationalism, and modernism, on the one hand, and neo-orthodoxy, as championed by the Wahhābis in Arabia, the Muslim Brotherhood in Egypt, and similar conservative groups, on the other.[91]

[90] Anawati and Gardet, *Mystique musulmane*, p. 70.

[91] *Ibid.*, pp. 72 f.

CHAPTER NINE

The Arab-Spanish Interlude and the Revival of Peripateticism

I

BEGINNINGS OF PHILOSOPHICAL SPECULATION IN MUSLIM SPAIN: IBN MASARRAH, AL-MAJRĪṬĪ, and IBN BĀJJAH

THE beginnings of philosophical speculation in Islam coincided, as we have seen, with the founding of the 'Abbāsid caliphate in the eighth century. A rival principality was set up in Spain by the only surviving Umayyad prince following the overthrow of the Umayyads in 749. This principality was able before long to challenge the 'Abbāsids not only politically but culturally as well. In due course, Umayyad Spain was able to write one of the most brilliant cultural chapters in the whole history of Islam and to serve as the bridge across which Greco-Arab learning passed to Western Europe in the twelfth century.

Despite the intense rivalries between the 'Abbāsids of Baghdad and the Umayyads of Cordova, however, the cultural relations of the eastern and western wings of the Muslim empire were not always warlike. From the ninth century on, scholars traveled from one end of the empire to the other, carrying books and ideas and thereby insuring what one might call the cultural unity of the Islamic world.

According to the Arab-Spanish historian of philosophy and medicine, Ṣā'id b. Aḥmad b. Ṣā'id (d. 1070), author of *Ṭabaqāt al-Umam*, interest in philosophy and science began in the ninth century during the reign of the fifth Umayyad ruler of Spain, Muḥammad b. 'Abdu'l-Raḥmān (852–886).[1] Although the interest of Spanish scholars so far had centered around astronomy and medicine, as well as the Islamic subjects of jurisprudence, *ḥadīth*, and linguistics, it took a whole generation for "ancient learning" to gain ground. On the initiative of al-Ḥakam II (al-Mustanṣir) (961–976), scientific and philosophical works were imported from the East on a large scale, so that Cordova with its huge library and university could now compete with Baghdad as a major center of learning in the Muslim world.[2]

However, a reaction set in during the reign of al-Mustanṣir's heir and successor, Hishām II (976–1009), who ordered the burning of books of ancient learning, especially logic and astronomy, in an attempt to placate the theologians and the masses who had always frowned upon the study of these subjects.[3] By the middle of the eleventh century the study of philosophy and science nevertheless was revived and numerous scholars flourished. Of these, 'Abdu'l-Raḥmān b. Ismā'īl (called the Eucledian) deserves special mention as an early student of logic. Like other Spanish scholars, 'Abdu'l-Raḥmān journeyed east in search of works of scholarship. Another, Abū Uthmān Sa'īd b. Fatḥūn, is mentioned as a leading grammarian and musicologist who wrote an introduction to the philosophical sciences entitled the *Tree of Wisdom*.[4]

The scholar who is generally regarded as the outstanding mathematician and astronomer of this period is Maslamah b. Aḥmad al-Majrīṭī. He appears to have traveled extensively in the East, and various traditions emphasize his association with the Brethren of Purity, whose *Epistles* he is said to have brought with him from the East. A

[1] Ṣā'id, *Ṭabaqāt al-Umam*, p. 64.
[2] See Hitti, *History of the Arabs*, pp. 530 f.
[3] Ṣā'id, *Ṭabaqāt*, p. 66; Hitti, *History of the Arabs*, p. 532.
[4] Ṣā'id, *Ṭabaqāt*, p. 68.

tradition even attributes to him the writing of the summary of the fifty-one *Epistles* known as *al-Risālah al-Jāmi'ah*,[5] and a voluminous treatise on magic and cosmology entitled *Ghāyat al-Ḥakīm* (*The Aim of the Sage*)[6] is also ascribed to him. This treatise embodies a great deal of hermetic and Neo-Platonic material and reflects the influence of the Brethren of Purity. Chronological inconsistencies make it doubtful, however, that al-Majrīṭī was the author of this work. Be this as it may, the chief influence of al-Majrīṭī was exerted through a long line of disciples who were never superseded, according to Ṣā'id, in Muslim Spain.[7]

Another scholar who has already been mentioned in connection with *Ṣūfism* is Muḥammad b. 'Abdullah b. Masarrah, designated by Ṣā'id as al-Bāṭinī (the adept of occultism or Shī'ism). Accused of heresy, Ibn Masarrah journeyed East, where he was drawn to Mu'tazilite theology, but he returned eventually to his homeland and settled down to an ascetic life.[8] He is particularly noted for his espousal of pseudo-Empedoclean doctrines, which are a mixture of genuine Empedoclean and Neo-Platonic theories of the conventional type.[9]

Of the eleventh-century authors who cultivated an interest in philosophy and logic, Ṣā'id mentions Abu'l-Ḥakam 'Amr al-Krimānī, who excelled particularly in geometry and journeyed as far east as Ḥarrān in search of mathematical knowledge. From the East he is reported to have brought with him a copy of the *Epistles* of the Brethren of Purity, which al-Majrīṭī is more frequently said to have introduced into Spain. Other authors of this period are Ibn al-Jallāb, Ibn al-Kannāri (or al-Kattārī), Ibn Ḥazm,[10] and Ibn Sayyidih.[11] Ṣā'id observes, however, that none of these Andalusian scholars made an appreciable contribution to physical and metaphysical studies, with the exception of a certain 'Abdullah b. al-Nabbāsh al-Bajjā'ī,[12] and perhaps Abū 'Uthmān b. al-Baghnūsh of Toledo.[13]

[5] See *supra* and Istanbul Ms., Raghib Pasha, 965, fol. 3.

[6] See H. Ritter's edition (Leipzig, 1933).

[7] Ṣā'id, *Ṭabaqāt*, p. 69; cf. Ibn Abī Uṣaybi'ah, *'Uyūn*, II, 39.

[8] *Ṭabaqāt*, p. 21; *'Uyūn*, II, 37. Cf. Asin Palacios, *Ibn Masarra*, pp. 36 f., and Cruz Hernandez, *Filosofia hispano-musulmana*, I, 221 f.

[9] For pseudo-Empedoclean theories in Arabic sources, see *Ibn Masarra*, pp. 40 f.

[10] *Infra*, pp. 348 f.

[11] *Ṭabaqāt*, pp. 70 f; *'Uyūn*, II, 40 f.

[12] *Ṭabaqāt*, pp. 77, 85; cf. *'Uyūn*, II, 49.

[13] *Ṭabaqāt*, p. 83; *'Uyūn*, II, 48.

The first major figure in the history of Arab-Spanish philosophy is without doubt Abū Bakr Muḥammad b. al-Ṣāyigh, better known as Ibn Bājah, or Bājjah (the Avempace of Latin sources). Born in Sarogossa, he later moved to Seville and Granada and died from poison at Fez in 1138.[14] Apart from those scant details very little is known about his life. Two of his disciples, however, have recorded their opinion of his standing in philosophy and science. The first is Abu'l-Ḥasan 'Alī b. al-Imām, who transcribed the only collection of his master's philosophical and scientific works to have come down to us.[15] The second is Ibn Ṭufayl, author of *Ḥayy b. Yaqẓān*, to which we will be turning shortly.

Ibn al-Imām speaks of his master with unqualified praise. Prior to Ibn Bājjah, he writes, the philosophical works imported by al-Ḥakam II into Spain had remained a mystery. He admits that his master's studies in the higher regions of metaphysics were perfunctory, but he deems them sufficiently learned to justify placing Ibn Bājjah on a footing equal with the two foremost philosophers of the East, Ibn Sīnā and al-Ghazālī.[16]

Ibn Bājjah's other disciple, Ibn Ṭufayl, was certainly more competent to judge, and yet he confirms Ibn al-Imām's impression, both of the history of philosophical studies in Spain and of Ibn Bājjah's standing in it. The first generation of Spanish scholars, he writes, concerned themselves primarily with the study of mathematics. The next generation made a certain contribution to the study of logic, but their contribution was somewhat meager. Eventually a new class of scholars, more skilled in the abstract disciplines of philosophy, appeared on the scene. Ibn Bājjah was in the forefront of this class. Two things, however, prevented the full flowering of his genius: his untimely death and his worldly ambition. As a result, most of his works are unfinished or perfunctory, as he himself admits in some of them.[17]

Ibn Ṭufayl's judgment is fully supported by internal evidence. Of

[14] Ibn Khallikān, *Wafayāt*, p. 681.

[15] Oxford, Pococke Ms. 206. The only other Ms. of these works, Berlin 5060, must be presumed lost. It was more complete than the Oxford Ms. and contained some of Ibn Bājjah's medical writings.

[16] See Ibn Bājjah, *Opera Metaphysica*, p. 177.

[17] See Ibn Ṭufayl, *Ḥāyy b. Yaqẓān*, p. 12.

the thirty-odd treatises to have come down to us, none exceeds thirty folios and the majority are no more than ten. Moreover, hardly any of the questions broached in them are adequately treated. Instead, the author is often content to refer the reader to "what Aristotle has stated in more than one place." The apparent vastness of his learning justifies the regard in which he was held by later scholars, although he had more than a few critics and detractors.[18] His introduction of serious philosophical discussion marks a turning point in the history of Islamic culture in the Iberian peninsula, since it set the stage for the most systematic Islamic exposition of Aristotelian doctrine and the most valiant defense of this doctrine by the greatest Aristotelian of Islam, Ibn Rushd of Cordova.

Like al-Fārābī and Ibn Sīnā, Ibn Bājjah's problem is essentially ethical or eschatological. The aim of philosophical thought for him is expressed in Avicennian terms such as "contact" or "conjunction" (*ittiṣāl*) with the active intellect, i.e., the attainment of a spiritual or intellectual condition in which the mind is united with this supermundane agency and thereby becomes a part of the intelligible world. We have called this problem ethical or eschatological, in so far as the ultimate preoccupation is with the destiny of the Soul in the after-life. Both al-Fārābī and Ibn Sīnā conceived of the two main divisions of philosophy, the theoretical and the practical, as complementary. Philosophy for them is the quest of knowledge in so far as it leads to happiness, or alternatively the gratification of the Soul's desire for happiness through the acquisition of knowledge. The theologians and jurists had insisted that this condition could not be attained in this life. The *Ṣūfīs* and the philosophers, though partially in agreement with this view, outlined what we may call a philosophico-ethical program of salvation whereby the Soul could partake of this condition in this life. The *Ṣūfīs* emphasized the practical and personal aspects of this program and referred to its culminating stages as union, whereas the philosophers emphasized its theoretical or speculative aspects and called it "contact" or "conjunction".

Both in his magnum opus, *Tadbīr al-Mutawaḥḥid* (*The Conduct of the Solitary*), and in his treatise on conjunction, *Ittiṣāl al-ʿAql bi'l-Insān*,

[18] See al-Fatḥ b. Khāqān, *Qalā'id al-ʿUqyān*, pp. 34 f.

Ibn Bājjah develops the classic themes of intellectual progression from the condition of potentiality to that of actuality and the eventual "contact" of the "acquired" with the active intellect, which only the privileged few are able to achieve.

The *Tadbīr* opens with a discussion of the various forms of direction, personal, political, and divine. The mark of the virtuous state, as al-Fārābī had shown, following Plato, is that it provides the framework for a truly virtuous existence and has no need for physicians or judges. However, when the virtuous state degenerates into one of the four corrupt or degenerate forms of which Plato and al-Fārābī had spoken, the plight of the philosopher living in it becomes acute, and unless he emigrates he will be forced to live as a stranger in the midst of his own people and associates.

The consideration of the plight of this stranger or solitary (*al-mutawaḥḥid*)[19] leads Ibn Bājjah to inquire into the varieties of human actions, and in particular those which lead to the final condition of union or conjunction with the active intellect. Some of those actions are common to both man and other animals, and therefore are not of the type suited for this purpose. Typically, human actions differ from these in that they are voluntary and arise from deliberation or reflection, whereas involuntary actions arise from impulse. In the degenerate forms of the state, all actions are involuntary and impulsive, because their inhabitants do not act rationally and voluntarily but are motivated for instance by provision for the necessities of life, pleasure, honor, or conquest.[20]

If the chief characteristic of man and of the actions proper to him is reason, then clearly he is one of the intellectual or "spiritual forms" that constitute the upper portion of the great scale of being. Hence Ibn Bājjah turns to determining the position of man along the scale of "spiritual forms" in the universal hierarchy of being which the Muslim Neo-Platonists had popularized. Of those forms, he recognizes four: (1) the forms of heavenly bodies; (2) the active and acquired intellects; (3) intelligible forms abstracted from matter; and (4) the forms or

[19] This term may also refer to the condition of union (*al-tawaḥḥud*) with the active intellect of which Ibn Bājjah speaks at the end of *Ittiṣāl al-'Aql*.

[20] Ibn Bājjah, *Opera Metaphysica*, pp. 62 f.

notions stored in the inner powers of the Soul, such as the *sensus communis*, the imagination, and retentive faculties.

The first category is entirely immaterial, whereas the second, though essentially immaterial, has a certain relation to matter. For the intellect perfects material intelligibles in its acquired capacity, or produces them in its active capacity. The third has a certain relation to matter, in so far as such forms are abstracted from their material substrata, whereas the fourth is a mean between material and spiritual forms.

Man's genuine vocation is essentially intellectual, and it is to the extent that those subordinate forms contribute to the fulfillment of this vocation that they are worthy of his interest or pursuit. When this objective has been achieved, the "solitary" is able to rise to that condition of permanence or immateriality which is the characteristic of all spiritual forms. Only this "spiritual man" is truly happy; the "corporeal man" is too engrossed in the pleasures of the body to desire anything beyond them. When this spiritual man has attained the philosophical ideal of wisdom and has partaken of the highest virtues, theoretical and moral, he becomes truly divine and joins the ranks of the intelligible substances. This, as al-Fārābī and Ibn Sīnā had argued, is the ultimate goal of man and the token of that union with the active intellect which Ibn Bājjah and Ibn Rushd also call *ittiṣāl* (contact or conjunction).

Faced with the problem of life in imperfect or degenerate regimes in which his higher intellectual aspirations are frustrated, the solitary ought either to emigrate to a perfect regime or, in the absence of such a regime, he should cut himself off from his fellow men as much as possible. To the objection that such antisocial action is incompatible with the Aristotelian dictum that man is a political animal by nature, Ibn Bājjah replies that such a dire act is the solitary's final recourse and that the solitary life, though evil per se, can be good *per accidens*. Where the ultimate aims of political association are frustrated, it is obvious that an apolitical life is the only life that can be morally justified.

Ibn Bājjah strikes the same note in *Ittiṣāl al-ʻAql*. However, as briefly hinted in *The Conduct of the Solitary*, the final stages in man's intellectual and spiritual progress are not entirely human; its consummation is brought about by an infusion of a light which God casts into the heart of His elects and which al-Ghazālī had described in a *Ṣūfī* context as the "key to all forms of knowledge."[21] Thus "upon departing the body," Ibn Bājjah writes, the one so favored by God "will become one of the [celestial] lights glorifying God and singing His praise and will join thereby the ranks of the prophets, saints, martyrs, and the blessed."[22]

This dependence of the mind on divine illumination in the final stages may be said to be Ibn Bājjah's concession to *Ṣūfism,* of which he had remained critical. Like Ibn Ṭufayl and Ibn Rushd, however, he categorically states that this divine favor is reserved for the philosophers and thereby arbitrarily limits the scope of this illumination, laying down, as it were, the conditions under which God may dispense it to the privileged few.

II

IBN ṬUFAYL AND THE NATURAL PROGRESSION OF THE MIND TOWARD TRUTH

THE second major figure in the history of Arab-Spanish philosophy is Abū Bakr b. Ṭufayl, a native of Wadī Āsh, a small village northeast of Granada. Very little is known about his life, education, or public career. We can only surmise that he was born in the first decade of the twelfth century, studied medicine and philosophy at Seville and Cordova, and was introduced to the Almohades caliph, Abū Ya'qūb Yūsuf, a generous patron of the sciences who cultivated a genuine interest in philosophy.[23] His relationship with this enlightened prince

[21] See *supra,* p. 246. [22] Ibn Bājjah, *Opera Metaphysica,* p. 162.

[23] Al-Marākushī, *al-Mu'jib fī Akhbār al-Maghrib,* p. 172; cf. Gauthier, *Ibn Thofail, a vie, ses œuvres,* p. 3.

is said to have been very cordial and he apparently was instrumental in presenting numerous scholars and philosophers to his patron. The most notable and felicitous presentation was without doubt that of the young Ibn Rushd, probably in 1169,[24] since it appears to have launched the latter on his career as the commentator of Aristotle. Apart from his service as royal physician to the caliph, Ibn Ṭufayl's functions at court are described in the vaguest terms by our authorities, and we can only infer that he probably acted as companion or *aide* to the caliph, but not necessarily as vizier. In 1184 his patron died, but he continued to enjoy the same privileged position at court during the reign of Abū Ya'qūb's son and successor until his death at an advanced age in 1185.[25]

Ibn Ṭufayl is said to have written numerous works on medicine, astronomy, and philosophy. The only philosophical work of his to survive is *Ḥayy b. Yaqẓān*, an allegorical novel in which he develops the esoteric themes of the solitary which Ibn Bājjah had placed at the center of his ethical and metaphysical system. Al-Marākushī, the historian of the Almohades dynasty, states, however, that he saw a treatise on the Soul by Ibn Ṭufayl in his own handwriting.[26] Apart from this treatise, our sources mention no other philosophical writing of his.

Ḥayy b. Yaqẓān, it will be recalled, is the title Ibn Sīnā gave to one of his esoteric works.[27] Whether anything can be made of the title, *Living, Son of Wakeful*, is a difficult and in some respects fruitless question. As will appear from our analysis, perhaps the chief merit of this work lies in its original literary form, which had been tried by Ibn Sīnā and was far from being common. Its subject matter is much more ordinary. It is essentially an exposition of general Neo-Platonic themes developed in the East by al-Fārābī and Ibn Sīnā and in the West by Ibn Bājjah. The first scholar to note its importance was Edward Pococke, the British Arabist of the seventeenth century who prepared an edition of the Arabic text accompanied by a Latin translation, with the informative, if long, title: *Philosophus autodidactus, sive epistola . . . qua ostenditur quomodo ex inferiorum contemplatione ad superiorum notitiam*

[24] Gauthier, *Ibn Thofail*, p. 17. [25] *Ibid.*, p. 19.
[26] *Al-Mu'jib*, p. 172. [27] *Supra*, p. 180.

ratio humana ascendere possit. The book was translated into English, Dutch, German, Spanish, and French,[28] and enjoyed a considerable vogue in some circles. The question is sometimes asked whether Daniel Defoe, author of *Robinson Crusoe* (1719), was not acquainted with Pococke's *Philosophus autodidactus*, but the question is purely academic, since apart from the literary form the two works have very little in common.

Another significant feature of this philosophical allegory is the deliberate attempt to show that, once the solitary has apprehended truth through unaided reason, he is able to verify, upon entering into converse with his fellowmen, the harmony of philosophy and dogma, of reason and revelation. This was, as we have seen, a major theme of Muslim Neo-Platonism, which Almohades rulers, with Abū Ya'qūb at their head, were particularly anxious to demonstrate.

In the preamble to *Ḥayy*, the author states that his aim is to expound the "illuminative wisdom" which Ibn Sīnā spoke of and which is reducible, according to Ibn Ṭufayl, to mysticism. What sets the philosophers apart from the mystics is that the former claim that mystical illumination can be attained through speculation only, whereas speculation leads the seeker at best to the threshold of that ineffable experience which is the crux of genuine mysticism. Even Ibn Bājjah had fallen short of that ideal, according to him.[29]

In order to describe that condition which cannot be expressed in words, he resorts to allegory, a more suitable method because it is less direct and less explicit. The scene is set on a desert island in the Indian Ocean and the chief actor is Ḥayy, an infant generated spontaneously on that island.[30] A deer who had lost her fawn gave Ḥayy suck until he grew strong and could vie with the beasts in their pursuits. However, although he had led the life of beasts, he was soon struck by the fact that his skin was bare and that he lacked the natural means of self-defense with which the beasts were provided. When he was seven he resorted to the expedient of covering himself with tree leaves or

[28] Gauthier, *Ibn Thofail*, pp. 44 f.

[29] *Ḥayy b. Yaqẓān*, p. 10.

[30] Though inclined to accept this mode of spontaneous generation, the author nevertheless gives an alternative theory, which makes Ḥayy the offspring of a forbidden union on the mainland (*Ḥayy*, p. 21).

animal hides to protect himself against the elements. Eventually the deer which had nursed him died; this caused him great distress and led him to ponder the mystery of death. A crude autopsy enabled him at length to identify the cause of death as a disorder of the heart resulting in the departure of the spirit, the body's vital principle. Noting that death was not accompanied by any visible corporeal damage, he concluded that it was simply the outcome of the dissolution of the union of Soul and body. Thus Ḥayy discovered life.

Ḥayy's second major discovery was fire, which he related to the phenomenon of life. His other empirical discoveries included the use of implements, the analogies between animals and plants, their various ranks or species, and the upward and downward movements of the elements. From these empirical observations he was able to rise to the discovery of the spiritual world. First, he noticed that every entity was made up of two elements: corporeity and the form of corporeity. In animate entities this form corresponds to the Soul, which is the principle of life in the animal and as such is not an object of sense but only of thought. Second, he reasoned that it was upon the complexity of the powers of the Soul belonging to each class of animate objects that its grade in the scale of life depended.[31]

By the age of twenty-eight Ḥayy was able to rise to the awareness of the incorruptible world of the stars and to recognize the necessity of a Creator thereof. As to the duration of the world as a whole, he was unable to arrive at a conclusion. But, as both Maimonides and St. Thomas Aquinas were to show later, he eventually understood that the problem of the eternity or noneternity of the world was entirely irrelevant to the demonstration of the existence of its cause.[32]

The contemplation of the beauty and order which are the unmistakable marks of the creation convinced Ḥayy that such a cause must be perfect, free and all-knowing, bountiful and beautiful; in short, it must possess all the perfections which we observe in the world and be free from all imperfection. By this time, Ḥayy was thirty-five years old.

[31] *Hayy*, pp. 41 f.

[32] *Ibid.*, p. 55; cf. Fakhry, "Antinomy of Eternity of the World," *Le Muséon*, XVI (1953), 143 f.

When he proceeded to inquire how he had attained this knowledge of a Supreme Being, who was altogether immaterial, he could not help concluding that it was not gained through a bodily organ or power but through the Soul, which is entirely distinct from body and which constituted the very essence of his selfhood.[33] This discovery brought him to a full awareness of the nobility of his Soul, its superiority over the whole material universe, and its independence of the conditions of generation and corruption which affect body alone. The ultimate happiness of this Soul, he also realized, was bound up with the recognition of its kinship to the Necessary Being and its diligence in contemplating this Being, who is the supreme object of knowledge.[34]

The same process of introspection that had led Ḥayy to an awareness of his genuine nature as a spiritual essence led him in fact to a threefold awareness of his kinship to: (1) the animal kingdom, by virtue of his animal impulses and faculties; (2) the celestial spheres, by virtue of the Soul, which they also possessed; and (3) the Necessary Being, by virtue of the immateriality and nobility of his Soul, which is his true self. As a practical consequence, he understood that he had a threefold vocation in the world. With respect to the corporeal or animal aspect of his nature, his duty was to tend the body and be mindful of its essential needs, but only to the extent that this enabled his Soul to achieve its highest and noblest vocation, namely, the contemplation of God. He knew, however, that in this type of contemplation (i.e., the intellectual) the Soul never loses the sense of its own identity and consequently its contemplation of God is not perfect or full. He who partakes of perfect contemplation will lose all consciousness of his self, since it is obliterated or annihilated in the process, like everything else save the True One or Supreme Being.[35]

The ultimate goal of the seeker after truth, then, was annihilation of the self or its absorption in God (*fanā'*), which al-Junayd had set up as the culmination of the mystical life.[36] To attain this goal, the seeker should dwell on the two aspects of God's nature: the positive and the negative. Since the positive attributes of God are all reducible to His unity or the identity of attribute and essence in Him, the genuine knowledge of God resolves itself to the knowledge of His absolute

[33] *Ḥayy*, pp. 60, 67 f. [34] *Ibid.*, p. 63. [35] *Ibid.*, p. 69. [36] *Supra*, p. 267.

unity. Since the negative attributes are reducible to His transcendence and incorporeity, knowledge rooted in these attributes is never adequate. The consciousness of the corporeal, as indeed of the seeker's own identity, constitute a bar to the pure or genuine knowledge of the Being who is fully other. Hence only once the finite self and the whole world of corporeal entities have been left completely behind and the seeker has risen to the realization that there is no other being except God, is it given him to "see what no eye has seen, no ear has heard, and has not occurred to anyone at all."[37] This final stage is a kind of intoxication, which has led some to identify themselves with the object of their contemplation, i.e., God.[38] Ḥayy, however, was guarded from this temptation by God's grace.

Like other *Ṣūfī* writers, Ibn Ṭufayl dwells on the ineffability of this ultimate condition of "utter annihilation." He does not refrain, however, from describing it in allegorical and oblique terms, although he held it to be clearly "far above reason."[39] The final vision of Ḥayy is thus described in graphic terms that represent a remarkable amalgam of Neo-Platonic and *Ṣūfī* doctrine, similar in many ways to that of al-Ghazālī. Upon attaining the final stage of utter annihilation (in which he presumably partook of the *visio Dei*), Ḥayy was able to see the highest heaven and that immaterial entity (*dhāt*) "which was neither the essence of the True One, the Soul of that heaven, nor something else."[40] That entity may be compared to the reflection of the sun in a mirror, from which it is nevertheless distinct. Next Ḥayy perceived the firmament and its Soul, the spheres of Saturn and the other planets, with the corresponding Soul of each of them, and finally the world of generation and corruption and its Soul. Each one of these Souls was resplendent with beauty and, like the Soul of the first heaven, was fully engrossed in the contemplation of God. Ḥayy was even able to perceive an immaterial prototype of his own Soul, reflected a thousandfold in the innumerable Souls which were once united to their bodies. Some, like his own Soul, shone with great splendor, whereas

[37] *Ḥayy*, p. 76.

[38] There is an obvious reference in this passage to the extravagant *Ṣūfīs* al-Basṭāmī and al-Ḥallāj.

[39] *Ibid.*, p. 79. [40] *Ibid.*

others looked like distorted reflections in a tarnished mirror. Ḥayy had in fact caught a glimpse of the intelligible world of Neo-Platonism.

The epilogue of this allegory develops the second major theme of Muslim Neo-Platonism: the harmony of reason and revelation, of philosophy and religion. In a neighboring island a religious creed introduced by an ancient prophet was current. Two of its adepts, Absāl and Salāmān, were typical. The former inclined toward the inward or esoteric, the latter toward the outward or exoteric interpretation of this creed. Having heard of the desert island on which Ḥayy lived, Absāl decided to retire there to spend the rest of his life in meditation and prayer; he was not aware of the existence of Ḥayy on that island. One day he sighted him from a distance but did not wish to disturb his peace. Ḥayy, for his part, did not realize what kind of creature this strange visitor was. Eventually they met and their friendship grew daily. When Absāl had taught him to speak, Ḥayy began to unburden himself of his experiences, especially the mystical ones. These revelations greatly impressed Absāl and he now understood that the references of Scripture to the angels, prophets, heaven, and hell were mere representations in sensible terms of the spiritual realities Ḥayy had perceived on his own. Ḥayy, on the other hand, realized that everything Absāl had recounted to him concerning revelation and ritual was in conformity with what he had experienced himself. Hence, he could not but have total faith in the law laid down by the Prophet and supported by his unquestionable authority.[41]

Two questions continued to puzzle him, however. (1) Why did the Prophet resort to such representations concerning the "divine world" instead of speaking directly and openly to mankind, which would avoid involving them inextricably in anthropomorphic difficulties? (2) Why did he prescribe particular rituals and permit the acquisition of wealth and the pursuit of the pleasures of food and sex, thereby encouraging people to occupy themselves with those vanities?

At the root of these questions, observes the author, lurked a grave misunderstanding. Ḥayy had started by assuming mistakenly that all men were of "superior parts." However, it did not take him long to discover how ignorant and dull the masses are. Thereupon he was

[41] *Ḥayy*, p. 88.

moved by compassion for them and felt the urge to go forth and preach the truth to them. He put his intention to Absāl, who finally agreed to join him. And so they set out together for Absāl's birthplace, where Absāl introduced Ḥayy to his friends, who, as he supposed, formed a privileged class. Salāmān had risen to the rank of head of the island, and so Ḥayy began by instructing him. This adept of the outward and literal, however, was not very disposed to listen to the mystical and allegorical disquisitions of Ḥayy. The others, who were addicted to mundane pleasures and pursuits, were even less interested. Gradually Ḥayy realized that his instruction or preaching would be in vain, since the majority of his hearers were no better than beasts. Scripture had indeed been right in speaking to them in the only language they understood; that of similes and sensible representations. By this time Ḥayy had learned his lesson. He apologized to Salāmān and his countrymen and admitted his own mistake in exhorting them to seek the hidden meaning of Scripture. His parting message was that they should carry on as they had done before and should cling to the prescriptions of the law (*al-shar'*). Together with Absāl, he now understood that this was the only secure path which the ignorant masses could follow and that if they were to forsake it they would be irretrievably lost. With a somewhat heavy heart, they returned to Ḥayy's island, where they resumed their worship of God in solitude. Having failed to win over those who were content with the "outward" aspect of truth, they felt the only course left for them was to continue their contemplation of the elusive truth in the only way suitable to the people of "superior parts" or exceptional ability.

Thus does Ibn Ṭufayl express the Neo-Platonic postulate of the harmony of religion and philosophy. Without doubting his sincerity or the sincerity of his predecessors, the reader of *Ḥayy b. Yaqẓān* cannot overcome the suspicion of misrepresentation. The religious and philosophical truths which are so artfully reconciled or accommodated are obviously not on the same level. As shown in the life of Ḥayy, its chief spokesman, philosophical truth attained through the natural process of experience or reflection is the only truth which is worthy of the privileged few. Religious truth, on the other hand, belongs to the many, who cannot and should not aspire to anything higher than a purely external or literal version of this genuine truth. Thus Ibn Ṭufayl gives the final touches to this sublime doctrine of a superior or privileged class of seekers after truth, who alone are worthy of the divine favor of illumination or election, as Ibn Bājjah had argued.

III

IBN RUSHD AND THE DEFENSE OF ARISTOTELIANISM

By the beginning of the eleventh century Ibn Sīnā had become the symbol of Greek philosophy in the eastern part of the Muslim world. Al-Ghazālī's attack on Neo-Platonism had radically jeopardized the whole cause of philosophy, but post-Avicennian developments in philosophy and theology revealed the durability of that intellectual spirit which had given a new dimension to the Islamic view of life. Aristotle, in whose name the whole issue had been joined, suffered most. As has been reiterated so often, he was confused with Plotinus, reconciled with Plato, declared to be a disciple of Hermes, and even hailed as a venerable monotheistic sage. It is no wonder that his genuine teaching had remained virtually unknown until the latter part of the twelfth century, which witnessed the appearance on the philosophical scene of the first and last great Aristotelian in Islam, Ibn Rushd of Cordova, known to the Latin authors of the late Middle Ages as Averroes.

Abu'l-Walīd Muḥammad b. Aḥmad b. Rushd, who was born in 1126, descended from a long line of distinguished scholars and jurists in Muslim Spain. His early education was of the traditional type and centered chiefly on linguistic studies, jurisprudence (*fiqh*), and scholastic theology. Soon his medical talents came to the fore, as can be judged from his early association with Ibn Zuhr, a leading medical authority of the time, and his composition of the major medical treatise *al-Kulliyāt* in 1169. His philosophical education is not sufficiently documented, but internal evidence shows definitely that his two chief masters were Ibn Bājjah and Ibn Ṭufayl. In fact, it was through the good offices of the latter that Ibn Rushd was introduced around the year 1169 to the caliph Abū Ya'qūb Yūsuf, whose interest in philosophy and science has already been noted.[42]

A detailed account of his meeting with this caliph is given by the historian al-Marākushī, on the authority of one of Ibn Rushd's disciples.[43] As soon as he was presented to Abū Ya'qūb, the latter engaged him in conversation on the thorny question of the eternity of the world. The philosopher was somewhat taken aback, since he was not conversant with the caliph's philosophical sympathies or Ibn Ṭufayl's understanding with him concerning their plans for him. As it turned out, the caliph had sought the advice of the aging Ibn Ṭufayl on a possible interpreter of the works of Aristotle, which he had found too abstruse. The meeting with the caliph had two concrete results: one was the appointment of Ibn Rushd as *qāḍī* or religious judge of Seville; the other was his undertaking, in deference to the wish of the caliph, to comment upon or paraphrase Aristotle's works. Two years later, however, Ibn Rushd returned to Cordova in the capacity of chief judge, a post which his father and grandfather had also filled.[44] Eventually he was attached to the Almohades court at Marakesh as the court physician of the caliph, succeeding Ibn Ṭufayl in 1182.

The death of Abū Ya'qūb in 1184 and the accession of his son Abū Yūsuf, surnamed al-Manṣūr, brought no immediate change in Ibn Rushd's preeminence at court. However, ten years later, possibly in response to public pressure or due to a personal grudge nursed against this old *habitué* at the Almohades court, Ibn Rushd suddenly fell out of favor. The caliph ordered his books to be burned and carted him off to Alisana (Lucena), a small town to the southeast of Cordova, together with other students of philosophy and science. At the same time, a prohibition was issued against the study of such subjects. Shortly after, however, Ibn Rushd was restored to favor and the

[42] *Supra*, p. 294. [43] *Al-Mu'jib fī Akhbār al-Maghrib*, p. 174.
[44] Gauthier, *Ibn Rochd (Averroès)*, p. 4.

caliph, we are told, resumed his own study of philosophy.[45] In 1198 Ibn Rushd died at the age of seventy-two.

The philosophical output of Ibn Rushd was as voluminous and varied as that of any of the greater philosophers of the East. Two characteristic features set his work apart from that of the two Eastern masters, al-Fārābī and Ibn Sīnā, his only two equals in the world of Islam: his meticulousness in commenting on the texts of Aristotle and his conscientiousness in grappling with the perennial question of the relation of philosophy and dogma. A third feature must also be mentioned: no other philosopher of note had either exercised the functions of canonical judge or composed systematic treatises on jurisprudence (*fiqh*). At least two such treatises are attributed to him, one of which, *Bidāyat al-Mujtahid*, is still extant. His medical writings, although they lie outside the scope of this study, may also be mentioned. Apart from his extant *al-Kulliyāt* and a series of original medical tracts, most of these works consisted of compendia (Arabic: *talkhīṣ*) of the works of Galen, the Alexandrian physician and philosopher of the second century, whose influence on Arabic philosophy and medicine has frequently been noted.

Although the widely accepted view that Ibn Rushd initiated the method of commentary[46] should now be abandoned, there is no doubt that he is the greatest medieval philosopher to exploit it to the full, prior to St. Thomas Aquinas. The method has an obvious analogy to the koranic method of *tafsīr* and was used frequently by al-Fārābī in his logical commentaries on Aristotle and by Ibn Sīnā to a lesser extent in his lost *Kitāb al-Inṣāf*.[47]

Ibn Rushd wrote three types of commentary on the works of Aristotle, generally designated as the large, the intermediate, and the short. Although it is true that, with minor exceptions, he wrote commentaries on all the works of Aristotle, the *Republic* of Plato, and the *Isagoge* of Porphyry, the only Aristotelian works on which a large,

45 Al-Marākushī, *al-Mu'jib fī Akhbār al-Maghrib*, p. 175; Ibn Abī Uṣaybi'ah, *'Uyūn*, II, 76. Cf. Gauthier, *Ibn Rochd*, pp. 9 f.

46 See, for instance, Gauthier, *Ibn Rochd*, p. 16; Rénan, *Averroës et l'averroïsme*, pp. 59 ff.

47 Important fragments of this work have survived. See Badawī, *Arisṭū 'ind al-'Arab*, pp. 22–74. As for al-Fārābī, see *Sharḥ Kitāb al-'Ibārah*.

intermediate, and short version of these commentaries were written are the *Physics*, the *Metaphysics*, *De Anima*, *De Caelo*, and *Analytica Posteriora*.[48] The distinction between the large and intermediate commentaries is not always easy to make. The paraphrases or compendia, on the other hand, are shorter summaries analogous to the earlier Greek paraphrases of Themistius, Galen, and Alexander of Aphrodisias.

In addition to these commentaries Ibn Rushd wrote a series of original works intended to show how far al-Fārābī and Ibn Sīnā had departed from the genuine teaching of Aristotle. One dealt with *The Divergence of al-Fārābī's Approach to Logic . . . from That of Aristotle*, another with *Al-Fārābī's Departure from Aristotle in the Arrangement, Canons of Proof, and Definition in Analytica Priora.* Another group of Peripatetic treatises was aimed at Ibn Sīnā. A general *Inquiry into Problems Discussed in Ibn Sīnā's Metaphysics of al-Shifā'* appears to have dealt with his general metaphysical strictures against Ibn Sīnā, the tenor of which may be gathered from his extant works. Another treatise dealt specifically with *Ibn Sīnā's Distinction between the Absolutely Possible, the Possible in Itself, the Necessary through Another and the Necessary in Itself.* To these last works must be added the copious references to al-Fārābī and Ibn Sīnā in the commentaries, in *Al-Tahāfut*, and the two important theological tracts, *Fasl al-Maqāl* and *Al-Kashf 'an Manāhij al-Adillah.*

In fact, the three major parts of Ibn Rushd's work could be seen as his commentaries upon or interpretation of Aristotle, his criticism of al-Fārābī and Ibn Sīnā in the name of a pure Aristotelianism, which they either distorted or misunderstood, according to him, and his demonstration of the essential harmony between philosophy properly understood and Scripture properly interpreted.

Historians of medieval philosophy have tended heretofore to concentrate on the study of Ibn Rushd as commentator and consequently to highlight his contribution to the exegesis of Aristotle. Ibn Rushd's place in the history of philosophical ideas in Islam is radically different, however. The error in perspective which has resulted from this

[48] For inventory of the Commentaries, see Wolfson, "Revised Plan for Publication of a Corpus Commentariorum Averrois in Aristotelem," *Speculum*, XXXVIII (Jan. 1963), 90 f.; cf. Rénan, *Averroês et l'averroïsme*, p. 62.

approach has been unfortunate. For one thing, it has led to the portrayal of "Averroes" as some kind of leader of a Latin rebellion against the established authority of the Church, a kind of Muslim Siger de Brabant, on the one hand, or the leader of a fresh intellectual wave among the Jews of Spain and Southern France, on the other. Furthermore, it has tended to ignore his original contribution to the perennial question of the relationship between philosophy and Scripture, in which his own deepest convictions appear to have been involved, and as a consequence denationalized him, so to speak. No one would wish to underrate Ibn Rushd's contribution to the interpretation of Aristotle. For in this lay his unquestioned right to stand in the foremost ranks of that international contingent of scholars who, from Theophrastus to al-Fārābī and St. Thomas Aquinas, have illustrated through their dedication to the same cause the philosophical unity of mankind. But if, in the process, his vital intellectual interests and his place in the historic context of Islamic thought are ignored, a grave injustice would be done him.

What contributed to Ibn Rushd's denationalization was the significant historical circumstance that, with the revival of Aristotelianism in Western Europe by the end of the twelfth century, he was soon recognized as an undoubted leader among both Jews and Christians. The great regard in which he was held by Moses Maimonides (d. 1204) and his disciple Joseph ben Judah established his reputation among the Jews as the outstanding interpreter of Aristotle. Before the end of the twelfth century Ibn Rushd's works were read in Arabic by Jewish scholars, whose philosophical culture was, as Rénan has put it, "nothing but a reflection of Muslim culture."[49] By the beginning of the thirteenth century, however, the Jewish dispersion beyond the Pyrenees and along the Mediterranean coast made it necessary to translate his works into Hebrew. Moses ben Tibbon, Jacob ben Abba Mari, Simeon Anatoli, Solomon ben Joseph ben Job, Zerachia ben Isaac, and Joseph ben Machis are his best-known translators in the thirteenth century; and in the fourteenth century his translators included Calonymus ben Calonymus, Calonymus ben Todros, and Samuel ben Judah ben Meshullan.[50] A characteristic feature of the fourteenth century is

[49] *Averroês et l'averroïsme*, p. 173. [50] *Ibid.*, pp. 186 f.

the rise of a whole wave of super-commentaries on the commentaries of Ibn Rushd.[51]

The Jewish phase was only the first in Ibn Rushd's westward migration. Owing to the closer cultural links between the Jews and the Christians and the fairly common knowledge of Hebrew in Western Europe, as illustrated by the cases of Roger Bacon (d. 1294?) and Raymond Martin (d. after 1284), the Latin translation of Arabic philosophical works, very often through Hebrew, had become highly developed by the beginning of the thirteenth century. Between 1217 and 1230 Michael the Scot translated into Latin Ibn Rushd's commentaries on *De Caelo et Mundo*, *De Anima*, *De Generatione et Corruptione*, *Physica*, *Metaphysica*, *Meteorologica*, as well as the paraphrases of *Parva Naturalia* and *De Substantia Orbis*. Hermann the German, on the other hand, translated the epitomes of *Poetica* and *Ethica Nicomachea* between 1240 amd 1256.[52] The remaining commentaries were gradually rendered by less celebrated scholars. All together, fifteen out of the thirty-eight commentaries of Averroes were translated into Latin directly from Arabic during the thirteenth century.[53]

Thereafter Ibn Rushd's commentaries may be said to have become part of the Aristotelian heritage of Western Europe. Ibn Rushd had scarcely any disciples or successors in the Muslim empire. Even his critics are of little consequence. With the possible exception of Ibn Taymiyah (d. 1327), none of them was of the stature of Ibn Sīnā's major critic, al-Ghazālī. His followers and critics in the West form a brilliant galaxy, however: Maimonides, Siger de Brabant, Moses ben Tibbon, Levi ben Gerson, Albert the Great, St. Thomas Aquinas.

For a correct understanding of the philosophical and theological ideas of the Muslim Ibn Rushd, the most important source is, without question, his *Tahāfut al-Tahāfut* (*Incoherence of the Incoherence*), one of the greatest philosophico-theological works. Written probably in 1180, it is the product of Ibn Rushd's maturest thought and constitutes a systematic rebuttal of al-Ghazālī's critique of Greco-Arab philosophy.

[51] *Averroès et l'averroïsme*, pp. 193 f.
[52] *Ibid.*, pp. 205 f.; cf. Wolfson, "Revised Plan," p. 92.
[53] See list in Wolfson, "Revised Plan," p. 92.

It is in addition a masterly exposition in which the author's most fundamental thoughts are brought into focus.

Al-Ghazālī, it will be recalled, had directed the brunt of his attack at al-Fārābī and Ibn Sīnā, the two foremost Muslim interpreters of Aristotle, according to him. Rather than defend those two Muslim philosophers, Ibn Rushd is often content to show the measure of their divergence from genuine Aristotelian teaching or the cogency of al-Ghazālī's arguments. His own careful study and analysis of the Aristotelian texts enabled him to determine, better than any other Muslim philosopher, the extent of that divergence and to reduce the issues which separated Islamic philosophers and theologians to their essential components. In some of his larger commentaries, such as the *Physics* and the *Metaphysics*, some of these issues are more fully explored than in the *Tahāfut*, but nowhere are they more dramatically and articulately set out than in this masterly treatise of philosophical debate.

Before we turn to the consideration of Ibn Rushd's estimate of the anti-Avicennian polemic of al-Ghazālī, it will be necessary to examine in some detail his important contribution to the ever-present question of the relation of philosophy to Scripture. From the time of al-Kindī, this question had been one of the major issues that had set the theologians against the philosophers and cast a dark shadow over the whole task of philosophizing in Muslim lands. Ibn Rushd, far more systematically than any of his predecessors, had developed a stringent theological method which enabled him to deal effectively with this question.

The starting point of this method is the late Neo-Platonic theme of the unity of truth in all its manifestations. The Brethren of Purity were perhaps the first to popularize this theme in the tenth century, but it is presupposed by al-Kindī, al-Fārābī, Ibn Sīnā, and the whole Illuminationist or Ishrāqī tradition, though certainly not by such *libre-penseurs* as Ibn al-Rāwandī or al-Rāzī. Obviously inherited from the Hellenistic Neo-Platonic tradition, as illustrated in the eclecticism of Jamblichus, Damascius, Syrianus and Simplicius,[54] the concept of the unity of all truth was the only logical way in which the philosophers of Islam could justify their philosophical

[54] See Zeller, *Outlines of the History of Greek Philosophy*; cf. Fakhry, "Philosophy and Scripture in the Theology of Averroes," *Mediaeval Studies*, XXX (1968), pp. 78 f.

pursuits, appease the theologians, and satisfy the mind's urge for internal coherence.

The anthropomorphisms in which the Koran abounds had from the start raised the crucial question of this unity. Both the koranic references to God's "sitting upon the throne" (Koran 7, 54 and 20, 5) and the possibility of perceiving Him on the Last Day (Koran 75, 22), to mention only the two most glaring instances, compelled the more rationally minded theologians, from the time of Wāṣil b. ʿAṭā' on, to resort to the only logical device possible, the interpretation of those anthropomorphisms in a way that would safeguard God's immateriality without sacrificing their intellectual content. Thus, the "sitting upon the throne" was interpreted by the Muʿtazilite and post-Muʿtazilite theologians as an allegory for majesty or sovereignty, and the "contemplation" of God's countenance as an allegory for the beatific vision.

The more literal-minded jurists and exegetes, like Mālik b. Anas (d. 795) and Aḥmad b. Ḥanbal (d. 855), were not particularly disturbed by such anthropomorphisms. In their unconditional belief in the infallibility and sanctity of the koranic text, they were simply content to accept its truth. But this attitude, which they and other literalists and semi-literalists in centuries to come were to assume, did not satisfy the nagging intellectual curiosity of the rationalist theologians or the philosophers. Ibn Rushd is fully committed to the infallibility of the Koran also, but he is equally committed to the postulate of the unity of truth.[55]

For Ibn Rushd this postulate not only involved the methodological necessity of recourse to interpretation (*ta'wīl*) only; in addition it implied the tacit recognition of the *parity* of philosophy and Scripture, of reason and revelation, as the two primary and infallible sources of truth. If some philosophers, such as Ibn Sīnā, had tended in their zeal for philosophy to sacrifice this parity, some like al-Kindī never doubted it. Better than any other Muslim philosopher, Ibn Rushd has given clear expression to this concept of parity and drawn all the logical corollaries implicit in it.

Two circumstances in particular enabled Ibn Rushd to maintain the difficult position which we have labeled the parity of philosophy and

[55] See, for instance, *Faṣl al-Maqāl* in *Falsafat Ibn Rushd*, p. 26; cf. Hourani, *Agreement of Philosophy and Religion* (p. 70).

Scripture, of reason and revelation. First, the distinction, which the Koran itself makes (Koran 3, 5) and which the commentators from al-Ṭabari (d. 923) down had recognized, between ambiguous (*mutashābih*) and unambiguous (*muḥkam*) Scriptual passages, and second, the absence of a teaching authority in (Sunnite) Islam who held the right to define doctrine. What the first circumstance entailed was the recognition that some Scriptural passages cannot be taken at face value. What the second circumstance entailed was the need for some authority in whom the right to arbitrate doctrinal conflicts was vested. In Shī'ite Islam this right was vested in the *Imām*, who was the spiritual and temporal head of the community, as well as its infallible teacher (*mu'allim:* magister). This explains how in Shī'ite circles from the time of the Brethren of Purity in the tenth century down to that of Nāṣir-i-Khusrū in the eleventh and al-Shīrāzī in the seventeenth, the conflict between philosophy and Scripture was never a serious issue.

In trying to determine the body in which this doctrinal authority should be vested, Ibn Rushd exhibits his greatest subtlety. The Koran again provides him with a clue to this determination. Having stated that "it is he who has revealed the Book to you [i.e., Muḥammad]," it goes on to state (at least according to a perfectly sound and respectable reading), "some of its verses are unambiguous [*muḥkamāt*] . . . and the others are ambiguous [*mutashābihāt*], and that "only God and those confirmed in knowledge know its interpretation [*ta'wīl*]" (Koran 3, 5).

It will be noted at once that the whole issue hinges on the interpretation of the phrase "those confirmed in knowledge." For Ibn Rushd, however, the phrase admits of one and only one interpretation, namely, the philosophers. His reasons are sometimes historically founded, sometimes purely a priori. Both on the basis of Aristotelian logical theory and that of his own estimate of the validity of scholastic theological methods, he arrives at this judgment, which for him is undeniable. Aristotle, as is well known, distinguishes in *Analytica Posteria* (I, 71^{b}) and *Topica* (I, 100^{a-b}) between scientific and sophistical arguments and lists in *Sophistica* (165^{b}) four types of sophistical arguments: didactic, dialectical, examination, and contentious (διδασκαλικοὶ, διαλεκτικοὶ, πειραστικοὶ, ἐριστικοὶ). In *Rhetorica* (I, 1354^{a}) he explains the nature of rhetorical or persuasive reasoning. Ibn Rushd reduces the list to the three principal types of argument: the demonstrative, the dialectical, and the rhetorical, and proceeds to identify the demonstrative method with that of the philosophers, the dialectical with that of the theologians, and the rhetorical with that of the masses at large.[56]

What further disqualifies the theologians (*al-mutakallimūn*), according to him, is the fact that they have unlawfully divulged the secrets of interpretation, which should be reserved for only those who are fit to comprehend them, and they have thereby sowed the seeds of heresy and discord in Islam.[57]

To make good his case against the theologians and particularly the Ash'arites, Ibn Rushd wrote his *Exposition of the Methods of Proof Concerning the Beliefs of the Community* (*al-Kashf*),[58] intended to serve as a sequel to his *Relation of Philosophy and Religion* (*Faṣl*). His aim in this treatise is stated to be "the examination of the external aspects [*al-ẓāhir*] of the beliefs which the lawgiver [i.e., Muḥammad] intended the public to adhere to," as distinct from those (false) beliefs which the unwarranted interpretations of the theologians have induced them into.[59] By those "external beliefs" he means those articles of faith which are indispensable for salvation, or as the text puts it, "those without which the faith [of the believer] is not complete." The determination of those articles provides him with the occasion to draw up a statement of orthodoxy, as he understood it, as well as to lay down the conditions and the limits of the method of interpretation.

The first condition is that, as already hinted, neither the theologians (whether Mu'tazilite or Ash'arite), nor the literalists (*ḥashwiyah*), nor the advocates of the esoteric method (i.e., the Ismā'īlīs or Bāṭinīs) are competent to formulate the "sound interpretations" which genuine faith requires. Only the philosophers are. The examination of his specific strictures against each of these groups lies outside the scope of this book, but it is noteworthy that the general charge leveled at them

[56] See *Faṣl* in *Falsafat Ibn Rushd*, pp. 19 f., and Hourani, *Agreement of Philosophy and Religion*, p. 64.

[57] *Faṣl*, pp. 22 f. *et passim*; see also Hourani, *Agreement of Philosophy and Religion*, pp. 65 f.

[58] In *Falsafat Ibn Rushd*, pp. 30 ff.; Spanish translation in Alonso, *Teología de Averroes*, pp. 203 ff.

[59] *Al-Kashf*, pp. 30 f.

is that most of their arguments or interpretations are "innovations" which have no basis in tradition.[60]

The second condition is that Scripture, which is addressed to all classes of men and not just the philosophers, uses the three types of proof already mentioned.[61] Each class, however, attains the degree of assent (*al-taṣdīq*) appropriate to it and which its salvation requires. And this, argues Ibn Rushd, is the token of God's wisdom: that in the Koran He has addressed each class according to the degree of their understanding.[62]

The third condition is that interpretation should be properly understood and applied. By interpretation, or *ta'wīl*, is meant "the act of extending the connotation of the term from the real to the figurative meaning, without violating the linguistic usage of the Arabs, which allows for giving a thing the name proper to its equal, its cause, its accident, or its concomitant."[63] Ibn Rushd asserts repeatedly that the masses should take the pronouncements of Scripture at their face value and that the divulging of the "secrets of interpretation" is a very grave sin, of which al-Ghazālī is particularly guilty. The obvious implication of this thesis is that there is an impious inquisitiveness which can only lead to damnation and from which the masses, who are not equipped to probe the hidden truths of revelation, should be guarded at any cost.

Where the line of demarcation between what ought and what ought not to be interpreted lies is not clearly spelled out by Ibn Rushd. It is fair to infer from his statements, however, that there are three cases in which interpretation is called for: (1) where no consensus (*ijmā'*) is possible on the legal or doctrinal significance of certain Scriptural passages; (2) where the pronouncements of Scripture appear to conflict with each other; and (3) where those pronouncements appear to conflict with the principles of philosophy or natural reason.

The first of these cases is doubtless the most fertile area of possible interpretation. *Ijmā'* itself is ill defined and, in the absence of a teaching religious authority, inconclusive.[64] It is possible theoretically, of

[60] *Al-Kashf*, p. 31. [61] See *Faṣl*, pp. 7, 19.
[62] *Ibid.*, p. 9, and *al-Kashf*, p. 79. [63] *Faṣl*, p. 8.
[64] On the general question of *Ijmā'* see Gauthier, *Ibn Rochd (Averroes)*, pp. 32 f., and Hourani, *Agreement of Philosophy and Religion*, pp. 28 f.

course, that consensus on all juridical and doctrinal matters could have been achieved during the life of Muḥammad and thereby the area of interpretation drastically restricted from the start. But the fact of theological discord in early Muslim history shows beyond question how idle is this supposition.

The second case is the one with which the commentators of the Koran and the theologians (particularly the Muʿtazilah) were primarily concerned. Ibn Rushd himself is naturally concerned with the third case, especially since the intermittent dialectical warfare between the theologians and the philosophers had seriously compromised philosophy in the Muslim world and brought it to the verge of bankruptcy following al-Ghazālī's classic onslaught. The rehabilitation of philosophy, he felt, could be achieved only once it is demonstrated that no genuine conflict between philosophy and religion could arise, and that Scripture properly interpreted is in complete harmony with philosophy properly understood.

It should be noted that nowhere does Ibn Rushd suggest that the philosopher is authorized to introduce any new doctrines, or, conversely, to eliminate any positively given ones, in attempting to harmonize philosophy and Scripture through *ta'wīl*. From this it follows that, like the commentator on the texts of Scripture, he is fully dependent on these texts. This is the first and perhaps the most important limit of the philosophical method of *ta'wīl*. But there are other and equally significant limits. Like the most humble member of the religious community, the philosopher has a personal stake in salvation, or, as Islamic sources express it, happiness in this world and the world-to-come. To safeguard his salvation the philosopher must subscribe to that system of beliefs that is indispensable for salvation.

The determination of the irreducible core of such beliefs thus becomes a decisive issue for the philosopher. As outlined in *al-Kashf* this irreducible core consists of the following articles or precepts to which the philosopher, the theologian, and the ordinary man must all subscribe. (1) The existence of God as Creator and providential ruler of the world. The most convincing arguments for this existence are not the cosmological or etiological ones developed by Aristotle, nor the argument from contingency advanced by Avicenna and the

Ash'arite theologians, but rather the argument from invention (or creation) and the argument from providence or design (*dalīl al-'ināyah*).[65] The Koran itself has drawn attention to those two arguments which are the most suited to the capabilities of all classes of men. (2) God's unity defined in three koranic verses (21, 22; 23, 33; 17, 44) which are at the basis of all the philosophical arguments for this unity. (3) The "attributes of perfection" which the Koran predicates of God and which every Muslim must believe to apply to Him.[66] These are knowledge, life, power, will, hearing, seeing, and speech. (4) God's freedom from any imperfection (*tanzīh*) clearly asserted in the Koran, especially in the classic verse (Koran 42, 9) "there is nothing like unto Him" and upon which the *via remotionis*, a favorite method of the Mu'tazilah and the Neo-Platonists, ultimately rests. Apart from the Koran, this concept is rooted in human nature. For man recognizes instinctively that the Creator must be unlike the creature and that any attributes common to both must belong to God in a preeminent way, or, as the Scholastics have put it, *modus eminenter*.[67]

The other articles are (5) the creation of the world, (6) the validity of prophecy, (7) the justice of God, and (8) resurrection or survival after death (*al-ma'ād*). The Koran has legislated unambiguously upon all those matters and consequently has left the philosophers, the theologians, and the masses no choice but to acquiesce. Here interpretation or controversy is entirely precluded. It is clear, however, that the *manner* in which these articles are to be understood is not unambiguously defined in the Koran. Let us take as an example the problem of creation. That the world is created by God is absolutely certain; however, whether the world was created *ex nihilo* and in time, as the theologians maintain, is far from being clear. There is not a single proposition in the Koran which states explicitly that "God existed together with non-being" and subsequently the world came into being after it was not. The import of a series of koranic passages appears, on the contrary, to suggest that the "form" of the world is created in time, whereas both its duration and matter are uncreated. Thus the

[65] *Al-Kashf*, pp. 45 f.; cf. Fakhry, "The Classical Islamic Arguments for the Existence of God," *Muslim World*, XLVII (1957), pp. 133 f.

[66] See *infra*, pp. 316 f. [67] *Al-Kashf*, pp. 60 f.; al-Ghazālī, *Tahāfut*, p. 463 *et passim*.

verse (Koran 11, 6) "He who created the heavens and the earth in six days, while His throne rested on water" implies the eternity of water, the throne, and time, which measures their duration. Similarly, the verse (Koran 41, 10) "Then He arose toward heaven, which consisted of smoke" implies that the heaven was created out of preexisting matter, smoke.[68]

Or let us take the equally knotty question of resurrection. This is a question "regarding the validity of which," writes Ibn Rushd, "the various religions are in agreement and the demonstrations of the learned have established its truth through necessary proofs."[69] The only difference between the philosopher and the theologian on this score is that the character (*ṣifat*) of this resurrection is differently understood. The Koran, in its concern for the welfare of the masses, has spoken of the pleasures and tribulations of the world-to-come in gross sensuous or corporeal terms so as to compel their assent. In so far as they serve a positive moral or spiritual purpose by encouraging a life of virtue, such "sensuous representations" can only be welcomed by the philosophers, who must piously defer to the authority of the prophets as the lawgivers of the community in these matters.[70]

Some scriptures, it is true, have dispensed with "sensuous representations." The Koran, however, has this advantage over them: it has coupled the sensuous or pictorial to the spiritual or nonsensuous method and has thereby safeguarded the salvation of the three classes.[71]

An obvious implication of this view is that the masses at large, as distinct from the philosophers and theologians, can only understand the pictorial language of sensuous representations. The theologians, misunderstanding the nature or purpose of this language, have extended to it the process of interpretation and thereby confused the masses and repudiated the divine wisdom underlying its use. However, since the sensuous representations with which the Koran abounds do not belong to the class of ambiguous statements, the duty of the masses is to accept them at their face value, and any attempt to elicit their hidden meaning for them through interpretation should be condemned.[72]

Another implication is that, despite the harmony of philosophy and

[68] *Faṣl*, p. 13. [69] *Al-Kashf*, p. 118. [70] *Tahāfut*, p. 584.
[71] *Al-Kashf*, pp. 102 f.; *Tahāfut*, p. 585. [72] *Al-Kashf*, p. 64.

Scripture where the fundamentals of belief are concerned, religion has a wider scope than philosophy. Whereas philosophy is concerned with "the intellectual felicity of a small group of men" (the philosophers), religion is concerned with the felicity of all and consequently has used the three types of argument: the rhetorical, the dialectical, and demonstrative.[73] Although different, those three types are not incompatible. The results arrived at through demonstration are not different in substance from the results arrived at through dialectical or rhetorical methods. Only the form in which they are expressed is different.

Moreover, there is a whole area outside the scope of reason into which philosophy cannot venture. Al-Ghazālī was therefore right to argue that "with respect to whatever lies outside the scope of human cognitions, it is necessary to resort to Scripture [*al-shar'*]."[74] In certain cases human reason is essentially incapable of acquiring a form of knowledge indispensable for man's felicity. In other cases, it is incapable because of accidental impediments or simply the difficulties inherent in the subject matter itself. In all such cases, revelation necessarily supplements rational knowledge.[75]

Let us now turn to Ibn Rushd's rebuttal of al-Ghazālī's chief anti-Avicennian strictures. A major criticism is the allegation that Ibn Sīnā and the Neo-Platonists in general have divested God of any positive attributes, in the manner of the Mu'tazilite theologians. Attributes are represented by them as distinct from the essence of the entity they qualify and adventitious to it. In God, who is absolutely simple, the composition of essence and attribute is logically impossible, according to them.[76]

In his rebuttal Ibn Rushd accuses al-Ghazālī of misunderstanding the nature of predication as it applies to God and the creature respectively. The philosophers do not deny the divine "attributes of perfection," i.e., knowledge, will, life, power, speech, hearing, and seeing. What they deny is that they apply to God and the creature *univocally* or that any proportion between the creature and God exists. The attribute of knowledge can be inferred from the magnificent order which we observe in the world and the manner in which the lower always

[73] *Tahāfut*, p. 582.
[74] *Ibid.*, p. 582.
[75] *Ibid.*, pp. 255 f.
[76] *Ibid.*, pp. 162 f.

subserves the higher in it. Thus knowledge belongs to God eternally but the mode of its bearing on created entities is unknown to us. Consequently we are not justified in asserting that God knows the coming-to-be of created entities (*al-muḥdathāt*) or their passing-away either through an eternal or through a temporal mode of knowledge.[77] Between the divine and the human (created or temporal) modes of knowledge there is no proportion, since, whereas God's knowledge is the cause of the object known, human knowledge is the effect. If so, then the Avicennian thesis that God has a universal knowledge of particulars must be rejected on the ground that universal and particular are categories of human but not of divine knowledge. In fact, the mode of God's knowledge, being entirely transcendent, can only be known by God Himself.[78]

Another attribute, which is a concomitant of knowledge, is life. We observe that, in the creature, knowledge is always accompanied by life and with that observation as a basis we assert that the Creator must possess life also. By the same token, we assert that He must have will, power, and speech. For the characteristic of a conscious act of an agent is that he willed it and had the power to do it. As for speech, it is simply the outward sign, verbal or other, expressing the agent's knowledge of the deed done. Finally, hearing and sight must be predicated of God, as corollaries of the all-embracing knowledge which He has of all possible objects of cognition, both rational and perceptual.[79]

Ibn Rushd does not explain how God can have knowledge of such *sensibilia*. The mode of God's knowledge, whether rational or perceptual, is stated categorically to be unknowable, because it is infinite or transcendent. He does not give up however the attempt to rationalize it and in particular to show its relation to the divine essence as self-thinking thought. Aristotle's reason for asserting that the only fit object of divine knowledge is the divine essence was the desire to spare God the indignity or mutability that knowledge of the particular involved. Ibn Rushd accepts the premises of this argument but

[77] *Al-Kashf*, p. 54; cf. *Tahāfut*, p. 443.
[78] *Tahāfut*, p. 446; *Ḍamīmah* (Appendix to *Faṣl*), pp. 28 f.
[79] *Al-Kashf*, pp. 55 f.

endeavors to save God from that condition of ignorance which Aristotle had declared to be the token of absolute divine bliss.

The nature of the knowledge of which immaterial entities partake is such, he argues, that the object and subject are fully identified. It follows therefore that "in knowing Himself, God knows all things which exist by virtue of that being which is the cause of their existence.... And so the First Being knows the nature of particular beings through that being per se, who is Himself."[80]

The second part of al-Ghazālī's *Tahāfut* deals with four physical propositions which he deemed to be in conflict with Islamic dogma. In the first question he contests the validity of the causal nexus on two major grounds. The first is the theological ground, which the Ash'arites from al-Bāqillānī on had rendered classical, namely, that it militated against the koranic concept of God's absolute power and His unconditional prerogative to act freely and miraculously in the world. The second is the more sophisticated epistemological argument that the alleged correlation between natural causes and effects is neither borne out by experience nor logic. First, sense experience does not warrant the claim that the effect happens through the cause, but simply with it, and it is a mistake to equate temporal conjunction with necessary causal determination. Secondly, there is no logical necessity binding an event "C" to event "E," but only the divine preordination (*taqdīr*) stipulating that they should occur together in succession. There is nothing to prevent such a divinely ordained sequence from being broken whenever God so desires, as happens in those extraordinary phenomena generally designated by the Muslims as miracles.[81]

In his rebuttal, Ibn Rushd observes that the denial of "efficient causation" is only possible verbally and for a sophist. The theological motive of the Ash'arites in general and al-Ghazālī in particular in denying the necessity of the causal nexus was to reserve to God the exclusive prerogatives of sovereignty and efficacy in the world. But such a denial would nullify the concept of action altogether, and

[80] *Grand Commentaire*, III, 1693; cf. St. Thomas Aquinas' statement in *Summa Theologia*, I[a], Q. 14, a. 6: "Ita Deus, inquantam cognoscit se, ut principium essendi, cognoscit naturam entis et omnia alia inquamtum sunt alia."

[81] *Tahāfut*, pp. 517 f.; cf. Fakhry, *Islamic Occasionalism*, pp. 60 f.

consequently the whole basis for referring the processes of generation and corruption in the world to God would be eliminated.[82] Al-Ghazālī had thus unwittingly destroyed the only logical ground upon which the concept of God's exclusive efficacy could rest.

Furthermore, genuine knowledge is essentially the act of eliciting the causes underlying a given process. To the extent such causes are unknown, the process is deemed to be unknown. It follows therefore that whoever repudiates causality repudiates reason.[83] The consequences of such repudiation are as disturbing for philosophy and science as they are for theology; for if everything happens in the world fortuitously or depends on the inscrutable decree of God, no rational pattern could be discerned in the Creation. And this would amount not only to a denial of the wisdom which has presided over the creation of the world, but also of the very existence of a wise Creator. On this view it is no longer possible to prove the existence of God from the beauty of order which we observe in the world or to refute the arguments of the Materialists who refer all happenings in the world to the blind forces of chance.[84] Such a thesis is incompatible with the teaching of the philosophers, on the one hand, and, on the other, is contrary to the express pronouncements of the Koran, which describes the world as the perfect workmanship of God.

The remaining physical questions of the *Tahāfut* turn on the self-subsistence, immateriality, and indestructibility of the Soul. The philosophers are unable to prove the first two alleged predicates of the Soul, according to al-Ghazālī, and consequently the third, which is supposed to follow logically from them, is gratuitous. The error is compounded by the fact that the indestructibility or immortality of the Soul, even if successfully demonstrated, would still fall short of the Islamic dogma of corporeal resurrection.

In countering al-Ghazālī's arguments on the first two scores, Ibn Rushd contents himself with reasserting the Aristotelian thesis according to which the intellectual element in the Soul alone is incorporeal and consequently capable of surviving the death of the body.[85] However, in the rebuttal of the third proposition, he brings to bear on the

[82] *Tahāfut*, p. 519. [83] *Ibid.*, p. 522. [84] *Al-Kashf*, pp. 41 f., 86.
[85] *Tahāfut*, p. 553 *et passim*.

whole controversy an entirely fresh interpretation of the relationship of philosophy and Scripture, which we have already mentioned.

Ibn Rushd's criticisms of al-Fārābī and Ibn Sīnā, both in the *Tahāfut* and the commentaries, are numerous and devastating. He argues that in their preoccupation with the problem of harmony the two Muslim Neo-Platonists had misunderstood or minimized the vast differences between Aristotle and his master, and in particular his sustained critique of the Platonic theory of ideas.[86] Moreover, the whole emanationist doctrine which forms the cornerstone of their cosmology and metaphysics is entirely un-Aristotelian. In ascribing it to Aristotle, the two Muslim philosophers have distorted his whole teaching.[87] According to this doctrine, the universe emanates necessarily from the First Being, through the intermediary of a series of separate intelligences that move the heavenly spheres, beginning with that of the empyrean and ending with that of the moon. Through the dual relationship of possibility and necessity in which they stand to the First Being, those intelligences bring plurality into a universe whose original cause is absolutely one.

This peculiar doctrine, which seeks to explain the emanation of plurality from unity by recourse to such devices, is not only un-Aristotelian, but it is fraught with logical fallacies as well. Starting with the gratuitous premise that the Invisible Agent (i.e., God) is analogous to the visible or particular agent, its exponents go on to assert that likewise he can only produce a single effect. But this is to misunderstand the nature of divine power and to limit its scope arbitrarily to a single mode of production.[88]

In an important passage of the *Large Commentary on the Metaphysics of Aristotle*,[89] Ibn Rushd examines the various theories of the origin of the world. There is first the doctrine of creation *ex nihilo*, advanced by the "theologians of our religion and that of the Christians," according to which the Supreme Agent produces the effect in its entirety by an act of "invention," without any preexisting matter upon which to act. Possibility inheres exclusively in the agent, according to this view.

The antithesis of this doctrine is the theory of latency (*al-kumūn*), according to which the agent simply elicits what is latent in the patient.

[86] *Paraphrase of Metaphysics*, p. 53 *et passim*. [87] *Tahāfut*, p. 182.
[88] *Ibid.*, pp. 176 f. [89] *Grand Commentaire*, III, 1497 f.

A related theory is that nothing comes out of nothing and no coming-to-be is possible without a preexisting subject or substratum upon which the action supervenes. Some, like Ibn Sīnā, held that the "Giver of Forms" or active intellect imparts the forms to material entities; others like Themistius and al-Fārābī referred this action either to material agents, as in natural processes, or to immaterial agents, as in supernatural or extraordinary processes.[90]

The third view is that of Aristotle, which "we have found," says Ibn Rushd, "the least doubtful and the most congruent with the nature of being." Although this statement is qualified by the parenthetical clause "as Alexander [of Aphrodisias] says," both in the *Metaphysics* and in the *Tahāfut*,[91] this theory is stated in terms of unqualified approval and consequently must be supposed to be the one to which Ibn Rushd unquestionably subscribed. According to this theory the agent does not produce anything out of nothing, but simply brings the form and the matter together, or, to be more exact, reduces what is potential in the patient into actuality. God is spoken of, by analogy, as the Maker of the world in the sense that He brings together the elements of which it is made up. In so far as "the cause of conjunction or composition [*ribāṭ* or *tarkīb*] is the cause of being" with regard to those entities whose being is the product of the union of form and matter (i.e., the whole world of generation and corruption), God should be designated as the Cause or Maker of the world.[92]

The case of incomposite entities—the separate intelligences which move the heavenly spheres in the Aristotelian system—raises certain difficulties. Their number is given by Ibn Rushd as thirty-eight, to correspond to the spheres of Ptolemaic cosmology.[93] The dualism of matter and form upon which Ibn Rushd bases his doctrine of production made it impossible to apply the same principle to those immaterial substances. Aristotle himself tended to pass over the question of their origin, as well as their specific relation to the Unmoved Mover. Ibn Rushd, however, states categorically that those intelligences derive their being, like everything else, from the Supreme Being. For, since

[90] *Grand Commentaire*, p. 1498. Ibn Rushd cites the example of animals and plants not produced by animals or plants of the same species.

[91] Pp. 180 f. [92] *Tahāfut*, p. 180. [93] *Paraphrase of Metaphysics*, pp. 131 f.

those intelligences form a hierarchy, and since they all share in the double property of being and immateriality which are their most distinctive characteristics, it follows that they must all derive their being from that Being who possesses those characteristics to the highest degree, i.e., the "Supreme Mover of the spheres" or God.[94]

Ibn Rushd's other criticisms of Ibn Sīnā in particular and Arab Neo-Platonism in general may now be outlined. First, he inveighs against Ibn Sīnā's whole concept of being in relation to essence, which, he believed, preceded existence logically and could be defined independently from the fact of whether its object existed or not. Only on the assumption that an entity actually exists can its essence be conceived or defined by a process of inference or abstraction. Ibn Sīnā made this error, according to Ibn Rushd, because he confused the two meanings of being, the real or ontological and the conceptual or intentional. The latter could be conceived or defined *in abstracto* but not the former.

Moreover, Ibn Sīnā, who identifies "being" and "one" following Aristotle, confuses the two senses of one, i.e., the numerical and the ontological. And since being and one are convertible, according to Aristotle, he infers from this that being is an accident, whereas the only correct inference is that being, conceived as synonymous with the true (i.e., conceptual being) or the numerical one is an accident.[95]

Having asserted the independence or self-subsistence of essence, on the one hand, and the accidental nature of being, on the other, Ibn Sīnā then goes on to assert that being is an adventitious quality which supervenes upon the essence and causes it thereby to come into being. The question could be asked here whether this accident through which an entity acquires being and unity derives its own unity and being from another accident or not. If it derives it from another accident, then this will depend on another accident, and so on, ad infinitum. If it derives it from itself, so that it belongs to it per se or essentially, then it has been granted that there is at least one entity which is per se, and whose existence does not depend on an adventitious quality or accident.[96]

Next Ibn Rushd criticizes Ibn Sīnā for tacitly accepting the Ash'arite metaphysics of contingency and thereby repudiating the causal nexus.

[94] *Paraphrase of Metaphysics*, p. 139. [95] *Grand Commentaire*, I, 313 f.; III, 1279 f.
[96] *Ibid.*, III, 1280.

For in his concept of the emanation of the "substantial forms" from the active intellect, once matter is "disposed" to receiving them, he obviously intends to credit this transcendent agent (called for that reason the "Giver of Forms") with all real efficacy in the world. The part which matter plays in natural processes becomes, on this view, purely passive and secondary.[97]

Another criticism is leveled at Ibn Sīnā's well-known distinction between the possible *simpliciter*, the possible in itself, though necessary through another, and finally the necessary in itself. Ibn Rushd, it will be recalled, composed a treatise on this question, to which he frequently returns in his extant writings. This whole distinction, he argues, is entirely gratuitous. A thing is either possible or necessary, so that the possible in itself, though necessary through another, is a contradiction in terms, since it implies that "the whole nature of the possible has been transmuted."[98]

Nor is it self-evident, as Ibn Sīnā contends in his argument for the existence of God, that the world as a whole is possible. For once we posit the series of natural and supernatural (transcendent or heavenly) causes impinging on a concrete entity, such an entity is no longer possible but both actual and necessary. Indeed, were one to remove from the whole Creation the mark of necessity decreed by divine wisdom, one would no longer have any basis upon which to posit the existence of its wise Creator.[99] Ibn Sīnā's argument *a contingentia mundi*, which he took over from the Ash'arite theologians, is purely "dialectical," since it rests upon such fallacious premises.[100]

Closely related to this fallacy is the Avicennian concept of the world as possible and eternal at the same time. Such a concept, Ibn Rushd observes, is clearly erroneous; for possibility is a predicate of what is in potentiality. As soon as it is actualized it is no longer possible but rather necessary. Moreover, as Aristotle has shown, in eternal entities possibility is identical with necessity, for what is eternally possible must exist eternally, unless it is assumed to be eternally impossible, which is absurd.[101]

[97] *Grand Commentaire*, III, 1498 *et passim*.

[98] *Ibid.*, p. 1632.

[99] *Supra*, p. 319, and *Tahāfut*, p. 413.

[100] *Paraphrase of Metaphysics*, p. 4; cf. *Al-Kashf*, p. 41.

[101] *Tahāfut*, p. 98.

Ibn Rushd then makes three subsidiary criticisms in the name of genuine Aristotelianism. (1) He challenges Ibn Sīnā's claim that the existence of matter is demonstrated in metaphysics rather than physics, and the parallel claim that the existence of nature is not self-evident but requires proof.[102] (2) Next, he questions the claim that the demonstration of the ultimate material cause and the Prime Mover is the concern of the metaphysical philosopher and not the physicist. According to Ibn Rushd, the metaphysician receives from the physicist the knowledge of the existence of those two ultimate causes of the world, in the first instance.[103] (3) And finally he attacks Ibn Sīnā's introduction of a separate faculty of the Soul called the estimative (*al-wāhimah*), by virtue of which the higher animals discriminate between what is harmful and what is useful. The ancients (i.e., Aristotle and his Greek commentators) ascribed this power to the imaginative faculty with which those animals are provided.[104]

Despite those devastating criticisms, Ibn Rushd remains in essential sympathy with Ibn Sīnā's whole doctrine of man's ultimate destiny. His two Spanish masters, Ibn Bājjah and Ibn Ṭufayl, had both stated that man's destiny consists in his eventual release from the prison of corporeal existence and his entry into a state of intellectual bliss, analogous to that which the separate intelligences enjoy. Ibn Rushd, who wrote no fewer than three tracts on the question of "conjunction" (*ittiṣāl*), states decisively, in the only tract to survive in Arabic,[105] that it is in the "conjunction" of the material or "possible" intellect with the active intellect that man's eternal bliss consists. On the general question of survival after death (*al-ma'ād*) we have seen what kind of concessions he makes to the theologians. Although in that context he recognizes willingly that an extraphilosophical or Scriptural solution cannot be excluded, he is nonetheless emphatic that, on strict philosophical grounds, the only form of survival possible is intellectual, i.e., that of the material or "possible" intellect, once it is reunited with the active intellect. In this way, man's destiny, as we have already seen,

[102] *Paraphrase of Physics*, pp. 6, 18.

[103] *Paraphrase of Metaphysics*, p. 4.

[104] *Tahāfut*, p. 547.

[105] See Appendix to *Paraphrase of De Anima*, pp. 119–24. In this *Paraphrase*, pp. 92 f., he expounds Ibn Bājjah's doctrine of *ittiṣāl* with approval and describes his method as "demonstrative."

is to rise by degrees to that intellectual or immaterial condition proper to the separate intelligences in general and the active intellect in particular. The token of this extraterrestrial condition is the fully actualized capacity of the mind to apprehend intelligible forms directly, without any intermediaries, and to apprehend itself as well. However, significantly enough, this whole eschatological view is not set forth without qualification. The attainment of this goal of intellectual excellence is the prerogative of the privileged few only. The masses at large can only achieve a measure of moral excellence by partaking of a life of practical virtue whose condition is not the theoretical apprehension of truth, but rather that uprightness or rectitude of the Soul whose conditions have been defined in Scripture.[106]

In the *Nicomachean Ethics*, it will be recalled, Aristotle had described man's ultimate destiny in terms of that contemplative life which is essentially a prerogative of God.[107] Man's intellectual goal thus becomes for him a kind of *imitatio Dei*, the conditions and stages of which he did not define. Ibn Sīnā and Ibn Bājjah, on the other hand, defined it as a kind of *conjunctio cum Intellectu*, which was for them the terminal stage in the Soul's heavenward journey. Despite a certain hesitation, Ibn Rushd recognized that such an account of the Soul's destiny was somehow inadequate and that the consummation of man's vocation belonged to the supernatural order. Thus, the discussion of the whole problem of "conjunction" in the *Paraphrase of De Anima* ends on this note: "This condition [i.e., *ittiṣāl*] is a kind of divine perfection of man. For natural perfections consist in acquiring the natural states of capacity in the theoretical sciences mentioned in the *Book of Demonstration* [*Analytica Posteriora*]. That is why those two capacities, i.e., for natural and divine perfection, are predicated of them equivocally, since the aptitude for the ultimate divine perfection has no part in material power or in personal individuality," but is rather a supernatural perfection and one of "nature's marvels" or "God's gifts."[108]

[106] *R. al-Ittiṣāl*, pp. 119 f., and *Paraphrase of De Anima*, pp. 92 f.
[107] *Nic. Eth.*, X. 1177[a]. [108] *Paraphrase of De Anima*, p. 95.

CHAPTER TEN

Post-Avicennian Developments: Illumination and the Reaction against Peripateticism

I

AL-SUHRAWARDĪ

We have already referred to a certain bipolarity in Ibn Sīnā's thought and an implicit dissatisfaction with Peripateticism (*al-Mashshā'iyah*), expressed particularly in his "Oriental" writings.[1] Whether Ibn Sīnā actually carried out his design to set forth in full this Oriental philosophy or not, it is certain that later in life he felt a distinct urge to move away from the well-trodden Peripatetic path, in the direction of a mystical and experiential approach to truth, which he designated illumination (*ishrāq*). In the mystical allegory of *Ḥayy b. Yaqẓān*, the East (*al-Sharq*) is represented as the home of light, and the West as the home of darkness,[2] and the light imagery is fully exploited for philosophical and mystical purposes.

Ibn Sīnā's design, expressed both in *al-Shifā'* and the *Logic of Orientals*, to write a treatise "embodying the fundamentals of the true science,"

[1] *Supra*, p. 178. [2] *Supra*, p. 181.

which was not to be divulged except to "ourselves—or those who are akin to ourselves," in the degree of their apprehension and dedication to truth, may never have been carried out. Two generations later, Shihāb al-Dīn Yaḥiā al-Suhrawardī (d. 1191) of Aleppo, nicknamed al-Maqtūl (the Murdered) or al-Shahīd (the Martyr), proceeded to carry out this design by capitalizing to the utmost on the anti-Peripatetic sentiments of Ibn Sīnā and the mystical and experiential aspirations which he and kindred spirits had sought to satisfy. One of his best-known biographers and commentators, Shams al-Dīn al-Shahrazūrī (d. ca. 1281), pays him the singular tribute of calling him the author who combined the "two wisdoms: i.e., the experiential [*al-dhauqiyah*] and the discursive [*al-baḥthiyah*]" and who attained a standing in the former which is recognized by its own adepts to be unsurpassed.[3] As to "discursive wisdom," this biographer states that in a major treatise, *al-Mashāri'*, he has fully exhausted the subject matter of both ancient and modern wisdom and has "repudiated the presuppositions of the Peripatetic philosophers and reestablished the doctrine of the ancient sages" in an unprecedented manner. Some *Ṣūfīs*, like al-Basṭāmī and al-Ḥallāj, may have attained an equal standing in the practical ways of mysticism, but none was able to combine the two ways, the theoretical and practical, with such consummate skill.

The *al-Mashāri'* forms part of a trilogy that embodies the substance of al-Suhrawardī's illuminationist thought; *Ḥikmat al-Ishrāq* and *al-Muqāwamāt* are the two other parts. Al-Shahrazūrī's praise of *Ḥikmat al-Ishrāq* (or *Wisdom of Illumination*) is hyperbolical: no one before or after has been or will be able to equal it, according to him. Even to glimpse the intent of its author requires the acumen and powers of a divinely assisted sage (*ṣiddīq*). To this trilogy should be added a fourth work, *al-Talwīḥāt*, a summary of Peripatetic themes intended to prepare the ground for a refutation of them.

Al-Shahrazūrī's testimony, as well as the evidence of the tetralogy in question, clearly indicates the tenor of al-Suhrawardī's thought, with its negative and its positive components. The reaction against Islamic Peripateticism in the name of a higher wisdom, which can be

[3] Al-Shahrazūrī, *Nuzhat al-Arwāḥ*; Fātiḥ Ms. 4516; and Spies and Khatak, *Three Treatises on Mysticism*, pp. 101 f.

found in Plato and Aristotle and goes back as far as the time of Hermes, Asclepius, Pythagoras, and Zoroaster, served simply as the substructure of a mystical philosophy, which Ibn Sīnā had projected but never fully set out.

In the introduction to *al-Talwīḥāt* the author states that his aim is to give the gist of the teaching of Aristotle, the First Master, without regard to the current interpretations of the Peripatetics. First he considers the categories of Aristotelian logic and takes the liberty of departing from the common doctrine, because "the Categories are not taken from the Master, but from a Pythagorian called Arkhūṭās [Archytas]."[4] Next he discusses the concepts of the universal and particular, finite and infinite, real and conceptual. An important problem broached in this context is that of being and essence, a legacy of Avicennian ontology of which al-Suhrawardī is partially critical. His own position is that "it is not correct to say that the being of particulars is superadded to their essence. For we can conceive of it [i.e., the essence] apart from being, and we cannot conceive of the being [of a fictitious animal] directly, without knowing whether or not it exists in any particular entity."[5] Therefore the two are clearly distinct, at least in thought. In things, the being and the essence are fully identified; for the mind does not recognize any duality in existing things, but rather sees the complete identity of being and essence, of particular and universal.[6]

Despite this identity, being is not to the essence, as some suppose, what the predicate is to the subject. For on the latter supposition the essence could exist before, after, or simultaneously with being in such a way that the particular does not exist through the being which determines its essence, but rather independently of it or alongside it, which is absurd.

The discussion of being leads al-Suhrawardī logically into the discussion of the Necessary Being. In this connection he is critical of Ibn Sīnā's proof of the existence of the Necessary Being on the ground that it is purely dialectical, since Ibn Sīnā maintains that being is an accident superadded to the essence and that consequently essence precedes

[4] *Al-Talwīḥāt*, in *Opera Metaphysica et Mystica*, I, 12.

[5] *Ibid.*, p. 22. [6] *Ibid.*, p. 24.

existence, which has been shown to be wrong. His own proof, though not radically different in logical structure, is more direct. Everything possible requires a cause, hence the whole series of possible entities in the world requires such a cause, which is not possible, because it would form part of the series and itself would require a cause, and so on ad infinitum. An infinite series, however, is absurd. Therefore a Necessary Being, who is not possible in any sense, must be at the basis of the whole series.[7]

Other proofs for the existence of God are given. (1) Neither the matter nor the form of bodies is necessary; therefore, bodies owe their existence to a Being who is necessary in every way. (2) Since motion does not belong to body essentially, the series of movements in the world requires a Mover who is unmoved. (3) The Necessary Being is not subject to any of the categories. For to every category belongs at least one particular, who is possible, and this would entail that possibility is a predicate of the genus to which this particular belongs. Therefore all the categories are possible and require a Necessary Being, who is not subject to any of them, but is pure being and is not susceptible of any plurality.[8]

Throughout his "Peripatetic" works, al-Suhrawardī claims to be simply expounding Peripatetic views without necessarily granting their validity. It is not always clear, however, how far he is willing to go in repudiating these views. In many cases he appears to concur in them or to choose the likeliest interpretation of them. Be this as it may, he asserts in numerous places that his own unequivocal position ought to be sought in his magnum opus, *Ḥikmat al-Ishrāq*, a work that he claims has never been equaled or surpassed.[9] Its aim, he tells us, is not to inveigh against adversaries, but to set the truth down in unadulterated form, as it had been revealed to him through "spiritual observation" and the practice of the mystical way, which is the way of illumination (*ishrāq*).

What the method of illumination involves as a first premise was conveyed to the author by Aristotle, who appeared in a dream and informed him that self-knowledge is the prelude to all higher

[7] *Al-Talwīḥāt*, in *Opera Metaphysica et Mystica*, pp. 33 f. [8] *Ibid.*, pp. 38 f.
[9] *Al-Mashāri'*, in *Opera Metaphysica et Mystica*, p. 401; also pp. 483, 505.

knowledge.[10] This knowledge is not purely discursive or speculative; it has an important experiential (*dhauqī*) component. Indeed, of the various grades of wisdom, some involve purely theoretical and some purely experiential knowledge. The highest of these grades is that of the adept of theosophy (*ta'alluh*) who is a master of the discursive method as well. To him indeed belongs the office of magistrate, as God's vicegerent (*khalīfah*) on earth. Next to him in rank is the adept of theosophy who lacks discursive acumen. The office of vicegerent might devolve upon this person also, but never upon the sage who is proficient in discursive knowledge only. Like the Shī'ite *Imām*, this vicegerent is indispensable, so that it is impossible for the world to be without one at any time. When he is not visible, he is only in concealment. He is generally called the "pivot" (*al-quṭb*).[11]

In his exposition of the "science of light," which represents the core of this illuminationist philosophy, al-Suhrawardī lays no claims to originality. This science has always had its exponents: Plato, Hermes, Empedocles, Pythagoras, Agathadaimon, Asclepius, Aristotle, and others, in the West; Jamasp, Farashaustra, Buzurjumhr, Zoroaster, and others, in the East.[12] Despite the differences of idiom or method of exposition that set them apart, says al-Suhrawardī, these sages have all shared in a universal and perennial wisdom, originally revealed to Hermes (identified in Muslim sources with the koranic Idrīs or Enoch) and handed down through an unbroken chain to al-Basṭāmī, al-Ḥallāj, and culminating in al-Suhrawardī himself.[13]

Although the *Ḥikmat* is said by the author to be a nonpolemical work, it starts nonetheless with a disquisition against the Peripatetics. Al-Suhrawardī's criticisms of Peripatetic logic and physics, as given in this allegedly more personal work, are numerous; we will consider only the three most important ones.

1. The Peripatetic doctrine of substance is fraught with difficulties.

[10] *Al-Mashāri'*, in *Opera Metaphysica et Mystica*, p. 484. The account of al-Suhrawardī's imaginary conversation with Aristotle in *Talwīḥāt*, pp. 70 f., clearly suggests the Aristotle of the *Theologia*, as we have seen.

[11] *Ḥikmat al-Ishrāq*, in *Œuvres philosophiques et mystiques*, p. 12.

[12] *Ibid.*, p. 10, and Prolégomènes, p. 25, for the identity of those figures.

[13] Nasr, *Three Muslim Sages*, pp. 62 f.

From Peripatetic premises it must be inferred that substance cannot be known, since its *differentiae* are unknown. The Soul and the separate intelligences cannot be known either. In fact, substance is generally defined by the Peripatetics in purely negative terms.[14]

2. Prime matter (*hayūlā*) is defined by the Peripatetics as the substratum of the continuous and the discontinuous. However, magnitude forms no part of body, according to them, but is continuous in the same sense that body is. Hence, instead of being extraneous to body, as they claim, magnitude must be identified with body and must be stated, for that reason, to be the genuine material substratum of body. What differentiates bodies, therefore, is not matter, as they claim, but rather the forms that supervene upon this magnitude in succession.

3. As for the Platonic ideas, the Peripatetics argue that if these ideas were self-subsistent it would not be possible for them to be embodied in their particular representations. If it is argued nevertheless that part of the idea requires a particular substratum only, the whole would require such a substratum also, in so far as the idea is indivisible. However, the Peripatetics admit that the forms exist both in the mind and in the objects outside. The ideas can equally well subsist on their own in the intelligible world, on the one hand, or be embodied in their material representations, on the other.[15] Al-Suhrawardī rejects, however, the Platonic view that the idea, being the common prototype of a multitude of particulars, must be numerically one. For were the idea essentially one, it would be impossible for it to become multiplied in these particulars. Nor does it follow from the fact that it is not multiple that it should be one, for the contrary of multiple is not one, but rather not-multiple, i.e., what cannot be logically predicated of the subject in question.[16]

The core of the whole illuminationist philosophy with which *Ḥikmat al-Ishrāq* is primarily concerned is the nature and diffusion of light. Light is stated here to be both immaterial and indefinable. For, if by "obvious" is meant that which requires no definition, clearly light, as the most obvious entity in the world, requires no definition either. As the all-pervasive reality, light enters into the composition of every entity, physical or nonphysical, as an essential component

[14] *Ḥikmat al-Ishrāq*, pp. 73 f. [15] *Ibid.*, pp. 92 f. [16] *Ibid.*, p. 161.

thereof. Everything other than the "Pure Light" consists either of that which requires no substratum, which is the dark substance, or of the form of this substance, i.e., darkness per se. Bodies, in so far as they are receptive of both light and darkness, may be called isthmuses (singular: *barzakh*). Considered in itself, every isthmus is dark. Whatever luminosity belongs to it must therefore be derived from an extraneous source.[17]

To these dark substances belong certain dark attributes, such as figure and magnitude, which derive from the dark nature inherent in dark substances. The Pure Light, on the other hand, is entirely free from darkness, and as such apprehends itself without any intermediary or representation.[18] It has in this regard an analogy with the human self, which is also apprehended without any intermediary whatsoever. Only what is corporeal or material requires a bodily organ for its apprehension, and as such is never the subject, but rather the object, of such apprehension. In the case of the self, the act of apprehension is not an adventitious aspect or quality, but the very essence of selfhood (*anā'iyah*). It is indivisible and depends on no agency outside itself, whereas every other act of apprehension depends on it.[19]

Light may thus be defined as that which is both manifest in itself and manifests other things. Indeed, it is manifest in a primary sense. Contrary to the opinion of the Peripatetics, who argued that an object is known negatively to the extent it is divested of matter, apprehension must be represented positively as the act of self-manifestation, predicated primarily of light and luminous objects. Were immateriality the condition of self-apprehension, prime matter (*hayūlā*) would be capable of knowing itself immediately, in so far as it inheres in no material substratum itself. Indeed, a close parallel between pure matter and the Necessary Being is drawn by the Peripatetics, since both are described as pure essences. If the Necessary Being were capable of apprehending itself and other things by virtue of its immateriality or simplicity, so also must be pure matter.[20]

From the standpoint of its relation to things beneath, light may be divided into light in-and-for-itself and light in-or-for-another. The

[17] *Hikmat al-Ishrāq*, pp. 106 f. [18] *Ibid.*, pp. 110 f.
[19] *Ibid.*, p. 114. [20] *Ibid.*, pp. 115 f.

second illuminates other things and is therefore light-for-another, but not for-itself. Whether for-itself or for-another, light is fully manifest and as such must be described as living, for life is this mode of actual self-manifestation.[21]

The pure lights form a hierarchy. At the top of the scale of pure light stands the Light of Lights, upon which the whole series of subordinate lights depends. As the origin or source of all the other lights, this light must necessarily exist. For the series of lights must terminate in a First or Necessary Light, because of the impossibility of an infinite regress. This Necessary Light al-Suhrawardī designates as the Light of Lights, the Self-subsistent Light, the Holy Light, etc.[22]

The first attribute of this Light of Lights is unity. To posit two such lights would involve the absurdity that they both share in and depend upon a *tertium quid*. Being essentially one, the Necessary Light generates by a process of emanation the first light, which is numerically one and uncompounded since it is impossible that an entity made up of light and its opposite, darkness, should emanate from a reality entirely free from darkness. This first light differs from its source in the degree of its perfection only.

Owing to its dependence on the Light of Lights, the first light has a double nature: penury in itself and plenty through the Light of Lights. As it apprehends its penury or dark nature, it gives rise to the first shadow or penumbra, called by al-Suhrawardī the "highest isthmus" (i.e., the empyrean heaven of Neo-Platonic cosmology). As it apprehends its penury in relation to its source, it generates the second light. This in turn generates both a light and an isthmus (i.e., a heavenly sphere), and the process continues until we come to the ninth isthmus or sphere and the world of the elements beneath it. As to the series of lights emanating from the necessary light, al-Suhrawardī argues that it does not terminate with the ninth (as the Arab Neo-Platonists maintained); he does believe, however, that this series is numerically finite.[23]

The relation of the higher to the lower lights is described by al-Suhrawardī in terms of domination (*qahr*, corresponding to the empedoclean *neikos*), whereas that of the lower to the higher lights is

[21] *Ḥikmat al-Ishrāq*, pp. 117 f. [22] *Ibid.*, p. 121. [23] *Ibid.*, pp. 131 f., 138 f.

described in terms of attraction or love (*ʿishq: philia*).[24] These two powers, domination and love, govern the world. The Light of Lights, which has nothing beyond it, dominates everything else and loves the highest and most beautiful entity, i.e., itself. In this act of self-love, it partakes of the highest pleasure—consciousness of the possession and contemplation of the most perfect.[25]

In the series of lights emanating from the Light of Lights we should distinguish between "dominant" (*qāhirah*) and "ministering" (*mudabbirah*) lights. The dominant lights consist of superior or separate luminous essences that are entirely self-sufficient, on the one hand, and formal or archetypal realities that contain the species or forms of corporeal entities corresponding to the Platonic ideas, on the other. The ministering lights direct or minister to the heavenly spheres, and might on account of their preeminence be called "commanding" (*isfahbad*). These lights form a hierarchy and act upon the spheres through the intermediary of the heavenly bodies, of which they are the absolute rulers. *Hurakhsh* or the sun, source of the diurnal light, is one of the paramount chiefs of this hierarchy, to which divine honors (*taʿẓīm*) are due as heavenly chief or lord.[26]

The world, which is made up of the elements and is, as it were, the penumbra of the Light of Lights as it is irradiated through all the luminous and nonluminous orders of being, is stated by al-Suhrawardī to be eternal like its author. His arguments for its eternity, which are essentially Aristotelian, are bound up with the eternity of motion. Every part of motion depends on a previous part. It is impossible, however, that these parts should coexist. Instead they must succeed one another eternally. Of the various types of motion, the only one which satisfies this condition is circular motion since it alone is without end or terminus, whereas rectilinear motion cannot go on forever, because, like everything in the sublunary world of which it is an attribute, it must eventually come to an end.[27]

[24] For Empedocles in the Muslim tradition, see M. Asin, *Ibn Masarrah*, pp. 40f. The Mazdean association between light (*khurrah*) and victory (*peruzih*) should also be noted. See Corbin's remarks in Prolegomènes to his edition of *Œuvres philosophiques et mystiques*, pp. 39 f.

[25] Cf. *Ḥikmat al-Ishrāq*, p. 136, and Aristotle, *Met.* XII. 1072^{b}23.

[26] *Ḥikmat al-Ishrāq*, pp. 149 f.

[27] *Ibid.*, pp. 173 f.; cf. Aristotle, *Physics* VIII. Ch. 8.

Time, which the author, again following Aristotle, defines as the measure of motion, is likewise eternal, without beginning or end. For if time were to have a beginning, it would have to be preceded either by nothingness (*nafs al-'adam*) or by some entity or other. In both cases, there would be a time prior to the beginning of time.[28]

The universe then is an eternal emanation (*fayḍ*) from the First Principle.[29] In addition to the series of immaterial substances or lights, whose number is undetermined, as we have seen, a series of higher material entities (the heavenly bodies) emanates directly from the first light and indirectly from the Light of Lights or God. From these heavenly bodies emanate the "elemental" bodies of the sublunary world. These bodies are called elemental, in so far as they ultimately derive from a "common matter," called in illuminationist literature the primordial isthmus. The simple elemental forms, as well as the less simple inorganic or organic forms, supervene upon this common matter by rotation: air is converted to water, water to earth, earth to air, air to fire. This convertibility proves, according to al-Suhrawardī, that the four primary elements of the Peripatetics are not primary, in so far as they are subject to this endless permutation and do not on that account retain any essential nature or form.[30]

The motions of terrestrial bodies are referable either to the Supreme Light, which is the source of all being, or to the subordinate lights of the luminous hierarchy emanating from it. Heat plays a major role in natural process; for what causes stones to fall, water to evaporate, water vapor to condense in rain, thunder or lightning to form, is not nature, as the Peripatetics claimed, but rather heat. Both heat and movement, which is most akin to heat, are ultimately due to a superior light.[31] Indeed "if you examine the multiplicity of entities in the world, you will find that the only entity which operates upon things remote or near is light. And since love and domination derive from light, and movement and heat are produced by it, light is at the basis of passion, appetite, and anger . . . and desire conduces to motion necessarily."[32] For these reasons, and owing to its nobility, fire

[28] *Ḥikmat al-Ishrāq*, p. 180. [29] *Ibid.*, p. 181 *et passim*. [30] *Ibid.*, pp. 192 f.
[31] *Ibid.*, pp. 194 f. [32] *Ibid.*, p. 196.

deserves, together with light, worship or adoration, as was the practice of the ancient Persians.

As a result of the combination of the contrary qualities in certain bodies, physical or terrestrial entities arise. The predominant element in these entities is the light, called "*sfendarmudh*," whose talisman or theurgy is earth. The most perfect combination is that which gives rise to man, who derives his perfection from the Light of Lights through the intermediary of Gabriel. This Holy Spirit confers on the embryo, as soon as it is disposed to receive it, the human light or Soul, called the "*isfahbad*" of humanity.[33] The creation or emanation of this light does not precede the formation of the body, since its manifestation in individuals depends on body. Moreover, were these Soul lights eternal and uncreated, both they and their prototypes in the immaterial world would be infinite, which is absurd.[34]

To the human light correspond two bodily faculties: the passionate, whose prototype is the power of domination; and the appetitive, whose prototype is love. Other inferior bodily powers, such as the nutritive and the reproductive, arise from the diverse relationships of the body to light and may be looked upon as so many corporeal manifestations of the terrestrial light. Their diversity is due to the diversity of the relationship of that light to the body.

The instrument of the terrestrial light in directing the body is the spirit (*rūḥ*), lodged in the left chamber of the heart. This spirit permeates the whole body and communicates to its various organs the light imparted by the terrestrial light.[35] Differences in functions, however, do not involve differences in faculties or organs, so that, *sensus communis*, the estimative faculty and the imaginative, are, contrary to the contentions of Ibn Sīnā, one and the same.[36] All these functions are referable to the terrestrial light, which perceives the objects of sense through the intermediary of the bodily organs, which are its penumbras, so to speak, and may on that account be designated the "sense of sense." However, it is possible for it to dispense altogether

[33] *Ḥikmal al-Ishrāq*, p. 201. Compare the role of the active intellect in Avicennian cosmology.

[34] *Ibid.*, p. 203.
[35] *Ibid.*, p. 207.
[36] *Ibid.*, pp. 209 f.

with bodily organs, as attested by the mystics, who have partaken of a vision of the higher lights clearer than physical sight.

The association of the terrestrial light with matter is brought about by its entanglement with "dark forces." In consequence, it became alienated from the world of light and was forced to dwell in the human body, which is its first and highest dwelling place, according to the Eastern sages. In its subsequent reincarnations this light could dwell in lower animal forms, but the process cannot be reversed. Al-Suhrawardī is fully aware of the incompatibility of this view with that of Plato and Pythagoras. However, he appears to suspend judgment on the whole question of the transmigration of the Soul, but he accepts the implications of the Platonic-Pythagorean view of the eventual release of the Soul from the "wheel of rebirth."[37] Thus the release of the ministering lights, which dwell in the body and direct it, occurs when the body disintegrates. Transmigration is not the necessary condition of this release. For, to the extent that the captive light yearns for the higher world of light and is not weighed down by the cares of the body, it is able to achieve contact (*ittiṣāl*) with it and be eventually released from the bondage of the body altogether and join the ranks of the holy spirits in the world of pure light. Even while it lingers in this lower world, the purified Soul can catch a glimpse of the higher world and its splendors and even partake of certain supernatural powers, such as foretelling or controlling events in the future.[38]

Such then is the substance of that philosophy of light which Ibn Sīnā had projected and al-Suhrawardī developed. Apart from the mystical or experiential element which pervades this philosophy, its cosmological and metaphysical groundwork is not altogether unfamiliar. It is essentially an Avicennian, Neo-Platonic groundwork to which certain mystical and religious elements from Zoroastrian and other Oriental sources have been added. What sets it apart from the traditional Neo-Platonism of Islam is primarily its attempt to exploit to the full the light imagery, which, as we have seen, Ibn Sīnā had first adumbrated and Zoroastrianism fully incorporated in its religious and metaphysical world-view.

We believe that despite these differences of idiom or emphasis,

[37] *Ḥikmat al-Ishrāq*, pp. 221, 230. [38] *Ibid.*, p. 252.

however, the metaphysical outlook of al-Suhrawardī remains essentially Avicennian or Neo-Platonic. This is perhaps nowhere better illustrated than in a short treatise entitled *The Philosophers' Creed*,[39] in which he seeks to defend the "theosophists" against the strictures and slanders of the masses, who accuse them of godlessness or irreligion. Al-Suhrawardī argues that the theosophists believe in the unity of God, the creation of the world, and the inevitability of judgment. The first entity created by God is the first intellect, which in turn gives rise, through emanation, to another intellect, from which the Soul and the body of the first heaven emanate. The process goes on in downward progression until we come to the last intellect and the world of generation and corruption, which it governs. This lowest intellect is called by them the "giver of forms" or the "holy spirit."

The rest of the cosmological and metaphysical world-view al-Suhrawardī ascribes to the philosophers is the familiar Avicennian one. Not only does he expound this world-view with tacit approval, he even tries to support his exposition by quotations from Scripture or *Ṣūfī* lore. The inference is thus inescapable that he fully endorses this world-view. Any refinements that he makes upon it are purely stylistic and are often drawn from mystical or Zoroastrian sources. Much more thoroughgoing in his mysticism than either al-Fārābī or Ibn Sīnā, he seeks to incorporate in his own system the cardinal elements of the practical "way" of the mystics, so far as this can be done in an articulate form. He is fully aware of the difficulties this articulation involves, difficulties that prevent his work from being as systematic and precise as that of other Neo-Platonic masters.

[39] *I'tiqād al-Ḥukamā*,' in *Œuvres philosophiques et mystiques*, pp. 261–72.

II

THE SUBSEQUENT DEVELOPMENT OF ILLUMINATIONISM: ṢADR AL-DĪN AL-SHĪRĀZĪ (MULLA ṢADRĀ) AND HIS SUCCESSORS

DESPITE his reaction against Muslim Neo-Platonism in the name of a higher wisdom with roots both in Greece and the East, al-Suhrawardī never questioned the right of reason to probe the deepest religious mysteries. This right had been questioned by the Traditionist or conservative theologians, the jurists, many *Ṣūfīs*, and the masses at large. The importance of al-Suhrawardī in the history of post-Avicennian thought lay in his vindication of the unity of religious and metaphysical truth and the duty of the conscientious searcher to seek truth wherever it can be found: in Greek philosophy, in ancient Persian thought, in Muslim Neo-Platonism, and in *Ṣūfism*.

The Ishrāqī current which al-Suhrawardī unleashed continued to swell, particularly in Shī'ite circles during the Ṣafawid period in Persia. The founder of the Ṣafawid dynasty, Shāh Ismā'īl (1500–1524), who claimed descent from a *Ṣūfī* order going back to the thirteenth century, undertook to enforce the Shī'ite creed throughout the whole of Persia in a determined manner.[40] As a consequence, interest in philosophy and theology, which had declined during the Mongol period, now revived, especially during the reign of Shāh 'Abbās (1588–1629). Numerous scholars flourished during this period, of whom Mīr Dāmād (d. 1631) and Bahā' al-Dīn 'Amilī (d. 1621) are noteworthy. Both were teachers of the most illustrious philosopher of the Ṣafawid period, Ṣadr al-Dīn al-Shīrāzī (d. 1641), "unanimously acclaimed as the greatest philosopher of modern times in Persia."[41]

Born in Shīrāz in 1572, al-Shīrāzī, more commonly referred to as Mulla Ṣadrā, moved to Isfahan, an important cultural center of the

[40] See Browne, *Literary History*, IV, 53 f. [41] *Ibid.*, p. 408.

period, and continued his studies with Mīr Dāmād as well as Mīr Abu'l-Qāsim Fendereski (d. 1640). Eventually he returned to Shīrāz to assume a teaching position at a religious school (*madrasa*) founded by the governor of the province of Fars.[42] It is said that he made the pilgrimage to Mecca on foot seven times and died at Basra on his way from the seventh in 1641.

In addition to numerous commentaries on *Ḥikmat al-Ishrāq* of al-Suhrawardī, on *al-Hidāyah fi'l Ḥikmah* of Athīr al-Dīn al-Abharī, on parts of Ibn Sīnā's *al-Shifā'*, he wrote many original works. Among those which have come down to us are treatises on *Creation in Time* (*Ḥudūth*), on *Resurrection* (*al-Ḥashr*), on the *Attribution of Being to Essence*, on *Predestination and Free Will*,[43] as well as *Kitāb al-Mashā'ir*,[44] *Kitāb Kasr Aṣnām al-Jāhiliyah*. But there is no doubt that his major work is the monumental *Kitāb al-Ḥikmah al-Muta'āliyah* (*Transcendental Wisdom*), also called *Kitāb al-Asfār al-Arba'ah* (*Four Journeys*). This work may be described as the *summa philosophiae* of al-Shīrāzī since it embodies the substance of many of his own shorter treatises as well as that of post-Avicennian thought in general.

In the introduction to this work, al-Shīrāzī comments in melancholy terms on the plight of philosophy in his day and the public's general departure from its study. Having applied himself to its study, he became convinced that ancient philosophy, conjoined to revealed truth as imparted to the prophets and the sages, was the highest expression of truth. Too sullen to express his ideas in writing, he cut himself off from the world for a long time and withdrew into himself, until his "heart caught fire," as he puts it, "and the light of the divine world shone forth upon me . . . and I was able to unravel mysteries which I had not previously suspected."[45] As a result, he was able to apprehend intuitively what he had originally learned discursively, as well as a lot more. By degrees, he realized that he was duty-bound to impart to others what he had been so privileged to receive as a grace from God. The result was this voluminous work, which he called the

[42] Introduction to al-Shīrāzī, *Kitāb al-Mashā'ir*, p. 7.
[43] See *Rasā'il Akhund Mulla Ṣadrā*.
[44] Or *Livre des pénétrations*, as translated by H. Corbin.
[45] *Al-Asfār al-Arba'ah*, I, 3.

"four journeys" (*al-Asfār al-Arba'ah*) of the Soul from the Creation (*al-Khalq*) to the Supreme Reality (*al-Ḥaqq*), then to Reality through Reality, then from Reality back to Creation, and finally to Reality as manifested in Creation.

The conception of the divisions of philosophy outlined in this work is essentially Avicennian. Philosophy has two such main divisions: the one theoretical, aimed at the knowledge of things as they really are; the other practical, aimed at attaining those perfections to which the Soul is fitted. The consummation of the first activity is the attainment of the ultimate goal of all theoretical pursuits, namely, duplicating or reflecting the intelligible world, whereby the Soul becomes an intelligible world of its own, as al-Fārābī and Ibn Sīnā had argued.[46] The consummation of the second is approximation to God, through a kind of *imitatio Dei* which makes the Soul worthy of such a privilege. The identity of the aims of philosophy and dogma on this view is complete, and the author cites various koranic verses, prophetic Traditions, and sayings of the first Shī'ite *Imām*, 'Alī, in support of this thesis. Nowhere does he express the type of reservations or qualifications which Sunnite writers on theological questions felt compelled to express when it came to the relationship of philosophy and dogma. Like al-Suhrawardī, al-Shīrāzī believed in the unity of truth transmitted in an unbroken chain from Adam down to Abraham, the Greeks, the *Ṣūfīs* of Islam, and the philosophers. In another treatise he describes at length how Seth and Hermes (corresponding to the koranic Idrīs and the biblical Enoch) were responsible for spreading the study of wisdom (*al-ḥikmah*) throughout the world.[47] The Greeks, who were originally star worshipers, according to him, were instructed in theology and the science of unity by Abraham. Of their ancient philosophers, he distinguishes between two groups associated with two different traditions: one initiated by Thales of Miletus and culminating in Socrates and Plato; the other initiated by Pythagoras, who received instruction in wisdom from Solomon, whom he met in Egypt, as well as from the Egyptian priests. The pillars of wisdom in Greece, according to al-Shīrāzī, were Empedocles, Pythagoras, Socrates, Plato, and Aristotle.

[46] *Supra*, p. 166.

[47] *R. fi'l-Ḥudūth* in *Rasā'il Akhund*, pp. 67 f.; cf. *al-Asfār*, II, foll. 246 f.

Plotinus (al-Shaykh al-Yūnānī) is frequently referred to as a great figure. Although the dissemination of wisdom through all lands is ascribed to those Greek sages, al-Shīrāzī often states, in the manner of most Muslim historians of philosophy from al-Sijistānī to al-Shahrazūrī,[48] that those sages received the "light of wisdom" from the "beacon of prophecy" in the first instance.[49] This explains their total agreement with the "prophetic tradition" on such questions as the unity of God, the creation of the world, and the resurrection which they continued.

We have seen how for al-Suhrawardī this historical chain is brought up to date[50] and how the *Ṣūfīs* are said to be the genuine successors of the early Greek sages. Al-Shīrāzī had the same regard for the *Ṣūfīs*, with Ibn 'Arabī (to whom he sometimes refers as Ibn al-A'rābī) at their head, and is in fundamental agreement with al-Suhrawardī on the role of mysticism in the development of philosophical and religious thought.

An important aspect of his thought is the application of philosophical and *Ṣūfī* concepts to Imamite (Shī'ite) theology. With the death of Muḥammad, he argues, the period of prophecy ended. This marked the beginning of the period of *imāmah* or *wilāyah* in Islam. This period starts with the twelve Shī'ite *imāms* and will continue until the return of the twelfth, who is in temporary concealment, at the end of the millenium. Generally speaking, however, the cycle of *wilāyah* begins with Seth, who was to Adam what 'Alī was to Muḥammad—his *imām* or successor.[51]

Al-Shīrāzī finds a philosophical basis for this doctrine in Ibn 'Arabī's concept of the reality of Muḥammad, i.e., the eternal, prophetic reality or "*logos*," of which Muḥammad is the last and fullest manifestation or embodiment.[52] According to him, this reality has two dimensions: one overt (*ẓāhir*), the other covert (*bāṭin*). As Muḥammad was the manifestation of the prophetic principle, the first *imām* ('Alī) and his successors are the manifestations of the *wilāyah*. When the "awaited" *imām* or Mahdī reappears at the end of time, the whole

[48] See *supra*, p. 327.
[49] *R. fi'l-Ḥudūth*, p. 69; cf. *al-Asfār*, II, foll. 246 f.
[50] *Supra*, p. 330.
[51] *Livre des pénétrations*, pp. 13 f.
[52] *Ibid.*, p. 14; cf. *supra*, p. 283.

meaning of the divine revelation will be revealed and mankind will revert to the original monotheistic cult initiated by Abraham and confirmed by Muḥammad.

The first part of *al-Asfār* deals with metaphysics or "divine science." As was customary in Avicennian and post-Avicennian circles, the analysis of the concepts of being and essence, and their interrelationship, formed a major part of metaphysical discussions. Al-Shīrāzī returns to these two themes with remarkable persistence in numerous other treatises and asserts that being is indefinable, in so far as it has no *differentia*, species, accident, or property.[53] It is, however, clearly distinguishable from essence in thought, so that the object of divine creation or production is not the essence, as al-Suhrawardī, al-Dawwānī, and others had argued, but rather being, in so far as it is made to supervene on the essence.[54] It follows from this that essences have a certain priority over being in relation to the divine act of creation, if not per se. Consequently al-Shīrāzī identifies them with the "fixed entities" of Ibn 'Arabī, which are the archetypal forms upon which the universe is patterned.[55]

Everything created is thus compounded of being and essence. The Necessary Being, however, is entirely free from such composition and imparts to every created entity the being which it possesses by a process of irradiation analogous to that of light. But since the effect must be proportionate to the cause, it is the being of created entities, not their essence, which emanates from the Necessary Being.[56] Being the Light of Lights or Light per se, He imparts to created entities their luminous nature, whereby they are analogous to Him. Their own essence, however, being precisely that whereby they differ from Him, cannot be attributed to His action, but is the darkness or isthmus, which in the language of Ishrāq sets the creature apart from the Light of Lights, who is its genuine author.

In his formulation of this and similar metaphysical problems, al-Shīrāzī continually strives to bring together Avicennian, Ishrāqī, and

[53] *Al-Asfār*, I, 10 f.; cf. *Livre des pénétrations*, pp. 6 f. (Arabic text), and *Rasā'il Akhund*, pp. 110 f.

[54] *Ibid.*, I, 14, and *Livre des pénétrations*, p. 37.

[55] *Ibid.*, I, 15 f., and fol. 95a, and *Livre des pénétrations*, p. 35.

[56] *Ibid.*, I, 104.

Ṣūfī elements. For one thing, he accepts the Avicennian concept of motion and its ultimate dependence on a first Unmoved Mover,[57] without a sufficient appreciation of its detrimental implications for a creationist thesis of the conventional type, which he accepts. For another, he tacitly accepts the emanationist presuppositions of Neo-Platonism but seeks to fit them into a *Ṣūfī*-Ishrāqī framework. Following Ibn 'Arabī, he distinguishes in the Supreme Reality (*al-Ḥaqq*) between the rank of unity or Godhead which the *Ṣūfīs* call the "blindness" or "mystery" (*al-ghayb*), on the one hand, and the series of subordinate manifestations or determinations of this Reality, on the other. The first phase of this manifestation corresponds to the order of essences or "fixed entities" that exhibit the Supreme Reality without being commingled with it.[58] The status of these entities, which he also calls "possible essences," is discussed at considerable length. They have, he argues, a conceptual reality which is often misunderstood but which has two aspects: one whereby they are necessary in relation to their cause and share with it in the universal attribute of being, and another whereby they fall short of this ideal and form so many subordinate rungs along the ladder of being. In short, they mark the first degree of diversification in the unity of the Supreme Reality, without being distinct from it, and while multiple they form part of a single universal substance or intellect called in the language of *Ṣūfism* the "world of command," and in the language of philosophy the "intelligible world."

The second degree of diversification corresponds to the universal Soul, of which all the particular Souls and cognitive faculties are the manifestation. This universal Soul is identified with the koranic Preserved Tablet, which embodies the eternal decrees of God, is the articulate expression of His will since all time, and serves for that reason as God's means of contact with the world, so to speak.

A characteristic feature of the Soul is that, unlike either the preceding or succeeding order, it is a mixture of light and darkness and serves thereby as a link between the intelligible and material realms. The latter realm begins with the universal sphere, which embraces all the subordinate spheres of Neo-Platonic cosmology. Owing to its subtlety,

[57] *Al-Asfār*, I, foll. 105a; cf. *R. fi'l-Ḥudūth*, p. 514. [58] *Ibid.*, I, foll. 95a, 97b.

this universal sphere is the borderline between the world of "intellectual forms" or Souls, on the one hand, and that of material entities in the world of nature, on the other.[59]

Despite this diversification, the whole universe forms a "single jewel" with many layers differing in the degree of their luminosity or subtlety, the higher being always the more luminous or fine. The whole hierarchy may be said to correspond alternatively to the varying degrees of divine knowledge, the manifestation of the divine attributes, the signs of the divine beauty, or the series of lights which exhibit God's "face".[60]

Despite his deference for Ibn Sīnā, al-Shīrāzī rejects two of his major themes, the eternity of the world and the impossibility of bodily resurrection. As to the first theme, his view is that all the ancient philosophers, from Hermes to Thales, Pythagoras, and Aristotle, are unanimous in their belief that the world is created in time (*ḥādith*). Their successors have simply misunderstood their teaching when they ascribed to them the contrary view. Be this as it may, the thesis of the eternity of time and of motion is untenable. The only reality which could precede the existence of time is God, who brings the world into being by His creative fiat (*al-amr*).[61] As a component of the created universe, neither the whole of time nor a part of it could have existed prior to this fiat. Both the sensible and intelligible worlds are subject to continuous permutation or change and cannot for that reason be eternal. The archetypal essences called "fixed entities" by the *Ṣūfīs*, and active intellects or intelligible forms by the philosophers, are no exception to this general law of mutation. Although they existed originally in God's mind, they had in that state of possibility no reality or being in themselves, but only the being they derived from the divine decree.[62]

The teaching of the ancient philosophers, which is fully in conformity with that of the prophets and the saints, is not only that the world is created in time, but that everything in it will ultimately

[59] *Al-Asfār*, III, foll. 304, 354. See also *R. fi'l-Ḥudūth*, pp. 358 f., where a clearly Plotinian theory of emanation is set forth.

[60] *Al-Asfār*, III, foll. 304, 354 f.

[61] *R. fi'l-Ḥudūth*, pp. 45 f.

[62] *Ibid.*, pp. 62 f.

perish. The only reality which will abide forever is, as the Koran has put it, "God's face".

From this brief survey, it will appear how vast was the learning of this seventeenth-century philosopher and mystic and how complex was the fabric of his metaphysical eclecticism. Three fundamental strains went into the making of this fabric: the Neo-Platonic or Avicennian, the Ishrāqī, and the *Ṣūfī*. It was primarily al-Suhrawardī, the founder of the Ishrāqī movement, and Ibn 'Arabī, the great exponent of unitary mysticism, who were his chief mentors. But in addition to those two and Ibn Sīnā, al-Shīrāzī drew freely on the whole philosophical tradition from Plato to Aristotle (or rather the pseudo-Aristotle of the *Theologia*, in the manner of most Ishrāqī authors), to the pseudo-Empedocles, to al-Ghazālī, Mīr Dāmād, al-Ṭūsī al-Shahrazūrī, F. D. al-Rāzī, and many others. Convinced of the unity of truth from whatever source it emanated and conscious of his vocation as its spokesman and advocate, he did not hesitate to draw on any source at hand. In the process a certain diffuseness and repetitiousness became unavoidable, but this should not detract from the achievement of al-Shīrāzī, who was the last great encyclopedic writer in Islam. His voluminous output is an eloquent disproof of the view expressed by many historians of Islamic medieval philosophy that al-Ghazālī had by the end of the eleventh century dealt philosophy a crippling blow from which it never recovered.

Mulla Ṣadrā's many disciples and successors attest to his lasting influence, as well as to the continuity of the Shī'ite Ishrāqī movement in Persia. Of his disciples we should mention his two sons Ibrāhīm and Aḥmad, his two sons-in-law Fayāz 'Abdu'l Razzāq Laḥijī (d. 1662) and Muḥsin Fayḍ Kāshānī (d. 1680), Muḥammad Bāqir Majlisī (d. 1700), and Nimatullah Shustarī (d. 1691). His successors include Muḥammad Maḥdī Burujirdī (d. 1743), Aḥmad b. Zain al-Dīn b. Ibrāhīm al-Aḥsā'ī (d. 1828), who reacted violently against Mulla Ṣadrā, and Mulla Hadī Sabzawārī (d. 1878), who commented upon *al-Asfār* and other works of al-Shīrāzī and has been called by E. G. Browne "the last great Persian philosopher".[63]

[63] Browne, *Literary History*, pp. 411, 408 f., 432 f.; cf. *Livre des pénétrations*, p. 19.

CHAPTER ELEVEN

Theological Reaction and Reconstruction

I

LITERALISM AND NEO-ḤANBALISM: IBN ḤAZM, IBN TAYMIYAH, AND MUḤAMMAD B. 'ABDUL-WAHHĀB

ALTHOUGH al-Ghazālī's attack on Arab Neo-Platonism was devastating, it nevertheless recognized the right of reason to arbitrate in theological disputes. In consequence, al-Ghazālī clearly distinguished between those aspects of philosophy which were incompatible with the fundamentals of belief and those which were not. Whereas physics and metaphysics contained the bulk of those propositions that were particularly pernicious from an Islamic point of view, logic and mathematics were deemed to be quite innocuous. Logic is in fact an indispensable instrument (*ālah*: organon) for settling controversial questions, not only in philosophy and jurisprudence (*fiqh*), but in theology as well.[1]

The progress of misology, whose seeds al-Ghazālī had been instrumental in sowing, continued in theological and philosophical circles

[1] Al-Ghazālī, *Tahāfut*, pp. 16 f.; *Mi'yār al-'Ilm*, pp. 60 f.; *supra*, pp. 249 f.

long after the twelfth century. The two forms it took were (1) a return to the literalism and traditionalism of the early theologians and jurists, whose champion Ibn Ḥanbal had been in the ninth century; and (2) a repudiation of the rational process as futile and irrelevant and the consequent withdrawal into the inner fort of the Soul, where the antirationalist hoped to discover the truth through a more direct experiential process called *al-dhauq* (taste) or *al-kashf* (revelation).

The second form of misology found expression in illuminationism at the speculative level, and in *Ṣūfism* at the more practical, religious level. The first culminated in the recrudescence of the literalist position at the hands of a series of well-known theologians, of whom Ibn Ḥazm of Cordova and Ibn Taymiyah of Damascus may be taken as the two prototypes, although there were many other important figures such as Ibn Qayim al-Jauziyah (d. 1350), disciple of Ibn Taymiyah, and Muḥammad b. 'Abdul-Wahhāb (d. 1792), founder of the Wahhābī movement.

Ibn Ḥazm was born at Cordova in 994. His father was a vizier to the Umayyad caliph, and his fortunes fluctuated with those of his master. When the Berbers rose in rebellion against the Umayyads in 1013, Ibn Ḥazm was expelled from Cordova and his property was confiscated. For ten years thereafter he traveled from one part of the realm to another, working actively for the restoration of the Umayyads, to whom he remained loyal despite the tenuousness of their position. His political activity, however, came to grief in 1023, when his patron al-Mustaẓhir was assassinated; he was forced to leave Cordova once more and to renounce his politics. The rest of his life, which ended in 1064, was devoted to writing.

Ibn Ḥazm's best-known work is perhaps a tract on courtly love (*Ṭauq al-Ḥamāmah*), which he wrote at the age of twenty-five, and which reflects the influence of Ibn Dāwūd al-Isfahānī (d. 909), the Ẓāhirite theologian and author of *Kitāb al-Zuhra*, the first tract on Platonic love in Islam.[2] Rich in psychological observations, this book has been translated into many languages, including English. It also includes many moral and autobiographical reflections and may be related for that reason to a more systematic moral treatise, *Al-Akhlāq*

[2] Corbin, *Histoire de la philosophie islamique*, pp. 278 f.

wa'l Siyar,[3] which has also come down to us. Considering the dearth of such ethical writings in Arabic, this treatise is not without interest. It belongs, however, like many such Arabic works, more to the genre of belles-lettres than to systematic ethical discussions.

We are interested here in Ibn Ḥazm as theologian and polemist. Continuing the Ẓāhirite tradition initiated in the East by Dāwūd b. Khalaf al-Isfahānī (d. 883), father of the above-mentioned author of *Kitāb al-Zuhra*, Ibn Ḥazm repudiates all forms of analogy or deduction and adheres to a strict literalism for which all forms of scholastic theology, whether liberal or conservative, Mu'tazilite or Ash'arite, are equally heretical.[4]

It will be recalled that the jurists had, from Abū Ḥanīfah's time (d. 767) on, used various rational devices to settle knotty legal or theological issues on which the Koran and the Traditions had not clearly or explicitly legislated. In a tract entitled *Kitāb al-Ibṭāl*,[5] Ibn Ḥazm inveighs against the use of analogy (*qiyās*), independent judgment (*ra'y*), preference (*istiḥsān*), imitation (*taqlīd*), and causal interpretation (*ta'līl*), and asserts the exclusive validity of the literal method as the only one rooted in the explicit statements of the Koran, the Traditions, or *ijmā'* (consensus). He accepted the last of these accredited sources of law and dogma with the important proviso that it should be limited to the consensus of the Companions (*al-Ṣaḥābah*), or close associates of the Prophet. In this way Ibn Ḥazm robs *ijmā'* of its chief value as a practical device for the solution of legal or dogmatic problems on which the Koran and the Traditions are silent.

Having repudiated all forms of analogy or deduction in juridical matters, Ibn Ḥazm next dismisses all forms of scholastic theology as vain and pernicious. The speculation of the theologians, whether Mu'tazilites, Ash'arites, or others, on such questions as the essence of God, the composition of substance, the nature of moral responsibility, etc., is entirely futile. Man must resign himself to the impossibility of plumbing such mysteries and, in particular, the mystery of God's essence and the rationality of His ways.[6] Only what lies within the

[3] *Epître morale*, translated into French and edited by Nada Tomiche.

[4] See Ṣā'id, *Ṭabaqāt al-Umam*, pp. 75 ff.

[5] Goldziher, *Die Zahiriten, ihr Lehrsystem und ihre Geschichte*, pp. 207–30.

[6] *Al-Fiṣal*, II, 81, 116, 121.

grasp of our senses or is an object of direct intellectual apprehension, on the one hand, or is laid down explicitly in Scripture, on the other, is a genuine object of knowledge. As for the nature and attributes of God, our knowledge is fully circumscribed by what is explicitly stated in the Koran. The rational content or significance of the names God has chosen to apply to Himself in the Koran is, however, entirely beyond our grasp. Indeed, we are not at liberty to apply to God any names or attributes other than those chosen by Himself.[7] The rationalization of these names and attributes, whether in negative or positive terms, is equally unjustified. We must affirm justice and goodness of God and deny injustice and wickedness of Him, not on the rational ground (proposed for instance by the Mu'tazilah) that this is what His perfection logically requires, but simply on the ground that justness and goodness are predicated of God, and unjustness and wickedness not predicated of Him in the Koran.

Ibn Ḥazm's polemics are thus leveled at liberal and conservative theologians of the Mu'tazilite and Ash'arite varieties alike and amount in fact to a repudiation of the validity of applying any of the methods of scholastic theology to questions of jurisprudence or dogma. In this repudiation, Ibn Ḥazm is simply content to cling to the authority of Scripture and resists any attempt by others to draw him into theological discussions.

The slavish traditionalism which Ibn Ḥazm upheld had many a champion. A major figure in the history of this traditionalism in the thirteenth century was the Syrian jurist and "reformer" Aḥmad b. Taymiyah, who was born in Ḥarrān in 1262 and died in Damascus in 1327. Separated by more than two centuries, Ibn Ḥazm and Ibn Taymiyah stand out as the two most forceful protagonists of traditionalism in the whole history of post-Mu'tazilite Islam. Although neither of them is comparable in intellectual stature to al-Ghazālī, both surpassed him in the vehemence of their antirationalist polemics. Like Al-Ghazālī, but without his moderation, they both attack Greco-Arab philosophy in unequivocal terms. Even more vehemently than Ibn Ḥazm, Ibn Taymiyah protests against the abuses of philosophy and theology and advocates a return to the orthodox ways of the ancients

[7] *Al-Fiṣal*, II, p. 74.

(*al-salaf*). It is as though in his religious zeal he is determined to abolish centuries of religious thought and devotion and to draw from the still waters of religious truth as they had been long before they became troubled by theological and philosophical controversies.

The source of all religious truth, according to him, is the Koran and the Traditions as interpreted by the Companions (*al-Ṣaḥābah*) of Muḥammad or their immediate Successors (*al-Tābi'ūn*). The Traditions themselves have clearly recognized the preeminence of those Companions and Successors; hence their authority in religious matters can never be equaled or questioned and their judgment, as expressed in *ijmā'* (consensus), is wholly infallible.[8] The consensus of their successors lacks this characteristic, as can be seen from the subsequent history of controversy in theology, philosophy, and *Ṣūfism*. Furthermore, since the Companions and their immediate Successors (i.e., the first generation of Muslim jurists and scholars) have settled conclusively all the religious problems which might interest the Muslim community, any opinion or practice which emerged subsequently must be declared heretical. Ibn Taymiyah does not hesitate to include among those guilty of such heresy the Khārijites, the Shī'ites, the Mu'tazilah, the Murji'ah, the Jahmites, and even the Ash'arites—in short, all the theological or religious groups or sects which stemmed from the main body of Islam following the death of the fourth caliph, 'Alī.[9]

The responsibility for corrupting or misleading those sectaries should be imputed, according to Ibn Taymiyah, to the unfruitful methods of the theologians, the philosophers, and the linguists, who have made bold to interpret the Koran in a manner which is at variance with the only authoritative interpretation, that of the ancients (*al-salaf*). "I have examined all the theological and philosophical methods," he writes, "and found them incapable of curing any ills or of quenching any thirst. For me, the best method is that of the Koran. In the affirmative, I read 'The Merciful sat upon the throne' [Koran 7, 54] . . . in the negative, 'Nothing is like unto Him' [Koran 42, 11]."[10] Indeed, he claims, no one who has partaken of his experience will

[8] Ibn Taymiyah, *Majmū'at al-Rasā'il*, Pt. I, p. 16.

[9] *Ibid.*, pp. 18 f., 76 f.

[10] *Ibid.*, p. 100. The reference is to the affirmative and negative methods of interpreting koranic passages.

doubt the futility of these methods. The philosophers and the theologians have been unable to prove conclusively the justice or the wisdom, the mercy or even the truthfulness of God. And although some of them might be closer to the truth than others, none is free from error altogether. In fact, the only safeguard against error is the unconditional submission to the authority of the ancients.

As one might expect, Ibn Taymiyah's harshest polemics are reserved for the philosophers. The substance of their teaching on the subject of religious truth is that Scripture, being addressed primarily to the masses at large, has been deliberately couched in metaphors and pictorial representations, in order that it may be readily accessible to them. Religious propositions on such questions as God and the life-to-come are at best morally and socially advantageous, but not necessarily true.[11]

Ibn Taymiyah's polemic against the philosophers is contained chiefly in his *Refutation of the Logicians*, his comments on Ibn Rushd's theological tract, *al-Kashf*, and his *Conformity of Revealed and Rational Knowledge*.[12] In the *Refutation of the Logicians*, he begins by attacking the claim of (Aristotelian) logicians that conceptions which are not self-evident can only be known through definition, on the ground that, not being self-evident, this claim requires proof or else should be dismissed as gratuitous.[13] Moreover, the difficulties attendant upon the attempt to define concepts are legion. Even writers who, like al-Ghazālī, have sought to defend logic, were forced to admit the difficulty for the learned, let alone the unlearned, to determine the "*infima* species" and the "essential *differentiae*" upon which definition rests.[14]

Another grave error of the logicians stems from their contention that definition conveys genuine knowledge of the *definiendum*. A definition is merely a statement or an assertion made by the speaker, which could obviously be entirely unwarranted. He might either know the truth of such a statement beforehand, in which case he does not learn anything new about the *definiendum*, or he does not, in which case he cannot admit it without proof.[15]

As for the validity of judgments resulting from the conjunction of

[11] Ibn Taymiyah, *Majmū'at al-Rasā'il*, pp. 160 f., 180 f.
[12] See Bibliography.
[13] *Al-Radd'ala 'l-Manṭiqiyīn*, p. 7.
[14] *Ibid.*, pp. 19 f.
[15] *Ibid.*, pp. 32 f.

other judgments in a syllogism, the theory of the logicians is also fraught with difficulties. First, logicians divide judgments into those which are self-evident and those which are not. But the basis of this division is far from clear, considering how radically people differ in their powers of apprehension. Thus some can apprehend the middle term, with which the validity of the syllogism is bound up, much more readily than others, owing to the acuteness of their powers of intuition (*al-ḥads*),[16] as Ibn Sīnā himself had shown.

Ibn Taymiyah next attacks one of the cornerstones of Aristotelian logic, the theory of demonstration (*burhān*). Demonstration, it will be recalled, was represented by Aristotle and the Arab Aristotelians as the highest form of proof. Ibn Taymiyah does not question the syllogistic process resulting in apodeictic proof, but rather observes that demonstration is quite vacuous. For, as the highest type of proof, demonstration must bear on universals which exist only in the mind. Since all being is particular, however, it follows that demonstration does not yield any positive knowledge of being in general or of God in particular.[17] It follows therefore that the demonstrative method, on the one hand, and metaphysics, on the other, which makes the greatest use of this method, according to them, can have no bearing on being.

Moreover, in their analysis of being they recognize five types of substance: form, matter, body, Soul, and intellect, and ten categories (the ten categories of Aristotelian logic). But these two lists have not been shown to be exhaustive, and do not at any rate apply to the highest entities such as God and the universal intelligences, or contribute anything to our knowledge of these entities.[18]

These strictures are enough to illustrate the futility or inadequacy of the logical methods used by the philosophers or the theologians who have been induced to emulate their example. Logic is, after all, a purely human convention susceptible to all the fallibility and confusion to which every human method or device is. It is unquestionably inferior to that indubitable method which is laid down in the Koran and the Traditions and to which the believer is duty-bound to cling, to the exclusion of any other.

[16] *Al-Radd 'ala 'l-Manṭiqiyīn*, pp. 88 f., cf. *supra*, p. 182. [17] *Ibid.*, pp. 124 f.
[18] *Ibid.*, p. 132.

Ibn Taymiyah's best-known disciple was Ibn al-Qayim al-Jaūziyah, another key figure in the history of the antirationalist reaction to theology, philosophy, and mysticism. The revival of Ḥanbalism culminated, however, in the Wahhābī movement, which was founded in the eighteenth century by Muḥammad b. ʿAbdul-Wahhāb and became the official creed of central Arabia following the success of the Saʿūdī dynasty in establishing its hegemony in Najd and Hijaz. What the Wahhābīs have in common with Ibn Taymiyah is, in addition to their literalist adherence to the text of the Koran and the Traditions, the emphasis on ritual observance and the condemnation of the cult of saints and similar excesses of the *Ṣūfī* orders. What all those Neo-Ḥanbalite movements have in common with the ninth-century theologian and jurist whose name they adopted and who was so inflexible in his opposition to rationalism, as we have seen,[19] is an insistence on the necessity of returning to the orthodox ways of the "pious forebears," or the first generation of Muslims, and the restoration of the common cult to its original purity.[20]

II

MODERATION AND DECLINE: F. D. AL-RĀZĪ, N. D. AL-NAṢAFĪ, AL-ĪJĪ, AL-JURJĀNĪ, AND AL-BĀJŪRĪ

THE extremism of the literalist reaction in theology had its liberal counterparts. Some of the outstanding theologians of the twelfth century continued the tradition championed by al-Ghazālī, who in his attack on the philosophers sought to meet them on their own ground

[19] *Supra*, p. 79.

[20] Cf. *EI*, art. Wahhābiya (D. S. Margoliouth) and Laoust, *Essai sur les doctrines sociales et politiques de T. D. Aḥmad b. Taimiya.*

and in the process made certain radical concessions to philosophy in general and to logic in particular.

The only equal of al-Ghazālī in philosophical and theological erudition in the twelfth century is Fakhr al-Dīn al-Rāzī, one of the last encyclopedic writers of Islam. Born in 1149 in Ray, like his countryman and namesake, the tenth-century physician and philosopher Abū Bakr b. Muḥammad b. Zakariyā al-Rāzī, Fakhr al-Dīn journeyed extensively throughout Persia. From Khwārizm he went to Ghaznah, and from Ghaznah to Herāt, where he eventually settled at the court of 'Alā' al-Dīn Khwārizm Shāh, whose generous patronage he enjoyed until his death in 1209.[21]

Apart from his own father, his teachers included al-Simnānī, al-Baghawī, and Majd al-Dīn al-Jīlī, the teacher of the other great thinker of the period, al-Suhrawardī. There is little doubt that the greatest formative influence on his thought was Ibn Sīnā, although he was also influenced by Abu'l-Barakāt al-Baghdādī (d. ca. 1166), author of a compendium of physics, logic, and metaphysics, *al-Mu'tabar fi'l-Ḥikmah*, and an important medical writer of the twelfth century.

Al-Rāzī's major philosophical works include his commentary on the two major works of Ibn Sīnā, *al-Ishārāt* and *'Uyūn al-Ḥikmah*, and his *al-Mabāḥith al-Mashriqiyah*, probably his most important work. The most noteworthy of his theological and exegetical works, are *al-Arba'īn fī Uṣūl al-Dīn*, *al-Muḥaṣṣal*, and *Mafātiḥ al-Ghayb*, a voluminous commentary on the Koran. The interest of these writings, as Ibn Khaldūn, the fourteenth-century historiographer has aptly remarked, consists in the fact that, like al-Ghazālī, al-Rāzī has fully exploited in them the methods of the philosophers in his rebuttal of those propositions which conflict with dogma.[22] More than al-Ghazālī, however, he combines philosophy and theology so completely that the separation between their respective spheres is hardly discernible. This is perhaps best illustrated in the above-mentioned *al-Mabāḥith al-Mashriqiyah* (*Oriental Investigations*), which, as its title suggests, forms a link in that chain of disquisitions on "Oriental philosophy," which as we have seen Ibn Sīnā had adumbrated in one of his later works, *al-Ishārāt*.

[21] Al-Subkī, *Ṭabaqāt al-Shāfi'iyah al-Kubrā*, V, 33–40.

[22] *Al-Muqaddimah*, pp. 466, 495.

In his commentary on this work of Ibn Sīnā, al-Rāzī sets out this philosopher's doctrine faithfully but does not hesitate to criticize it when the occasion arises. Some of his criticisms recur in *al-Mabāḥith* and will be mentioned below. The second best-known commentary on *al-Ishārāt* was written by the Shīʿite philosopher, astronomer, and theologian Naṣīr al-Dīn al-Ṭūsī and constitutes a defense of Ibn Sīnā against al-Rāzī's attack. According to this partisan of Ibn Sīnā, who also wrote a rebuttal of al-Ghazālī's *Tahāfut* entitled *al-Dhakhīrah*, al-Rāzī's work was a "diatribe not a commentary" (*jarḥ lā sharḥ*).[23]

The perusal of *al-Mabāḥith* is enough to convince the reader of al-Rāzī's debt to Ibn Sīnā. Many of the themes he broaches are reminiscent of classic themes discussed in Ibn Sīnā's *al-Shifā'*. Thus *al-Mabāḥith* opens, like *al-Shifā'*, with a long discussion of essence and existence and the general modes of being, such as unity, plurality, necessity, possibility, etc. Being, he argues, is indefinable, because our awareness of being, particularly our own, precedes any other awareness and cannot in consequence be referred to a more primary or defining concept.[24] Its relation to essence (*māhiyah*) is neither one of identity nor of entailment, but rather one of otherness, or else it would be tautological to predicate being of a given essence. Eleven arguments are then given to corroborate the view that being is other than or extraneous to essence. The gist of these arguments is that the conception of an essence does not necessarily involve that of its being, nor does the predication of a property or attribute of the former necessarily apply to the latter. Hence the two are entirely independent and the essence requires an extraneous existential determination before it can come to be.[25]

The process of cognition is described as one of illumination, originating in what he calls the world of emanation (*ʿālam al-fayḍ*), which differs little from the intelligible world of Neo-Platonism and is bound up with the disposition of the Soul to receive the cognitions in question. In this process, sensation plays the purely passive role of preparing the Soul for this reception, as Ibn Sīnā had also maintained. This is particularly true of the apprehension of the primary principles or axioms

[23] Commentary on *al-Ishārāt wa'l-Tanbīhāt*, I, 162.

[24] *Al-Mabāḥith*, I, 11, 16. [25] *Ibid.*, pp. 25 f.

which are known intuitively without any intermediary whatsoever[26] and which form the basis of all knowledge. Al-Rāzī inveighs against the Platonic view of knowledge as reminiscence, however, on the grounds that the Soul is created in time and cannot therefore have preceded the body, as the theory of reminiscence presupposes, and that recognition, which is advanced as evidence for this theory, does not necessarily entail that the Soul had a preexisting knowledge of what it learns in this life. What is learned may be said to be known merely in general or abstract terms, prior to the act of acquiring a concrete or specific knowledge of it.[27]

Al-Rāzī is critical, however, of the Avicennian doctrine of emanation. Thus, as had become customary in theological circles since al-Ghazālī's time, he rejects as groundless the maxim that out of one, only one entity can come. This maxim, it will be recalled, was one of the major theoretical props of the whole emanationist scheme. The First Being gives rise to the first intellect, which in turn gives rise to the second intellect, as well as the Soul and body of the first heaven. Unlike the First or Necessary Being, the first intellect involves an element of plurality, owing to its dual character as a being possible in itself, but necessary through its cause. This in fact is the ultimate cause of multiplicity in a world emanating from a First Principle, who is absolutely one.

As for God's knowledge of particulars, a question that set the theologians against the philosophers from the time of al-Fārābī on, al-Rāzī takes an equally anti-Avicennian stand. Being immaterial, God knows Himself, since it belongs to all immaterial beings to be capable of self-knowledge; and, being the cause of all the entities which have resulted from His creative act, He knows the whole order of created entities by the same act of self-knowledge.

Contrary to the contentions of Ibn Sīnā and his followers, God's knowledge of particulars does not necessarily involve plurality, change, or dependence on its object. For knowledge is not the act of assimilating the form of the knowable, as the Neo-Platonists generally assert, but is rather a special relationship to the object.[28] What changes in

[26] *Al-Mabāḥith*, I, 245 f. [27] *Ibid.*, p. 376.
[28] *Ibid.*, p. 470; cf. *al-Muḥaṣṣal*, pp. 127 f.

the process of knowing particulars, on this view, is not God's essence, but His relationship to the object. Consequently the chief Neo-Platonic objection to God's knowledge of particulars can be discounted. Thus al-Rāzī reaffirms, sometimes on his own authority and sometimes on that of Abu'l-Barakāt al-Baghdādī, God's all-embracing knowledge of Himself, of universals, and of particulars, and rebuts the classic objections of Neo-Platonic writers one by one. However, his rebuttal is neither more forceful nor more acute than that of al-Ghazālī, who, as we have seen, subverted the whole Avicennian thesis of divine knowledge of particulars, *more universale*, and reaffirmed in unequivocal terms the koranic concept of God's all-embracing knowledge.[29] More conscientious, perhaps, and more thorough than al-Ghazālī in reporting the views of the Neo-Platonists of Islam, al-Rāzī is nevertheless more diffuse, and his own position is not always stated incisively. Despite these shortcomings, there is little doubt that he stands out as a towering figure in the dialectical struggle between the philosophers and the theologians. Both in terms of his erudition and his earnestness he deserves a special place in the history of philosophical thought in Islam.

Subsequent developments in theology and the continuing rift between philosophy and theology need not concern us here. Suffice it to note that the thirteenth century marked the onset of the decline in theology. The period of original theological output and controversy was succeeded by a period of commentary and reaction. The last great theologian to follow in the footsteps of al-Ghazālī and al-Rāzī in the struggle against the philosophers was Ibn Taymiyah. The other noteworthy theologians of the thirteenth and fourteenth centuries are Ḥāfiẓ al-Dīn al-Nasāfī (d. 1301 or 1310), who is not to be confused with Najm al-Dīn al-Nasafī (d. 1142), another writer on dogmatic and other theological questions; 'Aḍud al-Dīn al-Ījī (d. 1355), author of *al-Mawāqif*; al-Taftazānī (d. 1390), who is famous for his commentary on the *Creed* of Najm al-Dīn al-Nasafī, which remained for centuries one of the chief textbooks of theology; and al-Sayyid al-Sharīf al-Jurjānī (d. 1413), best known for his commentary on al-Ījī's *al-Mawāqif* and his philosophical glossary of technical terms, *al-Ta'rīfāt*. The most

[29] *Supra*, p. 256.

important theologians of the fifteenth century are al-Sanūsī (d. ca. 1490) and al-Dawwānī (d. 1501). The theologians who kept the tradition of commentary or exposition alive after the fifteenth century are al-Birqilī (d. 1573); al-Laqānī (d. 1631), author of *Jauharat al-Tauḥīd*, which became famous as the basis of subsequent commentaries or glossaries; al-Siyalkūtī (d. 1657); and al-Bājūrī (d. 1860), author of a commentary on *Jauharat al-Laqānī*.[30] In the nineteenth century, Muḥammad 'Abdu (d. 1905), as we shall see, emerged as the major theological figure in this unbroken tradition which stems from al-Ḥasan al-Baṣrī and Wāṣil b. 'Atā' in the eighth century.

III

REACTION AND RECONSTRUCTION: IBN KHALDŪN

THE fourteenth century may be called the century of Neo-Ḥanbalism. Ibn Taymiyah and his disciples insured the victory of Neo-Ḥanbalism over scholastic theology and philosophy, and although the intellectual momentum of Islam had waned by this time, exceptions continued to arise here and there. Of these exceptions Ibn Khaldūn of Tunis is the most remarkable in the West, Mulla Ṣadrā[31] the most remarkable in the East. Both for the vastness of his learning and the originality of his sociological thought, Ibn Khaldūn occupies a place apart in the annals of Islamic philosophical thought.

Born in 1332 into a noble Arab-Spanish family of scholars and civil servants, 'Abdu'l-Raḥmān b. Khaldūn received the customary education of his class. He studied the koranic and linguistic sciences, the Traditions, and jurisprudence with a series of teachers whom he praises

[30] Watt, *Islamic Philosophy and Theology*, pp. 153 f.; Brunschvig and von Grunebaum, *Classicisme et déclin culturel dans l'histoire de l'Islam*, pp. 93 ff.

[31] See *supra*, pp. 339 f.

in a lengthy autobiography.[32] He traveled west in 1352, driven by the political squabbles of the times and the plague of 1348–1349, which took the lives of his parents and most of his teachers. After a short stay in Bougie he settled down in Fez at the court of the sultan Abū 'Inān, who was recruiting scholars for his new scientific council.[33] One of the scholars Ibn Khaldūn met at Fez was al-Sharīf al-Tilmisānī al-'Alwī (d. 1370) to whom he gives unqualified praise. In addition to jurisprudence, theology, and linguistics, this scholar reportedly introduced one of Ibn Khaldūn's teachers, Ibn 'Abd al-Salām, to the suspect study of the philosophical writings of Ibn Sīnā and Ibn Rushd.[34] From Fez, where he attained at one time a high administrative position under Abū Salīm, the successor to Abū 'Inān, he moved on to Granada, which he reached in 1362. Later he was lured back to Fez and Bougie, where he also occupied positions of eminence at court. But throughout those troubled years and despite the allurements of public office, which he often struggled with, Ibn Khaldūn yearned for a quiet life of study and meditation. During a short period of solitude in 1377 he was able to complete his most important work, *al-Muqaddimah*, which was the introduction to his world history, *Kitāb al-'Ibar*.[35] Tired of public life and the hazardous service of fickle rulers in North Africa, he sailed to Alexandria in 1382. In Cairo, the Mamlūk sultan, al-Malik al-Ẓāhir Barqūq, recognized his great achievement as a scholar and a jurist. In 1384 he was appointed Professor of Mālikī Law and subsequently Chief Mālikī Judge of Egypt. With intermittent interruptions he retained the position of Professor of Law at various Mamlūk institutions and the judgeship until his death. One final memorable episode in his life should be mentioned: in 1401 he encountered Tīmūr Lane outside the walls of Damascus. Tīmūr Lane apparently showed great regard for this scholar and may have wished to attach him to his court.[36] Ibn Khaldūn, however, returned to Egypt shortly after to resume his activities as jurist and scholar until his death in 1406.

The role of Ibn Khaldūn in the philosophical history of Islam is a

[32] *Al-Ta'rīf bi'bn Khaldūn wa Riḥlatuhu Sharqan*, pp. 15 f.

[33] *Ibid.*, p. 58; cf. *The Muqaddimah of Ibn Khaldūn*, tr. Rosenthal, xli.

[34] *Al-Ta'rīf*, pp. 62 f. [35] *Ibid.*, p. 229.

[36] *Ibid.*, pp. 366 f.; cf. Mahdi, *Ibn Khaldūn's Philosophy of History*, pp. 58 f.

complex one. We have already referred to his philosophical education and his possible introduction at an early age to the writings of Ibn Sīnā and Ibn Rushd by one of his most important teachers. One tradition even ascribes to him the writing of epitomes of Ibn Rushd's works.[37] But it is not clear whether these works are Ibn Rushd's theological and Mālikī writings or his commentaries on Aristotle. Be this as it may, the two most important aspects of his philosophical contribution are the extensive remarks on and criticisms of Greco-Arab philosophy and the formulation in original theoretical terms of the first and last major philosophy of history in Islam. To this should be added his contribution to scholastic theology and mysticism in two extant works, *Lubāb al-Muḥaṣṣal*,[38] a summary of F. D. al-Rāzī's compendium of theological and philosophical opinions, and *Shifā' al-Sā'il*, a mystical treatise of the conventional type.

Despite his ventures into those philosophical and semi-philosophical fields, Ibn Khaldūn remains essentially a historian with an empiricist's outlook on and instinctive suspicion of the flights of metaphysical fancy. In *al-Muqaddimah* he gives a very perceptive and succinct account of the whole range of Islamic learning. This, coupled with his critical remarks on the nature and scope of the philosophical sciences, is symptomatic of the state of philosophical learning in the fourteenth century and of the judgment which history, after five centuries of philosophical and antiphilosophical controversy, had passed on the whole attempt to establish a "national home" for Greek philosophy in Muslim lands. In this respect the foremost mentor of Ibn Khaldūn is al-Ghazālī, rather than Ibn Rushd. His most systematic and thoughtful estimate of the value of the philosophical method is contained in a critical disquisition entitled "The Repudiation of Philosophy and the Perversity of its Adepts,"[39] which sets the general tone of the whole discussion in this chapter and elsewhere.

As a prelude to his critique, Ibn Khaldūn gives a classification of the traditional (*naqlī*) and the philosophical (or natural) sciences, interspersed with brief comments on the rise and development of philosophy

[37] Maqqarī, *Nafḥ al-Ṭīb*, VIII, 286 f.; Mahdi, *Ibn Khaldūn's Philosophy of History*, p. 35 and n. 5.

[38] Escorial Ms. 1614.

[39] *Al-Muqaddimah*, pp. 514-19.

from the time of the Chaldeans and the Egyptians. His concept of the history of philosophy is the traditional Islamic one, associated with the names of the better-known historiographers such as Ṣā'id and al-Qifṭī.

His criteria for evaluating philosophy are essentially religious or theological. The philosophers claim, he argues, that the knowledge of reality both sensible and supersensible is possible through the theoretical devices of speculation and deduction only, and that the truth of the articles of faith themselves can be established through those devices without the assistance of revelation.[40] From the consideration of particulars in the world of sense, the mind is able to rise to the knowledge of the First Intellect, identified by the philosophers with God, and it is in the contemplation of that Intellect that man's ultimate happiness lies. This happiness, represented as purely intellectual, is possible without the assistance of revelation at all, they claim.

Against this general Neo-Platonic thesis of the hierarchy of being and of man's ultimate happiness, Ibn Khaldūn first argues that the assumption that the scale of being terminates with a First Intellect is purely arbitrary. The nature of reality is much more varied and complex than the philosophers, in their narrow-mindedness, have surmised. Their case is analogous in this regard to that of the Materialists, who refuse to entertain the existence of any entities other than the material because their knowledge cannot extend beyond them.[41]

Next, he observes, even in the physical sciences their procedure is an unjustified one. In reasoning about the external world, they tacitly assume that physical reality must conform to the logical pattern of their arguments, or, in other words, that what is so in thought must be so in fact. But, whereas their arguments belong to the order of general propositions, the physical entities they are supposed to describe belong to that of particulars, materially individuated. The only evidence that can be adduced in support of the alleged conformity between such particulars and the propositions describing them is the empirical. The resultant conformity, however, is not necessary, but depends on the accidental circumstance that the propositions in question are rooted in the "imaginative forms" (or phantasms) rather than the

[40] *Al-Muqaddimah*, p. 514. [41] *Ibid.*

"second intelligibles" upon which all philosophical abstractions rest. Apart from these difficulties, however, "physical enquiries are of no relevance to our religious faith or our livelihood and must for that reason be abandoned."[42]

The philosophers' use of metaphysics is even more erroneous, since its objects (the spiritual entities) lie outside the scope of our experience and their natures are entirely unknown to us. Our only basis for judging them is by analogy to what we observe in our own self, especially in that type of "inward vision" associated with mystical experience. Beyond this analogy, we have no means of characterizing such spiritual entities. The foremost philosophers concur in this result. For what has no material substratum cannot be demonstrated, according to them, since the premises of demonstration must ultimately have a concrete basis in fact. Even Plato has conceded that certainty is not possible in metaphysics, only probability or conjecture. But, concludes Ibn Khaldūn, if probability or conjecture is all that our demonstrations will yield after prolonged meditation or research, let us be content with the original probability or conjecture with which we started.

As for the philosophers' claim that human happiness consists in the intellectual apprehension or contemplation of intellectual realities, including the First Intellect, this too must be rejected as gratuitous. Man is made up of two parts: the corporeal and the spiritual (or intellectual). To each part belongs a series of cognitive objects (*madārik*). In both cases, however, the subject of cognition is the spiritual part. This part sometimes apprehends spiritual, sometimes corporeal objects. The former it apprehends directly, whereas the latter it apprehends through the agency of such corporeal organs as the brain and the various organs of sense. Now the pleasure which the cognitive power derives directly from what it apprehends directly and without any intermediaries is obviously greater than incidental or indirect pleasures. Hence, the "spiritual Soul" partakes of the highest pleasure only when in possession of its spiritual object. However, this pleasure is not attained through meditation or reasoning, but through direct mystical experience, in which "sensation has been completely transcended and

[42] *Al-Muqaddimah*, p. 516.

the sense organs dispensed with altogether." Even intellectual powers are transcended or dispensed with at this mystical level, because they too depend on "the brain activities of imagination, reflection, and memory."[43] Indeed, the more one becomes entangled in the philosophers' processes of reasoning or proof, the more difficult it will be to attain this ultimate goal of human happiness.

The whole basis of the philosophers' theory of happiness is the thesis that once conjunction (*ittiṣāl*) with the active intellect takes place, man's felicity is attained. What those philosophers, particularly al-Fārābī and Ibn Sīnā, mean by "conjunction" is "that direct apprehension of the Soul by itself and without any intermediary."[44] But the pleasure attendant upon this apprehension falls far short of that happiness the Soul has been promised in Scripture. Like the scale of being upon which their concept of happiness is predicated, this theory arbitrarily limits the higher reaches of reality created by God. The happiness we have been promised in Scripture far exceeds anything philosophical demonstrations can elicit or a life of moral uprightness can warrant. It is, in short, a supernatural gift of divine grace. Even Ibn Sīnā has admitted, in connection with the problem of corporeal resurrection, that it falls outside the scope of demonstration, because demonstration refers exclusively to what is "proportionate" to the natural order. Therefore it is necessary to seek in Scripture the truth about corporeal resurrection.[45]

From all this, Ibn Khaldūn concludes that metaphysics is incapable of solving any of the crucial problems affecting man's ultimate destiny or salvation. Its only "fruit" is to "sharpen the mind" by developing in us the "*habitus* of truth" through the prolonged use of the logical method. Despite its shortcomings, this method is the soundest known to us. The only condition Ibn Khaldūn lays down as a means of guarding the student of logic against error or perdition is not to broach its study before becoming fully proficient in the religious sciences, especially koranic exegesis (*tafsīr*) and jurisprudence (*fiqh*).[46]

[43] *Al-Muqaddimah*, p. 517. [44] *Ibid.*, p. 518.

[45] *Ibid.*, p. 519. Ibn Khaldūn quotes Ibn Sīnā's *Kitāb al-Mabda' wa'l-Ma'ād*; cf. *supra*, p. 165.

[46] *Ibid.*, p. 519.

Ibn Khaldūn's positivist method, tempered by mystical or religious elements, led him as it had led al-Ghazālī before to take this qualified view of logic as a valid instrument of thought, while dismissing the bulk of physical and metaphysical propositions as religiously pernicious. Like him also, he rejects secondary causality as incompatible with the explicit assertion of Scripture that all happenings in the "world of the elements" should be ascribed to God's direct initiative or power.[47]

It was his positivism, however, that led him to undertake a systematic codification of a "science of civilization" whose laws are reducible to geographic, economic, and cultural laws, or to a certain "dialectic" of historical development, which is partly immanent, partly determined by the transcendent decrees of the Almighty. The resultant theory of history and of civilization is without doubt his major claim to a position of preeminence in the history of philosophical ideas in Islam. For although he stands outside the mainstream of Islamic philosophy in its Neo-Platonic and Peripatetic forms, his philosophical erudition and his originality place him in the forefront of the more creative thinkers of Islam. Some of the topographic and demographic aspects of his science of civilization have a basis in the writings of al-Mas'ūdī (d. 956), Aristotle, or al-Fārābī,[48] but the systematic codification and analysis of the relevant data is entirely his own.

Despite his virtual repudiation of "secondary causality" and his recognition of the dependence of the historical process upon the will of the Almighty, Ibn Khaldūn sets out to establish the critical study of history upon a solid foundation of geographic, political, and cultural knowledge. The norms of such knowledge, as well as the laws governing the events or processes on which it turns, are essentially rational or natural and provide the student of history "with the criteria for discriminating between the truth or falsity of historical records . . . in a demonstrative or infallible way."[49]

The starting point of the underlying "science of civilization" is the Aristotelian maxim that man is a political animal by nature, since he

[47] *Al-Muqaddimah*, pp. 521, 143, *et passim*.

[48] Ibn Khaldūn refers to al-Mas'ūdī, Galen, and al-Kindī in connection with his theory of climatic determination (*al-Muqaddimah*, p. 87).

[49] *Ibid.*, p. 37.

is unable without assistance from his fellow men to provide for his essential material needs or for his protection against attack. Political association, however, presupposes a ruler who deters (*wāzi'*) individuals prone to aggression from encroaching upon the rights or security of others. This is what gives rise to the institution of monarchy (*al-mulk*), which is a perfectly natural institution. Above it, however, is the prophetic office, which the philosophers regarded as natural also, but Ibn Khaldūn, following the majority of scholastic theologians, regarded as lying outside the scope of demonstration. Its validity is to be sought in the authority of the religious law (*al-shar'*).[50]

The fallacies of the view of prophecy or theocracy elaborated by al-Fārābī and Ibn Sīnā are next set out. First, it ignores the historical realities of political power and the fact that the authority of the monarch is often maintained by force or rests upon the primitive basis of tribal solidarity (*al-'aṣabiyah*). Accordingly, a natural or rational form of government has often resulted. The laws by which this "natural monarchy" is governed are purely rational. A religious or theocratic regime, on the other hand, is one in which divinely ordained laws are enforced by a prophet or a successor of a prophet (*caliph*).[51]

Moreover, "natural monarchy" ministers to man's natural or terrestrial needs only. But man has a dual vocation, this-worldly and other-worldly. His short career in this world is simply a prelude to a higher life in the world-to-come, in which alone his genuine felicity can be achieved. It follows therefore that, since only in theocratic or prophetic forms of government man's felicity in this world and the world-to-come are safeguarded, the superiority of these forms over "natural monarchy" is unquestionable.[52]

The forms of human association, the distribution of the population, the rise and fall of states and empires, and even individual or ethnic character, are determined by numerous factors such as climate, geography, economics, religion, and ecology. Climatic and economic factors, such as heat and cold, abundance or scarcity of food supplies, may often determine the physical and psychological traits of whole groups. Thus the inhabitants of the torrid zone tend to be more volatile and less concerned about the morrow. Inhabitants of the colder zone

[50] *Al-Muqaddimah*, p. 44. [51] *Ibid.*, pp. 44, 187. [52] *Ibid.*, pp. 190 f.

tend to be more reserved or phlegmatic. Where food is more abundant, people tend to be somewhat relaxed, soft, and epicurean; where it is more scant, they tend to be frugal, sturdy, and devout.[53]

Ecological factors also determine the forms of human association and the laws of their development. Thus we observe that from the pastoral stage, in which the sole aim of man is to provide for his basic needs, society evolved into the agrarian and industrial phases of civilization, which are marked by strife for a higher level of livelihood. Thus the most primitive form of association, the pastoral or nomadic, gives way progressively to the "settled" or sedentary, and desert life is succeeded by city life, with which civilization (*al-'umrān*), in the strict sense, is bound up.[54]

If we compare the two, we find that the nomad's mode of life is more natural. He is in addition more rugged and more inclined to natural goodness. The city dweller is softer and more liable to corruption and vice. Like Rousseau, Ibn Khaldūn believed that originally good or neutral human nature is corrupted by civilization.

The political implications of this theory of society are obvious. In the nomadic condition, society is virile, healthy, and aggressive, whereas in the city it is lethargic, passive, and slothful. Eroded by its vices, such a society invites invasion, to which it falls an easy prey. But no sooner have its invaders settled down to a sedentary existence than they are gradually reduced to a condition of helplessness by the same forces of luxury and softness. A new wave of invasion now carries the denizens of the desert on its crest and the process goes on indefinitely. The nomadic-sedentary cycle of stimulus and response continues.

Issuing out of the state of nature, society, as we have seen, requires the strong hand of a monarch to hold it together. But the monarch himself is the product of the original force of tribal solidarity (*al-'aṣabiyah*) that gives the group its primordial unity. The monarch must depend on this solidarity, as well as on the principles of rational and religious justice in consolidating his power. Indeed, it is part of the divine plan for such a society that once such conditions have been obtained, it is "favoured" with a worthy holder of the royal office. But as soon as those conditions have ceased and corruption or strife have

[53] *Al-Muqaddimah*, pp. 86 f. [54] *Ibid.*, pp. 120 f.

set in within the state, the tide is ready to turn at the behest of God. The old must now give way to the new.[55]

Although this cycle is represented by Ibn Khaldūn as endless, the age of the state and the stages through which it passes are carefully worked out. The "natural" age of the state is equivalent to three generations of forty years each. The first generation is marked by the frugality of the nomadic life and the ardor of the spirit of solidarity holding them together and moving them to share in the authority of the monarch. The second is marked by the weakening of that spirit, in consequence of the transition to a civilized mode of life, and the unwillingness to share in monarchical authority. The third is marked by the complete loss of the spirit of solidarity and with it the loss of the militant spirit which was the rampart of the state. When this happens, the death of the state is imminent and is finally sealed by a timely decree of God.[56]

More specifically, we may distinguish five stages in the process of the growth and decay of the state:

1. The stage of consolidation, during which monarchical authority is established on a solid democratic base of popular support.

2. The stage of tyranny, during which the monarch resorts to the gradual monopoly of political power. The tribal bonds between him and his subjects are weakened and his dependence on foreign elements is intensified.

3. The stage of exploitation of the privileges of authority by accumulating wealth, levying taxes, and engaging in the construction of public buildings or monuments in an attempt to vie with other monarchs.

4. The stage of pacification, attended by the endeavor to continue the traditions and institutions of the ancestors.

5. The stage of dissolution and decay. During this stage the monarch squanders the public treasure in the gratification of his pleasures and those of his retainers. As a result decay sets in throughout the state, and the ground is prepared for a new wave of nomadic invasion.[57]

[55] *Al-Muqaddimah*, pp. 143 f., 157. [56] *Ibid.*, p. 171. [57] *Ibid.*, pp. 175 f.

This analysis of the ecological and historical laws that govern the growth, development, and decay of human institutions has an obvious natural or positive basis which is partly geographic, partly economic, and partly sociological. It is a mistake to assume however that the historical or ecological determinism is complete. Ibn Khaldūn's philosophy of history and the state has an important extranatural, extrarational component, bound up with what we may call his concept of the divine plan for the world. The two distinct lines of determinism work in conjunction. The will of God is always for him the decisive factor in bringing about the cyclical changes in the process of history. Even the age of the state, computed in multiples of forty years, is not arrived at through abstract analysis or deduction. It is derived instead from a koranic passage that equates the prime of the individual with this figure and is also related to the forty-year Israelite sojourn in the Sinai desert, according to the exegetical traditions of Islam.[58] What this dual determinism involved for this partly modern, partly traditionist philosopher of history is essentially the recognition of the fact that the historical process serves at best as the stage upon which the grand designs of the Almighty are realized in the world.

[58] *Al-Muqaddimah*, pp. 170, 141.

CHAPTER TWELVE

Modern and Contemporary Trends

I

THE EMERGENCE OF THE MODERNIST SPIRIT: J. D. AL-AFGHĀNĪ AND MUḤAMMAD ʻABDU

THE final reconciliation of philosophy and theology by Ishrāqī thinkers, from al-Suhrawardī to al-Shīrāzī, insured for philosophy a secure place in Persia and prepared the ground for the rise of "modernism" in Muslim lands. The continuity of Islamic thought, particularly in its Shīʻite form, is illustrated by the long line of philosopher-theologians who carried on the Ishrāqī tradition that culminates in Ṣadr al-Dīn al-Shīrāzī, its greatest champion in modern times. The first genuine modernist thinker in Islam, Jamāl al-Dīn al-Afghānī, was in part a product of the same tradition and the herald of the new spirit of liberalism which ushered Islam into the nineteenth and twentieth centuries.

Born in Asadabād in Persia, or according to his own account in Asʻadabād in Afghanistān[1] in 1839, Jamāl al-Dīn moved with his

[1] See Luṭfallah Khān, *Jamāl al-Dīn al-Asadabādī al-Afghānī*, pp. 49 f.; cf. Adams, *Islam and Modernism in Egypt*, p. 4, n. 1. See also Riḍa, *Tārīkh al-Ustādh al-Imām*, I, 27.

family to Qazwīn and subsequently to Teheran, where he studied at the feet of Aqāṣid Ṣādiq, the best known Shī'ite theologian of the time in Teheran. From Teheran he moved to al-Najaf in Iraq, the seat of Shī'ite religious studies, where he spent four years as the disciple of Murtaḍa al-Anṣārī, a leading theologian and scholar. In 1853 he journeyed to India, where he was introduced to the study of the European sciences. His travels eventually took him to the four corners of the earth: Hijaz, Egypt, Yemen, Turkey, Russia, England, and France. One of the most memorable of these travels was his visit in 1869 to Egypt and from there, after a brief stay, to Istanbul. His reception at Istanbul was cordial at first, but soon jealousy and suspicion drove him out of the Ottoman capital. In 1871 he returned to Egypt and settled for a period of eight years, during which his tremendous intellectual and political impact on the Egyptian intelligentsia began to bear fruit. His disciples in Egypt included distinguished writers such as Adīb Isḥāq, politicians such as 'Arābī Pasha, and many others. However, his greatest disciple and lifelong associate was the other pillar of the modernist movement in the Near East, Muḥammad 'Abdu.[2]

Another memorable trip was one he made to Paris, where in collaboration with M. 'Abdu in 1884 he began publishing an inflammatory gazette, *al-'Urwah al-Wuthqā*, which called for the union of all Muslims and the restoration of the caliphate. In Paris he also met and greatly impressed the French philosopher and historian Ernest Rénan, whose work on Averroes has already been mentioned. As he conversed with him Rénan felt that he was speaking with a familiar, if older, friend, and hearing once more the call for rationalism and free thought sounded centuries earlier by Ibn Sīnā and Ibn Rushd.[3] In 1892 he went to Istanbul for the second time and was accorded high honors by Sultan 'Abd al-Ḥamīd, who recognized the value, for the pan-Islamic movement of which he was the champion, of an intellectual and propagandist of the caliber of al-Afghānī. However, the association between the sultan and the scholar came to nought because of the inherent jealousies and incompatibilities which set one part of the Muslim world against the other. In 1897 he died of complications

[2] Riḍā, *Tārīkh*, I, 31 f. [3] *Ibid.*, p. 139.

resulting from oral surgery; according to some accounts, however, his death was due to poisoning.[4]

As will appear from his biography, al-Afghānī was essentially a revolutionary fired by an intense religious zeal for the emancipation and progress of the Muslim peoples, whose ignorance and backwardness his European travels had helped to reveal to him. His ill-starred association with Sultan 'Abd al-Ḥamīd gave substance to his ideal of a united Islamic caliphate, free from foreign rule. Despite the frustration of this goal, the intellectual impetus he gave to pan-Islamism and modernism found expression in the work of his disciples, especially M. 'Abdu, to whom we will turn presently.

As a systematic thinker or theologian, al-Afghānī does not stand out as a truly dominant figure. His only published work, the *Refutation of the Materialists* (or Naturalists), written originally in Persian, is an *œuvre de circonstance* which lacks the depth or acumen of polemical works of this type. Although his polemical weapons in this book are leveled primarily at the syncretic naturalism (*Nacheriya*) of Aḥmad Khān of Bahadūr (d. 1898), whom he met during his visit to India in 1879,[5] he casts his net much wider. Among the Materialists or Naturalists whom he castigates, chiefly on account of their denial, implicitly or explicitly, of the existence of God, are Democritus and Darwin.[6]

After repudiating the godless philosophies of materialism and naturalism he proceeds to demonstrate the invaluable contributions of religion to the causes of civilization and progress. Religion has taught man three fundamental truths: (1) the angelic or spiritual nature of man, who is the lord of creation; (2) the belief of every religious community in its own superiority over all other groups; and (3) the realization that man's life in this world is simply a prelude to a higher life in a world entirely free from sorrow and which man is destined eventually to inherit.

The first truth has generated in man the urge to rise above his bestial proclivities, to live in peace and concord with his fellow men, and to hold his animal impulses in check. To the extent that nations

[4] Riḍā, *Tarīkh*, I. 91; cf. Luṭfallah, *al-Afghānī*, p. 118, and Adams, *Islam and Modernism*, p. 12.

[5] See *al-'Urwah al-Wuthqā*, p. 384; cf. Gibb, *Modern Trends in Islam*, p. 58.

[6] See *al-Radd 'alā 'l-Dahriyīn*, pp. 15 f.

are willing to live up to this truth, they will strive incessantly to improve their lot, to foster the pursuit of knowledge, and to cultivate those arts and skills which are the genuine marks of civilization.

The second truth has generated in man the urge to fix his gaze upon the higher world to which he will eventually repair, to cleanse himself of all the wickedness and malice to which his nature is prone, and to live in accordance with the precepts of peace, justice, and love.

Religion has in addition implanted in its adepts three traits: (1) modesty, which guards them against evil actions and leads them to repent; (2) honesty, which is the bulwark of a healthy body-politic; and (3) truthfulness, without which human association is virtually impossible.

If we apply this analysis to the major nations of the world we find that their greatness has always been a function of their cultivation of these traits. Thus the Greeks, though a relatively small nation, were able, thanks to those virtues, to stand up to a mighty empire, Persia, and ultimately to destroy it.[7] The materialism and hedonism of Epicurus, however, soon eroded the Greek concept of man's dignity and his heavenly destiny and this resulted in cynicism and moral decay, which proved the undoing of the Greeks and led to their eventual subjection by the Romans.

Likewise, the ancient Persians, a very noble people, began with the rise of Mazdaism the same downward journey, which resulted in their moral dissolution and their subjugation by the Arabs.

The Muslim empire itself rose on the same solid moral and religious foundation. By the tenth century, however, the advent of materialism in Egypt and Persia, in the guise of (Ismāʿīlī) *bāṭinī* propaganda, undermined the faith of the Muslim peoples by sowing the seeds of doubt in their minds and releasing their followers from religious or moral obligations, on the insidious ground that such obligations were prescribed for the uninitiated only. As the Muslims lost their moral stamina, they were so enfeebled that a small band of Franks[8] were able to establish and maintain a firm foothold in their midst for two hundred years. Subsequently the hordes of Genghis Khān were able to trample the whole land of Islam, sack its cities, and massacre its people.

[7] *Al-Radd ʿalā 'l-Dahriyīn*, p. 47.

[8] I.e., the Crusaders.

Following the fall of the Roman Empire, the French had risen to a position of undoubted preeminence in the sciences and arts and became the foremost European nation. The eighteenth century witnessed a radical change in its history. During that century Voltaire and Rousseau revived, in the name of enlightenment and equity, the old "naturalism" of Epicurus. They dismissed religious beliefs as sheer superstitions and denied the existence of God, substituting for Him the Goddess of Reason. It was those pernicious doctrines, al-Afghānī declared, which finally plunged France into the bloody struggle known as the French Revolution, from which even Napoleon could not save this country. The general decadence and dissolution which ensued were attended by greater calamities in the nineteenth century, especially the rise of socialism and the Prussian occupation of France.[9]

Al-Afghānī concludes these reflections on European history by applying the same moral and philosophical categories to the nihilists, the socialists, and the communists of the nineteenth century. Under the pretext of championing the cause of the poor and the oppressed, they preached the abolition of all privilege and the communization of all property. How much blood they shed in the process and how much sedition they fomented in the name of justice and equality, everyone knows. Their attack on religion and monarchy stems from the premise that all economic goods are gifts of nature and their private possession is a violation of the "law of nature." Their agents are active throughout Europe and especially Russia, and if they were able to consolidate their power, the human race would be threatened with extermination. "May God protect us from their evil words and deeds," he wrote.[10]

This analysis of the religious and moral forces at work in the rise and fall of nations is remarkable for its consistency and for the religious pathos with which it is infused. Surprisingly enough, the nineteenth-century "naturalists" whom al-Afghānī attacks are the European nihilists and socialists and their predecessors, the *libre penseurs* of pre-Revolutionary France. Although he states in *al-'Urwah al-Wuthqā* that it was the *Nacheris* of India that he intended to criticize, they are not explicitly mentioned in the body of the text. The obvious implication is that al-Afghānī sets out to refute "naturalism" as a general theory

[9] Al-Afghānī, *al-Radd*, p. 59. [10] *Ibid.*, p. 62.

and thereby render the position of the Indian *Nacheris* theoretically untenable.

An interesting feature of his analysis is the theory of history upon which it rests, and the role of religion as a catalytic agent in the progress of mankind. Peculiarly enough, however, he reduces religion to a rationalist system of beliefs, shorn of any supernatural content. Genuine religious beliefs, he argues, must be founded upon sound demonstrations and valid proofs, rather than the doubtful fancies or opinions of the ancestors.[11] The superiority of Islam lies in the fact that it commands its followers to accept nothing without proof and admonishes them not to be led astray by fancies or whims:

> This religion enjoins its adepts to seek a demonstrative basis for the fundamentals of belief. Hence it always addresses reason and bases its ordinances upon it. Its texts clearly state that human felicity is the product of reason and insight, and that misery and perdition are the outcome of ignorance, disregard of reason, and the extinction of the light of insight.[12]

The mark of the superiority of Islam over other religions, from Hinduism to Christianity and Zoroastrianism, lay in that its fundamental dogmas can be fully rationalized and are free from any element of mystery. It is only too apparent that al-Afghānī is wholly modern in his conception of the "rationality" of dogma. His break with the traditional concept of a supernatural component of the religious cult, as expressed chiefly by the Ḥanbalites, the Ash'arites, and the *Ṣūfīs*, is equally apparent. Even the Mu'tazilah, the early rationalists of Islam, would have balked at these somewhat extravagant claims.

His rationalism, however, did not lead him, as it had led other Muslim thinkers, from Ibn al-Rāwandī to Abu'l-'Alā', to repudiate religious belief as either superfluous or unreasonable. On the contrary, as our analysis has shown, he remains fully aware of the reality of religion as an essential ingredient in the make-up of personal morality and the complex of human culture. Both the rationality and the cultural dimension of Islam (shorn, it is true, of any supernatural element) will become dominant themes in the modernist interpretation of Islam in the twentieth century.

[11] Al-Afghānī, *al-Radd*, p. 83. [12] *Ibid.*, p. 84.

During his second visit to Egypt in 1871, al-Afghānī met Muḥammad 'Abdu, the scholar who was to become his greatest disciple and the true propagator of the religious element in his teaching in the Near East. Born in 1849 in Maḥallat Naṣr in Egypt, Muḥammad 'Abdu later moved to Ṭanṭa, where he pursued his linguistic and religious education along traditional lines.[13] Despite his initial aversion to study, in Ṭanṭa he eventually met Shaykh Darwīsh, the first teacher to profoundly influence his life. In 1866 he entered al-Azhar, the great ancient center of Islamic learning, where he remained for four years; he was soon disillusioned, however, with the antiquated curriculum and the archaic methods of instruction used there. The greatest gaps in the curriculum were in theology and philosophy. Al-Afghānī, brought up in the Persian tradition which emphasized those sciences, started his public instruction in Egypt with those very subjects, identified at al-Azhar with heresy.[14] M. 'Abdu was drawn to this foreign teacher from the start, but before embarking on the study of those dangerous subjects he sought the advice of Shaykh Darwīsh. Not only did this *Ṣūfī* teacher allay his fears, but assured him that philosophy (*al-ḥikmah*) and science are the two most secure paths to the knowledge and worship of God. Only the ignorant or the frivolous, who are God's worst enemies, consider these subjects heretical.[15]

Al-Afghānī's instruction of M. 'Abdu centered on logic, theology, astronomy, metaphysics, and particularly Ishrāqī theosophy.[16] In addition to these abstract subjects, this versatile teacher infused in his disciple a public spirit which his early mystical interests had tended to dull. Concern about public affairs had been almost unknown in Egypt heretofore, owing to a general apathy and an absence of representative institutions. Al-Afghānī not only imparted the spirit of free expression to his students, but actively spearheaded the movement of national and intellectual emancipation in Egypt. M. 'Abdu recognized clearly in him the herald of the intellectual renaissance of modern

[13] Riḍā, *Tārīkh*, I, 21 f.; cf. Adams, *Islam and Modernism*, pp. 19 f.

[14] Riḍā has noted this difference in educational methods. He writes: "The philosophy of the Greeks and the Arabs is still studied in the country of the Persians, whereas few look into it in the Arab countries such as Egypt and Syria" (*Tārīkh*, I, 79; see also p. 39).

[15] *Ibid.*, p. 25. [16] *Ibid.*, p. 26.

Egypt.[17] Al-Afghānī's own mystical sympathies enabled him to win the confidence of his disciple and to rouse him eventually out of that lethargy which mysticism tended to generate in weaker spirits. His biographer and disciple, M. Rashīd Riḍā, has noted, however, the role which his first *Ṣūfī* mentor, Shaykh Darwīsh, had played in the final process of urging him to embark on a public career of active service, to which *Ṣūfism* had only been the prelude.[18]

In his public teaching M. 'Abdu soon came into conflict with reactionary theologians, who accused him of straying too far from tradition. His courses at al-Azhar drew large bodies of students, but the philosophical, ethical, and even theological subjects he broached aroused the suspicions of the conservative *Ulema* of that ancient institution. His approach to these subjects was not always purely academic or scholastic. Thus, in his lectures on the *Muqaddimah* of Ibn Khaldūn, he applied that famous historiographer's analysis to the Egyptian situation and infused in his disciples a new spirit of independence and free thought.

The checkered public career of this remarkable and versatile thinker does not concern us here except incidentally. From the editorship of the *Official Gazette*, to membership of the education council, from the executive council of al-Azhar to the office of Grand Mufti of Egypt, he was able to play a prominent role in the intellectual and religious awakening of Egypt. The two most important episodes in his life on the intellectual level were the joint editorship of *al-'Urwah al-Wuthqā* in 1884 and the assumption in the following year of a teaching post at the Sulṭāniyah school in Beirut. His lectures at this school covered the traditional linguistic and juridical subjects, but in addition he taught the long-forgotten subjects of philosophy, logic, and scholastic theology (*Kalām*).[19]

His lectures in theology at Beirut formed the substance of his most systematic work, *Risalāt al-Tauḥīd*, which represents an important link in that long chain of scholastic treatises which the Mu'tazilite doctors had initiated in the eighth century. This treatise starts off with the definition of theology or the "science of unity" as the study of God's existence, His unity, His attributes, and the nature of prophetic

[17] Riḍā, *Tarīkh*, I, 38, 74, 79. [18] *Ibid.*, pp. 107 f., 133. [19] *Ibid.*, p. 394.

revelation. Prior to the rise of Islam, he observes, theology was not unknown; however, the methods of demonstration used by pre-Islamic theologians tended to be of a supernatural or preternatural type, such as appeal to miracles, rhetorical disquisitions, or legend. The Koran changed all this. It revealed in an inimitable way what "God had permitted or prescribed the knowledge of . . . but did not stipulate its acceptance simply on the ground of revelation, but advanced proof and demonstration, expounded the views of disbelievers, and inveighed against them rationally."[20] In short it declared reason to be the ultimate arbiter of truth and established its moral commandments on sound rational grounds. Thus "reason and religion marched in unison for the first time in that sacred book revealed by God to a prophet commissioned by Him."[21] Muslims consequently realized that reason was indispensable for the reception of such articles of faith as God's existence, His commissioning of prophets, as well as the comprehension of the subject matter of revelation and compliance with it. They also realized that, although some of these articles may exceed the power of reason, they do not contradict it.

In due course, political divisions at first and theological differences subsequently began to split the ranks of Islam. The theological controversies were sparked by Wāṣil's revolt against Ḥasan al-Baṣrī and the consequent rise of the Mu'tazilite school. Eventually al-Ash'arī was able to effect a compromise between the extreme rationalism of the Mu'tazilah and the conservatism of their opponents and thereby became the champion of orthodoxy.[22]

The philosophers who soon appeared on the scene were primarily interested in rational knowledge. The religious received them at first with open arms, since their rational methods conformed to the rationalism prescribed by the Koran. However, their position was subsequently compromised on two grounds: (1) their extravagent adulation of the Greek philosophers, especially Plato and Aristotle, and their tendency to follow them uncritically; and (2) their involvement in the theological squabbles of the times, which exposed them to the wrath of the masses.

In due course al-Ghazālī engaged in a wholesale attack on the

[20] *Risālat al-Tauḥīd*, p. 24. [21] *Ibid.*, p. 25. [22] *Ibid.*, p. 36.

philosophers which exceeded the bounds of moderation. The animosities between the different religious and intellectual groups was later intensified by politicians, who added further to the general confusion. Eventually, ignorance and obscurantism became widespread, and the disjunction between religion and science, which the Koran had overcome, reappeared once more.[23]

This historical survey of the rise and fall of rationalism in Islam is interesting for its somewhat a priori character and the great vogue it subsequently achieved in modernist circles. Although the factual foundation upon which it rests may be questioned, M. ʻAbdu goes on to apply it to the fundamental tenets of Islamic belief. Thus the core of Islam, according to him, is belief in God's unity as established by reason and supported by revelation. The blind acceptance (*taqlīd*) of any precept or dogma is incompatible with the express teaching of the Koran, which had enjoined reflection upon the wonders of Creation and admonished believers against the uncritical acceptance of the beliefs of their forebears.

The Scholastic core of *Risālat al-Tauḥīd* follows familiar post-Avicennian lines. After a preliminary discussion of the concepts of necessary, possible, and impossible, he turns to the discussion of the Necessary Being. This being is characterized *ex hypothesi*, according to him, by eternity, indestructibility, simplicity, and incorporeity. His "existential" attributes include all the "perfections of being," such as life, knowledge, will, and the ability to impart or communicate those perfections to other beings.[24] The wonderful harmony and order in the universe further confirm His supreme knowledge and wisdom. This knowledge is free from all the imperfections to which finite knowers are subject, such as dependence on instruments or movement. Will belongs to Him as a corollary of His knowledge, since what is produced by Him is produced according to the dictates of His knowledge and in conformity with it. But the concept of the divine will excludes the popular concept according to which God is free to act or not to act, since the latter is incompatible with the immutability of His knowledge and will.[25]

Another group of attributes predicated of God by the Koran, such

[23] *Risālat al-Tauḥīd*, p. 40. [24] *Ibid.*, p. 56. [25] *Ibid.*, pp. 64, 66.

as speech, hearing, and sight, cannot be established through unaided reason, but is not on that account incompatible with reason.[26]

An interesting point made in connection with the scope of human knowledge illustrates M. ʿAbdu's hesitation between the rationalism of the Muʿtazilah and the philosophers and the Traditionism of the "pious forebears" (*al-salaf al-ṣāliḥ*), with whose stand the *Salafī* movement which he founded is identified. Like al-Ghazālī, he quotes a dubious tradition in which the Prophet commands the Faithful: "Reflect upon God's Creation, but not upon His nature, or else you will perish," in support of an agnosticism which is ill-suited to his much-vaunted rationalism. The proper object of reason, he argues, is the accidental aspects of things upon which its light comes to bear. From such accidental aspects, it can proceed to the discovery of their underlying causes, the species to which they belong, and the rules which govern them. Beyond this, however, reason cannot go. Thus the knowledge of the genuine essences of things is beyond its grasp and the simple components from which they are made up entirely incomprehensible to it.[27] The reason for this, according to him, is that the knowledge of the essences of things does not enter into the divine economy of salvation or the human economy of utility or pleasure. Such an economy prescribes that man should concern himself with what is proportionate to his powers and not what lies beyond them. For instance, it is enough that he should know that he has a Soul, but whether it is an accident or a substance, whether it is separate from body or not, are entirely fruitless questions. Similarly, it is enough that he should know that God is a Being who does not resemble any other being, that He is eternal, living, knowing, etc., but whether these attributes are other than His essence and whether His speech is other than the content of sacred Scripture, are equally fruitless questions. The philosophers or theologians who occupied themselves with such inquiries have been victims of presumption or frivolity.[28]

Other controversies which set the Muslim sects against one another have centered around the questions of responsibility and reward, free will and predestination, etc. With regard to the latter question, some (the Muʿtazilah) have argued that God must take account of the welfare

[26] *Risālat al-Tauḥīd*, p. 72. [27] *Ibid.*, p. 75. [28] *Ibid.*, pp. 78 f.

of His servants in whatever He does, whereas others (the Ash'arites and Ḥanbalites) have declared His actions entirely free from any determination. The former err in reducing God to the status of a servant who is subject to the dictates of his master. The latter have reduced Him to a capricious despot who acts arbitrarily and irresponsibly. Both sects agree, however, that His actions must manifest His wisdom and that irresponsibility or falsehood cannot be predicated of Him because of the perfection of His knowledge and His will. The differences between them are often purely semantic. In applying the categories of necessity to God, the former are guilty of impertinence. In applying caprice to Him, the latter are guilty of folly.[29]

The problem of free will has generated the same endless disputes. Common sense shows clearly, however, that a rational agent is conscious of his actions and consequently determines them. When his designs are frustrated or thwarted by forces beyond his control, reflection leads him to posit a transcendent power which superintends or disposes events in this world. And yet to deny that man has no part in the actions he performs consciously is to deny the whole concept of obligation, which is the basis of all religion. The whole difficulty turns on the relation of the providence of the Almighty to free choice (*ikhtiyār*) as a predicate of a rational agent. Its solution is part of that mystery of free will and predestination (*al-qadar*) which we have been admonished not to delve into.[30]

Free choice presupposes necessarily the distinction between good and evil. This distinction is analogous to the distinction between the beautiful and the ugly, the pleasant and the unpleasant, the useful and the harmful. All these categories, M. 'Abdu argues, are known intuitively and their objects form part of the general stock of facts in the universe. Only the ignorant or the foolish will deny that they are self-evident.[31]

Owing to the diversity of their intellectual aptitudes, men differ in their ability to know God, the nature of the other life, or the means to happiness in this life and the next. Hence the human mind stands in need of a helper to assist it in the knowledge of the virtuous actions

[29] *Risālat al-Tauḥīd*, pp. 84 f. [30] *Ibid.*, p. 91. [31] *Ibid.*, p. 103.

and the right beliefs upon which its felicity ultimately depends. This helper is the prophet.[32]

Much of *Risālat al-Tauḥīd* is taken up with the question of prophethood or revelation, which formed an integral part of scholastic treatises of this kind from the time of al-Bāqillānī. M. ʻAbdu asserts here the necessity of prophethood, the superiority of prophetic truth, and the role of miracle in supporting the claims of the divinely commissioned prophets. The view of miracle and its probative force which he expounds follows familiar traditional lines. He is emphatic, however, in stating that the miraculous is not synonymous with the irrational but rather the preterrational. And since it serves a higher religious purpose, miracle is radically different from sorcery or magic.

The primary function of revelation is moral edification. It is a mistake therefore to seek in Scripture (the Koran) answers to scientific or historical questions, as some apologists tended to do in recent times. Thus the geographical, historical, and astronomical references in the Koran are not instances of scientific discourse, but of moral or religious instruction only. The reader of the Koran is continually exhorted to consider the wonders of Creation in so far as they exhibit the wisdom of its Author and to work toward acquiring profitable knowledge.

Islam, as the final and consummate revelation to Muḥammad, the "seal of the prophets," has recognized better than any other religion the dual character of man as a citizen of two realms, the spiritual and the temporal, and his duty to submit to no authority other than God or accept any truth not substantiated by reason. In this way, Islam has liberated its followers from the bondage of political and ecclesiastical authority and recognized their right to shape their lives according to their best lights. In addition, it recognized their right to enjoy the good things of life, provided this is done in moderation. In some cases this enjoyment is a divine reward for their uprightness, in other cases a token of their personal liberty. The universality of Islam is such that it has left no fundamental order, spiritual, moral, or intellectual, for which it has not legislated.[33]

We need not consider here the extensive "publicist" activity of M. ʻAbdu. The essential components of his modernist theology are all

[32] *Risālat al-Tauḥīd*, p. 111. [33] *Ibid.*, p. 238.

contained in this treatise of scholastic theology, which makes up in vividness for what it lacks in systematic completeness. We cannot omit, however, the mention of his most heated confrontation with G. Hanotaux, the French Foreign Minister at that time, who raised what he labeled "the question of Islam,"[34] i.e., the problem of the capacity of Islam to cope with the stresses and strains of modern civilization—a problem which, more than half a century after, continues to exercise Muslim intellectuals today.

Against the strictures of Hanotaux and other European critics of Islam, M. 'Abdu like al-Afghānī before him employs the classic retort of modern apologists of Islam: the necessity to draw a clear line of demarcation between Islam and the Muslims, between the systems of beliefs and practices which was the signal of the awakening of mankind in the seventh century, and the subsequent political and military upheavals which destroyed the political and religious unity of the Muslim peoples. Foreign elements who had infiltrated the caliphate were responsible during the 'Abbāsid period for corroding this unity from within. The present decadence of Islam is only a phase in a long cycle of events which began with the rise of Islam and culminated a century later in an era of splendor unmatched in the history of man. At a time when Europe was wrapped in total darkness, the East shone with the light of tolerance and rationalism, which was to spread in due course across the Iberian peninsula into Western Europe.[35]

He counters the charge that Islam has, owing to the fatalism it fostered, impeded the progress of the Muslim peoples by noting, in the first instance, that fatalism in its various forms is not an exclusively Islamic doctrine. In the second instance, the Koran has affirmed free choice and "acquisition" (*al-kasb*) in approximately sixty-four verses, while underscoring the all-pervasive sway of divine providence. Similarly Muḥammad and his successors rejected the implications of fatalism and condemned the lethargy it was prone to generate. Eventually, however, the infiltration of Islam by foreign elements, coupled

[34] In the *Journal de Paris* (1900), under the rubic "Face to Face with Islam and the Muslim Question" (see Adams, *Islam and Modernism*, p. 86, and Riḍā, *Tārīkh*, I, 789 f.

[35] *Al-Islām Dīn al-'Ilm wa'l-Madaniyah*, pp. 53 f., 60 f., 138 f.

with the diffusion of the order of dervishes, deluded the masses into supposing that fatalism was of the essence of religion.[36]

Another issue raised by Hanotaux was that the disassociation in Christianity between the spiritual and the temporal orders, between what is God's and what is Caesar's, had left the door wide open for the progress of the European peoples, whereas their necessary correlation in Islam led to the immobility of the Islamic peoples.[37] M. 'Abdu's retort became the standard one of Muslim apologists ever since. Its substance is the reassertion of the organic unity of the Islamic world-view and the claim that this unity is the mark of the superiority of Islam, which does not recognize the arbitrary disjunction between the spiritual and the temporal. As the "religion of nature" (*dīn al-fiṭra*), its motto is not to give to Caesar what is Caesar's and to God what is God's, but rather to subordinate Caesar to God and to hold him accountable for both his deeds and misdeeds.[38] Unlike Christianity, Islam does not command its followers to cut themselves off from the world or to give up worldly pleasures completely. Instead, it has prescribed that "the soundness of body is prior to the soundness of religion," and has permitted the enjoyment of the good things of life such as food, drink, adornment, sex, and property, provided it is done in moderation and in conformity with the precepts of the Koran.[39]

M. 'Abdu's most important disciple and successor was M. Rashīd Riḍā (d. 1935). Born and educated in Tripoli, Lebanon, he emigrated to Egypt in 1897 with the express purpose of studying under M. 'Abdu. Although he was inclined originally to *Ṣūfism*, the reading of *al-'Urwah al-Wuthqā* fired him with an intense zeal for the reform and rejuvenation of Islam which al-Afghānī and M. 'Abdu had set as the only task worthy of a true Muslim in modern times. His activity as a publicist found expression in *al-Manār*, a journal dedicated to the preaching of Islam and the vindication of its perennial character, which he founded in 1898.[40] This periodical may be regarded as the successor to *al-'Urwah*, discontinued at the end of its first year of publication. Like *al-'Urwah*, *al-Manār* was dedicated to the cause of

[36] *Al-Islām Din al-'Ilm wa'l-Madaniyah*, pp. 59 f. [37] *Ibid.*, pp. 40 f.
[38] *Ibid.*, p. 77. [39] *Ibid.*, pp. 111 f. [40] Adams, *Islam and Modernism*, p. 180.

pan-Islamic union and the creation of a pan-Islamic empire, with the Ottoman Sultan at its head.[41] The cornerstone of the reform program of *al-Manār* was the assertion of the finality of the Islamic system of beliefs and the necessity of returning to the straight path of the "good forebears" (*al-salaf al-ṣāliḥ*), who were guided by the light of the Koran and the Traditions prior to the dissemination of heresy and strife.

This "fundamentalist" interpretation of Islam contained hardly any elements which had not been introduced or expressed either by Ibn Taymiyah in the fourteenth century or by al-Afghānī and M. 'Abdu in the nineteenth. It was at best a restatement of the same Neo-Ḥanbalite exhortation to return to the orthodox ways of *al-salaf*, phrased in terms more suited to the political and cultural conditions of the Muslim peoples at the turn of the century, and which continues to echo in contemporary intellectual circles in Egypt and the rest of the Muslim world.

II

MODERNISM IN INDIA: SAYYID AḤMAD KHĀN, AMEER ALI, AND MUḤAMMAD IQBĀL

THE first important modernist in the history of Indian Islam was Sayyid Aḥmad Khān of Bahadur. Born in 1817 at Delhi, he received the conservative religious education of well-to-do Muslims and wrote theological and historical treatises which reflected the Traditionist sympathies of the Wahhābīs.[42] After the Mutiny of 1857 he worked actively for an Anglo-Muslim *rapprochement* and developed a syncretic brand of Islam which did not differ radically from Christianity. For him, the essential similarity of the two faiths was reducible to a natural

[41] Adams, *Islam and Modernism*, p. 183.

[42] Wilfred C. Smith, *Modern Islam in India*, p. 16.

morality from which the supernatural element had been expunged and which was the occasion of al-Afghānī's *Refutation of the Naturalists*, as we have seen. After a brief visit to England in 1870, Aḥmad Khān's enthusiasm for Western (British) culture reached extravagant proportions, and upon his return to India he started the publication of an Urdu journal entitled *Tahzīb al-Akhlāq* (*Cultivation of Morals*) and an Urdu commentary of the Koran conceived in entirely modern, rationalist terms. He also founded in 1875 the Muḥammadan Anglo-Oriental College, which later grew into the University of Aligarh.

The test of religious truth, according to Aḥmad Khān, is conformity with the norms of natural reason. Hence, in his interpretation of the Koran, miraculous or extraordinary episodes are interpreted in a manner which conformed with those norms, in other words, naturalistically. Other sources of religious belief or practice, such as the Traditions and *Ijmā'*, were rejected, and the koranic text, especially the Meccan *sūrahs*, became the basis of a morality and spirituality in complete conformity with reason and nature (hence the name *nechari* [i.e., naturalist] for this movement). According to him, whatever beliefs and practices can be shown to be incompatible with this morality were to be disavowed, such as warfare, slavery, and the subjugation of women.[43]

The liberalism of Aḥmad Khān had other champions in India. Of those, Sayyid Ameer Ali (d. 1928) is perhaps the most noteworthy during the three decades following his death. Essentially in sympathy with Aḥmad Khān's liberal views, Ameer Ali goes a step further in his apology for Islam. His veneration for the Prophet of Islam, who is set up as the paragon of moral and spiritual excellence, is far more pronounced. Rather than show the compatibility of Islam and modern liberalism, Ameer Ali argues that the spirit of Islam is reducible to those very ideas which make up the core of liberalism. As many another Muslim intellectual, such as Rashīd Riḍā, have contended, the novelty of modern liberalism is an illusion; Western Christendom and Western science have a solid basis in Islamic teaching.[44]

As might be surmised, Ameer Ali's sense of history was much more acute than Aḥmad Khān's and his grasp of the historical dimension of

[43] Wilfred C. Smith, *Modern Islam in India*, pp. 20 f.
[44] Ali, *The Spirit of Islam*, pp. 371 f.

Islam as a religion much firmer. This is illustrated in the extensive allusions he makes to the history of Islamic literature, philosophy, and science, and his well-known *Short History of the Saracens*, first published in 1899. The darker periods in Muslim history are not ignored but are explained away as natural consequences of the corruption or decadence to which every culture has been prone. The fault in such cases, as M. ʿAbdu and al-Afghānī have also argued, is not to be laid at the doorstep of Islam, but rather that of the Muslim peoples, who either misunderstood their religion or fell short of the ideals it set. Obsession with history, he warns, should not serve, however, as a bar to progress, but as a spur to infinite progress through the exploitation of the judicial methods of independent judgment (*ijtihād*) which had been the glories of early Islam.[45]

Ameer Ali was much less tolerant of other religions, such as Buddhism, Hinduism, and Christianity, than was Aḥmad Khān. His estimate of Buddhism and Hinduism borders on contempt, Christianity, of which he sometimes speaks with sympathy, does not escape his criticism or derision. On the whole, he reiterates uncritically the classic Islamic thesis that the historical Christianity which Muḥammad came into contact with in the seventh century was a corrupted Christianity that had been corroded by centuries of political and doctrinal strife. He attributes the spectacular success of Islam in the seventh century to the general decadence and depravity into which the world had been plunged by Christianity and from which Islam was to rescue it.[46] Even today, despite the vicissitudes of time and the erosion of centuries of strife, the purity of Islam remains for him untarnished, by virtue of a certain immunity to corruption which none of the other religions has enjoyed. His conception of historical Islam, therefore, despite his vast erudition, remains essentially romantic.

The romantic liberalism of Ameer Ali is one of the earliest expressions of a general spirit of apology which permeates intellectual circles in Islam today, from India and Pakistan to Egypt and Morocco. With more eloquence and scholarship than many of his contemporaries or his successors, he has stressed the enduring spiritual and ethical values

[45] Ali, *The Spirit of Islam*, pp. 183 f.; cf. Wilfred C. Smith, *Modern Islam in India*, pp. 51 f.
[46] *The Spirit of Islam*, pp. xlv ff. and 143 f.

which have made of Islam, according to him, "a religion of right-doing, right-thinking, and right-speaking, founded on divine love, universal charity, and the equality of man in the sight of the Lord."[47] In short, it is a religion "in complete accord with progressive tendencies" and a dynamic agent of civilization.[48]

Despite his importance as an apologist for Islam, Ameer Ali remains dependent in his interpretation of Islam on historical scholarship. The most significant, if not the only, attempt to interpret Islam in modern philosophical terms is that of another important Indian thinker, Muḥammad Iqbāl (d. 1938), a poet of profound sensibility and a scholar of vast philosophical culture. Rather than draw on history, in his attempt to restate the Islamic world-view in modern terms, as Ameer Ali had done, he draws upon the philosophical heritage of the West without reservation. His aim, it is true, is not to demonstrate the validity of the Western outlook, but rather its essential conformity with the koranic *Weltanschauung*. Thus the synthesis he attempts in his *Reconstruction of Religious Thought in Islam* may be compared in its magnitude to the synthesis attempted a millennium earlier by al-Ghazālī in his *Revival of the Religious Sciences* (*al-Iḥyā'*). In substance it is more analogous, however, to the syntheses attempted by al-Kindī and Ibn Rushd, who set out to harmonize the philosophical world-view of the Greeks and the religious world-view of Islam. The fundamental difference between them is that, whereas the philosophical categories employed by al-Kindī and Ibn Rushd were drawn from Plato, Aristotle, and Plotinus, those employed by Iqbāl are drawn from those of Hegel, Whitehead, and Bergson. The masters have changed, but the problem remains essentially the same, namely, the attempt to bridge the gulf between speculative thought and religion.

Born in Sialkūt in the Punjab in 1878, Iqbāl received his early education in Sialkūt and Lahore. In 1905 he went to England and Germany, where he pursued his philosophical studies; he returned to India three years later to practice law. As Wilfrid C. Smith has put it, three things impressed him most about Europe: the vitality and dynamism of European life, the immense possibilities open to man, and the dehumanizing influence that capitalist society had on the European

[47] Ali, *The Spirit of Islam*, p. 178. [48] *Ibid.*, p. 180.

soul.[49] The last circumstance strengthened his faith in the superiority of Islam as a moral and spiritual ideal, and he consequently dedicated himself to the defense and development of this ideal. The six lectures on the *Reconstruction of Religious Thought in Islam* that he delivered in Madras in 1928–1929 were his major contribution to the task of reawakening his coreligionists in India and to the rethinking of Islam in modern, dynamic categories, derived primarily from nineteenth- and twentieth-century European thought.

Iqbāl's concept of religion is that of a complex, partly rational, partly ethical, and partly spiritual experience. Religion, he writes, "is neither mere thought nor mere feeling, nor mere action; it is an expression of the whole man."[50] Hence it is not in opposition to philosophy, but is rather an important feature of that total experience of reality upon which philosophy must reflect. This is clearly borne out by the central position which the Koran assigns to knowledge and reflection. Historically, it was the Ash'arite theologians who exploited to the full the dialectical processes of Greek thought in the defense and the definition of orthodoxy.[51] The Mu'tazilah and Ibn Rushd went too far in their reliance on reason, and consequently they failed to recognize that in the domain of scientific and religious knowledge disassociation from "concrete experience" is a fatal error. Al-Ghazālī, on the other hand, jeopardized the structure of religion by basing it upon the precarious foundation of philosophical skepticism, rooted in the contention that finite thought cannot apprehend the Infinite.

If thought, so narrowly conceived, is unable to apprehend the Infinite, it is because (1) it mistakes the nature of this Infinite as an immanent reality of whose several manifestations the multitude of finite concepts are no more than particular moments or phases, and (2) it misconceives the dynamic character of thought as it unfolds itself in time through a "series of definite specifications," whose embodiment is designated by the Koran as the "Preserved Tablet."

The concept of the concrete world embodied in the Koran is essentially one of a created reality in which the actual and the ideal merge and intertwine and which exhibits a distinct rational pattern. But it is not,

[49] Smith, *Modern Islam in India*, p. 102.

[50] *Reconstruction of Religious Thought in Islam*, p. 2.

[51] *Ibid.*, pp. 4 f.

for that reason, a "block universe" or finished product, which God has completed, but rather a universe that continually realizes itself across the vast expanses of space and time. Man, as the most dynamic force in this universe, is the principal agent, or coworker with God, in the process of realizing the infinite potentialities of reality.[52]

It is in religious experience that man apprehends the complex aspect of this dynamic reality which is in the process of continual unfolding. This experience has an outward or empirical character as well as an inward or mystical one. The test of its genuineness is not exclusively pragmatic; it is philosophical or speculative as well, since such an experience is not without cognitive content. After criticizing the three traditional arguments for the existence of God, on the ground that either they demonstrate the existence of a Being, who though supposedly infinite is really finite, or on the ground that they presuppose an unbridgeable gulf between being and thought, which renders the process of proof entirely futile, Iqbāl asserts the unity of thought and being; and upon this as a premise he proceeds to demonstrate the existence of God. The clue to his demonstration is provided by the koranic conception of God as "the First and the Last, the Visible and the Invisible."[53] But instead of exploiting this clue directly, Iqbāl follows a circuitous philosophical path leading through Berkeley to Whitehead, Russell, Einstein, and Bergson. What all those philosophers deny, according to him, is the "hypothesis of pure materiality" rendered untenable by recent developments in relativity physics and the metaphysical concepts of process and creative evolution.

None of those concepts, however, is accepted by Iqbāl without reservation. Thus the creative evolution of Bergson is open to the charge that it rejects teleology, which it mistakenly identifies with rigid determinism. Teleology, however, need not be conceived as closed. In the Koran, for instance, the universe is conceived as being liable to continuous development, but the pattern of this development is not fixed or static. "To my mind," he writes, "nothing is more alien to the Quranic outlook than the idea that the universe is the temporal working out of a preconceived plan."[54]

52 *Reconstruction of Religious Thought in Islam*, p. 11. 53 *Ibid.*, p. 30.
54 *Ibid.*, p. 52.

Bergson's concept of pure duration gives us, however, a "direct revelation of the ultimate nature of Reality" as a spiritual principle or ego continually realizing itself, not in serial time, but in the inward movement of dynamic growth or duration. The scene upon which the creative drama of God's boundless self-manifestation, or the uniform pattern of behavior appropriate to him as Absolute Ego, is enacted, is nature. Hence "nature is to the Divine Self what character is to the human self."[55] Not only Bergson, but Goethe also, has given expression to the same dynamic concept of the unceasing realization of God's creative possibilities.

Apart from modern scientific and philosophical theories, Iqbāl finds parallels for this dynamic concept of God as Creative Will or Energy in the atomistic occasionalism of Ash'arite theology. For the Ash'arite, the world is not a fixed system of substantial entities, similar to Aristotle's, but rather a stream of continually created atoms, conjoined to a stream of positive or negative accidents upon which the nature of created entities in the world depends.[56]

To insure its conformity with the spirit of Islam, Iqbāl reinterprets the atomism of the Ash'arites in terms of a "monadology" or spiritual pluralism, in which every particle or element of reality is spiritual, i.e., an ego or a self. The higher the selfhood or consciousness, the greater the reality of the entity in question and the closer it is to God. The Ash'arite concept of the self (*al-nafs*) as an accident is rejected as inadequate, and in its stead is upheld the concept of a spiritual ego as a simple, indivisible, and immutable soul substance, serving as the center of man's mental states or emotions. The chief exponent of this view in Islam, according to him, is al-Ghazālī. In this view the artificial dualism of soul and body is overcome and the finite ego is shown to be an aspect of an Ultimate Ego immanent in nature and referred to by the Koran as "the First and the Last, the Visible and the Invisible."[57] The great mystics, al-Ḥallāj, al-Basṭāmī, and Rūmī, gave graphic expression to this truth in their extravagant utterances identifying their finite egoes with the Infinite Ego.[58]

[55] *Reconstruction of Religious Thought in Islam*, p. 54.

[56] *Ibid.*, pp. 66 f.; cf. *supra*, pp. 242 f.

[57] *Ibid.*, pp. 67, 95 f.

[58] *Ibid.*, p. 104; cf. *supra*, p. 273.

In Iqbāl's opinion, Muslim thought had, in its reaction against Greek philosophy, reasserted the koranic sense of the concreteness of reality, both in its empirical and spiritual aspects. In this sense, the birth of Islam marks the birth of the "inductive intellect," which made possible the rise of a scientific culture of the modern type. The reactions of numerous theologians, such as Ibn Ḥazm and Ibn Taymiyah, against Aristotelian logic set the stage for the rise of the inductive logic of J. S. Mill and the empiricism of modern scientific thought. Roger Bacon is generally credited by European historians with the introduction of the new spirit of scientific inquiry, but "where did Roger Bacon receive his scientific training?" Iqbāl asks. "In the Muslim universities of Spain," he hastens to reply.[59] This proves conclusively, according to him, that the contention that Greek philosophy determined the character of Muslim culture is entirely unfounded. For, whereas Greek thought was primarily interested in abstractions, Muslim thought turns primarily on the concrete; and, whereas the ideal of Greek thought was proportion, that of Muslim culture in its speculative and mystical aspects was the possession and enjoyment of the Infinite.[60]

We will not dwell much longer on Iqbāl's general characterization of Muslim culture and the Islamic concept of reality. Very often he reads into classic Islamic themes purely Hegelian or Bergsonian concepts. The relationship between such concepts and the koranic verses cited in their support is often very tenuous. Like other liberal interpreters of the Koran, particularly in India, the chief fault of his exegetical method lies in its disregard for the contextual character of koranic revelation, of what the commentators normally refer to as *asbāb al-nuzūl'*, the historical circumstances in which the revelation was made.

Be this as it may, the reader of Iqbāl's *Reconstruction of Religious Thought in Islam* is overwhelmed with the vastness of his learning and the scope of his metaphysical and religious speculation. His versatility and eclecticism, however, are often exasperating. For one thing, he often rambles from one theme to another and provides only the most

[59] *Reconstruction of Religious Thought in Islam*, p. 123. He quotes as his authority Briffault, *The Making of Humanity*.

[60] *Ibid.*, p. 125.

tenuous links. For another, he frequently invokes the authority of illustrious philosophers and scientists in support of his own major themes, only to turn on them later and show their inadequacy or incoherence. Very often the multiplication of authorities, ancient or modern, Western or Islamic, is done at such a pace that the reader is left breathless. In the scope of six pages, for instance, the following names are cited: Berkeley, Whitehead, Einstein, Russell, Zeno, Newton, al-Ash'arī, Ibn Ḥazm, Bergson, Cantor, and Ouspensky—to mention only the principal figures or authorities.[61]

Despite these shortcomings, it cannot be denied that, better than any other twentieth-century thinker, Iqbāl has made an impressive and conscientious attempt to rethink the basic problems of Islam in modern categories. It need not surprise us that in the process he tended to lose sight of the premises of this rethinking and has unwittingly turned over to a strange assortment of modern philosophers and scientists, from Berkeley to Einstein, the task of interpreting the Koran. Almost all Islamic modernists and liberals have committed the unforgivable sin of ignoring and underrating the historical dimension of Islam. Very often in their appeal to the authority of the Koran in support of theological or metaphysical claims of which the ancients never dreamed, they quite naturally draw on the hidden meaning of koranic passages. The *Ṣūfīs*, the Isma'īlīs, and many others were particularly skilled at this art, but traditional Islam has always frowned upon this unorthodox procedure. Today this art can be practiced in the name of rationalism or progress only in moderation; otherwise it threatens to destroy the very foundations of the cult and replace it with the fantasies of dreamers or visionaries.

Finally, by wedding the Islamic or koranic view of man and the world to the current phase of scientific development, as Iqbāl particularly has done, the modernists make their second most dangerous error, since they stake the religious truth of Islam on the doubtful truth of a scientific phase. And if there is anything the history of scientific discovery teaches us, it is the ephemeral character of such scientific phases, whether associated with the venerable names of Aristotle or Ptolemy or modern pioneers such as Newton, Eddington, or Einstein.

[61] *Reconstruction of Religious Thought in Islam*, pp. 31–37.

III

THE PHILOSOPHICAL SCENE TODAY

AL-AFGHĀNĪ, M. ʿAbdu, Ameer Ali, and M. Iqbāl, each in his own way, addressed himself to the problem of modernism and isolated the elements in the Islamic view of life in a progressive age dominated by Western categories of thought. Although each had received the impact of Western ideas, there remained at the basis of their modernist outlook an element of mistrust of Western culture and a sense of the superiority of the Islamic view of life.

All modernist thought in the last three decades has been dominated by the same anti-Western spirit. In many cases, the new generation of modernists has proved more radical, if less erudite. On the whole, it continues the same lines of speculation initiated by these pioneers and develops the same grand themes outlined in their more creative writings.

It would be pointless to list here all or even most of the contemporary thinkers who have simply popularized themes developed by the more original thinkers previously discussed. Sayyid Quṭb and Muḥammad al-Bahī illustrate the more militant current of anti-Western polemic in the Arab Near East today. In his recent work *Islam and the Problems of Civilization* (1963), S. Quṭb starts from the premise that Western civilization has completely failed to solve the problems of modern man chiefly because of its commitment to the hollow, spiritual ideal of life preached by Christianity. Only Islam with its global and concrete view of life, in its double spiritual and temporal aspects, is capable of ensuring the salvation of contemporary man. For Islam, the artificial disjunction between the religious and practical dimensions of life does not arise. Even the antithesis between science and religion which has been a feature of Western culture is unknown to Islam. As both Ameer Ali and Iqbāl have argued, Islam has been at peace with science and was in fact directly responsible for the growth of the scientific spirit in the Middle Ages. But the evils which have resulted from the abuse of that spirit in modern times, in industry, in technology, in economics, and in biology are not the responsibility of Islam.

M. al-Bahī's polemic in his *Islamic Thought and its Relation to Western Imperialism* (1957) is even more militant and is leveled not only at the Western enemies of Islam, but at the Muslim advocates of liberalism and modernism as well, from Iqbāl to Ṭāha Ḥusain, who are accused of having been servile disciples of the West. The former applied Western philosophical categories to the interpretation of Islam, and the latter subjected the study of pre-Islamic poetry (in 1926) to the critical methods of Western scholarship and destroyed thereby the whole literary and theological fabric of Muslim thought. On a different level, the secularists from ʿAlī ʿAbd al-Rāziq to Khālid M. Khālid are reproached for having distorted or misrepresented the nature of Islam, which, as has often been explained, recognizes no distinction between the spiritual and temporal dimensions of life. Their secularism is ultimately inspired, according to him, by Western or Christian concepts.

A more moderate and thoughtful exponent of the modernist thesis is the late Egyptian critic and essayist who achieved, up to his death in 1965, a very high standing in literary and intellectual circles, namely, ʿAbbās Maḥmūd al-ʿAqqād. In a series of important theological works that span a quarter of a century, this author has addressed himself to some of the most crucial theological questions facing Muslim intellectuals today. In a comparatively early work, *The Genius of Muḥammad* (1943), he undertakes the defense of the Prophet of Islam against attack or criticism and displays his nearly superhuman genius in the military, political, scientific, moral, and religious fields. He also undertakes to give an historical analysis of the religious, political, and cultural context in which Islam arose in the seventh century, redeeming humanity from all the ills which corruption and obscurantism had inflicted upon it and which had rendered its rise a necessary part of the divine economy of salvation, as Ameer Ali had also argued.

Part of al-ʿAqqād's criticism is aimed at those rationalists or agnostics who regard religious faith as either superfluous or illusory. The two principal arguments advanced against the validity of such faith are, according to him, the incompatibility of evil in the world with the existence of a just and omnipotent God, on the one hand, and the superstitious character of many religious dogmas which cannot be justified on the basis either of sense experience or rational argument, on the other.

In refuting the argument from the reality of evil in the world, al-'Aqqād shows considerable perspicacity. The existence of evil in a created universe is logically necessary, since it is not possible for a perfect being to create his own equal in perfection. Consequently, a certain imperfection is inseparable from a finite creation, and it is with this imperfection that the evil we observe in the world is ultimately bound up. That God could refrain from creating such an imperfect world altogether, while remaining an all-powerful Being, involves a logical absurdity; for power denotes precisely this ability to bring what is possible into being.[62] Nor is the reduction of all religious belief to superstition justified, for the critics of religious belief are not able to unravel all the mysteries of creation or to produce a substitute for religion which could fulfill the same cultural and moral function in the history of mankind which religion has fulfilled.

The primary role of religion is essentially to regulate the "relationship between the individual and the universe as a whole." "Its scope extends to everything which is, whether external or internal, public or private, past or future to an infinite extent."[63] From this it follows that the broader the scope of a religion and the nobler its dogmas and rituals, the higher it is on the scale of spiritual values. Thus, if we find a religion which introduces a cleavage between the corporeal and the spiritual, the heavenly and the terrestrial, then such a religion is inferior to one which conceives life as an undivided whole. This indeed is the token of the superiority of Islam over Christianity and heathenism.

A second group of contemporary Arab thinkers reflect current philosophical trends in the West. Of the exponents of existentialism, A. R. Badawī in Egypt and René Habachī in Lebanon are perhaps the most noteworthy. In *Existential Time* (1943) and *Studies in Existentialist Philosophy* (1961) Badawī examines the fundamental tenets of existentialism as interpreted particularly by Martin Heidegger. The essential feature of temporal existence, according to him, is existence or being-in-time (*Dasein*). The continuity attributed to being and its extension into past and future are an illusion born of man's desire to

[62] *Ḥaqā'iq al-Islām wa Abāṭīl Khuṣūmih*, p. 11. [63] *Ibid.*, p. 17.

curb the tyranny of time which destroys everything, i.e., his desire for survival. This continuity or permanence, however, is a property of essential being, that is, the bare possibility which is prior to existence only. Actual being is always temporal and contemporary, and everything else has no being at all. For "every being conceived outside time is an unreal being, generated by the illusory distractions of a deluded mind, endeavoring to force existing entities into its stereotyped molds. The source of this conception is man's wish to conquer his horror of time."[64]

This shows how close the relationship is between time and man's conception of it. To actual being-in-time there attaches a cosmic sense of anxiety from which man can never be freed. When he becomes aware of his condition in the world, he rebels against time, negates it, or runs away from it by seeking refuge in eternity as a type of timeless mode of being. All this, however, is to no avail, since it only results in the disorientation of man, his disparagement, and the raising of false hopes. It is much more fitting that man should accept the fact of his temporal being and face up to his destiny with a fortitude worthy of a free agent.

Another property of being-in-time is the conjunction in it of being and not-being, or the fact that not-being enters into its composition as an essential ingredient thereof. Thus actual being is the resultant tension of this reciprocity or antithesis between being and not-being. It follows that time is the cause of the essential conjunction of being and not-being and is in that sense the creator (*khāliq*).[65]

The logical consequences of this existentialist analysis are primarily the necessity of confining the scope of philosophical inquiry to concrete existence, understood both in the sense of human existence and that of the world of possible experience; and accordingly the denial of the validity of any speculation about any order of reality lying outside this world and man's place in it, i.e., the traditional theological or metaphysical subjects of God and the other life.

Other existentialists in the Arab Near East do not feel compelled to accept those anti-theistic and anti-metaphysical implications of existentialism. René Habachī, for instance, bases on analogous existentialist

[64] *Al-Zamān al-Wujūdī*, p. 251. [65] *Dirāsāt fi'l-Falsafah al-Wujūdiyah*, p. 237.

premises a "personalist" philosophy which looks upon not-being and death as an illusion and calls upon man to transcend the limits of finite personality and to engage in the search for a higher reality rooted in a "transcendent personality" to which man's existential experiences, especially his sense of inadequacy, dependence, and need for compassion, clearly point. Man's existence, it is true, is a temporal existence, not in the sense that time is an evil which ought to be overcome or that it is the only reality there is, but rather in the sense of personal commitment (or *engagement*). Hence the essence of existentialism is the recognition of the reality of the self as the center of man's whole experience and its progressive superseding in the direction of a higher experience. In this approach to reality, the philosopher must accept with gratitude whatever elements can contribute to his total comprehension of this reality, whether they derive from Greek, medieval, or modern thought.

What distinguishes this type of existentialism from other a-metaphysical or a-theological types is the reassertion of the validity of spiritual experience and the whole scale of supernatural and theological values. In this regard, "personalism" is able to elicit, better than any other existentialist system, a divine meaning or purpose immanent in history.[66]

Other contemporary Western philosophical currents have had their followers. The most articulate and erudite exponent of logical positivism and analysis in Arabic is Zakī Nagīb Maḥmūd of Egypt. In three important works, the *Myth of Metaphysics* (1953), *Positivist Logic* (1957), and *Towards a Scientific Philosophy* (1958), he has stated in eloquent terms the case for positivism in a cultural milieu which had not been roused from its traditionalist dogmatic slumber. Zakī Nagīb has described his own position as a frank invitation to philosophy to comply with the criteria of scientific truth, namely, to define its terms with precision and to conform to the accepted procedures of scientific methodology. The function of philosophy, however, should be clearly understood. It is not the description of the external world or the factual analysis of its content. Its proper objects are the symbolic forms and categories, mathematical and other, which the scientist

[66] Habachi, *Falsafah li Zamānina'l-Ḥāḍir*, p. 137.

applies to the objective world. With this as his material, the philosopher can analyze, interpret, or coordinate those forms and categories so as to ascertain the degree of their logical coherence. The exact connotation of terms or idioms is always a function of the empirical data which they designate. As soon as we pass beyond these data our statements are without empirical content and consequently utterly meaningless.[67]

Of the more traditional philosophers, we may mention one of the earliest authors to write in Arabic, between 1931 and 1949, a systematic narrative of Greek, medieval, and modern philosophy. Yūsuf Karam (d. 1959) was one of the leading pioneers in the field of systematic philosophical studies and acknowledged master of the younger generation of Arab philosophers. Shortly before he died he developed in two major works, *Reason and Being* (1956) and *Physics and Metaphysics* (1959), a theory of knowledge and an ontology that reflect the traditional outlook of Aristotelian-Thomist realism. The argument is conducted in both works against the background of empiricism and rationalism, which he dismisses as equally untenable. Unlike some of the contemporary philosophers mentioned above, Y. Karam's sense of history is very acute. He is willing to learn from pagan, Muslim and Christian philosophers and he emerges with a comprehensive and all-round world-view which sacrifices nothing. His method illustrates an important characteristic of contemporary Arabic thought—the urge to harmonize conflicting philosophical and theological trends, ancient, medieval, and modern. In this sense his outlook and method are analogous to those of the whole series of Arabic philosophers, from al-Kindī to Ibn Rushd and al-Shīrāzī, in whose thought theological and philosophical concerns have always coalesced. Accordingly, he stands out as the most typical product of the Arab Near Eastern intellectual tradition with its profound sense of history, its veneration for authority, and its utter inability to divorce philosophy from religion. It is fitting therefore that we should conclude a history of Islamic philosophy with this account of his thought.

[67] Nagīb, *Falsafah wa Fann*, p. 26.

BIBLIOGRAPHY

Al-ʻAbbāsī, A. R. *Maʻāhid al-Tanṣīṣ.* Cairo, 1947.

ʻAbdal-Rāziq, M. *Failasūf al-ʻArab wa'l-Muʻallim al-Thānī.* Cairo, 1945.

ʻAbdel-Kader, A. H. *The Life, Personality and Writings of al-Junayd.* London, 1962.

ʻAbdu, M. *Al-Islām Dīn al-ʻIlm wa'l-Madaniyah.* Cairo, 1964.

——— *Risālat al-Tauḥīd.* Cairo, 1963.

Abū Rīda, M. ʻA. H. *Rasā'il al-Kindī al-Falsafiyah.* Cairo, 1950, 1953.

Adams, Charles C. *Islam and Modernism in Egypt.* London, 1933.

Affifi, A. E. *The Mystical Philosophy of Ibnu'l-ʻArabī.* Cambridge, 1938.

Al-Afghānī, J. D. *Al-Radd ʻala'l-Dahriyīn* (Arabic trans.). Cairo and Baghdad, 1955.

——— and M. ʻAbdu. *Al-ʻUrwahal-Wuthqā.* Cairo, 1958.

Afnan, Soheil M. *Avicenna: His Life and Works.* London, 1958.

Ali, Ameer. *The Spirit of Islam.* London, 1955.

Alonso, M. *Teología de Averroes.* Madrid and Granada, 1947.

Anawati, G. C. *Essai de bibliographie avicennienne.* Cairo, 1950.

——— and L. Gardet. *Introduction à la théologie musulmane.* Paris, 1948.

——— *Mystique musulmane.* Paris, 1961.

——— "Prolégomènes à une nouvelle édition du *De Causis* Arabe," *Mélanges Louis Massignon.* Institut Français de Damas, 1956, pp. 75 ff.

Al-ʻAqqād, A. M. *Haqā'iq al-Islām wa Abāṭīl Khuṣūmih.* Cairo, 1962.

Aquinas, Thomas. *Liber de Causis,* in *Opuscula Omnia.* Prais, 1929.

Arnold, T. W. (ed.). *Al-Muʻtazilah,* from Ibn al-Murtaḍā, *Kitāb al-Munya wa'l-Amal.* Leipzig, 1903.

Al-Ashʻarī, Abdu'l-Ḥasan. *Al-Ibānah ʻan Uṣūl al-Diyānah.* Hyderabad, 1948.

——— *Istiḥsān al-Khauḍ fī ʻIlm al-Kalām,* in R. J. McCarthy, *Theology of Al-Ashʻarī.* Beirut, 1953.

——— *Maqālāt al-Islāmiyīn.* Istanbul, 1939–40.

Asin Palacios, M. *Ibn Masarra y su escuela.* Madrid, 1949.

——— (ed. and trans.). *El regimen del solitoria.* Madrid and Granada, 1946.

Averroes (see Ibn Rushd).

'Awa, Adel. *L'esprit critique des Frères de la Pureté*. Beirut, 1948.
Bacon, Roger. *Opus Majus*. London, 1900.
Badawī, A. R. (ed.). *Arisṭū 'ind al-'Arab*. Cairo, 1947.
——— *Dirāsāt fi'l-Falsafah al-Wujūdiyah*. Cairo, 1961.
——— (ed.). *Faḍā'iḥ al-Bāṭiniyah*. Cairo, 1964.
——— (ed.). *Manṭiq Arisṭū*. Cairo, 1948.
——— (ed.). *Neoplatonici apud Arabes*. Cairo, 1955.
——— (ed.). *Plotinus apud Arabes*. Cairo, 1955.
——— (ed.). *Shahīdat al-'Ishq al-Ilāhī*. Cairo, N. D.
——— *Al-Zamān al-Wujūdī*. Cairo, 1955.
Al-Baghdādī, A. Q. *Al-Farq bain al-Firaq*. Cairo, 1910.
——— *Uṣūl al-Dīn*. Istanbul, 1928.
Al-Bāqillānī, A. B. *Al-Tamhīd*. Beirut, 1957.
Baumstark, A. *Die Christlichen Literaturen des Orientes*. Leipzig, 1911.
——— *Geschichte der Syrischen Literatur*. Bonn, 1922.
Al-Bayhaqī, Z. D. *Muntakhab Ṣuwān al-Ḥikmah*, Bodleian Ms. Marsh 539 and Koprülü 902.
——— *Tārīkh Ḥukamā' al-Islām*. Damascus, 1946.
Al-Bīrūnī, M. *Indica*. London, 1887.
Browne, E. G. *Literary History of Persia*. Cambridge, 1924.
Brunschvig, R., and G. E. von Grunebaum. *Classicisme et déclin culturel dans l'histoire de l'Islam*. Paris, 1957.
Al-Bukhārī, M. *Al-Jāmi' al-Ṣaḥīḥ*. Leyden, 1862–1908.
Carra de Vaux, B. *Les penseurs de l'Islam*. Paris, 1921–26.
Corbin, H. *Avicenne et le récit visionnaire*. Paris and Tehran, 1954.
——— *Histoire de la philosophie islamique*. Paris, 1964.
Cruz Hernandez, M. *Filosofía hispano-musulmana*. Madrid, 1957.
De Boer, T. J. *Geschichte der Philosophie im Islam*. Stuttgart, 1901. English translation by E. R. Jones. London, 1903.
Duhem, P. *Le système du monde*. Paris, 1953–59.
Dunlop, D. M. "The Translations of al-Biṭrīq and Yaḥia (Yūḥannā) b. al-Biṭrīq," *Journal of the Royal Asiatic Society*, 1959, pp. 140 ff.
Duval, P. *Histoire d'Edesse*. Paris, 1892.
——— *La littérature syriaque*. Paris, 1899.
Fakhry, M. *Islamic Occasionalism*. London, 1958.
——— "Some Paradoxical Implications of the Mu'tazilite View of Free Will," *Muslim World*, XLIII (1953), 98–108.
——— "A Tenth-Century Arabic Interpretation of Plato's Cosmology," *Journal of the History of Philosophy*, VI (1968), 15–22.
——— (ed.). "Ibn Bājjah (Avempace)," *Opera Metaphysica*. Beirut, 1968.
——— "The Classical Islamic Arguments for the Existence of God," *Muslim World*, XLVII (1957), 139 ff.

Fakhry, M. "Al-Kindī and Socrates," *Al-Abḥāth*, March 1963, pp. 23 ff.
——— "Reconciliation of Plato and Aristotle," *Journal of the History of Ideas*, XXVI (1965), 469–78.
Al-Fārābī, A. N. *Falsafat Arisṭūṭālīs*. Beirut, 1961.
——— *Fī Ithbāt al-Mufāriqāt*. Hyderabad, 1345 A.H.
——— *Fuṣūl al-Madanī*. Cambridge, 1961.
——— *Iḥṣā' al-'Ulūm*. Cairo, 1949.
——— *Al-Jam' bayna Ra'yay al-Ḥakīmayn*. Beirut, 1960.
——— *Al-Madīnah al-Fāḍilah*. Beirut, 1959.
——— *Majmū' Rasā'il*. Cairo, 1907.
——— *Risālah fi'l-'Aql*. Beirut, 1938.
——— *Sharḥ Kitāb al-'Ibārah*. Beirut, 1960.
——— *Al-Siyāsāt al-Madaniyah*. Hyderabad, 1346 A.H.
——— *Taḥṣīl al-Sa'ādah* (in *Majmū'*, above).
Al-Fatḥ b. Khāqān. *Qalā'id al-'Uqyān*. Paris, 1277 A.H.
Furlani, G. "Avicenna e il cogito ergo sum di Cartesio," *Islamica*, III (1927), pp. 53–72.
Gabrieli, F. *Alfarabius compendium legum Platonis*. London, 1952.
Gauthier, L. *Ibn Rochd (Averroes)*. Paris, 1948.
——— *Ibn Thofail, sa vie, ses œuvres*. Paris, 1909.
Georr, Kh. *Les catégories d'Aristote dans leurs versions syro-arabes*. Beirut, 1948.
Al-Ghazālī, A. H. *Faḍā'iḥ al-Bāṭiniyah*. Cairo, 1964.
——— *Iḥyā' 'Ulūm al-Dīn*. Cairo, 1348 A.H.
——— *Al-Iqtiṣād fi'l-I'tiqād*. Cairo, N.D.
——— *Al-Jawahir al-Ghawālī*. Cairo, N.D.
——— *Maqāṣid al-Falāsifah*. Cairo, 1331 A.H.
——— *Mishkāt al-Anwār*. Cairo, 1964.
——— *Mi'yār al-'Ilm*. Cairo, 1961.
——— *Al-Munqidh mina'l-Ḍalāl*. Beirut, 1959.
——— *Tahāfut al-Falāsifah*. Beirut, 1927.
Gibb, H. A. R. *Modern Trends in Islam*. Chicago, 1945.
Gilson, E. "Les sources gréco-arabes de l'augustinisme avicennisant," *Archives d'histoire doctrinale et littéraire du moyen âge*, 1929, pp. 5–27.
Goichon, A. M. *La distinction de l'essence et de l'existence d'après Ibn Sina*. Paris, 1937.
——— *Lexique de la langue philosophique d'Ibn Sina (Avicenne)*. Paris, 1938.
——— *La philosophie d'Avicenne et son influence en Europe médiévale*. Paris, 1944.
Goldziher, I. *Le dogme et la loi de l'Islam*. Paris, 1930.
——— *Die Zahiriten, ihr Lehrsystem und ihre Geschichte*. Leipzig, 1884.
Guillaume, A. *The Traditions of Islam*. Oxford, 1924.
Habachi, R. *Falsafah li Zamānina'l Ḥāḍir*. Beirut, 1964.

Hastings, J. *Encyclopaedia of Religion and Ethics.* Edinburgh, 1908–26.
Henning, W. B. "Eine Arabische Version Mittel-Persischen Weisheitschriften," *Zeitschrift der Deutschen Morgenländischen Gesellschaft,* Vol. 106 (1956), pp. 73–77.
Henry, P., and H. R. Schweyzer. *Plotini Opera.* Paris and Brussels, 1959.
Hitti, Ph. *Al-Bābu'l-Ḥādī 'Ashar: A Treatise on the Principles of Shī'ite Theology* (transl. William M. Miller). London, 1928.
——— *History of the Arabs.* London, 1953.
Hourani, G. *Agreement of Philosophy and Religion.* London, 1961.
Hauréau, B. *De la philosophie scholastique.* Paris, 1850.
Ibn Abī Uṣaybi'ah, A. *'Uyūn al-Anbā'.* Cairo, 1882.
Ibn 'Adī, Y. *Tahdhīb al-Akhlāq.* Cairo, 1913.
Ibn 'Arabī, M. D. *Fuṣuṣ al-Ḥikam* (edition and commentary by A. E. Affifi). Cairo, 1949.
——— *Al-Futūḥāt al-Makkiyah.* Cairo, N.D.
Ibn 'Asākir, 'A. *Tabyīn Kadhib al-Muftarī.* Damascus, 1347 A.H.
Ibn Bājjah (Avempace). *Opera Metaphysica* (edition and introduction by Majid Fakhry). Beirut, 1968.
Ibn Fātik, Al-M. *Mukhtār al-Ḥikam.* Madrid, 1958.
Ibn Ḥajar Al-'Asqalānī. *Tahdhīb al-Tahdhīb.* Hyderabad, 1325 A.H.
Ibn Ḥazm, M. *Al-Akhlāq wa'l-Siyar.* Beirut, 1961.
——— *Al-Fiṣal fi'l-Milal wa'l-Aḥwā' wa'l-Niḥal.* Cairo, 1317 A.H.
Ibn Al-'Ibrī, A. F. *Mukhtaṣar Tārīkh al-Umam.* Beirut, 1958.
Ibn Juljul, S. *Ṭabaqāt al-Aṭibbā'.* Cairo, 1955.
Ibn Khaldūn, A. R. *Al-Muqaddimah.* Cairo, N.D.
——— *Al-Ta'rīf bi'bn Khaldūn wa Riḥlatuhu Sharqan.* Cairo, 1951.
Ibn Khallikān, A. *Wafayāt al-A'yān.* Cairo, 1949.
Ibn Al-Marzubān, B. *Kitāb al-Taḥṣīl.* Cairo, 1329 A.H.
Ibn Al-Muqaffa', A. *Risālah fi'l Akhlāq.* Nurosmaniye, Ms. 2392.
Ibn Al-Nadīm, M. *Kitāb al-Fihrist.* Cairo, N.D.
Ibn Qutaybah, M. *K. al-Ma'ārif.* Gottingen, 1850.
Ibn Rushd (Averroes), M. *Faṣl al-Maqāl,* in *Falsafat Ibn Rushd.* Cairo, N.D.
——— *Al-Kashf 'an Manāhij al-Adillah,* in *Falsafat Ibn Rushd.* Cairo, N.D.
——— *Paraphrase of Metaphysics.* Cairo, 1958.
——— *Tafsīr mā Ba'd al-Ṭabī'ah.* (Grand commentaire de la Métaphysique). Beirut, 1938–55.
——— *Tahāfut al-Tahāfut.* Beirut, 1930.
——— *Talkhīṣ Kitāb al-Nafs.* Cairo, 1950.
Ibn Sīnā (Avicenna), H. *Aḥwāl al-Nafs.* Cairo, 1952.
——— *Fi'l-Fi'l wa'l-Infi'āl.* Hyderabad, 1353 A.H.
——— *Al-Ishārāt wa'l-Tanbīhāt.* Cairo, 1957–60.
——— *Kitāb al-Mabda' wa'l-Ma'ād.* Istanbul Ms., Sulaymaniya 1584.

Ibn Sīnā (Avicenna), H. *Manṭiq al-Mashriqiyīn*. Cairo, 1910.
——— *Al-Najāt*. Cairo, 1938.
——— *Al-Shifā'*. (*Ilāhiyāt*). Cairo, 1960.
——— *Tis'u Rasā'il*. Cairo, 1908.
Ibn Taymiyah, A. *Majmū'at al-Rasā'il*. Cairo, 1323 A.H.
——— *Al-Radd 'alā'l-Manṭiqiyīn*. Bombay, 1949.
Ibn Ṭufayl, A. B. *Ḥayy b. Yaqẓān*. Damascus, 1962.
Ikhwān Al-Ṣafā. *Rasā'il*. Beirut, 1957.
——— *Al-Risālah al-Jāmi'ah*. Damascus, 1949.
Iqbal, M. *The Development of Metaphysical Thought in Persia*. Lahore, N.D.
——— *The Reconstruction of Religious Thought in Islam*. London, 1934.
Al-Iskandar (of Aprodisias). *Maqālah fi'l-Laun*.
——— *Maqālah fi'l-Nushū'*.
——— *Maqālah fi'l-Ṣuwar al-Rūḥāniyah*, in Escorial Ms. No. 798.
Jabre, F. "La biographie et l'œuvre de Ghazali considérés à la lumière des *Tabaqats* de Subki," *Mélanges de l'Institut Dominicain d'Etudes Orientales du Caire*, 1954, pp. 83 f.
Al-Jāḥiẓ, 'A. *Kitāb al-Bukhalā'*. Leyden, 1898.
——— *Kitāb al-Ḥayawān*. Cairo, 1906.
Jeffrey, A. *Materials for the History of the Text of the Qur'ān* Leiden, 1937.
Jourdain, A. *Recherches critiques sur l'âge et l'origine des traductions d'Aristote*. Paris, 1819.
Al-Jurjānī, A. *Kitāb al-Ta'rīfāt*. Leipzig, 1845.
Al-Juwaynī, A. M. *Kitāb al-Irshād*. Paris, 1938.
Khalīfah, Ḥājjī, M. *Kashf al-Ẓunūn*. Leipzig and London, 1835–58.
Al-Khayyāṭ, A. Ḥ. *Kitāb al-Intiṣār*. Beirut, 1957.
Khusrū, N. *Jāmi' al-Ḥikmatayn*. Paris and Tehran, 1953.
——— *Zād al-Musāfirīn*. Berlin, 1341 A.H.
Al-Kindī, A. Y. *Rasā'il al-Kindī al-Falsafiyah*. Cairo, 1950, 1953.
Kraus, P. *Epître de Béruni*. Paris, 1936.
——— *Jābir ibn Ḥayyān*. Cairo, 1942–43.
——— (ed.). Al-Rāzī, *Opera Philosophica*. Cairo, 1939.
——— "Plotin chez les Arabes," *Bulletin de l'Institut d'Egypte*, Vol. 23 (1941), p. 267.
——— *Revista degli Studi Orientali*, 1933, No. 4, pp. 1–14.
——— and R. Walzer (see Walzer).
Laoust, H. *Essai sur les doctrines sociales et politiques de T. D. Ahmad b. Taimiya*. Cairo, 1939.
Lutfallah Khān, M. *Jamāl al-Dīn al-Asadabādī al-Afghānī*. Cairo, 1957.
McCarthy, R. J. "Al-Kindi's Treatise on the Intellect," *Islamic Studies*, III (June 1964), 119 f.
——— *Al-Taṣānīf al-Mansūbah ilā Failasūf al-'Arab*. Baghdad, 1962.

McCarthy, R. J. *Theology of al-Ash'arī*. Beirut, 1953.
Madkour, I. *L'organon d'Aristote dans le monde arabe*. Paris, 1934.
——— *La place d'al-Fārābī dans l'école philosophique musulmane*. Paris, 1934.
Mahdi, M. (ed.). *Al-Fārābī's Philosophy of Aristotle*. Beirut, 1961.
——— (trans.). *Al Fārābī's Philosophy of Plato and Aristotle*. Glencoe, 1962.
——— *Ibn Khaldūn's Philosophy of History*. London, 1957.
Maimonides, M. *Guide des égarés*. Paris, 1856–66.
Al-Malaṭī, A. *Kitāb al-Tanbīh*. Leipzig, 1936.
Al-Maqqarī, A. *Nafḥ al-Ṭīb*. Cairo, 1949.
Al-Marakushī, A. W. *Al-Mu'jib fī Akhbār al-Maghrib*. Leyden, 1881.
Marmura, M. "Avicenna and the Problem of the Infinite Number of Souls," *Mediaeval Studies*, XXII (1960), 232 ff.
Massignon, L. *Essai sur les origines du lexique technique de la mystique musulmane*. Paris, 1922.
——— *La passion d'al-Ḥallāj*. Paris, 1922.
——— *Recueil des textes inédits concernant l'histoire de la mystique*. Paris, 1929.
Al-Mas'ūdī, A. *Murūj al-Dhahab*. Paris, 1861–77.
——— *Al-Tanbīh wa'l-Ishrāf*. Leyden, 1893.
Mehren, A. F. Traités mystiques d'Avicenne. Leyden, 1889–91.
Meyerhof, M. "Transmission of Science to the Arabs," *Islamic Culture*, XI (1937), 20.
Migne. *Patrologia Graeca*. XCIV, Col. 1589f.
Miskawayh, A. *Al-Fauz al-Aṣghar*. Beirut, 1319 A.H.
——— *Jawidān Khirad*. Cairo, 1952.
——— *Tahdhīb al-Akhlāq*. Beirut, 1966.
Munk, S. *Mélanges de philosophie juive et arabe*. Paris, 1859.
Muslim, Ibn Al-H. *Al-Jāmi' al-Ṣaḥīḥ*. Al-Azhar, 1929.
Nagīb Maḥmūd, Z. *Falsafah wa Fann*. Cairo, 1963.
——— *Naḥwa Falsafah 'Ilmiyah*. Cairo, 1958.
Nallino, C. *Tārikh al-Falak 'inda'l-'Arab*. Rome, 1911.
Nasr, S. H. *Three Muslim Sages*. Cambridge, Mass., 1964.
Al-Naubakhtī, M. *Firaq al-Shī'ah*. Istanbul, 1931.
Nicholson, R. *Mystics of Islam*. London, 1914.
——— *Studies in Islamic Mysticism*. Cambridge, 1921.
Al-Nīsābūrī, A. S. *Kitāb al-Masā'il*. Leyden, 1902.
Nock, A. D., and A. J. Festugière. *Corpus Hermeticum*. Paris, 1945.
O'Leary, De Lacy. *Arabic Thought and Its Place in History*. London, 1922.
Patton, W. M. *Aḥmad b. Ḥanbal and the Miḥna*. Leyden, 1897.
Périer, A. *Petits traités apologétiques de Yaḥia ben 'Adī*. Paris, 1920.
——— *Yaḥia b. 'Adī*. Paris, 1920.
Pines, S. *Beiträge zur Islamischen Atomenlehre*. Berlin, 1936.

Pines, S. "Le texte inconnu d'Aristote en version Arabe," *Archives d'histoire doctrinale et littéraire du moyen âge*, 1956, pp. 5–43.
Plotinus. *Opera.* Paris and Brussels, 1959.
Porphyry. *Al-Isāgugī* (Arabic). Cairo, 1952.
Al-Qifṭī, 'A. *Tārīkh al-Ḥukamā'*. Leipzig, 1903.
Quadri, G. *La philosophie arabe dans l'Europe médiévale.* Paris, 1947.
Al-Qushayrī, 'A. K. *Al-Risālah al-Qushayriyah.* Cairo, 1330 A.H.
Radhakrishnan, S. *History of Philosophy, Eastern and Western.* London, 1952.
Rahman, F. *Avicenna's Psychology.* London, 1952.
Al-Rāzī, A. B. *Opera Philosophica.* Cairo, 1939.
Al-Rāzī, F. D. *Al-Mabāḥith al-Mashriqiyah.* Hyderabad, 1343 A.H.
——— *Al-Muḥaṣṣal.* Cairo, 1323 A.H.
Rénan, E. *Averroês et l'averroïsme.* Paris, 1882.
——— *De philosophia peripatetica apud Syros.*
Rescher, N. "Al-Kindī's Sketch of Aristotle's Organon," *The New Scholasticism*, January 1963, pp. 44 ff.
——— *The Development of Arabic Logic.* Pittsburgh, 1964.
Riḍā, M. Rashīd. *Tārīkh al-'Ustādh al-Imām.* Cairo, 1931.
Ritter, H., and R. Walzer. *Uno scritto morale inedito di al-Kindī.* Rome, 1938.
Rosenthal, F. *Aḥmad b. at-Ṭayyib as-Sarahsi.* New Haven, 1943.
——— *The Muqaddimah of Ibn Khaldūn.* London, 1958.
——— "As-Shaykh al-Yūnānī and the Arabic Plotinus Source," *Orientalia*, Vol. 21 (1952), pp. 461–529; Vol. 22 (1953), pp. 370–400; Vol. 24 (1955), pp. 42–66.
——— and R. Walzer (see Walzer).
Ross, W. D. *Aristotle.* London, 1956.
——— *Select Fragments.* Oxford, 1952.
Ruska, J. *Arabischen Alchemisten.* Heidelberg, 1924.
Sachau, E. (ed.). *Indica.* London, 1887.
Ṣā'id, Ibn Ṣ. *Ṭabaqāt al-Umam.* Beirut, 1912.
Al-Salhajī, M. *Manāqib al-Bisṭāmī.* Cairo, 1949.
Salman, D. "Algazel et les Latins," *Archives d'histoire doctrinale et littéraire du moyen âge*, 1935–36, pp. 103–27.
Sarton, G. *History of Science.* Cambridge, Mass., 1959.
Al-Shahrastānī, M. *Al-Milal wa'l-Niḥal.* London, 1892.
——— *Nihāhayt al Iqdām.* London, 1934.
Al-Shahrazūrī, Sh. D. *Nuzhat al-Arwāh*, in Spies and Khatak, *Three Treatises on Mysticism* and Fatiḥ Ms. 4516.
Sharif, M. M. *History of Muslim Philosophy.* Wiesbaden, 1962.
Shaykho, L. *Maqālāt Falsafiyah.* Beirut, 1911.
Al-Shīrāzī, S. D. *Al-Asfār al-Arba'ah.* Teheran, 1865.
——— *Kitāb al-Mashā'ir (Livre des pénétrations).* Paris, 1964.

Al-Shīrāzī, S. D. *Rasā'il Akhund Mulla Ṣadrā.* Teheran, 1302 A.H.
Al-Sijistānī, A. S. (see al-Bayhāqī). *Muntakhab Ṣuwān al-Ḥikmah.* Koprülü Ms. 902 and Bodleian Ms. Marsh 539.
Smith, M. *Studies in Early Mysticism in the Near and Middle East.* London, 1931.
Smith, Wilfred C. *Modern Islam in India.* London, 1946.
Spies, O., and S. Khatak. *Three Treatises on Mysticism.* Stuttgard, 1935.
Steinschneider, M. *Die Arabischen Uebersetzungen aus dem Griechischen.* Graz, 1960.
Al-Subkī, T. D. *Ṭabaqāt al-Shāfi'iyah al-Kubrā.* Cairo, 1324 A.H.
Al-Suhrawardī, Sh. D. *Oeuvres philosophiques et mystiques.* Teheran and Paris, 1952.
——— *Opera Metaphysica et Mystica.* Istanbul, 1945.
Ṣuyūṭī, J. *Tārīkh al-Khulafā'.* Calcutta, 1857.
Al-Ṭabarī, M. *History.* Leyden, 1879–1901.
——— *Tārīkh.* Cairo, 1939.
Al-Tauḥīdī, A. H. *Al-Hawāmil wa'l-Shawāmil.* Cairo, 1951.
——— *Al-Imtā' wa'l-Mu'ānasah.* Cairo, 1939–44.
——— *Al-Muqābasāt.* Cairo, 1929.
Taylor, A. E. *Commentary on the Timaeus.* Oxford, 1928.
——— *Plato.* London, 1960.
Tomiche, N. (see Ibn Hazm). (ed. and trans.). *Epître morale.* Beirut, 1961.
Al-Ṭūsī, Naṣīr-al-Dīn. *Commentary on al-Ishārāt wa'l Tanbīhāt.* Cairo, 1960.
Van den Bergh, S. (trans.). *Averroes' Tahāfut al-Tahāfut.* (*The Incoherence of the Incoherence*). London, 1954.
Van Riet, Simone. "Joie et bonheur dans le traité d'al-Kindī sur l'art de combattre la tristesse," *Revue philosophique de Louvain,* Vol. 61 (1963), pp. 13–23.
Walzer, R. *Greek into Arabic.* Oxford, 1962.
——— and P. Kraus. *Galeni compendium Timaei Platonis.* London, 1951.
——— and H. Ritter (see Ritter).
——— and F. Rosenthal. *Alfarabius de Platonis philosophia.* London, 1953.
Watt, W. M. *Free Will and Predestination in Early Islam.* London, 1948.
——— *Islamic Philosophy and Theology.* Edinburgh, 1962.
Wensinck, A. J. *The Muslim Creed.* Cambridge, 1932.
——— *La pensée de Ghazzali.* Paris, 1940.
Wolfson, Harry A. "Revised Plan for Publication of a Corpus Commentariorum Averrois in Aristotelem," *Speculum,* XXXVIII (Jan. 1963), 90 f.
Wright, W. *History of Syriac Literature.* London, 1894.
Yahia, O. *Histoire et classification de l'œuvre d'Ibn 'Arabī.* Damascus, 1964.
Zaehner, R. C. *Hindu and Muslim Mysticism.* London, 1960.
Zeller, E. *Outlines of the History of Greek Philosophy.* New York, 1931.
Zurayk, C. K. (trans.). *Miskawayh, the Refinement of Character.* Beirut, 1966.

INDEX

NAMES: Paging of major treatment is italicized. The principal titles will be found on these pages.

TITLES are listed alphabetically in the original language. Alternate titles in English are entered alphabetically with a cross reference to the foreign language title. Selected major works are listed under subjects.